WHO IS MY NEIGHBOR?

WHO IS MY NEIGHBOR?

Personalism and the Foundations of Human Rights

Thomas D. Williams

The Catholic University of America Press
Washington, D.C.

Copyright © 2005 Thomas D. Williams
All rights reserved

The paper used in this publication meets the minimum requirements of American National Standards for Information Science—Permanence of Paper for Printed Library materials, ANSI Z39.48-1984.

∞

Library of Congress Cataloging-in-Publication Data
Williams, Thomas D., LC
Who is my neighbor? : personalism and the foundations of human rights
/ Thomas D. Williams.
p. cm.
Includes bibliographical references and index.
ISBN 978-0-8132-3156-3 (alk. paper)
1. Human rights—Religious aspects—Catholic Church. 2. Natural law—Religious aspects—Catholic Church. 3. Neo-Scholasticism. 4. Personalism. I. Title.
BX1795.H85W55 2005
172'.2—dc22
2004001569

CONTENTS

Foreword by Mary Ann Glendon   vii
Introduction   xiii

PART ONE. RIGHTS IN THE CROSSHAIRS

1. Defining Human Rights   3
2. Some Needed Nuances   14
3. The Church and Human Rights   31

PART TWO. THE CASE AGAINST RIGHTS

4. The Accusation of Nonexistence   53
5. The Accusation of Inseparability   65
6. The Accusation of Innovation   82

PART THREE. A NEW SOLUTION TO AN OLD PROBLEM: THOMISTIC PERSONALISM

7. A Personalism Primer   108
8. The Person according to Personalism   125
9. Dignity and Its Due   146
10. The Two Loves   165
11. From Love to Human Rights   182
12. Christ and Human Dignity   204

PART FOUR. HUMAN RIGHTS AND CLASSICAL ETHICS

13. Natural Law	219
14. Natural Justice	256
15. Natural Rights in Classical Theory	283

PART FIVE. TOWARD AN ETHICS OF SOLIDARITY

16. Who Is My Neighbor?	302
Select Bibliography	321
Index	335

FOREWORD

Mary Ann Glendon

In 1998, while immersed in the history of the framing of the Universal Declaration of Human Rights, I gave a lecture at Notre Dame University titled, "Foundations of Human Rights: The Unfinished Business."[1] I deplored a fact I had only just discovered: that so little progress had been made on a project that the framers of that 1948 document had left for future generations, the task of demonstrating that universal human rights could be placed on a solid philosophical basis. With a postmodern deconstruction derby threatening to make nonsense of the Declaration, I expressed the hope that philosophers and theologians would soon come to the aid of the embattled human rights project.

It is somewhat disconcerting, to say the least, to think that a great transformative international movement might rest on nothing more substantial than a hunch that foundations could be found—if only someone looked for them. Yet in his 1989 address to the Vatican diplomatic corps, the philosopher-Pope John Paul II, a long-standing admirer of the 1948 Declaration, warned that the document "does not present *the anthropological and ethical foundations of the human rights* which it proclaims."[2] In 1997, the Pope's countryman Czeslaw Milosz expressed a similar concern

---

1. Mary Ann Glendon, "Foundations of Human Rights: The Unfinished Business," *American Journal of Jurisprudence* 44/1 (1999).

2. John Paul II, address to the diplomatic corps accredited to the Holy See, 9 January 1989, par. 7; emphasis in original. In earlier speeches, the Pope had described the Declaration as "one of the highest expressions of human conscience of our time" (address to the United Nations, October 2, 1979, par. 7) and as "a real milestone on the path of the moral progress of humanity" (address to the United Nations, October 5, 1995, par. 2).

in more alarming terms. Musing about "those beautiful and deeply moving words which pertain to the old repertory of the rights of man and the dignity of the person," the poet wrote: "I wonder at this phenomenon because maybe underneath there is an abyss. . . . How long will they stay afloat if the bottom is taken out?"[3]

An inquisitive person might well ask how it happened that such an imposing edifice was constructed with so little attention to foundations. The fact is that the fathers and mothers of the post–World War II human rights project were well aware of the omission. They just didn't have time to remedy it. When the U.N.'s first Human Rights Commission, chaired by Eleanor Roosevelt, began to draft a "bill of rights" to which persons of all nations and cultures could subscribe, the commission members were immediately faced with two problems: no one really knew whether there were any such common principles and if so, what they might be. Anticipating those difficulties, UNESCO had asked a group of philosophers (some, such as Jacques Maritain, well known in the West and others from Confucian, Hindu, and Muslim cultures) to look into the matter.

The philosophers sent a questionnaire to leading thinkers all over the world, from Mahatma Gandhi to Teilhard de Chardin. In due course, they reported that—somewhat to their surprise—there were a few common standards of decency that were widely shared, though not always formulated in the language of rights. They pronounced themselves "convinced that the members of the United Nations share common convictions on which human rights depend." At the same time, however, they cautioned that "those common convictions are stated in terms of different philosophic principles and on the background of divergent political and economic systems."[4]

The UNESCO group's bottom line was that agreement could be reached across cultures concerning certain rights that "may be seen as implicit in man's nature as an individual and as a member of society and to follow from the fundamental right to live."[5] But they harbored no illusions about how deep that agreement went. As Maritain famously put it when someone asked him how consensus had been achieved among such

---

3. Czeslaw Milosz, "The Religious Imagination at 2000," *New Perspectives Quarterly* (Fall 1997): 32.

4. UNESCO, *Human Rights: Comments and Interpretations* (London: Wingate, 1949), 268.

5. Ibid., 271.

diverse informants: "We agree about the rights but on condition no one asks us why!"⁶

Maritain and his colleagues did not view that problem as fatal to proceeding. For the time being, he maintained, the only feasible goal was to reach agreement "not on the basis of common speculative ideas, but on common practical ideas."⁷ Since there was consensus that some things are so terrible in practice that no one will publicly approve them, and some things are so good in practice that virtually no one will openly oppose them, a common project could go forward even in the absence of agreement on the reasons for those positions. That practical consensus, the UNESCO philosophers said, was enough "to enable a great task to be undertaken."⁸

The philosophers' judgment proved correct. The delegates on the Human Rights Commission had remarkably few disagreements over which principles should be included in the Declaration.⁹ (Their disputes were chiefly political, arising out of the antagonistic relations between the Soviet Union and the United States.) On December 10, 1948, the document was adopted by the U.N. General Assembly as a "common standard of achievement."

Against the predictions of skeptics, the nonbinding Declaration quickly showed its moral force. It became the principal inspiration of the postwar international human rights movement, it remains the most influential model for the majority of rights instruments in today's world, and it continues to serve as the single most important reference point for discussions of human rights in international settings.

Still, the decision to proceed "without asking why" had costs, as one of the UNESCO philosophers foresaw it would. In a prescient essay titled, "The Philosophic Bases and Material Circumstances of the Rights of Man," Richard McKeon warned that so long as the business of foundations remained unfinished, the Declaration would be highly vulnerable to struggles for the control of its interpretation "for the purpose of advancing special interests."¹⁰ That is precisely what happened throughout

6. Jacques Maritain, "Introduction," in ibid., 9.
7. Ibid., 10.   8. Ibid.
9. For a detailed account, see Mary Ann Glendon, *A World Made New: Eleanor Roosevelt and the Universal Declaration of Human Rights* (New York: Random House, 2001).
10. Richard McKeon, "The Philosophic Bases and Material Circumstances of the Rights of Man," in *Human Rights: Comments and Interpretations* (London: Wingate, 1949), 35–36.

the Cold War and in the culture battles that succeeded it. But Mrs. Roosevelt's commission was under such pressure to proceed, and the philosophers were so confident that foundations could be found, that they left the job of proving it for another day.

Now that day has come. What needs to be investigated is not whether agreement can be reached on a single foundation. Maritain and his colleagues considered that to be a fruitless endeavor. More promising, they thought, was to demonstrate that human rights could be firmly grounded in the world's major cultural, philosophical, and religious traditions. John Paul II concurred in their view, writing: "It is . . . the task of the various schools of thought—in particular the communities of believers—to provide the moral bases for the juridic edifice of human rights."[11]

Friends of human rights should be grateful, therefore, to Thomas Williams for taking up that challenge and for demonstrating with depth and brilliance how, and in what sense, foundations for human rights can be found in Thomistic personalism. The study presented here abundantly confirms the observation of Cardinal Avery Dulles that "[t]he Catholic doctrine of human rights is not based on Lockean empiricism or individualism. It has a more ancient and distinguished pedigree."[12]

Another important contribution of Father Williams's work is that it effectively counters the reservations expressed by many Catholic thinkers about the Church's adoption of the modern discourse of rights. His study reveals that human rights ideas are so deeply rooted in Christian tradition that the modern human rights project is not only compatible with Catholicism, it is profoundly indebted to it. He is, to be sure, appropriately cautious about the fact that the Church does not use the language of rights in the same way as it is used in some secular circles. (As the Fathers of Vatican II pointed out in *Gaudium et Spes,* the movement to respect human rights "must be imbued with the spirit of the Gospel and be protected from all appearance of mistaken autonomy. We are tempted to consider our personal rights as fully protected only when we are free from every norm of divine law; but following this road leads to the destruction rather than to the maintenance of the dignity of the human person (41).")

---

11. John Paul II, address to the diplomatic corps accredited to the Holy See, 9 January 1989, par. 7.

12. Avery Dulles, *Human Rights: The United Nations and Papal Teaching* (New York: Fordham University, 1999), 12.

Finally, one should take careful note of Father Williams's title. The question "Who is my neighbor?" suggests a far more promising starting point for the analysis of human rights issues than the radically individualistic paradigm that has gained prominence within the human rights establishment. By inviting deeper reflection on the nature of the human person, Father Williams has not only helped to place human rights on a firmer foundation but has also suggested promising lines for their future development. He has thus contributed to the development of modern Thomism while performing a great service to the cause of human freedom and dignity.

MARY ANN GLENDON
Learned Hand Professor of Law
Harvard University
President, Pontifical Academy for Social Sciences

INTRODUCTION

Human rights language poses serious problems that require a reasoned response. The ubiquity of references to human rights in secular and ecclesiastical circles could give the impression that a common understanding exists regarding rights. Such an impression vanishes, however, when one listens closely. It seems that everyone—within the Catholic Church and without—talks about rights, but the more they talk, the less they agree.[1] In fact, many users of rights language do not even share enough common ground to have an argument, much less a dialogue or discussion. Some of the disagreements are superficial, but many go deep, so deep that some respected thinkers have concluded that rights do not even exist. These controversies are of far more than academic interest, for the language of rights has become—for better or worse—the principal language in which men and women the world over discuss weighty issues that bear upon the human future. The inherent importance of the questions and the chaotic state of rights literature highlight the urgency that rights be placed on secure ethical foundations.

The problem is of particular interest to Catholics, since the Catholic Church has not only acquiesced to the contemporary trend to couch ethical discourse in the language of human rights, it has even taken a leading role in the process. Especially since the Second Vatican Council, the papal Magisterium has consistently adopted rights language in framing many of its moral teachings. The conciliar documents *Gaudium et Spes* and *Dignitatis Humanae* are replete with talk of human rights and their

---

1. Thus James Schall points out that rights "are not merely a common easily agreed upon tradition, but rather a field of struggle and controversy among differing world-views and values" ("Human Rights: The 'So-Called' Judaeo-Christian Tradition," *Communio: International Catholic Review* 8/1 [Spring 1981]: 61).

basis in the dignity of the human person. Numerous references to rights, in a variety of contexts, can be found in the 1983 *Code of Canon Law* and the 1992 *Catechism of the Catholic Church*. Pope John Paul II appeals to human rights over and over in his many encyclicals, apostolic exhortations, apostolic letters, and discourses. In fact, the language of rights is so fully ensconced in official Church documents that it can fairly be said to constitute an integral part of Catholic social thought.

Nevertheless, more than a few serious thinkers express misgivings about the espousal of human rights language and theory. One writer, J. B. Benestad, speaks of a "quiet revolution" brought about by the adoption of rights talk. "Many citizens," he writes, "including Church leaders, do not realize that rights are not simply another way of talking about classical virtue or the teaching of Jesus Christ. In fact, the doctrine of rights presupposes an understanding of human nature 'which is no longer defined in terms of its highest aspirations,' but rather assumes that people cannot really rise above preoccupation with their own interests."[2] Another commentator, Kenneth R. Craycraft, has contended that the very notion of rights employed in recent official Church documents is "problematic at best." According to Craycraft: "The Church has adopted a language that may be irreconcilable with its more ancient and basic claims about man and his relationship to God."[3] The philosopher Alasdair MacIntyre denies the existence of rights altogether. "The truth is plain," MacIntyre writes. "[T]here are no such rights, and belief in them is one with belief in witches and in unicorns." Furthermore, "every attempt to give good reasons for believing that there *are* such rights has failed."[4]

Besides these theoretical criticisms, reservations based on more practical considerations are also voiced. As Harvard Law School professor Mary Ann Glendon has noted, rights talk often impoverishes public dis-

---

2. J. Brian Benestad, foreword to *Human Rights, Virtue, and the Common Good: Untimely Meditations on Religion and Politics*, vol. 3 of *Ernest L. Fortin: Collected Essays*, ed. J. Brian Benestad (Lanham, Md.: Rowman & Littlefield, 1996), xii–xiii.

3. Kenneth R. Craycraft Jr., "Religion as Moral Duty and Civic Right: *Dignitatis Humanae* on Religious Liberty," in *Catholicism, Liberalism, and Communitarianism: The Catholic Intellectual Tradition and the Moral Foundations of Democracy*, ed. Kenneth L. Grasso, Gerard V. Bradley, and Robert P. Hunt (Lanham, Md.: Rowman & Littlefield, 1995), 60.

4. Alasdair C. MacIntyre, *After Virtue: A Study of Moral Theory*, 2nd ed. (London: Gerald Duckworth, 1985), 69.

course instead of enriching it, because it tends to oversimplify and trivialize ethical and social problems. Moreover, the accelerating proliferation of new rights has resulted in lengthy catalogues of rights, some of which contradict each other and many of which, detached from any reference to human goods, are simply unacceptable from the Christian perspective.[5] Talk of the rights of trees and animals, or of human rights to abortion, euthanasia, or assisted suicide, highlights the aberrant uses for which the term can be employed.

Intense controversy rages in contemporary political life over which interests constitute rights and which do not. For example, how many of the myriad proposed women's rights, family rights, children's rights, and reproductive rights are truly human rights, and how many are merely personal desires or interest-group agendas dressed up in rights language? Women's reproductive rights are often pitted against a child's right to life, while pornographers' rights to self-expression clash with parental rights to a healthy moral ecology for the raising of their children.

Wherein lies the solution to these dilemmas? How can true rights claims be distinguished from false ones? Do rights in fact exist as an objective, ethical reality, or are they a mere convention? Does rights language represent a real departure from traditional Christian and classical ethical categories, or does it merely approach ethical problems from a new perspective, one that is complementary and fully compatible with the traditional concepts?

The solution can lie only in excavating beneath the level of utility and convention to reach the very bedrock of rights, their ultimate ethical foundation. What does it actually mean to say that people "have rights," that someone is "owed" something by others? Why should people be treated in a determined way? What is it about the human person that makes him worthy of certain things? And exactly which things is he worthy of?

Unless human rights have an objective foundation, they are little more than a verbal fiction. Yet the challenge of finding that foundation has proved so daunting that many modern thinkers have simply given up on

---

5. "The prevailing consensus about the goodness of rights, widespread though it may be, is thin and brittle. In truth, there is very little agreement regarding *which* needs, goods, interests, or values should be characterized as 'rights'" (Mary Ann Glendon, *Rights Talk: The Impoverishment of Political Discourse* [New York: Free Press, 1991], 16).

it.[6] They have settled for the politically expedient solution of merely agreeing that some specific rights should be recognized, defended, and promoted. The problem with that approach, of course, is that opinions change over time, and conventional agreements alone cannot provide long-term security for rights or stand up to those who would propose contrary agendas.

As a result, surprisingly little has been written on these foundational questions. Most of the vast literature on rights is devoted to legal considerations, history, or pragmatic matters of rights accords, rights violations, and lists of rights agreeable to certain parties. For its part, the Church's Magisterium often speaks of rights being grounded in man's dignity but offers little explanation as to what this means and how it can be theoretically defended and justified.

Many today decry the seemingly unrestrained proliferation of rights and the effects of the rights revolution on culture and politics. Far fewer are those who attempt to explain what rights are, where they come from, and how they fit in with Christian moral tradition, if at all. Nonetheless, the necessary tools—especially the insights offered by Thomistic personalism—are available to make a compelling case for the objective reality of natural human rights and their grounding in the dignity of the human person. In the face of the rampant propagation of rights and seemingly irresolvable disputes as to their practical application, this foundational investigation can no longer be put off. Ending its postponement is the aim of this book.

6. See for example Richard Rorty, "Human Rights, Rationality, and Sentimentality," in *On Human Rights*, ed. Stephen Shute and Susan Hurley (New York: Basic Books, 1993), 111–34.

PART ONE

RIGHTS IN THE CROSSHAIRS

Many arguments end once terms are carefully defined. How many times do people ardently debate issues only to find that their differences boil down to equivocal terminology? How often do we assume that others share our perception of the terms and concepts we use, only to learn much later that such a common understanding never existed at all? A clarification of terms seems especially necessary to traverse the linguistic minefield of human rights. Not only does the abstract concept of rights lend itself to a variety of interpretations, but the term itself has suffered disfigurement in political and cultural debates where language is routinely manipulated to advance a given agenda. Thus a careful delineation of terms from the outset can anticipate possible misunderstandings and allow for a more transparent discussion of foundational questions.

A clarification of language also calls for a clarification of history, especially as regards the Catholic Church's rocky relationship with human rights. What evidence do we find of hostility to rights in the Magisterial texts of past centuries? Does the Church's contemporary embrace of rights language represent as violent a sea change as some writers would assert, or did the Church gradually assimilate rights into her proper vocabulary according to the needs of times and situations? A basic understanding of the Church's historical relationship with rights language will provide helpful background for understanding deeper questions concerning the compatibility or incompatibility of human rights with the Christian view of the human person and morality.

The following three chapters intend to clarify these key points and in so doing to set the stage for the remainder of the work. The first chapter analyzes rights from a linguistic perspective in an attempt to arrive at a clear working definition that can serve for the rest of the study. At the same time, faulty definitions are discarded, and unhelpful or confusing notions regarding rights are culled. Chapter 2 picks up where chapter 1 leaves off, further honing the idea of human rights by examining a series of qualifiers often employed together with rights that can attenuate or even alter the meaning of rights. Finally, the third chapter examines the Catholic Church's historical relationship with rights, both as a tenet of Liberalism and as a proper ethical category when disentangled from dubious political theory. These pages should furnish the necessary tools and background to examine deeper criticisms of rights and embark on an investigation into their philosophical and theological foundations.

1. DEFINING HUMAN RIGHTS

IF ASKED TO LIST SPECIFIC human rights, most people raised nowadays in the Western tradition could easily come up with a considerable number. Answers would range from the right to life and liberty to the right to free speech and from the right to assembly and self-expression to reproductive rights. Yet if these same people were asked for a definition of rights, most would flounder. While nearly everyone has at least a rudimentary notion of rights, especially as regards their particular instantiations, the concept itself often remains nebulous and elusive. A good definition of rights, however, is of more than academic concern. Many misunderstandings concerning specific rights and their proper application seem to proceed from a shallow understanding of exactly what rights are.[1]

The present study delves into the anthropological and ethical foundations of human rights. At the outset of such a project it is vital to determine as precisely as possible the nature of the phenomenon whose foundations are being explored. An adequate understanding of the term "rights" will allow access to the ethical bedrock upon which rights rest.[2] What exactly are these rights that cry out for a foundation? What does the statement that X has a right to Y actually *mean*? Do the right to life, the right to vote, the right to bear arms, the right to an education, and

---

[1]. John Finnis, for example, states that the "grammar of rights is so extensive and supple in its reach that its structure is generally rather poorly understood; misunderstandings in discussions about rights, and about particular (alleged) rights and their extent, are consequently rather frequent" (*Natural Law and Natural Rights* [Oxford: Clarendon Press, 1980], 198).

[2]. "The struggle over human rights," writes James Schall, "is not just whether the Russians or the Chinese or the Europeans or the Americans or the Third World respect them, but what it is that these rights are that deserves respect" ("Human Rights: The 'So-Called' Judaeo-Christian Tradition," 61).

the right to abortion all have the same root and foundation? These are pressing questions that require a reasoned response.

Since language evolves, a first matter to address is what the word "rights" means to men and women of our time. A simple phenomenological survey of common usage can illuminate essential characteristics of rights and help delimit the object of this study. A second step involves comparing the results of this survey with accepted definitions of rights from different epochs. This comparison will show that the basic concept of rights in modern parlance is far from arbitrary; it sinks its roots into a long-standing tradition of philosophical and theological reflection. A clear understanding of that comparison will provide an accurate working definition of human rights that will in turn serve as a dependable point of reference throughout this study.

LINGUISTIC ANALYSIS

Phenomenology involves the description and study of observable events in order to better understand what underlies them. To determine what rights are, a phenomenological-linguistic analysis of the way the word is used in everyday conversation can be helpful. What do people have in mind when they speak of rights? What common elements can be discerned between one rights claim and another? Regardless of the *validity* of specific rights claims, the way the word is used will shed light on its meaning and allow the distinctive features of rights to emerge.

Random examples from everyday usage reveal much about how people understand rights. "I have a right to think what I want." "A woman has a right to do what she wants with her body." "All people have a right to employment." "The poor have a right to housing and healthcare." Typical rights claims like these reveal several key characteristics of rights.

A Right Is Something One Has

First of all, the words "I *have* a right . . ." or "The poor *have* a right . . ." imply something that can be *possessed* by a subject. People speak of individuals (or families, or nations, or even animals) as *having* rights, rather than *being* rights or *righting* someone else. A right is understood as separate from the bearer of the right but somehow within his ownership or jurisdiction. And regardless of whether one exercises one's rights or not, one continues to possess them. For example, if someone has a right to migrate, the possession of the right is not contingent on the person choosing to leave her country.

This, of course, leads to many corollary questions. How, for instance, do rights come to be possessed? Are they acquired or innate? Once they are possessed can rights subsequently be forfeited, or are they inalienable? These are questions to be addressed further along. The relevant issue here is the character of rights as something that can be possessed.

A Transitive Term: Always a Right to Something

Common usage of the term suggests that what one possesses is always qualified as a right *to* something. This could be the right to perform an action ("to think what one wants") or to an object (housing or healthcare) or to the performance (or nonperformance) of an act by a third party (a right "to be left alone"). It would seem that rights are always qualified in this way, with a referent object. Even when rights (or "human rights") are spoken of in general, they always call to mind a collection of particular rights, or rights to particular things. A "right" in the abstract, with no referent, is an incomplete concept. Similarly, the phrase "human rights violations" always indicates that concrete actions have been committed that violate particular human rights.

Nonetheless, the unqualified statements "I have rights" or "I want my rights" or "These people have rights, too" are not without meaning. Asserting that a person possesses rights in general means that the person deserves to be taken into consideration and treated as a human being and not as a member of an inferior species. Nowadays affirming one's own— or others'—rights in the abstract calls attention to one's dignity as a person or to one's "status" as a human being, worthy of being treated as such. To say "I have rights" is to say "I am the sort of being that is capable of having rights" or "I belong to the human community and everything that is due to a member of this community is likewise due to me."

A Moral Faculty

This "right" that is possessed is clearly no tangible, material reality but rather a moral power or capacity or, in more classical language, a *faculty*. The word "power" (or "capacity" or "faculty") denotes the stable quality of being able to do something (such as to perform, possess, or demand), even when such a power is not exercised. The word "moral" denotes the quality of normative propriety, or conformity with what is just and fitting. A moral power ought not be confused with a physical power. To possess a right—say, to food or shelter—does not mean that one in fact *possesses* food or shelter, nor that one possess a *physical* power to procure for oneself food or shelter. Similarly, to possess a right "to think what we want" does not mean that we in fact *do* think what we want, nor even that we have the capacity to think what we want in the sense of a mental ability to do so (though this may be understood). Rather, such a statement proposes that we enjoy a relationship with independent thought such that to engage in it is proper and good and thus "belongs" to us. We can justly claim it as our own.

The very word "right" draws attention to moral or legal correctness. That is to say, by affirming a right to something, one at least implicitly affirms that it is *right* or *just* to have or do whatever it might be that one has a right to. In this sense, the assertion of a right seems to include but exceed the assertion of moral or legal *permission.* A different nuance of meaning and force is discernible between the expressions "I am permitted to think what I want" and "I have a right to think what I want." The first expression gives the sense that to think what one wants is lawful and violates no contrary norm of conduct. Either that or a concession has been made and one has been granted permission to think what one wants, despite whatever norms may exist to the contrary. "I have a right," on the other hand, makes a stronger statement. Whereas permission reflects the absence of a contrary law or a concession on the part of authority, right suggests a positive good.[3]

The superiority of a claim to a right as compared with a claim to permission is still more evident when speaking of a right not to an action but to a thing. For instance, the statement that "Children have a right to an education" goes beyond the statement that "It is permissible for chil-

---

3. "The difference between a right and a simple subjective pretension consists in the fact that the latter can show no intrinsic justification valid *erga omnes,* whereas with the former a value is evinced that man cannot be deprived of without harm and injustice, and in which is expressed something of the essence of humanity. In a proper and rigorous sense a 'human right' is something owed to the persona as such by dint of his being a human being" (Vittorio Possenti, "Diritti umani e natura umana," *Rivista di filosofia neo-scolastica* 2 [1995]: 250; author's translation).

dren to be educated." The first statement (rights claim) bears a connotation that children somehow *should* have an education, and that education is in fact good for them. The second statement (permission) gives the idea that an allowance has been made, and despite possible arguments to the contrary, education of children is not forbidden.

Rights Describe a Reciprocal Interpersonal Relationship

A fourth discernable characteristic of rights is the effect they produce in the social order. An assertion of right is other-directed and therefore passes from the sphere of personal morality to the juridical sphere.[4] Rights always bear a relational connotation and describe a moral relationship with other persons. In classical language, rights therefore fall within the domain of the virtue of justice.[5]

By proclaiming a right to something, one affirms not only that it is morally proper for one to have or do something but also that a moral relationship exists with other persons as regards the matter of the right.[6] In other words, rights always imply corresponding duties. For example, there is a difference between stating that X is good for Y, or even that Y should pursue X, and stating that Y has a right to X. The first two affirmations speak only of a relationship between the subject and the thing or action, that is, between Y and X, whereas the latter implicitly includes a

---

4. "Juridical" here refers to the order of justice, the virtue that directs interpersonal relations, and is not intended to refer specifically to the civil order. De Finance notes that the difference between obligation and duty parallels the difference between what is lawful and a right. In both instances, "the difference is due to the relational aspect, the 'other-directed' aspect, social in the broad sense, which characterizes the juridical order" (*An Ethical Inquiry*, trans. Michael O'Brien [Rome: Editrice Pontificia Università Gregoriana, 1991], § 200, p. 353). In other words, an "obligation" speaks only of the moral agent, whereas "duty" is necessarily other related (a duty to someone). In the same manner, "lawfulness" speaks only of correspondence to an objective code of conduct, whereas "right" necessarily includes a relational aspect to other persons.

5. See Thomas Aquinas, *Summa Theologiae*, trans. English Dominicans (*1912–36*; repr., New York: Christian Classics, 1981; hereafter *S. Th.*), II-II, 57.

6. Right, therefore, means more than "lawfulness" or "uprightness." De Finance has written: "It is morally permissible to do everything that is not evil and this, of itself, involves nothing more than a relationship with right reason. But we could not, strictly speaking, say that we have a right to perform actions of this kind, unless all we intended to express was that the Supreme Legislator did not require us to abstain from these actions. The reason for this is that rights, in common with justice . . . involve not only a relationship with right reason, but also a relationship with others. It is only as 'facing towards' others and in reference to them that we have rights" (*An Ethical Inquiry*, § 194, p. 344).

moral relationship involving X, Y, and another person or persons.[7] A rights claim always entails the affirmation of a duty to respect or satisfy that right. "Children have a right to an education" could be reworded to "It is just that children receive an education" or "Children are owed an education" and, as a corollary, "It is unjust for children not to receive an education." If one proposes that children have a right to an education, one also proposes that others (exactly who we are not yet sure) have a duty to provide children with an education.

Drawing Phenomenological Conclusions

An assertion of a right always involves, at least implicitly, four components: a rights-bearer (Y), a thing or action to which Y has a right (X), a third party (P), and a reciprocal moral or legal obligation between P and Y as regards X.[8] Among these four components exist certain relations. Between Y and X exists a relation of belonging. X in some way "becomes" Y, is proper to Y, such that for Y to possess or perform X is in harmony with the moral order. Between Y and P as regards X exists a relation of justice, whereby Y is "entitled" to X from P, and P "owes" X to Y. The form of this entitlement and owing will depend chiefly on the nature of X. If X is an *action* that Y has a right to perform, then P's "owing" may take the form of noninterference and respect of Y's performance of X. An example of this would be Y's right as a citizen to vote. In this case, P owes Y respect in Y's exercise of his right to vote and may not justly impede such exercise. If X is a *thing* that Y has a right to possess or use, but which Y is incapable of procuring for himself, then P's owing may take the form of an obligation to provide Y with X or facilitate Y's acquisition of X. For instance, if Y has lent P the sum of $100, then Y has the right to repayment of $100, and P has the correlative duty to restore to Y his $100. The four components of "rights" as commonly understood, then, are: the possessor of the right, the possessor of the duty to respect or satisfy the right,

---

7. As Alasdair MacIntyre notes, "the claim that I have a right to do or have something is a quite different type of claim from the claim that I need or want or will be benefited by something. From the first . . . it follows that others ought not to interfere with my attempts to do or have whatever it is. . . . From the second it does not" (*After Virtue*, 67).

8. Victor Cathrein asserts that "we may distinguish in right four elements: the holder, the object, the title, and the terminus of the right" ("Right," *The Catholic Encyclopedia*, vol. 13 [1914]).

the thing or action in question, and a reciprocal moral relationship that binds them all together.

DEFINITIONS OF RIGHTS

The aspects of rights drawn from a phenomenological-linguistic analysis correspond to key aspects contained in some of the more compelling definitions of rights in Western philosophical and juridical tradition. This shows that these essential characteristics are not arbitrary, and that they can serve as dependable parameters in formulating an accurate working definition of rights. The immense literature that has been generated on the question of rights has produced hundreds of definitions—though it is also worth noting that many who write on the subject of rights do not take the trouble to define them, preferring to take for granted a common understanding of the concept.[9] A look at one of the earlier definitions, offered by Hugo Grotius in the seventeenth century, and one of the most recent, that of Germain Grisez in the late twentieth century, will suffice to show that the contemporary understanding of the nature of rights is not new and will allow the formulation of a legitimate working definition.

Grotius

In 1625, the Dutch jurist Hugo Grotius defined a right as "a moral quality of a person, making it possible to have or to do something lawfully."[10] This definition includes three of the four characteristics gleaned from the phenomenological-linguistic analysis: the possessor of the right, the thing or action in question, and the moral force that links them.

---

9. Consider, for example, the description of rights given by Francesco Compagnoni in his dictionary of moral theology, which, despite its many valid observations, never reaches a true definition of what rights *are*. "[O]ne can say that the rights of man are prior to and above the state; they are innate in man and unrenounceable; their validity is independent from recognition or disregard by the state; they issue from a source of right that is supra-positive and of natural or divine law, or—renouncing attempts at a metaphysical foundation—from the very fact of being human beings. Their acceptance in the positive constitutional order of the state has only a declarative, and not a constitutive character" ("Diritti dell'uomo," in *Nuovo Dizionario di Teologia Morale*, ed. F. Compagnoni, G. Piana, and S. Privitera [Cinisello Balsamo: Edizioni Paoline, 1990], 220; author's translation).

10. Hugo Grotius, *De Iure Belli ac Pacis Libri Tres* (1625), vol. 2 of *Classics of International Law*, trans. Francis W. Kelsey (Oxford: Clarendon Press, 1925), bk. I, ch. I, IV, 35.

Conspicuous by its absence in Grotius's definition of rights is reference to the fourth characteristic—another person. Such an omission muddles the complementarity of rights and duties: a merely moral relationship between subject and some thing or action would imply duties only indirectly.

Later, however, Grotius refers to this moral quality as a *facultas* ("power" or "ability"), which he describes as "the right to one's own" *(suum)*.[11] This echoes the classical definition of justice: the habitual disposition to render to each his due, i.e., what is "his own" *(suum)*.[12] For Grotius, therefore, rights stand squarely in the domain of justice, which brings in—at least implicitly—the relations of rights to a third party. Consequently, even though the fourth characteristic of rights is not denoted by Grotius's definition, in his mind it is certainly connoted. This becomes even clearer in his discussion of law. Grotius first defines law as "what is just" and subsequently refers to "another meaning of law as a body of rights, different from the one just defined but growing out of it, which has reference to the person."[13] In other words, "what is just," when applied to persons, gives rise to "a body of rights" that are "moral qualit[ies] of a person, making it possible to have or to do something lawfully." When speaking of "contractual rights," in fact, Grotius explicitly makes mention of "contractual obligations" that correspond to them.[14]

Thus although the explicit terms differ, the four essential characteristics of rights implied by contemporary common usage of the word appear even in the thought of one of the most influential precursors of the Enlightenment.

Grisez

That these four characteristics also appear (though imperfectly) in the thought of the influential contemporary moral theologian Germain Grisez further demonstrates their importance. In the glossary of the first volume of his monumental work on moral theology, *The Way of the Lord Jesus,* Grisez succinctly defines rights as "moral or legal claims on others"

---

11. Ibid., bk. I, ch. I, V, 35.
12. *S. Th.,* II-II, 58, 11; see also Augustine, *De Civitate Dei,* XIX, 21, 2; *De Libero Arbitrio,* bk. I, 27 B.
13. Grotius, *De Iure Belli ac Pacis, b*k. I, ch. I, III, 1, 34; bk. I, ch. I, IV, 35.
14. Ibid., bk. I, ch. I, V, 35–36.

and asserts that rights "do not constitute a basic category but are correlative to duties, which are the social aspects of one's moral or legal responsibilities."[15] Grisez's emphasis on the third party (the person who must provide or respect someone's rights) complements Grotius's emphasis on the possessor of the right. Grisez's glossary definition found at the back of the text neatly sums up what he explains in an earlier section, where he says that "right and duty are the same reality, 'right' signifying its bearing upon the person or group affected by the action which the duty specifies."[16] Therefore, "there are as many meanings of 'rights' as of 'duties,' and all distinctions made concerning duties must also be made concerning rights."[17] Grisez also states that rights are not basic moral principles because they are not self-evident; they are intelligible only in terms of duties.[18] In the second volume of Grisez's series, he offers a more precise definition: "[A] right is a relational moral attribute of a person or group which corresponds to a responsibility that another or others have toward that person or group."[19] As Grisez explains, a person's right is a consequence of a corresponding responsibility: "[I]f X would act unjustly toward Y by doing or not doing A, then Y has a right that X do or not do A." Moreover, rights "are consequences, not principles, of justice."[20]

Both Grisez's brief glossary definition and his more developed discussion bring out important points, notably the essential aspect of the correlativity of rights and duties, but they also underestimate three key components. First, the relationship between the rights-bearer and the object of the right remains, at best, vague. Rights are always rights to something, not merely a moral relationship between two individuals. The word "claim" at best implies an object, which in turn suggests that, for Grisez, the object is not essential to the definition. Second, Grisez fails to specify that the moral or legal claim must be in accord with justice, though this too could be inferred from the context. As it stands, a claim

---

15. Germain Grisez, *Christian Moral Principles*, vol. 1 of *The Way of the Lord Jesus* (Chicago: Franciscan Herald Press, 1983), p. 924.

16. Ibid., 10.E.7, p. 264. Grisez further develops this thought when analyzing the issue of animal rights. See *Living a Christian Life*, vol. 2 of *The Way of the Lord Jesus* (Quincy, Ill.: Franciscan Press, 1993), 10.C.1, pp. 783–85.

17. Grisez, *Christian Moral Principles*, 10.E.7, p. 265.

18. See ibid., 10.E.8, p. 265.

19. Grisez, *Living a Christian Life*, 6.B.6, p. 329.

20. Ibid.;6.B.6.c, p. 330.

to anything, regardless of its validity, would qualify under Grisez's definition of a right simply by the fact of its being claimed. The chief difference, in fact, between a "right" and a generic "claim" is precisely this element of justice, the quality of being due. Third, it would seem that Grisez misses the mark in assigning a genus to rights in his definition. Grisez affirms that rights are "claims," but a phenomenological analysis revealed that rights are possessed whether a claim is lodged or not; thus, rights cannot be identified with the claim itself but rather with a moral or legal capacity in justice to make such a claim.[21]

More problematic still is Grisez's assertion that rights are consequences, and not principles, of justice. If indeed rights correspond to one's due and the moral capacity of claiming one's due, then they are indeed principles, rather than consequences, of justice. Justice is done, in fact, when all render to others their due, i.e., what they have a right to.

Filling in the Gaps

In spite of their lacunae, Grisez's definitions clearly touch on the same aspects of rights that appeared in Grotius's definition and in the phenomenological-linguistic analysis of common terminology—aspects that have been present throughout the history of philosophical reflection on the nature of rights. The centuries that passed between Grotius and Grisez exhibit a noteworthy consistency in the core concept of what rights really are.

Unfortunately, however, this underlying consistency has not yet yielded a complete, dependable definition, as modern reference books clearly evince. For example, the *Random House Webster's Electronic Dictionary and Thesaurus* reads: "Right *n.* 16. something that is due to anyone by just claim, legal guarantees, moral principles, etc.: the right to free

21. "A right is commonly said (by Paul Vinogradoff, for instance) to be a claim upheld by the law. As in the case of 'power,' however, there is an ambiguity between the positive and the normative sense of 'claim.' If by a claim were meant a demand actually made, it might be objected both that men possess rights to things they never claim, and that it makes sense to talk of the rights of infants incapable of demanding anything. On the other hand, 'to have a claim' as against 'to make a claim' means that if one were to make a demand, it would be justified or, at least, defensible. But as with 'power,' this would then locate the concept not in the language of description but in that of norms. Vinogradoff may well be right in saying that men have acquired legal rights only by claiming them, yet it would be a mistake to confuse a historical fact with an account of the meaning of 'rights'" (Stanley I. Benn, "Rights," in *The Encyclopedia of Philosophy*, vol. 7, edited by Paul Edwards. New York: Macmillan, 1967).

speech; children's rights." Similarly, in the *American Heritage College Dictionary* one reads: "Right *n.* 6. Something due to a person or community by law, tradition, or nature. 7. A just or legal claim or title."[22] The chief imprecision in both cases is that of identifying the "right" with "something due" rather than as a *power* to possess, do, or demand something. A sum of money can be due to someone by just claim, but the *money* itself is not a right. The right involved would be a moral capacity to demand that the money be repaid. Rights are always *to* something else, which implies a nonidentity between the right and the thing or activity connected to the right. Rather than equate a right with the object of the right, it would be more precise to say that a right is "something by which" a person may possess, do, or demand something. As a moral principle, "right" is an exact ethical counterpart to "duty." This "something by which" corresponds to the moral power (or faculty or capacity) referred to earlier as one of the four essential characteristics of rights.

The *Catholic Encyclopedia* offers a more nuanced definition of right. "Right," one reads, "may . . . be defined as a moral or legal authority to possess, claim, and use a thing as one's own."[23] Here "authority" takes the place of "faculty," of which it is basically a synonym in the present context. Though the definition omits reference to justice, the very fact of right being described as a "moral or legal" authority locates rights in the realm of justice, whence proceeds their force. The definition lacks breadth, however, as it contemplates only rights to "things" and fails to mention rights to activities.

Perhaps the reason that five centuries of reflection on the concept of rights has failed to produce a satisfactory definition is precisely because no one has yet clarified the ultimate foundation of human rights, which is the task of the current study. In the meantime, however, the results of comparing a phenomenological-linguistic analysis of the term with two definitions representative of the long philosophical tradition is sufficient to devise a reliable working definition: A right is the moral capacity or power to possess, to do, or to demand one's due. In still simpler terms, a right is the moral capacity to claim from another what one deserves.

22. *Random House Webster's Electronic Dictionary and Thesaurus,* college ed., version 1.0, s.v. "Right"; *American Heritage College Dictionary,* 3rd ed., s.v. "Right."
23. Cathrein, "Right."

2. SOME NEEDED NUANCES

The difficulty of defining rights is further aggravated by the appendage of numerous adjectives to the noun "rights," resulting in a broad range of "classes" of rights. Thus even a good definition of rights still does not tell the whole story. Rights often appear together with modifiers that alter their meaning, sometimes substantially. Human rights are not the same as civil rights, and positive rights are not the same as negative rights. In fact, the term positive rights means one thing when contrasted with negative rights and another thing altogether when contrasted with natural rights. Other adjectives—inviolable, objective, subjective, legal, inalienable, absolute, active, passive, strong, weak, and moral—often accompany "rights," and each of these qualifiers adds a particular nuance that differentiates it from the others.

These adjectives address aspects such as the genesis of rights (e.g., some proceed from contract or civil decree, others from nature), their sphere of influence, or their degree of moral binding power. It is essential to examine these adjectives closely, since in some cases they radically change the meaning of rights and therefore their foundation. Moreover, people frequently have one of these adjectives in mind when they speak of "rights" *tout court,* a practice that easily leads to misunderstandings. If by "rights" one person understands natural rights, and another understands legal or civil rights, confusion is sure to follow. To come to an adequate understanding of rights, therefore, it is important to offer some distinctions of different classes of rights. Eight sets of adjectives comprise the basic spectrum of rights taxonomy.

MORAL VS. LEGAL

Though a good definition identifies right as a "moral capacity," in the sense that rights describe a normative relationship between one person and another in relation to certain goods, rights can be further divided into moral and legal.[1] In fact, such a distinction is critical. Western society increasingly tends to conflate the moral and legal realms, generally absorbing the moral into the legal. Such an identification is unsound. When morality becomes legality, moral virtue is reduced to being "law-abiding." Lawfulness, however, embraces only an external conformity to a legal code, while morality encompasses the whole sphere of free human action and extends to deeds, words, thoughts, and even omissions.[2] Moreover, many cultural mores and manners skirt legal codification but make social relations human and ethical. A reduction of the ethical question of "what one ought to do" to legal obligation necessarily results in a minimalist ethics that lacks the elasticity and "humanity" proper to interpersonal relations and demands more of civil law than the law is capable of providing.[3]

There are, in fact, many moral duties that lie outside the purview of the law but oblige in conscience nonetheless.[4] John Courtney Murray summarizes this point in *We Hold These Truths:*

---

1. Here "legal" refers specifically to civil law, as distinct from moral law, and thus such legal rights are subject to enforcement by public authority.

2. The precedence of morality over legality is brought out forcefully in a comment made by Orthodox rabbi David Kaye, a U.S. Air Force chaplain, in an address delivered at the annual Canterbury Medal Award dinner in 1997. Kaye remarked that during the Holocaust, "no Jew was killed illegally, only immorally" (reported in the *National Catholic Register,* March 30–April 5, 1997).

3. The present inquiry into the foundations of rights deals with the broader and more fundamental area of *moral* rights, not simply legal rights. Hence the ability or inability of a rights-holder to take remedial legal action in the event of another's failure to comply with his duty falls outside the compass of this investigation. The subject at hand is the foundation of moral entitlement and conversely of natural moral duty. This will sometimes coincide with legal rights and duties, but often it won't. Throughout this inquiry, references to "rights," as such, will always be understood as moral rights.

4. Therefore Thomas Aquinas asserts that human laws should not attempt to repress all vices. "Now human law is framed for a number of human beings, the majority of whom are not perfect in virtue. Wherefore human laws do not forbid all vices, from which the virtuous abstain, but only the more grievous vices, from which it is possible for the majority to abstain; and chiefly those that are to the hurt of others, without the prohibition of which human

[M]orals and law are differentiated in character, and not coextensive in their functions. It is not th pe function of the legislator to forbid everything the moral law forbids, or to enjoin everything the moral law enjoins. The moral law governs the entire order of human conduct, personal and social; it extends even to motivations and interior acts. Law, on the other hand, looks only to the public order of human society; it touches only external acts, and regards only values that are formally social.[5]

As principles of justice, moral rights, too, extend beyond what can be codified into civil law. Nonetheless, some view only legal rights as true rights, since only rights that are encoded in law and backed up by legal sanctions can be guaranteed.[6] In this vein Russell Kirk wrote:

> Rights can take on flesh only if they are derived from some body of law. The abstractions we call "human rights" have no sanction in the positive laws of most countries; the Universal Declaration of Human Rights may receive the formal assent of various governments, but nowhere is that Declaration observed and enforced.
>
> "Rights" are immunities, guarantees that certain things may not be done to a person against his will. Rights can be secured only in a civil social order. In a condition of anarchy, no one enjoys rights, because there exists no just authority to which a person may appeal against the violation of rights. Therefore what we call the state, or organized political community, is necessary for the realizing of any rights.[7]

---

society could not be maintained: thus human law prohibits murder, theft and such like" (*S. Th.*, I-II, 96, 2).

5. John Courtney Murray, *We Hold These Truths: Catholic Reflections on the American Proposition* (Garden City, N.Y.: Image Books, 1964), 163–64.

6. It is typical to find definitions of rights that assume a juridical structure. Dario Composta, for example, defines human rights as the "legitimate faculty of being, having, or doing, protected by the juridical order" ("Prassi e coscienza dei diritti umani nella storia," *Seminarium* 23 [1983], 332; author's translation). According to such a definition, rights legislation would not merely recognize existing human rights but would bring such rights into existence, since their protection under the law would form part of their essence.

"For Bentham and Austin, a duty exists only where the law imposes (and enforces) a sanction for a breach of it. Bentham wrote in his *Fragment on Government* (1776), 'Without the notion of punishment . . . , no notion could we have of either *right or duty.*' There are two points here: first, whether duties really depend on consequential sanctions for their meaning or only for their effectiveness, or perhaps for neither; second, whether every right has its correlative duty, such that the right of X can always be stated without alteration of meaning as a duty of Y" (Benn, "Rights," 196).

7. Russell Kirk, *Redeeming the Time* (Wilmington, Del.: ISI Books, 1996), 232.

According to Kirk's reasoning, rights without legal sanctions are "abstractions," but by the same token, so is the entire moral law, in the sense that it preexists civil society and indeed serves as a yardstick for the justice of a given rule of law. In line with Aquinas's cogent explanation of virtue and the scope of civil law, it is not always possible or even desirable to suppose a *legal* obligation corresponding to every right.[8]

This being the case, it may again be objected: What good is a right that cannot be enforced? A right not backed up by the state's power of coercion, some contend, is a hollow concept. In reflecting on Pope John Paul's advocacy of rights for children, Jewish thinker Matthew Berke, while praising the Pope's efforts, considers that "[s]uch a prospect is perhaps not practicable—how does one guarantee children their 'right' to 'a united family' and a 'moral environment'?"[9]

Yet are rights always limited to what can be legally guaranteed? In proclaiming the rights of children, the Pope assuredly does not wish to unleash a spate of lawsuits brought by or on behalf of children demanding their legal right to a united home, nor is he calling for detailed legislation laying out exactly what must be provided to children to satisfy their rights. In fact, it is probable that the Pope is addressing parents in the first place, not public authorities or legislative bodies, since parents are chiefly responsible for seeing that children's rights are satisfied. Rights, after all, are not limited to relations between state and citizens but, like justice, encompass all interpersonal relations. Public authorities can of course help create a social and legal environment conducive to the satisfaction of these rights (e.g., regarding fiscal policy and divorce law where children are involved). Yet the fact that given rights are legally unenforceable in no wise strips them of moral value.[10]

What, then, is the relationship between the moral and legal spheres as

---

8. See *S. Th.*, I-II, 96, 2–3.

9. Matthew Berke, "A Jewish Appreciation of Catholic Social Teaching," in *Catholicism, Liberalism, and Communitarianism: The Catholic Intellectual Tradition and the Moral Foundations of Democracy*, ed. Kenneth L. Grasso, Gerard V. Bradley, and Robert P. Hunt (Lanham, Md.: Rowman & Littlefield, 1995), 247. Berke was responding to John Paul's *Centesimus Annus*, 47.

10. Thus de Finance writes, "It can undoubtedly happen that a person will be forcibly prevented from exercising a right: but this does not mean that the moral power which is his is diminished in any way. Trampled on and flouted though it may be, it still remains a *right*. Force neither creates nor destroys it, for it is of quite a different order" (*An Ethical Inquiry*, § 204, p. 359).

regards rights? Some see a direct correspondence between rights claims and legislation. Mary Ann Glendon, for example, has written: "When we assert our rights to life, liberty, and property, we are expressing the reasonable hope that such things can be made more secure by law and politics."[11] While Professor Glendon's contention generally holds true in practice, an assertion of rights is not necessarily a legal proposition at all.[12] Rather, when one affirms fundamental rights to determined goods, one affirms in the first place a moral claim to such goods and thus a moral duty on the part of others to respect those goods. In other words, like moral duties, moral rights appeal to conscience, not to civil law. They are statements of normative moral principle, regardless of whether they are legally codified.

Even so, since law exists to promote the common good and secure a just social order, it will naturally draw on basic moral rights or principles and codify many of them into civil rights, producing a substantial overlap between legal and moral rights. That is, since moral rights encompass the order of social justice, which is the proper domain of civil society, moral rights and civil rights will often coincide. Nevertheless, many moral rights will never, and should never, be formulated as civil laws.[13] In these cases, however, their force is not diminished, because it derives from their morality, not their legality.

Despite their essential differences, moral and legal are not two dis-

---

11. Glendon, *Rights Talk*, 45. It should be noted that in this context Professor Glendon was referring specifically to the rights asserted in the Declaration of Independence, a political document meant to be reflected in the rule of law.

12. For example, the Vatican II document *Dignitatis Humanae*, in speaking of religious liberty, appeals for legal recognition of this basic moral principle: "The right of the human person to religious freedom must be given such recognition in the constitutional order of society as will make it a civil right" (2). Moreover, in the same document we read that the "protection and promotion of the inviolable rights of man is an essential duty of every civil authority" (6). See also John XXIII, *Pacem in Terris* (hereafter *PT*), 60; Pius XII, radio message of Pentecost, June 1, 1941, in *Acta Apostolicae Sedis* (hereafter *AAS*) 33 (1941): 200). Nonetheless, two distinctions must be made. First, moral rights are always prior to civil rights and exist independently of them, and second, though basic, *inviolable* rights—which fall into the category of *negative* rights—should be protected by civil law, not all human rights fall into this category.

13. An example of such rights are those so-called positive rights to specific goods. One of the dangers of codifying such rights lies in the assignment of duties to meet specific needs. When codified, such duties often fall on the shoulders of the state, resulting in the inflation of government programs, as if government were responsible for satisfying all the needs of the populace. A strictly moral appeal to the rights of persons allows mediating institutions to intervene on behalf of those in need without doing so under legal constriction. This is not to say that

parate categories but two distinct realms that exert a considerable mutual influence on one another. Morality gives legality its binding force, but legality, in turn, helps educate the moral conscience. As Glendon has pointed out, law has an important pedagogical role in "forming or reinforcing a common moral sense."[14] Especially in societies with a vigorous rule of law, legislation sends important messages to citizens about morality itself. Actions that are "against the law" are frowned upon and judged as unacceptable behavior by society. In this sense, law is, in Glendon's words, a "repository of moral norms."[15] In its pedagogical function, the law teaches citizens what is important and what is not, what is acceptable and what is not.[16] Thus the law helps shape society's moral self-conception and identity.

The legal codification of rights, therefore, does not immediately spring from rights claims but involves manifold prudential considerations. The fact remains that an essential distinction exists between moral rights and legal rights, and the two, while often overlapping, operate on distinct levels.

NATURAL VS. POSITIVE

A second distinction separates rights that inhere in human nature itself from those that proceed from decree, contract, or convention. The former bear the title "natural rights" and the latter "positive rights." Natural rights, as the name suggests (from the Latin *nascor*, to be born), stem from a common human nature and are universally predicated of all human beings. Positive rights are those granted by some authority such as the state, obtained through contract or convention, or acquired through membership in a group (an association, society, etc.) that enjoys such rights or confers such rights on its members.

The fact that some rights are "natural" carries with it three further

---

government has no part in satisfying basic human rights, but only that discernment is needed in allocating such responsibilities.

14. Glendon, *Rights Talk*, 85.   15. Ibid.

16. "Members of the legal profession may understand that a judge's emphatic denial of a legal duty to snatch my neighbor's child from the path of an oncoming threshing machine has no bearing whatsoever on my moral duty to do so. . . . But when reported in the larger society, technically proper legal negations of responsibility can easily miseducate the public about what it means to be a citizen. Careless judicial pronouncements can harden the lines on a cultural grid which already seems to have decreasing room for a sense of public obligation" (ibid., 104).

corollaries, viz., that natural rights are objective, innate, and universal. Since natural rights inhere in human nature itself, they are objective in that they do not depend on the subjective perceptions, preferences, or dispositions of other persons. They are the same for everyone and can be objectively ascertained.[17] Because of their objective character, a distinction can be made between "true" natural rights and "false" natural rights, where the latter would be seen to proceed from subjective desire rather than from nature.[18]

Because the "natural" in natural rights refers to their innate quality, they can be contrasted to "acquired" rights. Natural rights do not depend on the actions of the individual who possesses them, because they are not earned. Nor do they depend upon outside authority, such as that of the state. Even when they are not recognized, they do not cease to exist and to oblige morally. Since they are not granted by the state, neither can they be revoked or annulled by political authority,[19] except when the misuse of such rights results in disturbance of the public order.

Finally, natural rights, by the very fact that they inhere in the human person qua human person, are universal. They are predicated equally of all members of the species, though specific applications of general rights may vary according to circumstance. The acknowledgment of the universality of natural rights eliminates the danger that some members of socie-

17. "It is an important element in human rights that the rights of one person should not be made dependent on the way the conscience of another person judges the situation. There is no reason why one should not discuss the legal rights of unborn children, even if the West German constitution already gives a positive answer to it. However, slogans stating that this should be decided by the conscience of individuals are nonsensical. Either it is the case that children have no right to life, in which case there is no need even to mention conscience, or else the unborn have a right to life, in which case the right cannot be made to depend on the disposition of other people's consciences" (Robert Spaemann, *Basic Moral Concepts,* trans. T. J. Armstrong [London: Routledge, 1991], 66).

18. The *Catechism of the Catholic Church* assigns to the Church the role of distinguishing true rights from false claims. "Respect for the human person entails respect for the rights that flow from his dignity as a creature. . . . It is the Church's role to remind men of good will of these rights, and to distinguish them from unwarranted or false claims" (1930).

19. "It is evident that these rights were inscribed by the Creator in the order of creation; so we cannot speak of concessions on the part of human institutions, on the part of states and international organizations. These institutions express no more than what God Himself inscribed in the order He created, what He Himself has inscribed in the moral conscience, or in the human heart, as St. Paul explains in the Letter to the Romans (cf. Rom 2:15)" (John Paul II, *Crossing the Threshold of Hope,* ed. Vittorio Messori, trans. Jenny McPhee and Martha McPhee [New York: Alfred A. Knopf, 1994], 196–97).

ty (e.g., the poor, the handicapped, the unborn, members of certain races or religions, women) could be excluded from the exercise of rights attributed to others.

Positive rights often correspond to natural rights as regards their content. For example, the Bill of Rights appended to the U.S. Constitution guarantees that a person not be randomly deprived of life, liberty, and property. A person has a natural right to the same things. Here the difference lies not in the content of the right but rather in its form and in the civil sanctions attached, since positive rights are formally declared and backed up by a ruling authority, whereas natural rights are unwritten and have their locus in human nature itself. But positive rights may also exceed natural rights even in content. The right to a specified minimum wage, for instance, or the right to drink alcohol at a given age, are not determined by human nature but by the prudential judgment of public authority. Some positive rights may even contradict natural rights, though in this case, from a Catholic perspective, such rights would not be binding in conscience. Government may grant, for instance, positive rights to immoral behavior or behavior that harms other people, where no natural rights could possibly exist.

HUMAN VS. CIVIL

A third classification distinguishes between human rights and civil rights. In reality, the concept of human rights overlaps that of natural rights almost to the point of synonymity, and civil rights coincide almost exactly with legal rights. Still, certain shades of meaning and emphasis make the distinction worthwhile.

"Human rights" is a newer term for natural rights and likewise underscores universality: certain rights belong to every member of the human family. The term, which became current in 1948 with the Universal Declaration of Human Rights, stresses that all human persons are entitled to a particular standard of treatment simply by virtue of their membership in the human race. Whereas "natural rights" could conceivably be applied to any species of creature, since the term designates the source of rights as being a common nature without specifying what that nature is, the expression human rights restricts the assignment of such rights to members of the human species.

The newer term is not without its opponents. Russell Kirk finds the concept suspect. "From the first," he writes, "the odor of demagoguery has clung to the political use of 'human rights' language. For all rights are human rights. Does anyone suggest a code of inhuman rights? Dogs and cats do not enjoy rights. States have no rights (despite constitutional arguments); states enjoy powers. God is above rights, and humankind can claim no rights against God."[20] Others see "human rights" as a corruption of "natural rights" and fear it may reflect doubt as to the origin of rights in human nature.[21]

Yet the modifier "human" when attached to rights is neither redundant nor superfluous. Despite Kirk's commonsense assertion that dogs and cats do not enjoy rights, not everyone shares his conviction, and animal rights activists exert considerable pressure on public opinion and legislators.[22] As for his contention that all rights are human rights, the rights comprised by this term are those shared universally by the entire human race and are thus distinct from rights enjoyed by certain individuals, such as those conferred on members of voluntary associations (rights of access to a clubhouse, for example). The adjective "human" also distinguishes the quality of originality and indicates that such rights precede human institutions and undergird human laws. Where civil rights, for instance, are the creation of the state, human rights are part and parcel of the universal human condition itself.

In contrast with human rights, civil rights refer to those entitlements encoded in civil law.[23] In this sense, "civil" refers to official sanction by public authority and thus such rights are legally enforceable.[24] In this sense, civil rights are synonymous with legal rights as defined earlier.

20. Kirk, *Redeeming the Time*, 228.

21. Lloyd Weinreb, for example, writes that in the twentieth century natural rights have flourished "more recently under the ambiguous rubric of 'human rights.' The switch from the 'natural' to the 'human' surely reflects doubt as to whether nature—or any of the equivalent terms for the world as it is—is intelligibly the source of any normative principles at all; 'human' rights can be understood to refer not to the source of the rights in question but to those who possess them, the basis of such universal (human) rights being left uncomfortably unclear" ("Natural Law and Rights," in *Natural Law Theory: Contemporary Essays*, ed. Robert P. George [Oxford: Oxford University Press, 1995], 279–80).

22. For a comprehensive exposition of the position in favor of animal rights, see Thomas Regan, *The Case for Animal Rights* (Berkeley: University of California Press, 1983).

23. Among its various definitions, "civil" means "of or pertaining to civil law." See *Random House Webster's Electronic Dictionary and Thesaurus*, definition 9.

24. Kirk continues: "A 'civil right' is a guarantee that the citizen is protected against certain

Yet civil and political rights refer not only to their locus as encoded in civil law but also to the *matter* of the rights, i.e., the sort of activities protected by them. Civil rights, therefore, refer also to the rights of the citizen, such as the right to vote or otherwise participate in government, and so forth.[25]

SUBJECTIVE VS. OBJECTIVE

Another pair of adjectives differentiates so-called objective right from subjective rights. These adjectives easily lend themselves to confusion, since "objective" often implies what is real or discernible to an unbiased observer, and "subjective" implies what exists only in the mind or the realm of personal opinion. A different distinction is in play when using these terms in reference to rights. Objective right refers to the "just order," that is, "the establishment and preservation of a certain equality between man and man (between individual human beings, or between one society and another)."[26] When people speak of "justice" (as in "working for justice"), they are speaking of objective right, a situation in which the common good is realized.[27] Right, according to Aquinas, is the object of the virtue of justice, and the etymological link between *ius* (right) and *iustitia* (justice) is evident.[28] The singular term "right" is rarely employed in this sense nowadays, but the distinction is important in order to understand the evolution of the word "rights" and the understanding that earlier generations had of this notion.

---

actions that otherwise the state might take to the citizen's disadvantage. Such rights commonly are stated in the negative—that troops shall not be quartered in private dwellings, for instance, or that punishments shall not be cruel and unusual. Civil rights are understood to entail corresponding civil duties, the most important of which is the duty to maintain the rule of law by which such rights are given flesh" (*Redeeming the Time*, 231).

25. "civ-il adj. 1. of, pertaining to, or consisting of citizens: civil life; civil society" *(Random House Webster's Electronic Dictionary and Thesaurus)*.

26. De Finance, *An Ethical Inquiry*, § 194, p. 342.

27. The "common good of society consists in the sum total of those conditions of social life which enable men to achieve a fuller measure of perfection with greater ease" (*Catechism of the Catholic Church* [hereafter *CCC*], 1906. See also *Dignitatis Humanae* [hereafter *DH*], 6; John XXIII, *Mater et Magistra* [hereafter *MM*], 65; *PT,* 58).

28. St. Thomas affirms that "justice has its own special proper object over and above the other virtues, and this object is called the just, which is the same as 'right.' Hence it is evident that right is the object of justice" (*S. Th.,* II-II, 57, 1). Furthermore, "the word *'ius'* [right] was first of all used to denote the just thing itself" (ibid., II-II, 57, 1, ad 1).

The term "subjective rights" describes what most people today understand by rights in general. Subjective rights are rights ascribable to individuals and groups rather than a state of equilibrium or just order. At the same time, subjective rights form part of the objective moral order. Their "subjectivity" does not denote a lack of objective validity; it underlines the locus of such rights in the personal subject.

Subjective rights are, in fact, directly related to objective right. Subjective rights "define for the individual subject the sector of the practical objective field in which he can exercise his liberty without violating the virtue of justice" while imposing a specific moral duty on other people.[29] "For what is a subjective right," de Finance observes, "but the just order (what is objectively right) considered in relation to the aims and interests of the subject, that is, as capable of promoting these? Undoubtedly, in order to be a genuine right, a subjective right has to be in conformity to the just order."[30] Moreover, objective right exists only when subjective rights are fully satisfied.[31]

It will be noted that "objective right" is used in the singular, since it refers to a just social ordering, whereas subjective rights are multiple and deal with specific areas of human action or specific human goods. When used in the singular, "right" (such as in "natural right") generally refers to objective right, whereas "rights" in the plural (or as a single member of this plural genus) most often refers to subjective rights.

TWO-TERM VS. THREE-TERM

The expression "two-term rights" denotes a simple moral relationship between a person and a particular good, such as when one speaks of the "right to medical care." When speaking of rights to certain human goods, one asserts "two-term relations between a (class of) persons and a (class of) subject matter (life, body, free speech, property or ownership of property . . .)."[32] Rights are often expressed in this way, with no explicit refer-

---

29. de Finance, *An Ethical Inquiry*, § 194, p. 344.

30. Ibid., § 194, p. 345.

31. The just order—which is a state of objective right—embraces the common good, and the common good, in turn, embraces natural rights. "The common good that authority in the State serves is brought to full realization only when all the citizens are sure of their rights" (John Paul II, *Redemptor Hominis* [Rome: Libreria Editrice Vaticana, 1979], 17; hereafter *RH*). See also *CCC*, 1907.

32. Finnis, *Natural Law and Natural Rights*, 218.

ence to the bearer of a corresponding duty. Nonetheless, since all rights entail not only a relationship between the right-bearer and a good but also comprise a social dimension involving another person or persons, all two-term rights are in theory convertible into three-term rights, though in practice this may be difficult. "Before such assertions [two-term rights] can reasonably be accorded a real conclusory force, they must be translated into specific three-term relations."[33]

A claim-right always includes the right to an *action* by another party. Though rights claims are often expressed as two-term relations between a person and a subject matter (free speech, healthcare, privacy, education), such rights claims can be translated into three-term relations between a person, a subject matter, and another person.[34] The omission of the other party in the formulation of a right does not mean that no corresponding duty exists, it simply leaves open the attribution of such a duty.

Though expressing rights as two-term relations may be less precise, this practice has a certain advantage. The heart of a moral right is the relationship of the right-bearer to the good or action in question, and from this relationship springs the duty of the third party to respect or promote this relationship. In other words, the moral goodness of obtaining a particular good makes it wrong for someone else to interfere in one's pursuit of it and may even call for positive intervention to ensure that the good is secured. As a principle of justice, rights always involve a relationship between persons. Still, the fact that others are obliged in justice to respect specific actions of the rights-bearer or promote his access to specific goods means that a prior relationship exists between the rights-bearer and such actions or goods.[35] By pointing to a certain good as a "right" of persons, we point to the underlying foundation of natural rights by manifesting explicit requirements of man's nature and of human flourishing.

---

33. Ibid.
34. See Robert P. George, *Making Men Moral: Civil Liberties and Public Morality* (New York: Oxford University Press, 1996), 119.
35. Such a relationship can be described as moral in two distinct senses, depending on whether the right refers to an action or to a particular good. In the case of an action, the existence of a right means that a person's performance of the action is in conformity with the moral law. In the case of a right to a particular good, it means that the person's possession and use of the good, or at least of his access to it, is a condition of the just order (objective right).

POSITIVE VS. NEGATIVE

Some rights, especially those that express a moral liberty to perform specified actions, impose no other duty on others than that of noninterference. A right to free speech, for example, entails only a corresponding duty that others refrain from impeding the exercise of that right. Other rights, however, especially those to particular goods (or services), imply a corresponding duty of others to assure that the rights-bearer has access to such goods. The former sort are commonly called negative rights and the latter positive rights.[36] On the part of the rights-bearer, this would translate into "No one can morally hinder my pursuit of such-and-such" vs. "Someone has a moral duty to provide me with such-and-such."[37]

This distinction becomes clear when we examine certain specific rights. The right to life, for instance, furnishes perhaps the most patent example of an inviolable right.[38] It is also, at least in its immediate scope, a *negative* right. The corresponding duty extends only to the abstention from that which would violate this right. No one is obliged to provide life for another, only to respect the life he already has. The obligations pertaining to other rights, however, are less easily delimited. Does the right to education, for example, mean that no one can impede a person from seeking an education, or does a positive obligation exist for someone to provide an education? The distinction between negative and positive rights is not as cut and dried as it may appear at first glance. Even absolute (negative) rights like the right to life can generate derivative (positive) rights such as the right to food, clothing, and medicine, which are necessary to the preservation of life. Here one crosses immediately into the realm of positive rights.

Both positive and negative rights have corresponding duties. To infringe another's rights is an injustice, and consequently a moral evil, whether or not such an action runs contrary to civil law. This infringe-

---

36. Others, such as Grisez, speak of "immunities" and "entitlements." See Grisez, *Living a Christian Life*, 6.B.6.a.ii, p. 330.

37. "A claim-right is always either, positively, a right to be given something (or assisted in a certain way) by someone else, or, negatively, a right *not* to be interfered with or dealt with or treated in a certain way, by someone else" (Finnis, *Natural Law and Natural Rights*, 200).

38. "For man, the right to life is the *fundamental right*.... there is no other right that so closely affects the very existence of the person" (John Paul II, *Crossing the Threshold of Hope*, 204–5).

ment can take the form of an active violation, in the case of negative rights, or a failure to deliver what is justly owed, in the case of positive rights. Here Aquinas's distinction between sins of transgression and sins of omission is illuminating.[39] In the present context, *transgression* would refer to an active violation of another's natural rights, whereas *omission* would refer to the failure to satisfy a right where one is morally obliged to do so.

ABSOLUTE VS. RELATIVE

Though by definition all rights are moral powers to do, possess, or demand something, the power varies considerably among different rights, depending on the strength of the bond between the rights-bearer and the object of the right. Some rights are termed absolute or inviolable, meaning that they must be respected in all situations, while others depend on additional factors or circumstances for their exercise. In this regard we can speak of a hierarchy among rights.

Benedict Ashley distinguishes between primary or basic rights, grounded on the fundamental needs of the human person, and secondary rights, which are "relative to social roles and which may differ among humans, provided they do not detract from their basic rights and are appropriate to legitimate social roles."[40] Following Joseph Fletcher, Ashley posits primary rights as deriving from four kinds of necessary goods: life, reproduction, society, and truth. "These primary rights," Ashley affirms, "belong to every human person, since without their satisfaction the human community cannot be preserved or its members achieve fulfillment."[41]

The respect for and defense of particular goods of the person obliges according to the strength of association between these particular goods and the person himself. Goods that are more closely associated with the person, or on which his dignity most depend, bear a greater weight of obligation than those that are more extrinsic to the person. Respect for the life of another, for instance, is more strictly binding than respect for his

---

39. See *S. Th.*, I-II, 71, 5; II-II, 79, 3.
40. Benedict M. Ashley, *Living the Truth in Love: A Biblical Introduction to Moral Theology* (Staten Island, N.Y.: Alba House, 1996), 281.
41. Ibid.

television set, because property is extrinsic to the person, whereas life is central to his identity and thus to his dignity. Life is most *his,* because it is most identifiable with *him.* To harm the life of the person is to do violence to the person himself, whereas to damage his property, while clearly an assault on his rights, is a more peripheral offense. Inviolable rights are always negative rights, just as exceptionless moral norms are always stated negatively. There are some things that may not ever be done, but the same absoluteness does not apply to positive precepts, except in a general way. For example, the precept of charity absolutely excludes certain actions (rape or torture, for instance) that are absolutely incompatible with charity, but it obliges positively only in general.[42] Similarly, the positive commandment to honor father and mother obliges absolutely only in the negative (to avoid behavior that would dishonor parents), but it prescribes no concrete absolute positive behavior. Positive expressions will vary with time and place. In the case of rights, something similar occurs. The very words "inviolable" and "inalienable"[43] bespeak a certain absoluteness that commands respect and cannot be violated but that does not mandate specific positive actions of others.

42. Due to an excessive emphasis on obligation that characterized a certain understanding of morality, some moral theologians in the past found themselves in the awkward situation of trying to establish obligatory minimums for such basic positive moral precepts as prayer and love of neighbor. This impossible venture resulted in the almost comical conclusions of otherwise serious moralists such as St. Alphonsus Liguori and the Carmelites of Salamanca. Thus Servais Pinckaers notes that the Carmelites, in their *Treatise on Moral Theology,* came to the conclusion that "we are obliged to make an explicit act of love at least once a year," while St. Alphonsus (*Theologia Moralis,* I.2.8) preferred the opinion that this act should be performed "at least once a month" (*The Sources of Christian Ethics,* trans. Mary Thomas Noble [Edinburgh: T&T Clark, 1995], 16).

43. Though the qualifiers "inalienable" and "inviolable" are often used interchangeably, "inalienable" properly refers to rights that cannot be forfeited, whereas "inviolable" refers to rights that may never be infringed. Thus there could be inalienable rights that are not strictly inviolable, meaning that the subject never ceases to possess such rights, even though in extreme circumstances he may be denied their exercise. Certain inalienable economic rights, for instance, may be infringed in cases of emergency, whereas the inviolable right to life may never be directly infringed. Sufficient care has not always been taken to respect the proper meaning of these adjectives. Pope John XXIII, for example, wrote of rights "which derive directly from [man's] dignity as a human person, and which are therefore universal, inviolable and inalienable" (*PT,* 145). Yet not all natural rights (those that flow from man's dignity as a human person) are inviolable. A simple example is the right to private property, which, though indeed a natural right, is not an absolute (inviolable) right (see, for instance, John Paul II, encyclical letter *Centesimus Annus* [Rome: Libreria Editrice Vaticana, 1991], 30; hereafter *CA*).

THREE GENERATIONS OF RIGHTS

A final distinction can be drawn among rights according to their "generation," a concept developed by French jurist Karel Vasak, who assisted Nobel Prize winner René Cassin in the founding of the International Institute of Human Rights, Strasbourg, and also served as Director of Human Rights for UNESCO.[44] Vasak categorizes rights according to three generations, using the tripartite motto of the French Revolution: *Liberté, Égalité, Fraternité.*

According to Vasak, the first generation of human rights corresponds to the idea of liberty and comprises the civil and political rights that were central to the French and American revolutions,[45] which in turn drew heavily on the classical Liberal tradition. As the heading "liberty" suggests, such rights are basically negative in character and express "freedom from" outside intervention, especially government intervention, in the activities they protect. These first-generation civil liberties "epitomize the Western liberal-political ideal of individual freedom over against the encroaching power of the state,"[46] and were incorporated, inter alia, into the first ten amendments of the U.S. Constitution as well as the Universal Declaration of Human Rights (Art. 2-21).

Following Vasak's taxonomy, a "second generation" of human rights, correlative to equality, embraces economic, social, and cultural rights. According to J. W. Montgomery, these second-generation rights take their modern origin from the socialist traditions of the early nineteenth century, as well as from Marxist socialism, and include such rights claims as the right to work, to rest, to leisure, to education, to social security, and to the protections of intellectual property such as inventions and literary works.[47] In contrast to first-generation rights, those of the second generation are essentially positive in character; they directly imply an obligation on the part of others to supply or ensure certain basic goods.

A third generation of human rights can be termed "solidarity rights"

---

44. See John Warwick Montgomery, *Human Rights and Human Dignity* (Edmonton: Canadian Institute for Law, Theology, and Public Policy, 1995), 26.

45. Though Montgomery lumps these two revolutions together, there are notable differences in the underlying ideology of the French and American revolutionaries and even in the specific rights included in their respective bills of rights.

46. Montgomery, *Human Rights and Human Dignity*, 27.

47. See ibid. Though the right to intellectual property could clearly be classified as a

and corresponds to the third of the watchwords of the French Revolution: fraternity, or brotherhood.[48] These rights, broader and more general in character, proceed from a more recent vintage of rights theorizing and have gone hand in hand with the growing phenomenon of globalization. In their concrete instantiations, such rights include national sovereignty and self-determination, economic and social development, a healthy environment, peace, and humanitarian disaster relief.[49]

On a political and national scale, first-generation rights are often advocated by the more culturally individualistic West, second-generation rights by socialist and communist countries, and third-generation rights by Third World nations such as many Latin American and African countries.

The distinctions in kinds of rights outlined in this chapter help paint a clearer picture of the contemporary landscape regarding human rights theory and clarify the subject matter of the task at hand: the establishment of a solid grounding for human rights. The final chapter of this first part will examine the historical relationship of the Catholic Church to the human rights project.

"second-generation right" as far as its chronological appearance on the rights scene, it would seem to be simply a new form of the classical right to property (see *CA*, 32).

48. Literature on "third-generation" rights includes: Mario Bettati, *Le nouvel ordre économique international* (Paris: Presses Universitaires de France, 1983); W. Paul Gormley, *Human Rights and Environment: The Need for International Cooperation* (Leyden, the Netherlands: A. W. Sijthoff, 1976); Jean-François Guilhaudis, *Le droit des peuples à disposer d'eux-mêmes* (Grenoble: Presses Universitaires de Grenoble, 1976); International Commission of Jurists, *Development, Human Rights, and the Rule of Law* (Oxford: Pergamon, 1981). On the part of the Papal Magisterium, see Pope John Paul's address to the Fiftieth General Assembly of the United Nations Organization, given in New York on October 5, 1995, and his social encyclical *Sollicitudo Rei Socialis* (Rome: Libreria Editrice Vaticana, 1987; hereafter *SRS*).

49. See Montgomery, *Human Rights and Human Dignity*, 28.

3. THE CHURCH AND HUMAN RIGHTS

To the surprise of many—and the dismay of some—the Catholic Church has not only kept pace with the rest of society in its espousal of rights language, it has led the way in introducing such language into social dialogue and has stood out as a defender of human rights on the international scene.[1] Even in the midst of mounting misgivings about rights talk, especially among cultural and political conservatives, the Catholic Church has assumed a leading role in promoting human rights and adopts rights language in her teaching.

The documents of the Second Vatican Council, notably *Dignitatis Humanae* and *Gaudium et Spes*, abound with references to human rights.[2] The 1983 *Code of Canon Law* speaks of "the fundamental rights of human beings" (CIC 747 §2) and gives special treatment to "the obligation and rights of all the faithful" (CIC 280–83) in the life of the Church. And the *Catechism of the Catholic Church,* promulgated in 1992, is likewise replete with rights language.[3] In fact, official Church documents are so suffused with rights language that it can safely be said that rights constitute an integral part of Catholic social thought.

Many wonder how the Church's enthusiasm for human rights in the

---

1. This is true in a general sense and also specifically as regards the United Nations Universal Declaration of Human Rights. Mary Ann Glendon has written that "the Church has emerged as, intellectually and institutionally, the single most influential champion of the whole, interconnected, body of principles in the Universal Declaration" ("Rights Babel: The Universal Rights Idea at the Dawn of the Third Millennium," *Gregorianum* 79/4 [1998]: 623).

2. In the Pastoral Constitution on the Church in the Modern World, *Gaudium et Spes* (hereafter *GS*), for example, the promotion of rights is put forward as an expression or derivative of the Church's evangelizing mission. "In virtue of the Gospel entrusted to it, the Church proclaims the rights of man" (41).

3. The *CCC* speaks of rights in a variety of contexts in the following numbers: 912, 1269, 1631, 1807, 1882, 1886, 1889, 1901, 1907, 1925, 1930, 1931, 1935, 1944, 1945, 1956, 1978, 2032, 2070,

latter half of the twentieth century can be reconciled with its earlier diffidence toward human rights theories, especially those bound up with Liberalism. Does this rapprochement with human rights represent a shift in Church teaching, a development of doctrine, or simply a rephrasing of perennial Church teaching in matters of theological anthropology and ethics?

If, as I contend throughout this study, justice and rights are so tightly intertwined that to speak of justice is necessarily to speak of rights, then the Church has affirmed the rights of man since her founding, albeit using different terminology.[4] Nonetheless, rather than look at the Church's theoretical and practical commitment to justice, here we will limit our survey to the Church's relationship with rights per se. As we have seen, some assert that the Church's recent adoption of human rights language represents a departure from traditional Catholic ethics. It will be helpful, therefore, to see whether this is so from a historical perspective.

THE CHURCH AND LIBERALISM

Though today the Catholic Church finds itself on the front line in the promotion of human rights, at the beginning of the modern rights movement the Church's position stood at odds with the thesis on which the movement was based as well as with some of its expressions. It is vital to distinguish from the outset between rights as a *concept* and *sociopolitical reality* on the one hand, and rights as a *historical movement* on the other.[5] Whereas the moral and political concept of rights had been present in some way in Catholic moral thought since the beginning of Christianity,

---

2186, 2203, 2213, 2237, 2242, 2243, 2246, 2254, 2270, 2273, 2294, 2298, 2306, 2344, 2375, 2378, 2381, 2383, 2407, 2411, 2414, 2420, 2424, 2430, 2431, 2458, 2492, 2494, 2498.

4. Thus Edouard Hamel asserts that "in the history of the Church, praxis has often preceded theory. The defense and promotion of the rights of man were often lived under different names. We can think, for example, of care for the sick, children, the poor, and the elderly. Was there not, in fact, constant attention to the rights of the little ones, the poor, and the oppressed?" ("Fondement théologique des droits de l'homme," *Seminarium* 23 [1983]: 311; author's translation).

5. "Although rights as a concept and as a socio-political reality existed prior to seventeenth and eighteenth century natural rights, *rights as a historic movement* was inaugurated with the natural rights schools and the accompanying socio-political revolutions" (Mary Elsbernd, "Rights Statements: A Hermeneutical Key to Continuing Development in Magisterial Teaching," in *Ephemerides Theologiae Lovanienses*, t. 62 [Leuven, 1986], 309n4; emphasis in original).

the natural rights movement brought with it a series of premises and corollaries that were viewed as hostile to the Catholic Church. The Church was especially cautious about embracing a Liberal concept of rights whose foundations were riddled with deistic and rationalistic suppositions and whose visible fruits were political structures antagonistic to Catholicism.

As Mary Elsbernd notes in her linguistic and historical study of rights in papal encyclicals, it was the French Revolution that sparked the confrontation between the natural rights movement and the Church. "Due at least in part to its alliance with the French monarchy," she writes, "the Catholic Church found itself the object of anticlerical activity and of legislation directed towards its restructuring into a national church."[6] Thus the rights movement came to be seen as one of the banners of Liberal anticlericalism and as a justification for actions directed against the Church. The magisterial pronouncements of this time reflect this atmosphere of antagonism between the Church and the Liberal rights movement.

Pius VI had already condemned the thesis that placed absolute liberty at the source of individual rights.[7] This condemnation evolved into a denunciation of the rights outlined in the French Declaration of the Rights of Man and of the Citizen as "adverse to religion and society."[8] The mix of theoretical and political factors prompting this condemnation is noteworthy. The papal bull that contained the condemnation was addressed to the inhabitants of one of the papal states that wanted to join the French Revolution and rid itself of papal rule. Thus Elsbernd writes, "this initial confrontation between the Catholic Church and the historical rights movement resulted in an identification of rights with anticlericalism, with attempts to subjugate church to state and with the rejection of papal temporal rule."[9] Outside of the political context of European Liberalism, however, the Church adopted a friendlier human rights doctrine, such as can be seen, for instance, in the 1741 papal bull *Immensa Pastorum* by Benedict XIV on the treatment of the Indians of Latin America.

Throughout the nineteenth century the Church continued to associ-

---

6. Ibid., 309.
7. Pius VI, *Quod Aliquantum*, in *Collection générale des brefs et instructions de notre Très-Saint Père Pie VI relatifs à la révolution française*, vol. 1, ed. M. Guillon (Paris, 1798), 124.
8. Pius VI, *Adeo Nota*, in Guillon, *Collection*, 38.
9. Elsbernd, "Rights Statements," 309.

ate the rights movement with Liberal political revolutions. Beginning with Pope Gregory XVI (1831–1846) and his 1832 encyclical on Liberalism and religious indifference, *Mirari Vos,* however, a certain rights vocabulary began to enter papal encyclicals.[10] Gregory likewise appealed to rights against Liberal governments and referred to a *ius proprium ac nativum,* which indicated a natural rights influence.[11]

During the reign of Pope Pius IX (1846–1878), the papal states were gradually absorbed into the kingdom of Italy. Despite this ongoing practical threat to the papacy in the name of Liberal rights, the vocabulary of *ius* increased and diversified in the encyclicals of Pius IX.[12] Noteworthy are his encyclicals on the adversaries of the Catholic religion (*Qui Pluribus* 1846), on the error of naturalism (*Quanta Cura* 1864), and his catalogue of the errors of modern times (*Syllabus* 1864). While rights were claimed principally for the Church, references to the rights of others, such as emperors and rulers, gradually began to appear. As Elsbernd notes, in speaking of rights Pius IX offered distinctions and nuances that already "could suggest a certain reinterpretation of the liberal rights concept."[13] For instance, Pius IX qualified rights with such adjectives as "legitimate"and "inviolable" and also made reference to a "genuine notion of right."[14] Furthermore, Pius IX declared the right of parents as first educators of their children.[15] Little by little, the language and concepts of the secular rights movement were introduced into Church teaching by the very pope who simultaneously faced the rebellion of his own temporal subjects as they demanded a Liberal constitution based on individual rights.

10. See Gregory XVI, *Mirari Vos,* in *Acta Gregorii Papae XVI,* ed. A. Bernasconi (Rome, 1901), 1:169–74; *Quo Graviora,* in ibid., 1:307–10; *Commissum Divinitus,* in ibid., 2:33–36. In these three encyclicals, Gregory uses a variation of the term *ius* a total of thirty times.

11. Gregory XVI, *Commissum Divinitus,* in Bernasconi, *Acta Gregorii Papae XVI,* 2:nos. 12, 35.

12. Elsbernd notes that twenty-five of Pius IX's thirty-seven encyclicals employ the term *ius* at least once, with a total frequency of once every 530 words. Prior to *Quanta Cura,* in *Acta Sanctae Sedis* (hereafter *ASS*) 3 (1867): 160–67, the frequency was once every 980 words, in *Quanta Cura* once every 140 words, and subsequent to it once every 395 words ("Rights Statements," 310n8).

13. Ibid., 310.

14. *Quanta Cura,* § 4, p. 163 ("legitimate"); Pius IX, *Respicientes,* in *ASS* 6 (1870): § 2, p. 137 ("inviolable"); *Quanta Cura,* § 4, p. 163 ("genuine notion of right").

15. *Quanta Cura,* § 4, pp. 163–64.

Like his predecessors, Pope Leo XIII (1878–1903) continued to appeal to rights for the Catholic Church based on divine right.[16] At the same time, the broadening and diversification of rights language and the adoption of terminology from the Liberal rights movement continued. Leo XIII speaks of the rights of civil authorities, of parents over children, and of masters over slaves, but also of members of a social class, of family members, and of individuals as such. He also echoes the Liberal tradition's proclamation of a number of rights such as rights of marriage, of association, of property, of life sustenance and, following Pius IX, of education.[17] In his 1888 encyclical *Libertas Praestantissimum,* Leo speaks of obedience to God's authority as conducive to a situation where "the interests and rights of all will be safeguarded—the rights of individuals, of domestic society, and of all the members of the commonwealth."[18] In the same document, Leo denounces some of the unconditional rights espoused by Liberalism by asserting that man never has a natural right to do wrong.[19] *Rerum Novarum* (1891), in particular, marked the beginning of a new era. This encyclical is a veritable Magna Carta of rights: the rights of man in general (32), of the family (10–11), of the common good (26–29), of workers (29), to private property (5, 30, 38), to leisure (33–34), to a just wage (36–37), and to association (31, 40–49). In his encyclicals Leo XIII not only invoked rights more frequently, he also showed an increased affinity to the Liberal use of the term.

Under the pontificate of Pius X (1903–1914), this rapprochement with

---

16. Elsbernd has computed that 60 percent of Leo's references to rights where the possessor is named refer to rights of the Church or of an ecclesiastical figure ("Rights Statements," 310n11).

17. For the right of marriage, see Leo XIII, *Arcanum,* in *ASS* 12 (1879): § 14, p. 390. For the right of association, see *Custodi di quella fede,* in *Codex Juris Canonici Fontes* 3 (1925): § 5, p. 388. For the right to property, see *Rerum Novarum,* in *ASS* 23 (1890–1891): § 6, p. 643. For the right to sustenance, see ibid., § 14, p. 662.

18. Leo XIII, *Libertas Praestantissimum,* June 20, 1888, in *Acta Leonis XIII* 8 (1888): 13.

19. "From what has been said it follows that it is quite unlawful to demand, to defend, or to grant unconditional freedom of thought, of speech, or writing, or of worship, as if these were so many rights given by nature to man. For, if nature had really granted them, it would be lawful to refuse obedience to God, and there would be no restraint on human liberty. It likewise follows that freedom in these things may be tolerated wherever there is just cause, but only with such moderation as will prevent its degenerating into license and excess. And, where such liberties are in use, men should employ them in doing good, and should estimate them as the Church does; for liberty is to be regarded as legitimate in so far only as it affords greater facility for doing good, but no farther" (ibid., 42).

the Liberal notion of individual rights slowed considerably, though Pius X continued to use the word *ius* in his writings with nearly the same frequency as had his predecessor.[20] For Pius X, all right was grounded in God's right of ruling, and every right derived from a God-given participation in that right.[21] The rights of the Church proceeded from her divine constitution; to assert that they flowed from the nature of the Church was modernism.[22] Pius X added further elements from the rights movement into his writings, such as the right to participation in political life and the right to religious practice, though with limitations.[23] Pius X also employed the term "civil rights," something Leo XIII had avoided in favor of "civil liberties." Pius encouraged Catholics to appeal to civil rights to further the recognition of the rights of the Church and of religion.[24] Most of Pius X's references to rights, however, are in the context of jurisdictional and ecclesiastical claims. So while Pius X continued to employ a vocabulary of rights in his encyclicals, it was of a different sort from that articulated by the Liberal rights movement, which stressed the rights of individuals vis-à-vis the state.

Pius XI (1922–1939) appealed to rights more frequently and in a wider range of formulations than any of his predecessors.[25] During his pontificate the world economic crisis; the rise of German national socialism, Italian fascism, and Spanish communism; and hostile leftist governments in Mexico led Pius XI to comment on sociopolitical and economic issues. He intervened in rights-related questions in *Quadragesimo Anno* (1931) on the imperialism of money, in *Non abbiamo bisogno* (1931) against fascism, in *Mit brennender Sorge* (1937) against Nazism, and in *Nos es muy conocida* (1937) on the religious persecution in Mexico. Though Pius XI's adoption of rights echoed that of his predecessors, he tied rights expressly to a

---

20. Elsbernd calculates the appearance of *ius* in Pius X's corpus as once every 613 words, as compared with once every 637 words for Leo XIII. She notes, however, that some 60 percent of the occurrences of *ius* can be found in twelve of Leo's eighty-six encyclicals ("Rights Statements," 311n15).

21. Pius X, *E Supremi*, in *ASS* 36 (1903–1904): § 6, p. 132.

22. Pius X, *Pascendi Dominici Gregis*, in *ASS* 40 (1907): §§ 23–24, p. 614. See also *Une fois encore*, in *ASS* 40 (1907): § 12, p. 7.

23. Pius X, *Il fermo proposito*, in *ASS* 37 (1904–1905): § 18, p. 757; Pius X, *Vehementer Nos*, in *ASS* 39 (1906): § 9, p. 10.

24. Pius X, *Gravissimo Officii Munere*, in *ASS* 39 (1906): § 6, p. 389; also *Il fermo*, § 18, p. 757.

25. Elsbernd cites the frequency as circa once every 430 words ("Rights Statements," 312).

Christian anthropology. Rights were fruit of a God-given human dignity through nature as well as grace. As Elsbernd observes, in the writings of Pius XI "rights had become an integral, foundational concept to a Christian anthropology, albeit transformed from the liberal description of the secular, rational individual."[26]

Throughout the nineteenth century and into the beginning of the twentieth, a number of magisterial writings document the points of greatest conflict in the realm of political philosophy. Among these are Leo XIII, *Inscrutabili* 1878 (the Catholic religion as the basis of civilization); *Diuturnum Illud* 1881 (the divine origin of state authority); *Humanum Genus* 1884 (freemasonry); *Immortale Dei* 1885 (Christian doctrine on the state); *Libertas Praestantissimum* 1888 (the errors of liberalism); *Rerum Novarum* 1891 (the condition of workers); *Graves de Communi* 1901 (Christian democracy as a social program); Pius X, *Lacrimabili Statu* 1912 (slavery among the Indians of South America).

Throughout this period popes made use of the terminology of rights with varying frequency, but none questioned the appropriateness of this language. In fact, the Church's separation of the wheat of rights language from the chaff of an anticlerical Liberal context suggests the need to evaluate the concept of rights on its own merits, not just in terms of the philosophical and political context in which rights theories grew.

POPE JOHN XXXIII AND 'PACEM IN TERRIS'

The term "human rights" per se does not appear in a magisterial document until the time of John XXIII (1958–1963). Other expressions prevailed earlier, such as "the rights of man," "natural rights," or simply "rights." John XXIII commented extensively on rights in *Mater et Magistra* (1961),[27] but it is the encyclical *Pacem in Terris* (1963) that expressly makes "human rights" the central subject of its study. The anticlerical vir-

---

26. Ibid.
27. For example, in this 1961 encyclical marking the seventieth anniversary of Leo XIII's *Rerum Novarum*, John XXIII asserted that men are becoming more and more conscious of "their rights as human beings" (*MM*, 211) and spoke of the rights of workers (§§ 16, 99, 103, 147), the duty of the state to protect the rights of the people (§ 20), the right to freedom of action and productive activity (§ 55), the right to private property (§ 109), and "personal rights" including those touching on the necessities of life, healthcare, education, professional training, housing, work, and leisure (§ 61). Many of these themes are repeated and amplified in *PT*.

ulence that had marked earlier discussions had ceased, and now the Church could devote itself to a deeper study of the topic from its own original point of view.

In *Pacem in Terris,* John XXIII proclaims the existence of rights, delving into their foundation in human nature. Every human, as a person, is a natural subject of rights and duties. The human dignity underlying these rights and duties is thrown into still greater relief when one considers the human person in the light of divine revelation.

> Any human society, if it is to be well ordered and productive, must lay down as a foundation this principle, namely, that every human being is a person, that is, his nature is endowed with intelligence and free will. Indeed, precisely because he is a person he has rights and obligations flowing directly and simultaneously from his very nature. And as these rights and obligations are universal and inviolable so they cannot in any way be surrendered.
>
> If we look upon the dignity of the human person in the light of divinely revealed truth, we cannot help but esteem it far more highly; for men are redeemed by the blood of Jesus Christ, they are by grace the children and friends of God and heirs of eternal glory. (9–10)

Taking these paragraphs as a starting point, the encyclical develops the rights and duties of man, using a great richness of references to previous teachings to illustrate the continuity with prior magisterial doctrine. The rights announced by John XXIII comprise a broad range of human goods: from the right to life, bodily integrity, and the indispensable and sufficient means for a dignified level of life to the natural right of man to access the goods of culture and a basic education to the right to honor God according to the sincere dictates of one's conscience and to profess religion in private and in public.

Man's natural rights also give rise to duties in other persons, "the duty, namely, of acknowledging and respecting the right in question." John XXIII repeats that every fundamental human right "draws its indestructible moral force from natural law, which in granting it imposes a corresponding obligation" (30).

Throughout the encyclical, John XXIII develops a doctrine of human rights as flowing from man's personal dignity and as an integral part of the natural law. For John XXIII, these rights are, very simply, what is due to man as man, and which therefore deserve respect and protection from other individuals and groups and from the state.

THE SECOND VATICAN COUNCIL

Though the Second Vatican Council promulgated no document on human rights per se, conciliar documents contain numerous references to human rights, most notably in the Declaration on Religious Freedom, *Dignitatis Humanae,* and in the Pastoral Constitution on the Church in the Modern World, *Gaudium et Spes,* both promulgated in 1965.

Dignitatis Humanae adopted some of the same thinking on rights that can be found in *Pacem in Terris,* though in a deeper and more nuanced way. Here the topic is specifically religious liberty, but the logic employed can be applied to rights in general. So, while it seeks to "leave intact the traditional Catholic teaching on the moral duty of individuals and societies towards the true religion and the one Church of Christ," the council expressly "intends to develop the teaching of recent popes on the inviolable rights of the human person and on the constitutional order of society" (1).

The right to religious freedom was a much disputed topic in Vatican II, especially in the drafting of *Dignitatis Humanae.* The letter *Mit brennender Sorge* by Pius XI and the rich humanism of all Vatican II contained many determining elements regarding religious freedom. Pius XII had likewise spoken of the right to worship and the freedom of religious practice in his discourse of December 15, 1945. Nonetheless, the path that the decree was to follow was very difficult. It was initially destined to be a "constitution" (the highest form of document) but wound up being a "declaration" (of a less solemn character).

The final approved text of *Dignitatis Humanae* expressly declared that "the human person has the right to religious freedom." The document goes on to state that "the right to religious freedom is based on the very dignity of the human person as known through the revealed word of God and by reason itself" (2).[28] In other words, a particular right—religious freedom—finds its roots, as do all natural rights, in the dignity of the human person. Furthermore, the dignity of the human person is knowable through revelation but also by human reason, such that rights are understood here as pertaining to natural law.

---

28. To show continuity with earlier teachings, *Dignitatis Humanae* here cites: *PT; AAS* 55 (1963): 260–61; Pius XII, radio message, December 24, 1942, in *AAS* 35 (1943): 19; Pius XI, *Mit brennender Sorge,* March 14, 1937, in *AAS* 29 (1937): 160; Leo XIII, *Libertas Praestantissimum,* 237–38.

In addressing the situation of the Church in the modern world, the Pastoral Constitution *Gaudium et Spes* treats both the foundation and the specific instantiations of human rights. Two sections of the document are particularly significant. *Gaudium et Spes* devotes the entire first chapter to "the dignity of the human person." This personal dignity, rooted in man's creation in God's image and likeness, provides the groundwork for all natural rights. It is Christ himself, "the perfect man," who "fully reveals man to himself and brings to light his most high calling" (22). This chapter treats man's nature and the dignity of intellect, freedom, and moral conscience; it also explores death, sin, and atheism and its causes.

The section on the common good addresses the question of the community of mankind. The council pointed out man's communitarian vocation as well as the interdependence among persons and between the person and society. *Gaudium et Spes* states that

> there is a growing awareness of the sublime dignity of the human person, who stands above all things and whose rights and duties are universal and inviolable. He ought, therefore, to have ready access to all that is necessary for living a genuinely human life: for example, food, clothing, housing, the right freely to choose his state of life and set up a family, the right to education, work, his good name, to respect, proper knowledge, the right to act according to the dictates of conscience and to safeguard his privacy, and rightful freedom even in matters of religion. (26)

Moreover, *Gaudium et Spes* reasserts the basic equality of all men as endowed with a rational soul and created in God's image and likeness, with the same nature and origin and the same divine calling and destiny. Therefore, basic personal rights are possessed equally by all, and forms of discrimination in this area are to be "eradicated as incompatible with God's design" (29).[29]

---

29. A similar statement can be found in the council document on the relation of the Church with non-Christian religions, *Nostra Aetate*, where one reads that there is no basis in theory or in practice for discrimination among persons "arising either from human dignity or the rights which flow from it" (§ 5).

POPE JOHN PAUL II

Though the trend toward human rights language clearly did not begin with him, Pope John Paul II has given it a decisive push forward.[30] As bishop during the Second Vatican Council, Karol Wojtyła played an active role in the drafting of both *Gaudium et Spes* and *Dignitatis Humanae*.[31] In a radio address broadcast over Vatican Radio on October 19, 1964, Wojtyła emphasized the personalist character of the council's teachings. "Although none of the completed constitutions or directives has the human person as its specific topic," Wojtyła noted, "the person lies deep within the entire conciliar teaching that is slowly emerging from our labors."[32] From his earliest days both as pastor and as academic, Wojtyła had a deep concern for the human person, his dignity, and the rights that flow from it.

Wojtyła brought all of this with him when elected Pope in 1978. In his programmatic encyclical, *Redemptor Hominis*, promulgated just months after his election, John Paul II set forth key thoughts that had been "pressing with particular forcefulness in my mind" and "had already been maturing in me previously, during the years of my service as a priest, and then as a bishop."[33] Among these key thoughts we find the issue of human rights, to which John Paul devoted number 17 of the encyclical. Speaking within the context of man's situation in the modern world, he praises "the magnificent effort made to give life to the United Nations Organization, an effort conducive to the definition and establishment of man's objective and inviolable rights" and expresses hope that "human rights will become throughout the world a principle of work for man's welfare" (17).

---

30. George Weigel, for example, speaks of a "Catholic human rights revolution" under the pontificate of this pope (*The Final Revolution: The Resistance Church and the Collapse of Communism* [New York: Oxford University Press, 1992], 70). Given the extensive and continual use of rights language in previous magisterial teaching, such an expression seems hyperbolic, but it underscores the importance of John Paul's contribution to this trend. According to Avery Dulles, "Of all the popes, no other has given so much emphasis to human rights as John Paul II, who confidently asserts that these rights have their foundation in Christ and the Gospel" ("Human Rights: Papal Teaching and the United Nations," *America*, December 5, 1998, 15).

31. See George S. Weigel, *Witness to Hope: The Biography of Pope John Paul II* (New York: HarperCollins, 1999), 163–69.

32. Karol Wojtyła, "On the Dignity of the Human Person," a talk broadcast in Polish over Vatican Radio on October 19, 1964, printed in *Person and Community: Selected Essays*, ed. Andrew N. Woznicki (New York: Peter Lang, 1993), 177.

33. John Paul II, Angelus message, March 11, 1979, *L'Osservatore Romano*, March 19, 1979, 2.

Concern for human rights, in the mind of John Paul, far from being foreign to the mission of the Church, stands at its center. Man is "the primary and fundamental way for the Church" (14), while human rights violations represent "an incomprehensible manifestation of activity directed against man" (17). Thus there is "no need for the Church to confirm how closely [the problem of human rights] is linked with her mission in the modern world." The defense and promotion of human rights is a necessary expression of the defense and promotion of the human person.

After speaking of human rights abuses that continue despite external adherence to the "letter" of the Universal Declaration of Human Rights, John Paul addresses the nature of the state and its fundamental duty of "solicitude for the common good of society" (17). Therefore, the state's rights of power "can be understood only on the basis of respect for the objective and inviolable rights of man." The common good, in fact, "is brought to full realization only when all the citizens are sure of their rights," and so "the principle of human rights is of profound concern to the area of social justice and is the measure by which it can be tested in the life of political bodies."

In this same number, Pope John Paul touches on the natural foundation of human rights in referring to the conciliar declaration *Dignitatis Humanae*. Therein, writes John Paul, "is expressed not only the theological concept of the question but also the concept reached from the point of view of natural law, that is to say, from the 'purely human' position, on the basis of the premises given by man's own experience, his reason and his sense of human dignity" (17). In this way, Pope John Paul II began his pontificate with a strong statement on the dignity and value of the human person and on the rights that flow from this dignity. This was to form a central leitmotiv of his entire pontificate.

Among the many specific human rights that John Paul has consistently defended, two stand out as particularly noteworthy. John Paul has singled out religious freedom as the "source and synthesis"of human rights, since it represents the right to live in the truth of one's faith and in conformity with one's transcendent dignity as a person.[34] Religious freedom

---

34. *CA*, 47. See also, for example, message for 1988 World Day of Peace, January 1, 1988, in *AAS* 80 (1988): 1572–80; message for the 1991 World Day of Peace, January 1, 1991, in *AAS* 83 (1991): 410–21; as well as *DH*, 1–2. Furthermore, in his 1995 address to the United Nations, John Paul referred to the fundamental right to freedom of religion and freedom of conscience as "the cornerstones of the structure of human rights and the foundation of every truly free society" (§ 10).

goes to the core of what it means to be human and touches on the heart of man's vocation as a being called to intimate communion with God. To deny this right is to trample man's dignity in its very essence.

John Paul has also frequently cited the right to life as among the most basic and important of human rights.[35] Though it is not an absolute value, since man may be asked to sacrifice his life for a higher good, man's life on earth is "the fundamental condition, the initial stage, and an integral part of the entire unified process of human existence."[36] Rights, for John Paul, are tied to man's flourishing as a human being, and they take on greater importance and force as they more closely affect man's perfection as a person. Thus the right to life is "the *fundamental right*" precisely because "there is no other right that so closely affects the very existence of the person."[37]

The association of rights with basic human goods needed for human flourishing can be seen elsewhere in John Paul's writing. As just one example, we could take the right to work. The Pope defends such a right not only on the grounds that employment is needed for subsistence but also on his understanding of work as a perfective good for man—a good, in other words, that makes him more human. "Work," writes John Paul, "is a good thing for man—a good thing for his humanity—because through work man *not only transforms nature,* adapting it to his own needs, but he also *achieves fulfillment* as a human being and indeed, in a sense, becomes 'more a human being.'"[38]

References to human rights in the writings and discourses of John Paul are far too numerous to enumerate, but we may take one particularly significant moment as a case in point. On October 5, 1995, the Pope addressed the United Nations General Assembly on the occasion of the fiftieth anniversary of its foundation. John Paul reiterated a message he had delivered to the United Nations on October 2, 1979, namely that the quest for freedom "has its basis in those universal rights which human beings enjoy by the very fact of their humanity." He also noted that it was precisely outrages against human dignity which led the United Nations Organization to formulate the Universal Declaration of Human

---

35. See, for example, John Paul II, *CA,* 47; *Evangelium Vitae* (Rome: Libreria Editrice Vaticana, 1995), 2; hereafter *EV.*

36. See *EV,* 2, 47.

37. John Paul II, *Crossing the Threshold of Hope,* 204–5; emphasis in original.

38. See John Paul II, encyclical letter *Laborem Exercens* (hereafter *LE*) (Rome: Libreria Editrice Vaticana, 1981), 9; emphasis in original. See also 16–23.

Rights just three years after its foundation, a document John Paul refers to as "one of the highest expressions of the human conscience of our time" (2).

John Paul stressed that human rights are not an abstraction but an objective ethical reality. He noted that a global movement toward freedom and full participation in society "confirms that there are indeed universal human rights, rooted in the nature of the person, rights which reflect the objective and inviolable demands of a universal moral law" (3). In other words, rights are not merely helpful conventions that lead to peace but are the reflection of the objective truth about man and about the moral law rooted in his nature. Natural rights form an essential part of the natural law, and it is this universal law that makes ethical dialogue among peoples possible. John Paul asserted that "there is a moral logic which is built into human life and which makes possible dialogue between individuals and peoples. . . . The universal moral law written on the human heart is precisely that kind of 'grammar' which is needed if the world is to engage this discussion of its future" (3).

In this regard, John Paul said that "it is a matter for serious concern that some people today deny the universality of human rights, just as they deny that there is a human nature shared by everyone" (3). Though there is no single model for organizing the politics and economics of human freedom, "it is one thing to affirm a legitimate pluralism of 'forms of freedom,' and another to deny any universality or intelligibility to the nature of man or to the human experience." The latter, he remarked, makes the international politics of persuasion extremely difficult, if not impossible.

Contemporary movements toward freedom, John Paul suggested, reflect many of the moral commitments inscribed in the United Nations charter. He made express reference to the commitment to "reaffirm faith in fundamental human rights (and) in the dignity and worth of the human person" contained in the preamble to the U.N. charter (4).

Pope John Paul's 1995 U.N. address is remarkable as well for its affirmation of the rights of nations, which "are nothing but 'human rights' fostered at the specific level of community life" (8). On this occasion the Pope made an important distinction in noting that the concept of *nation* "cannot be identified a priori and necessarily with the State." Here, a "nation" would more closely resemble a "people" than a state. First and foremost among a nation's rights is its right to exist, which "does not necessarily call for sovereignty as a state, since various forms of juridical aggregation between different nations are possible." Its right to exist naturally does, however, imply that every nation "enjoys the right to its own language and culture, through which a people expresses and promotes that which I would call its fundamental spiritual 'sovereignty.'" Thus every nation also has the right to shape its life according to its own traditions and to build its future by providing an appropriate education for the younger generation. The rights of nations are necessarily balanced by reciprocal duties among nations, which allow for "a fruitful 'exchange of gifts,' which strengthens the unity of all mankind."

From the foregoing brief reflections on the Magisterium from Pope John XXIII to Pope John Paul II regarding human rights, four simple axioms can be extracted that are especially relevant to a study on the foundations of human rights. First, according to the papal Magisterium, human rights are an objective reality, a component of the universal natural moral law. By his very nature and prior to any positive legislation, man possesses certain rights. Second, these rights flow from the dignity of the human person, made in the image and likeness of God, a dignity revealed by God in sacred scripture but also discernible to man's reason. Third, human rights reflect the truth about man and about man's genuine good. The goods that the popes defend and promote contribute to man's integral fulfillment as a person. Fourth, these rights are ordered according to a hierarchy of importance. Thus because of their centrality to man's existence and vocation, certain rights such as religious freedom and the right to life stand at the core of human rights. These four axioms undergird the encyclicals *Mater et Magistra* and *Pacem in Terris* of Pope John XXIII as well as the conciliar documents *Dignitatis Humanae* and *Gaudium et Spes* and they are explicitly evident in the Magisterium of Pope John Paul II.

CONTINUITY OR INNOVATION?

Despite the increase in references to rights and the absence of reservations in using such language, both of which distinguish *Pacem in Terris* from earlier Church documents, it is evident that John XXIII understood himself to be writing within the tradition of Catholic social thought. In laying out the foundation of rights in this encyclical, John XXIII uses traditional language in referring to an order that God "has imprinted in man's heart" (5) as well as in speaking of laws that the Father has written "in the nature of man" (6). Rights and duties "find their source, their sustenance and their inviolability in the natural law which grants or enjoins them" (28). Succeeding popes have explicitly affirmed the unbroken continuity of Catholic teaching regarding rights.[39]

Other scholars, as noted above, have questioned the harmony of recent Church teaching regarding rights with earlier teaching. Some, such as Ernest L. Fortin, believe that the Church ambled into a moral morass and effectively deviated from traditional natural law doctrine when it adopted the language of rights.[40] Some have noted a change in form but no significant change in content. Mary Ann Glendon has remarked:

> Many Catholics were surprised, and some were even shocked, at the extent to which the documents of Vatican II, and John XXIII's encyclicals *Pacem in Terris* and *Mater et Magistra* seemed to effect a shift from natural law to human rights. I agree with those who regard this shift as more rhetorical than theoretical, an effort on the part of the Church to make her own teachings intelligible to all men and women of good will.[41]

Francis Canavan draws on the Pope's assertion that man "has rights and obligations flowing directly and simultaneously from his very nature" to say: "This statement of John XXIII's casts doubt on the notion, advanced by some, that the recent popes have switched from traditional natural law to a modern natural-rights theory. It would be more accurate to say that . . . they have incorporated human rights into their doctrine of natural law."[42]

---

39. John Paul II, for example, in his 1980 address to the Fourth International Congress of Canon Law, stated: "There has never been a time when the Church has not protected these rights. . . . Likewise, there has never been a time when the Church has not proclaimed the duty both of private individuals and of public authorities to respect and promote the rights of the human person" (*L'Osservatore Romano*, English edition, November 17, 1980).

40. See, for example, Ernest L. Fortin, "The New Rights Theory and the Natural Law," in *Classical Christianity and the Political Order: Reflections on the Theologico-Politico Problem*, vol. 2 of *Ernest L. Fortin: Collected Essays*, ed. J. Brian Benestad (Lanham, Md.: Rowman & Littlefield, 1996), 265–86; Fortin, "From *Rerum Novarum* to *Centesimus Annus*: Continuity or Discontinuity?" in *Human Rights, Virtue, and the Common Good*, 223–29.

41. Mary Ann Glendon, "Catholic Thought and Dilemmas of Human Rights" (address given at the Higher Learning and Catholic Traditions Conference, University of Notre Dame, October 14, 1999).

42. Francis S. Canavan, "The Image of Man in Catholic Thought," in *Catholicism, Liberalism, and Communitarianism: The Catholic Intellectual Tradition and the Moral Foundations of Democracy*, ed. Kenneth L. Grasso, Gerard V. Bradley, and Robert P. Hunt (Lanham, Md.: Rowman & Littlefield, 1995), *19–20*. The quote Canavan is commenting on is from *PT,* 9.

Objections to rights language and the assertion that—consciously or not—recent popes have departed from a traditional moral framework by embracing such language deserve a more careful and nuanced treatment. The following part of this book will expressly address the criticisms of those who view the modern shift toward rights language as a break with, rather than a development of, classical ethical theory. Later, in the fourth part of the book, I will return to this question and will show how natural rights theory fits into traditional Christian thinking regarding natural law and justice.

PART TWO

THE CASE AGAINST RIGHTS

Though human rights are more accepted today than ever before, they are not without serious opponents. In the political arena some countries—China comes immediately to mind—refuse to subscribe to international rights accords for reasons of political expediency. Accepting the notion of universal human rights would lead to practical consequences and policy changes to which such countries are unwilling to submit. Other opponents resist for more theoretical reasons. Some simply do not agree that persons deserve the sorts of things proposed in human rights documents. A certain mindset considers the individual human person as subordinate to the collectivity and thus places emphasis not on the rights of the person but on the duties of citizens to the state.

But even within the democratic and Judeo-Christian tradition, where the individual human person is considered precious and worthy of protection, serious objections arise regarding the language of human rights. Among Catholics, for example, while many have supported the Church's enthusiastic endorsement of human rights, others have expressed misgivings, or even outright disapproval, of such an alliance. "Some have wondered," writes political science professor Kenneth Grasso, "how the

Council's embrace of freedom and human rights is to be reconciled with the traditional emphasis of Catholic thought on duty, virtue, and the common good."[1] Theologian Kenneth R. Craycraft, Jr. has contended more forcefully that the very notion of rights employed in recent official Church documents is "problematic at best." According to Craycraft: "The Church has adopted a language that may be irreconcilable with its more ancient and basic claims about man and his relationship to God."[2]

Nor have critics of human rights been wanting outside the Church, especially among cultural conservatives. Russell Kirk, patriarch of conservative politics in the Realpolitik tradition, warns that "human rights" is an elusive and manipulable term, "a Newspeak term, often supercilious, readily employed to advance causes hostile to genuine order and justice and freedom." To play with rights talk is to risk "hoist[ing] ourselves by our own verbal petard."[3]

Theoretical objections to rights take different forms. Some refer to the prudential dimension of rights language, arguing that society would be better off adhering to the traditional language of virtue, duty, and responsibility, since talk of rights inevitably encourages a self-centered approach to morality and interpersonal relations. Other adversaries of a more theological bent propose a discontinuity and even an incompatibility between rights language and traditional Christian moral vocabulary. Others would throw out entirely the concept of human rights on the grounds that rights are a vacuous, insubstantial human invention with no corresponding referent in the real world. Still others accept the validity and

---

1. Kenneth L. Grasso, "Beyond Liberalism: Human Dignity, the Free Society, and the Second Vatican Council," in *Catholicism, Liberalism, and Communitarianism: The Catholic Intellectual Tradition and the Moral Foundations of Democracy*, ed. Kenneth L. Grasso, Gerard V. Bradley, and Robert P. Hunt (Lanham, Md.: Rowman & Littlefield, 1995), 33.
2. Craycraft, "Religion as Moral Duty and Civic Right," 60.
3. Kirk, *Redeeming the Time*, 239.

usefulness of the term "human rights" yet express reservations regarding its indiscriminate propagation and highlight multiple dangers associated with the abuse of rights talk in political and social discourse.

Some of the more substantive arguments directly attack rights in their foundation and thus immediately touch on the subject matter of the present inquiry. Consequently, those who consider the very idea of human rights to be an empty concept merit a hearing and require a response, one that shows how rights not only have a referent in the real world but also correspond to the truth of the human person.

Those who object to rights on theological grounds bring to light the important issue of the theological foundation of rights and question the compatibility of rights with the Christian moral tradition. From a Christian perspective, it is insufficient to propose a philosophical basis for rights, if this basis runs counter to the Christian faith. Theology bears the responsibility of evaluating the harmony of ethical theories with the Gospel. Prudential arguments against rights will be useful in assessing the Church's choice to adopt rights terminology, especially in its social teaching, although these arguments will carry less weight in the present study since they involve the foundational question only tangentially. Finally, other objections to the application of rights to political and social discourse also deserve consideration, chiefly because the use or misuse of rights language can be shown to derive from a correct or incorrect understanding of the nature, and consequently of the foundation, of human rights. Clarification of the foundation of human rights will be conducive to a correct application of rights language and the distinction between use and abuse of this terminology.

The following three chapters will examine and answer the objections to human rights voiced by three representative contemporary thinkers:

Alasdair MacIntyre, Joan Lockwood O'Donovan, and Ernest L. Fortin. Though these authors are far from alone in their opposition to rights language, their arguments sum up in an exceptional way the central case against rights.[4] Each author's position will be summarized and refuted.

[4]. These three have been selected from among the many thinkers and writers who see natural rights as a modern innovation, unrelated to and even incompatible with classical and Christian ethical theory. Though we will not deal with him specifically here, another writer who deserves special mention is the French jurist Michel Villey (1914–1988), who wrote extensively on this theme and who saw the modern idea of individual rights, even in such Christian writers as De Vitoria and Suárez, as fruit of nominalism. See especially Michel Villey, *Le droit et les droits de l'homme* (Paris: Presses Universitaires de France, 1983).

4. THE ACCUSATION OF NONEXISTENCE

AMONG THE PHILOSOPHERS who reject wholly or in part the concept of human rights, perhaps none does so in as bold and thoroughgoing a manner as the American philosopher Alasdair MacIntyre (1929–). For this reason, as well as for his status as a believing Catholic, MacIntyre makes a good representative for those who oppose rights on behalf of philosophy in the classical and Christian tradition. MacIntyre's objections fall into three basic arguments:[1] an argument by default, whereby MacIntyre asserts that no compelling explanation of human rights has yet been made; an argument that rights are unintelligible without local social structures, which would invalidate claims of the universality of rights; and a historical-linguistic argument, in which MacIntyre asserts that the relatively recent origins of the word "rights" cast doubt on the existence of such an ethical reality, since it is unlikely that so important a concept would have lain undiscovered by ethicists for so long.

OBJECTIONS

The Argument by Default

In his celebrated 1981 work *After Virtue*, MacIntyre denies outright the existence of natural rights. "The truth is plain," he writes, "there are no such rights, and belief in them is one with belief in witches and in uni-

---

1. Others have drawn longer lists of anti-rights arguments from MacIntyre's writings. Kristin Shrader-Frechette, for example, enumerates six specific arguments: "the Witch Argument," "the Taboo Argument," "the Commonality Argument," "the Primacy Argument," "the Historical Argument," and "the Independent-Standard Argument" (see "MacIntyre on Human Rights," *Modern Schoolman* 79 [November 2001]: 4).

corns." What would lead a serious thinker like Professor MacIntyre to place rights in the same class with witches and unicorns? "The best reason for asserting so bluntly that there are no such rights is indeed of precisely the same type as the best reason we possess for asserting that there are no witches and the best reason we possess for asserting that there are no unicorns: every attempt to give good reasons for believing that there *are* such rights has failed."[2] Thus in one fell swoop MacIntyre disqualifies every argument hitherto made to ground natural rights.

MacIntyre likens belief in rights to superstition: the irrational belief in something that does not exist and for which—obviously, given its nonexistence—there is no proof. In Thomistic terms, one could say that MacIntyre admits the "essence" of rights while denying their "existence" or *actus essendi*. "Natural or human rights, then, are fictions but fictions with highly specific properties. . . . A central characteristic of moral fictions . . . : they purport to provide us with an objective and personal criterion, but they do not."[3] That is, just as in the case of unicorns, we can identify specific rights, describe their characteristic features, and discourse on their interrelations, but all this says nothing about their existence in the real world. The reason MacIntyre provides for his assertion of the nonexistence of rights rests on default. He has encountered no satisfactory explanation to convince him of the existence of such rights, and thus his disbelief hinges on the absence of positive reasons to believe. This, according to MacIntyre, is "the best reason" for refuting rights.

How does MacIntyre understand the "essence" of these rights whose "existence" he denies? In what do they consist? MacIntyre distinguishes rights from needs or preferences by highlighting the interpersonal and ethical dimension of the former, which is not present in the latter. He notes that "the claim that I have a right to do or have something is a quite different type of claim from the claim that I need or want or will be benefited by something. From the first . . . it follows that others ought not to interfere with my attempts to do or have whatever it is, whether it is for my own good or not. From the second it does not."[4] In the case of rights,

---

2. MacIntyre, *After Virtue*, 69.
3. Ibid., 70.
4. Ibid., 67. MacIntyre's words echo those of the utilitarian philosopher Jeremy Bentham, who wrote that rights are merely the utopian expression of needs we wish to have met: "A reason for wishing that a certain right were established, is not that right—want is not supply—

a third party is introduced who was not present in claims of needs or wants or benefits. Claims of needs or wants describe a bipartite relationship of a subject who pursues an object that he needs or desires. To make a rights claim, however, brings another into the picture and creates for him a duty of noninterference in the rights-bearer's pursuit of his needs.

MacIntyre's first objection throws down the gauntlet to moral philosophers and theologians, since it disqualifies an entire ethical category. To claim, as MacIntyre does, that rights do not exist, goes much further than to question the validity of a specific right or set of rights or to attenuate the absolute nature of certain rights claims. In order to reply satisfactorily to MacIntyre's objection, then, it is insufficient to begin with rights as a premise. It will first be necessary to show the existence of an ethical reality comprised by the term "human rights."

The Dependence of Rights on Local Social Structure

The distinction between rights claims and the expression of needs and wants opens into a second reason MacIntyre gives for refuting the existence of rights. To speak of "the rights of man" is to speak of a presumably universal phenomenon. Yet whereas needs and wants are universally experienced and thus universally intelligible, rights claims presuppose social and ethical structures that are *not* universal. MacIntyre argues against the "universalizability" of rights claims, even as regards universally necessary goods, on the grounds that rights claims require certain social arrangements that are not universally present. "One reason why claims about goods necessary for rational agency are so different from claims to the possession of rights," MacIntyre argues, "is that the latter in fact presuppose, as the former do not, the existence of a socially established set of rules only come into existence at particular historical periods under particular social circumstances. They are in no way universal features of the human condition."[5]

MacIntyre goes on to explain that "those forms of human behavior which presuppose notions of some ground to entitlement, such as the notion of a right, always have a highly specific and socially local character" and that "the existence of particular types of social institution or

---

hunger is not bread" ("Anarchical Fallacies," in *Society, Law, and Morality*, ed. Frederick A. Olafson [Englewood Cliffs, N.J.: Prentice Hall, 1961], 347).

5. MacIntyre, *After Virtue*, 67.

practice is a necessary condition for the notion of a claim to the possession of a right being an intelligible type of human performance."[6] In other words, and as we saw in the first argument, MacIntyre impugns not only the universal character of particular rights (such as, say, the right to free speech) but the very concept of rights claims as a universally "intelligible type of human performance." For MacIntyre, then, the very idea of a person claiming to naturally deserve something from someone else is socially determined and would be foreign to the mentality of certain cultures. Or, to cite MacIntyre's analogy, in the absence of the requisite social customs, "the making of a claim to a right would be like presenting a check for payment in a social order that lacked the institution of money."[7]

MacIntyre places much stock in the influence of what he calls "incommensurability," which he describes as a phenomenon whereby two large-scale systems of thought and practice contrast radically such that "there is and can be no independent standard or measure by appeal to which their rival claims can be adjudicated, since each has internal to itself its own fundamental standard of judgment."[8] This incommensurability between systems results in an "untranslatability" among terms from one system to another. In other words, "the terms in and by means of which judgment is delivered in each are so specific and idiosyncratic to each that they cannot be translated into the terms of the other without gross distortion." Examples of such incommensurable systems cited by MacIntyre are the physics of Aristotle opposed to the physics of Galileo or Newton and the belief in witchcraft by some African peoples compared to the cosmology of modern science.[9]

In making this argument, MacIntyre takes a phenomenon characteristic of scientific theories and applies it to moral systems. MacIntyre speaks of historians and philosophers of science, such as Thomas Kuhn, who have "identified in different periods of the history of physics different and incompatible standards governing rational choice between rival theories

---

6. Ibid.
7. Ibid.
8. For "incommensurability," see, for example, Alasdair C. MacIntyre, *Whose Justice? Which Rationality?* (Notre Dame: Notre Dame University Press, 1988), chapter 19. The quote is from MacIntyre, *Three Rival Versions of Moral Enquiry: Encyclopaedia, Genealogy, and Tradition: Being Gifford Lectures Delivered in the University of Edinburgh in 1988* (Notre Dame, Ind.: University of Notre Dame Press, 1990), 4.
9. MacIntyre, *Three Rival Versions*, 4–5.

and indeed different standards concerning what is to be accounted an intelligible theory."[10] Hence rights become a phenomenon endemic to a particular moral vision, outside of which they lose all meaning.

The Historical-Linguistic Argument

In MacIntyre's third argument, closely related to the first, he appeals to the history of moral discourse and the nonexistence of a *term* for rights all the way up to the late Middle Ages. Since the word "rights" itself appears relatively late on the scene, MacIntyre argues, one cannot help but doubt how such an important concept could have remained hidden for so long if rights actually existed. In *After Virtue,* he writes:

> It would of course be a little odd that there should be such rights attaching to human beings simply *qua* human beings in light of the fact . . . that there is no expression in any ancient or medieval language correctly translated by our expression "a right" until near the close of the middle ages. . . . from this it does not follow that there are no natural or human rights; it only follows that no one could have known that there were. And this at least raises certain questions.[11]

Thus not only have rights never been convincingly explained, says MacIntyre, but the concept was not so much as articulated until just a few centuries ago. If the word did not exist in ancient or medieval language, we can deduce that thinkers were unaware of the existence of rights. This ignorance could be due to one of two causes: either rights did not (and therefore *do not*) exist, or for millennia rights existed but without being discovered until recently. For such a fundamental ethical reality to lie undiscovered for so long leads to serious doubt regarding its existence.[12]

---

10. Ibid., 13.
11. MacIntyre, *After Virtue,* 69.
12. This is not the only instance where MacIntyre resorts to the historical-linguistic argument to cast doubt on words and concepts. In his 1988 Gifford Lectures, MacIntyre speaks of the blindness of late nineteenth-century Edinburgh encyclopaedists "to the local and parochial nature of their own assimilation of impropriety to immorality, just because they imputed to contingent features of their own morality a universality which they took to be the mark of rationality" (*Three Rival Versions,* 28). MacIntyre faults these Victorians for attributing a universal value to what was a distinctive feature of their own local understanding of morality. More specifically, he takes Henry Sidgwick to task for the latter's *Britannica* article on "Ethics." Sidgwick, writes MacIntyre, fails to notice "that the word 'morality' as used by his contemporaries has no equivalent expression in biblical or medieval Hebrew or in either classical or *koiné* Greek, or in either classical or high medieval Latin."

If "rights" were only unearthed several centuries ago, what was the cause of their appearance? Why did the term present itself when and as it did? As MacIntyre sees things, rights are a modern invention that emerged from a "distinctively modern moral scheme," which for him means a morality that conceives of man as an autonomous moral agent, unfettered by "the externalities of divine law, natural teleology or hierarchical authority." By "rights" MacIntyre understands "those rights which are alleged to belong to human beings as such and which are cited as a reason for holding that people ought not to be interfered with in their pursuit of life, liberty and happiness. They are the rights which were spoken of in the eighteenth century as natural rights or the rights of man."[13] The rights MacIntyre is talking about are specifically the "negative"rights (see chapter 2) proposed by the likes of Thomas Hobbes and John Locke and later adopted by American colonists such as Thomas Paine and French thinkers such as Rousseau and Voltaire and encoded in the American Declaration of Independence (1776), the French Declaration of the Rights of Man and of the Citizen (1789), and the American Bill of Rights (1791).

Moreover, MacIntyre sees these rights as part and parcel of a larger project. They are linked to anthropological assumptions that may or may not coincide with the classical, and especially the Christian, view of man. "The concept of rights," he continues, "was generated to serve one set of purposes as part of the social invention of the autonomous moral agent."[14] Therefore, not only is the concept of rights tied to local social structures, as explained in the preceding section, but these structures usher in a new understanding of man as autonomous moral agent, representing a radical departure from the classical view.

---

13. MacIntyre, *After Virtue*, 68–69. MacIntyre's reference to the "pursuit of life, liberty and happiness" evidently comes from the second line of the American Declaration of Independence. "We hold these Truths to be self-evident, that all Men are created equal, that they are endowed by their Creator with certain unalienable Rights, that among these are Life, Liberty, and the Pursuit of Happiness." MacIntyre is not alone is his criticism of the Declaration and its underlying conception of rights. Walter Berns writes: "This country was officially founded on the principle of self-interest. 'To secure these rights,' says the Declaration of Independence, and these rights are private rights, 'governments are instituted among men.' Men institute government for selfish reasons. That was, and is, the principle on which we built" ("The Need for Public Authority," in *Freedom and Virtue: The Conservative/Libertarian Debate,* ed. George W. Carey [Wilmington, Del.: Intercollegiate Studies Institute, 1998], 65).

14. MacIntyre, *After Virtue*, 70.

MacIntyre specifically takes issue with rights arguments advanced in the eighteenth century and the twentieth. He dismisses the former with a categorical declaration: "The eighteenth-century philosophical defenders of natural rights sometimes suggest that the assertions which state that men possess them are self-evident truths; but we know that there are no self-evident truths." Similarly, MacIntyre makes quick work of more recent attempts to ground rights on intuition: "Twentieth-century moral philosophers have sometimes appealed to their and our intuitions; but one of the things we ought to have learned from the history of moral philosophy is that the introduction of the word 'intuition' by a moral philosopher is always a signal that something has gone badly with an argument."[15]

RESPONSE
The Argument by Default

MacIntyre's sweeping affirmation that "every attempt to give good reasons for believing that there *are* such rights has failed" is a subjective opinion, not a statement of fact. Good reasons are reasons that convince, and MacIntyre is not convinced. Thus his assertion could be restated: "None of the arguments I have encountered in favor of rights has convinced *me* of their existence." In a sense, a response to MacIntyre's argument of default constitutes the basis for this entire work, which is an attempt to provide a coherent explanation of rights and their foundations. Nonetheless, a summary reply can be offered here; the compatibility of human rights with classical Christian ethics will be shown later along with a further development of the foundations of such rights.

Simply stated, the denial of rights is self-defeating, since it implicitly carries with it the denial of natural law, something neither MacIntyre nor anyone else in the classical tradition would be prepared to do. MacIntyre, like the other writers considered here, accepts the existence of universal natural duties, which in turn form the core of natural law.[16] A natural duty differs from an acquired duty in that it does not come about as a re-

---

15. Ibid., 69.
16. MacIntyre sees the precepts of the natural law as inherently bound up with the essence of cooperative social relationships. "And how can I trust without qualification, unless I recognize myself and others as mutually bound by such precepts as those that enjoin that we *never* do violence of any sort to innocent human life, that we *always* refrain from theft and fraud,

sult of anything man *does* but only from what he *is*. All people have duties or obligations toward God, toward other people, and toward themselves. Our focus here are natural duties whose object is other people. Whence do such duties arise?

A concrete example may prove illuminating. The Ten Commandments, or Decalogue, form the core of the moral code taught in the Old Testament. Midway through the list figures the injunction: "Thou shalt not kill." This moral duty—not to kill another human being—is conveyed as a divine mandate. At the same time a consensus among moralists of the classical tradition holds that the commandment against killing the innocent forms part of the natural moral law. That is to say that even had God not revealed this commandment, people would have been able to discern it by the unaided light of human reason. The revealed commandment serves to elucidate and confirm what is already accessible to reason.

On a natural level, how does this rational discernment come about? What cognitive process comes into play? Does man discover within himself an innate knowledge of this prohibition, infused in his intellect as a self-evident norm of conduct? The Christian tradition rejects such an understanding of natural law. The precepts of the natural moral law are *natural* for man, not in the sense that they are innate or infused, but in the sense that they are *intelligible* to human reason, and thus can be reasoned to.

The moral injunction against "killing" does not present itself in the abstract, without a referent object, but specifically as regards other human beings. There is no moral comparison between swatting a mosquito and killing a person. The fundamental difference between the *object* (which defines the "moral species")[17] of the act of swatting a mosquito and that of killing a human being, and consequently the determining factor in the moral evaluation such an act deserves, lies not in the moral agent nor in the physical action but in the *recipient* of the act. In other

---

that we *always* tell each other the truth, and that we *always* uphold justice in our relationships" (Alasdair C. MacIntyre, "Theories of Natural Law in the Culture of Advanced Modernity," in *Common Truths: New Perspectives on Natural Law,* ed. Edward B. McLean [Wilmington, Del.: ISI Books, 2000], 109–10). The question remains how one can affirm, for example, that we are bound to *always* tell others the truth without simultaneously admitting that others *deserve* to have the truth told to them, that is, that they have a *right* to be told the truth.

17. See John Paul II, encyclical letter *Veritatis Splendor* (*http://www.vatican.va/edocs/ENG0222/_INDEX.HTM;* hereafter *VS*), 77, 78; *S. Th.,* I-II, 18, 6.

words, killing a mosquito and killing a person are similar in that the moral agent (the perpetrator of the act) and the type of action (deliberate killing) are common to both, but the two are radically different in that a mosquito is not a person. Therefore the evil of the act of killing a human being must somehow proceed from the nature of the human being as recipient of the action and not from the moral agent nor from the generic sort of action (killing). One naturally discerns something about the human being that affirms: "I am not to be killed," or "To kill me would be morally evil." Something about the human being therefore confers a moral quality on actions that other persons may perform on him. When certain actions relating to the human person possess a moral quality of prohibition or obligation, one can say that these are things that a human being *deserves in justice*. And to deserve something in justice is to possess a moral right.

A counterexample may also be helpful. Suppose for a moment that MacIntyre is correct in saying that natural rights do not exist. This is equivalent to saying that no person can naturally claim to deserve anything from anyone else. It follows that when I come upon a person, that person deserves nothing from me. Barring some positive moral injunction to the contrary, I can treat him as I please without incurring any moral guilt. I can ignore him, spit at him, or trample him as if he were one more cobblestone under my feet. One could object that the absence of *rights* does not eliminate the moral *duties* of the agent, but this does not hold in the case of natural duties. Absent a civil law to the contrary, why must someone be treated in a given way just because he is a human person? One could always fall back on divine commandment, but this is the domain of positive (albeit divine) law and therefore no longer represents a natural duty. Moreover, in this case the obligation of the moral agent has God as its object, not the person, and thus is no longer a requirement of justice to the person but of obedience to God. It logically follows that if a person deserves nothing from me, I owe him nothing. The denial of natural rights necessarily entails the denial of natural duties and the denial of the entire natural law.

The Dependence of Rights on Local Social Structures

No one would refute MacIntyre's claim that many rights depend on existing social structures for their intelligibility. Many social habits to which people grow accustomed, and to which they feel entitled, may be foreign to another social milieu and could not be expected, much less demanded. Forms of courtesy or greeting, manifestations of deference or attention—to take an obvious example—vary widely from culture to culture. But what is true for particular customs is not necessarily true for more general human experiences. For example, outside of a particular social context, a bow as an expression of deference may be unintelligible, but deference itself, as a human attitude with manifold expressions, remains intelligible to all. In the case of "rights," what particular types of social institution or practice are necessary to make intelligible the notion of a claim to entitlement?

It would seem that the moral experience of debt—owing something to someone else—is a universal phenomenon, even if the content of the obligation may vary considerably. The corresponding moral experience of entitlement—to expect something from someone else as due in justice and to feel wronged by not receiving it—is likewise universal. For example, when a person receives a promise from another person, regardless of the content of the promise, he expects the promise to be fulfilled. He feels *entitled* to what has been promised. When money is lent with the understanding that it is not a gift, the lender entertains not only the hope to be repaid but understands himself to possess the moral *right* to be repaid, regardless of his culture. It seems that the burden of proof lies with those who would deny the universality of this basic experience, and MacIntyre offers no empirical evidence leading to such a conclusion. There may indeed be people whose culture or society has led them to believe that nothing is due to them, but even members of such a nondeserving caste can understand the concept that *something* is due to *someone,* for example the king or tribal chief. The idea of debt is universally intelligible.

If, then, entitlement is a universal human experience, even though the content of particular claims may vary widely, it seems unreasonable to sustain, as MacIntyre does, that "the existence of particular types of social institution or practice is a necessary condition for the notion of a claim to the possession of a right being an intelligible type of human performance." Anyone who can understand what it means for someone to owe something to someone else can understand, at least in theory, what it means for someone to be entitled to something simply because he is a human being. Not all share this understanding of the human person or accept the assertion that all men are entitled to certain things, but it remains "an intelligible type of human performance."

The Historical-Linguistic Argument

MacIntyre shores up his case against the existence of rights by citing the lack of a term for the concept of human rights until relatively recent times. It is true that neologisms sometimes arise because of discoveries or inventions of realities hitherto unknown (such as with the element molybdenum or the microchip). Sometimes, however, they reflect a new perspective on or a new classification of concepts that are already familiar. In the case of rights, it is clear that the concept of "deserving" or "being owed" was part and parcel not only of classical theory of justice but of the everyday experience of ancient peoples. Calling this ethical phenomenon "having rights" or calling it "flexopopoly" does nothing to change the underlying reality. Curiously, in the very volume where MacIntyre so categorically excludes the notion of rights, he praises the classical Aristotelian virtue of *phronesis*, which "characterizes someone who knows what is due to him, who takes pride in claiming his due."[18] For all intents and purposes, such a description could be perfectly well restated as "characterizing someone who is familiar with his rights and takes pride in demanding that they be respected." The choice of vocabulary does not alter the underlying meaning expressed.

Words evolve in meaning over time and even vary in meaning between one culture and another. Nevertheless, the evolution of language does not necessarily invalidate a particular proposition involving a specific use of a word, simply because other people meant different things by the same word or never used the word at all. Again, "words" are neither true nor false; rather, truth and falsehood are correctly applied to propositions involving words with some specific meaning in that particular context. A much more important question regarding the origin of rights is not when the word came into existence but whether it expresses a reality with which our ethical forebears were familiar and whether specific claims of rights can be correctly predicated of the human person.

As MacIntyre sees things, the word "rights," as well as the concept underlying the word, sprang from a specific mentality corresponding to a

---

18. MacIntyre, *After Virtue*, 154.

"distinctively modern moral scheme." This scheme conceives of man as an autonomous moral agent, unrestrained by "the externalities of divine law, natural teleology or hierarchical authority." By "rights" MacIntyre understands essentially the rights proclaimed by eighteenth-century thinkers. What does this delimitation mean for MacIntyre's argument? The historical genesis of rights theories can indeed be traced to particular individuals living in particular historical circumstances. Thomas Hobbes, for instance, espoused a conception of man as an autonomous moral agent, unrestrained by the externalities of divine law, natural teleology, or hierarchical authority. Here MacIntyre's stereotype holds good. The same cannot be said, however, for Francisco de Vitoria who, a full century before Hobbes, argued forcefully for the natural rights of the natives of the New World while simultaneously professing an unswerving belief in divine law, natural teleology, and hierarchical authority. Nothing about natural rights as an anthropological/ethical concept inherently conflicts with these "externalities" nor demands an understanding of man as an autonomous moral agent. The fact that certain exponents of rights theories denied these realities and had such a conception of man does nothing to dismantle the fundamental idea of natural rights themselves. The Liberal explanation of rights is just one possible explanation among several, and the present volume offers a theory of rights that is thoroughly non-Liberal in its approach and premises.

Finally, MacIntyre's wholesale dismissal of "self-evident truths" seems hasty and unwarranted.[19] Practical reasoning depends on nondemonstrable first principles just as speculative reasoning does, and any first principle must be, in some form, self-evident.

MacIntyre's accusation of nonexistence simply cannot be sustained. If the idea and language of rights are to be impugned, a more cogent case must be made.

---

19. Finnis, for one, has written: "Nowadays, any claim that something is self-evident is commonly misunderstood by philosophers. They think that any such claim either asserts or presupposes that the criterion of the truth of the allegedly self-evident principle, proposition, or fact is one's *feeling of certitude* about it. This is indeed a misunderstanding. Self-evident principles . . . are not validated by feelings. On the contrary, they are themselves the criteria whereby we discriminate between feelings, and discount some of our feelings (including feelings of certitude), however intense, as irrational or unwarranted, misleading or delusive" (Finnis, *Natural Law and Natural Rights*, 69).

5. THE ACCUSATION OF INSEPARABILITY

A SECOND REPRESENTATIVE of the reaction against rights language is Joan Lockwood O'Donovan (1950–), political philosopher from Oxford, England. While MacIntyre attempts to show the philosophical nonexistence of rights, O'Donovan adopts a different approach. She argues that the concept of rights is inseparable from its origins in an Enlightenment, Liberal philosophy that is simply incompatible with Christian theology.

In March 1996, O'Donovan presented a provocative paper entitled "The Concept of Rights in Christian Moral Discourse" at a two-day colloquium on Christian approaches to natural law sponsored by the Washington-based Ethics and Public Policy Center as part of its Evangelical Studies Project. In her paper O'Donovan revisits some of MacIntyre's arguments but also offers a unique historical analysis of the genesis and development of rights discourse in ethics and politics. She adopts this analysis as a basis for asserting the incompatibility of such language with Christian ethics—a common accusation among rights-theory critics. Making a case for the historical alliance of rights with classical Liberalism, O'Donovan asserts that since the two cannot be separated, Christian ethicists and theologians should refrain from using rights language.

O'Donovan contends that Christian thinkers absorb rights talk uncritically, incorporating its language into Christian ethics without weighing its negative effects. Noting the "entrenchment of rights language in contemporary political and legal discourse," O'Donovan laments the less obvious "indications that the concept of rights is itself passing beyond dispute, and possibly even beyond discussion." She registers her impression that "theologians often engage in a naïve and facile appropriation of the language of rights," simply tacking on theological arguments like man's creation in God's image and the unique dignity of persons to the Enlightenment construct of human rights. O'Donovan attempts to awaken discontent with this undiscriminating assimilation of rights language by offering a critical analysis of the dubious origins of rights and the latent philosophical presuppositions underlying them. She challenges "the adequacy of 'rights' as an element of theological-moral discourse . . . in the light of the pre-modern traditions of Christian natural law, particularly the Augustinian tradition with its evangelical and Christological approach to natural law."[1]

OBJECTIONS

The Ties of Rights to Liberal Contractarianism

The core of O'Donovan's case against rights talk consists in its ties to Liberalism, specifically to what she sees as Liberalism's indissoluble union with contractarianism. She notes that the concept of subjective rights entered contemporary legal and political currency "primarily through the liberal contractarian tradition bequeathed by Hobbes and Locke, Rousseau and Kant, and the theoretical exponents of the American and French Revolutions" and therefore the meaning ascribed to rights in contemporary popular and academic use "cannot be properly ascertained in detachment from this theoretical context." Moreover, these meanings carry with them a whole train of political, legal, philosophical, and theological concepts: "concepts of divine, natural, and positive law, of justice, freedom, and equality, of reason and will, of sovereignty and property, of covenant and contract."[2]

O'Donovan distinguishes two antagonistic views of political right. One, the older patristic and medieval tradition of political right, held that God's right established a matrix of divine, natural, and human laws that constituted the ordering justice of the political community. The central political-moral obligation of ruled and ruler alike was to abide by the demands of this objective justice, manifested in communal obligations

---

1. Joan Lockwood O'Donovan, "The Concept of Rights in Christian Moral Discourse," in *A Preserving Grace: Protestants, Catholics, and Natural Law,* ed. Michael Cromartie (Grand Rapids, Mich.: Ethics and Public Policy Center/William B. Eerdmans, 1997), 143, 144.

2. Ibid., 144.

according to divine intention, and rationally conceived as laws. The newer tradition of political right, whose beginnings O'Donovan places in the fourteenth and fifteenth centuries, carried a voluntarist, individualist, and subjectivist orientation, whereby God's right "established discrete rights, possessed by individuals originally and by communities derivatively, that determined civil order and justice."[3]

As society shifted from the older tradition of objective right to the newer tradition of subjective rights, the individual occupied an ever more prominent position, both for ruler and ruled, in interactions among citizens. Nevertheless, not until the seventeenth and eighteenth centuries, writes O'Donovan, did "the subjective rights of individuals supercede the objective right of divinely revealed and natural laws as the primary or exclusive basis of political authority, justice, and law."[4]

Throughout this social and political transition, theorists elaborated explanations of rights that kept pace with, undergirded, and provoked a change in mentality as regards political right. These theoretical elaborations of the concept of rights "have invested it with lasting intellectual content." Therefore, though Christian theorists have wished to divorce themselves from the encumbrances of Liberalism while clinging to its vocabulary, such a separation is impossible:

> Christian political thought (both Catholic and Protestant) that is not wholly satisfied with this fabric [of democratic, pluralistic, technological Liberalism] recognizes the need to divest the concept of rights of its offensive theoretical material. But when it attempts to separate some conceptual threads from the fabric, the result inevitably falls short: either too much of the fabric adheres to the threads, or the threads lose their coherence.[5]

O'Donovan does not set out to substantiate this judgment in her paper, a task that would require, as she acknowledges, reviewing the range of contemporary theological treatments of human rights and demonstrating in each case the occurrence of one or the other of the fatal flaws to which she alludes. Rather, she proceeds to consider the central historical content of rights theories.

---

3. Ibid.   4. Ibid., 145–46.
5. Ibid., 146.

The Problematic Content of Liberal Rights Theory

O'Donovan delineates three theologically problematic characteristics of rights theories: (1) the role of property rights; (2) the role of contract; and (3) the notion of freedom of choice.

In the first place, O'Donovan notes the paradigmatic position occupied by proprietary rights from the earliest definitions of subjective rights and how that preeminence influenced subsequent theories. She traces property rights from Pope John XXII's opposition to the Franciscan Order's vow of poverty in the 1320s, on the grounds that the lawful consumption of material goods was inseparable from the property right in them, all the way through John Rawl's attempt to synthesize negative libertarian and positive welfare principles. Along the way she cites the Parisian nominalist Jean Gerson (1363–1429) and his idea of right *(ius)* as "a dispositional *facultas* or power, appropriate to someone and in accordance with the dictates of right reason,"[6] as well as Luis de Molina, Francisco Suárez, and Hugo Grotius. The latter provided the definition of a right as "the faculty of demanding what is due . . . [to which] answers the obligation of rendering what is owing."[7] O'Donovan continues through Hobbes, Locke, and the Levellers, seeing in Hobbes's theory of unlimited natural right the beginning of "a model of social relationships as generally acquisitive, atomistic, and competitive."[8]

She sums up the influence of this centrality of property rights in Liberal rights theory as follows: "The continuing predominance of property right within the negative libertarian tradition . . . sustains the concept of a right or freedom as a power of acting possessed by a subject that entails the obligation of non-interference on the part of all other subjects, and especially of government."[9] In other words, rights conceived as powers of acting that impose on others the obligation of noninterference is the legacy of a conception of rights whose prototype is proprietary right.

O'Donovan also tries to explain how property right has influenced the

---

6. See Richard Tuck, *Natural Rights Theories: Their Origin and Development* (Cambridge: Cambridge University Press, 1979), 25–7, as cited in Joan Lockwood O'Donovan, "The Concept of Rights in Christian Moral Discourse," 147.

7. Grotius, *De Iure Belli ac Pacis*, bk. *I, ch. I, chs. IV–VIII*, as cited in Tuck, *Natural Rights Theories*, 56.

8. O'Donovan, "The Concept of Rights in Christian Moral Discourse," 148.

9. Ibid., 150–51.

more recent tradition of positive rights as entitlements of subjects to goods or opportunities rather than to noninterference, though, as she admits, the relation here is less obvious. A possible explanation to save the relation of positive rights to property is "that individuals are impeded in fully using their personal property (their freedoms, powers, or capacities) because the necessary means are unavailable to them."[10] In other words, the unavailability of certain requisite means effectively "interferes with" the subject's exercise of his power. To provide such means merely removes this interference.

In the discussion that followed the presentation of her paper and the rebuttal by Princeton professor Robert George, O'Donovan clarified what she sees as the relationship between property rights and rights in general. In the course of the discussion, she asserted that the very term "to have" situates rights in a mentality of ownership, specifically self-ownership. "My argument," O'Donovan explained, "is that the use of the word 'have' does imply self-ownership.... As soon as you get into the language of having rights, you are into a language of proprietary subjectivity." In other words, the very language of "having" rights is tainted with the Liberal idea of self-possession. "The only way out of the impasse is to break through into the language of justice and law and goodness, a language that does not depend on or evoke the concept of proprietary rights."[11]

The second problematic characteristic of Liberal rights theory is the role played by contract. O'Donovan underscores the importance of the idea of contract in Western theories of individual natural rights for the theoretical transition from original right to civil and social rights. Whereas pre-Renaissance political covenants typically expressed the mutual obligation between ruler and ruled, rooted in the subordination of both to divine and natural law, later theories of political covenant integrated individualist and naturalist ideas, such as "the pre-political natural equality of men, their primitive solitary existence, and the inauguration of society by a deliberate agreement among free individuals."[12]

---

10. Ibid., 151.
11. O'Donovan, "Comments," in *A Preserving Grace: Protestants, Catholics, and Natural Law*, ed. Michael Cromartie (Grand Rapids, Mich.: Ethics and Public Policy Center/William B. Eerdmans, 1997), 164, 165.
12. O'Donovan, "The Concept of Rights in Christian Moral Discourse," 152.

What O'Donovan calls the "crucially novel element" introduced into social and political contract conceptions by English Puritans and Whigs beginning in the mid-seventeenth century was the idea of an exchange of natural rights for civil rights, a concept with commercial overtones. The principal effects of bringing the idea of social and political contract into the sphere of economic transaction "was to accentuate the superior bargaining position and adjudicating power of contracting individuals . . . and the dominant role of calculative rationality in setting the terms of the contract" as well as "to deprive the sphere of *public* welfare and public law of a moral basis independent from that of *private* welfare and private law." This would have the long-term effect of undermining "the independent purposes and operation of the public realm." As political authorities succumb to the logic of market economics, citizens similarly take on a consumer mentality in their relations with the state, seeking "the best possible protection and provision for their infinitely expanding range of personal rights in return for surrender of some freedom and material property."[13] O'Donovan sees this tendency toward political contractualism as the reduction of public law and the common good to private law and private good.

A third problematic characteristic of Liberal rights theories flows from the particular understanding of human freedom they necessarily entail. O'Donovan discerns a common thread running through rights theories from their inception, "the idea of the bearer of rights as a self-transcending will who *uses* the world around as well as his own body and capacities to achieve certain self-referential ends."[14] This emphasis on the sovereign subject leads to competition between autonomous individuals, each of whom struggles to maximize the protection and provision of his subjective rights. Likewise, as the sovereign self acknowledges fewer and fewer external obligations and objective goods, rights tend to agglomerate into one universal, all-encompassing right: the right to freedom. "In a society whose only coherent public moral language is that of subjective rights, the only universally respected right is that of freedom, understood as the sovereignty of the subject over his physical and moral world—that is, his emancipation from all externally imposed material and spiritual constraints on his freedom of choice and self-determination."[15] With in-

---

13. Ibid., 152–53.   14. Ibid.
15. Ibid., 154.

dividual freedom of choice as the pivotal right, resolving conflicts of interest becomes increasingly difficult.

Though O'Donovan prefaces her arguments by asserting that these three characteristics are theologically problematic, she offers no analysis of where the problems lie. She limits her work to delineating the inherited theoretical content of the Western "rights" tradition, "with the hope of helping readers judge for themselves the historical and theological plausibility of contemporary Christian appropriations of the language of rights," while at the same time expressing her conviction regarding the incompatibility of such language with Christian theology. In the end, "the question that has yet to be satisfactorily answered . . . is why Christian thinkers have been and are willing to adopt a child of such questionable parentage as the concept of human rights."[16] After seeing whence rights proceed and the philosophical baggage with which they are historically associated, why would Christians want to incorporate such a concept into moral theology?

RESPONSE

In this presentation of the case against rights, readers will discover much overlap among the objections to rights presented by the three authors studied. This cannot be avoided, since the objections themselves wind back over each other, both within the exposition of each author and among the three different writers. Therefore the responses already given to certain arguments will assuredly also throw light on subsequent arguments against rights. To avoid needless repetition, arguments already answered adequately will receive less attention.

The Ties of Rights to Liberal Contractarianism

O'Donovan's case can be summed up as a logical sequence. (1) The concept of rights is inextricably bound up with Enlightenment Liberalism; (2) Enlightenment Liberalism embodies a morality and philosophical anthropology that are incompatible with Christianity; (3) therefore, rights language promotes a morality and philosophical anthropology incompatible with Christianity.

---

16. Ibid., 146, 155.

The logic is solid; the premises are not. O'Donovan successfully analyzes the origins of a certain strain of rights in Enlightenment Liberalism and shows how Liberalism and those rights advanced in lockstep. The claim, however, that the word itself and its basic moral referent are necessarily wrapped up in the philosophical and political baggage of Liberalism cannot be proved by a historical argument alone.[17] The fundamental question is whether "rights" must necessarily be Liberal rights as understood by Hobbes and his followers. Do rights carry with them ipso facto the assumptions of the Liberal school? Cannot the word "rights" be used without endorsing a whole series of propositions that would be judged incompatible with the Christian tradition?[18] To establish more than a mere historical connection between rights and Liberalism would require demonstrating that the Liberal conception of rights is the only possible way to understand the term.[19] Nowhere in her paper does O'Donovan succeed in establishing such a connection, nor does she indicate that such a demonstration is possible.

Before going on to examine the problems O'Donovan sees with Liberal rights theory, a word should be addressed to her understanding of the progression from objective right to subjective rights and from common good to individual good. O'Donovan sees a seventeenth- and eighteenth-

17. Lockwood's assumption reflects the case spoken of by Jacques Maritain on referring to systems that "jeopardize an authentic acquisition of moral experience by linking it to some theoretical error or some false philosophy" (*Man and the State* [Washington, D.C.: Catholic University of America Press, 1998], 80).

18. Robert George has answered this question in the affirmative. Though Liberalism cannot get along without rights, "surely no merely historical connection is sufficient to establish that those who reject possessive individualism cannot now deploy the language of rights without thereby importing into their thought features of that philosophy that mark it as antithetical to the value of community and other important goods. Here, I would suggest, only a logical (or, at a minimum, a very strong psychological) connection will suffice" ("A Response to Joan Lockwood O'Donovan," in *A Preserving Grace: Protestants, Catholics, and Natural Law*, ed. Michael Cromartie [Grand Rapids, Mich.: Ethics and Public Policy Center/William B. Eerdmans, 1997], 157).

19. Grasso notes that whereas "there can be no denying that liberalism has dominated modern theorizing about human rights . . . it simply does not follow that liberalism provides the only possible intellectual foundation for the institution, practices, and principles that are constitutive of the free society. . . . simply stated, the Catholic human rights revolution demonstrates that the institutions and practices of constitutional democracy and human rights can be projected from foundations other than the premises of liberalism, and thus that a principled commitment to democracy and human rights does not entail the acceptance of the liberal model of man and society" ("Beyond Liberalism," 53).

century phenomenon whereby the "subjective rights of individuals supersede the objective right of divinely revealed and natural laws as the primary or exclusive basis of political authority, justice, and law." Whereas a shift in emphasis from objective right to subjective rights undoubtedly occurred, and has endured up to the present, that shift did not produce the antagonism that O'Donovan posits between the two.

Objective right, as a just moral order, remains at the level of abstraction until it is made concrete and real through discrete subjective rights, which it naturally and necessarily entails. A situation of objective justice, both commutative and distributive, where all are treated fairly, is by definition a situation in which all receive their "due." Thus the establishment and preservation of a certain equality among persons means that each receives his "due," which can only be expressed in concrete terms. The "what is due" *(debitum)* is the proper matter of particular (subjective) rights. Each and every person enjoying what is due (subjective rights) yields a situation of objective right. Where subjective rights are not satisfied, objective right does not exist. It could of course be argued that the shift in emphasis from the language of "right" to the language of "rights" has been counterproductive, but it is misleading to speak of the two terms as if they were mutually exclusive, when in fact they are mutually indicative.

O'Donovan may have fallen into the error of associating subjective rights with rights flowing from the will of individuals, as opposed to objective right, whose origins are in God and in the divinely established laws of His creation. In reality, in standard ethical vocabulary, the word "subjective" when applied to rights refers not to a supposed issuance of rights from the subjective will of the individual but to what is just for the individual human subject.[20] It is the right that resides in the individual person (or "subject") rather than the right that describes a situation of justice and equilibrium residing in the whole of society. Therefore, these individual "subjective" rights are no less "objective," in the sense of absolute or real, than "objective right." In this regard, O'Donovan mistakenly contrasts subjective rights with an "objective right of divinely re-

---

20. "For what is a subjective right but the just order (what is objectively right) considered in relation to the aims and interests of the subject, that is, as capable of promoting these? Undoubtedly, in order to be a genuine right, a subjective right has to be in conformity to the just order" (de Finance, *An Ethical Inquiry,* § 194, p. 345).

vealed and natural laws." Subjective rights, as understood by the Catholic tradition, do not stand apart from natural law; far from contrasting with it, they form an integral part of it.

A similar relationship exists between the common good and the good of the individual person. Barring a collectivist philosophy that mistakenly sees the "collectivity" (state, commonwealth, etc.) as a subsisting entity above and apart from the individuals who compose it, the common good is always the good of persons. Since the human person is naturally social and finds perfection in interpersonal relationships and in the good of others, "common good" and "personal good" are bound up one with the other. By contriving a polarization between personal good and common good, O'Donovan loses sight of their natural and necessary complementarity.

The Problematic Content of Liberal Rights Theory

O'Donovan is not alone in pointing out the exaggerated role that property rights played in the development of rights theory in the Liberal school and the dangers of seeing such rights as absolute.[21] Seeing rights as principally a means of securing one's personal belongings against incursions from other (hostile) human beings represents an impoverishment of the concept of rights and an overly individualistic understanding of human flourishing. While acknowledging a real right to private property, one can warn against the danger of reducing human rights to property rights or of exalting property rights as absolutes.

Even among orthodox Catholic moral theologians one discerns at times the tendency to place the question of human rights within the framework of property. In his work *Living in Christ,* Carlo Caffarra locates his discussion of rights within his explanation of the seventh and tenth commandments. He begins this section by saying: "The seventh and tenth Commandments require respect for what is owed, for what belongs to the human person as such, for what is *his.*"[22] This placement is unfortunate. What is owed to the human person extends well beyond the matter of the seventh and tenth commandments. The seventh, according to the *Catechism of the Catholic Church,* refers specifically to "justice and

---

21. See, for example, Glendon, *Rights Talk,* especially 18–46.
22. Carlo Caffarra, *Living in Christ: Fundamental Principles of Catholic Moral Teaching,* trans. Christopher Ruff (San Francisco: Ignatius Press, 1989), 220–21.

charity in the care of *earthly goods and the fruits of men's labor*" as well as "respect for the right to *private property.*"[23]

Human rights are protected by all the precepts of the second tablet of the Decalogue, not just by these two, and thus it would seem more reasonable either to regard rights without reference to specific Commandments or to consider the place of rights in all of them. To treat them under the heading of the seventh and tenth Commandments implies a reductive understanding of the human goods protected by rights, as if these were limited to the material goods that are the proper matter of these two precepts. To limit rights to questions of property reflects either a misunderstanding of justice (i.e., justice as embracing not all the goods of the person but only his material goods) or a misunderstanding of the relationship between justice and rights (i.e., rights applying only to a limited subset of the matter of justice, specifically, the matter of earthly goods).

Caffarra does not relegate rights to a subset of justice, but he does treat justice within the context of the seventh and tenth commandments. "In short, these two commandments sanction what is *just,* founding the concept of *rights* on the dignity of the human person. The violation of these two Commandments occurs precisely in the violation of these rights."[24] But is not justice also the basis of the fourth commandment (what is owed to one's parents), the sixth (what is owed to one's spouse), and the eighth (what is owed to one's interlocutor)?[25] Why limit justice, and consequently rights, to respect for our neighbor's material goods?

On the other hand, property rights are in fact a logical prototype for human rights in general, precisely because they refer to "goods" in the most normal, tangible sense of the word. It makes perfect sense to take such a concrete example as a sort of analogy for less tangible goods. What "belongs" to one *(suum),* what is "due" to one *(debitum)* can most easily

---

23. *CCC,* 2401; emphasis added. The full text reads: "The seventh commandment forbids unjustly taking or keeping the goods of one's neighbour and wronging him in any way with respect to his goods. It commands justice and charity in the care of earthly goods and the fruits of men's labour. For the sake of the common good, it requires respect for the universal destination of goods and respect for the right to private property. Christian life strives to order this world's goods to God and to fraternal charity."

24. Caffarra, *Living in Christ,* 220–21.

25. See, for example, *CCC,* 2381, which describes adultery as "an injustice," whereby he who commits it "transgresses the rights of the other spouse."

be understood in terms of physical property. As explanations of justice often take property as their point of departure, so it is with rights. Such an explanation is not improper, as long as one understands it is not complete: that is, justice (and rights) include, but do not end with, a discussion of material property.

O'Donovan's objection to the role of property rights in Liberal theory goes still further, however. She sees the use of the language of "having" rights as necessarily bearing within it the Liberal understanding of self-ownership. That is, to speak of "having rights" creates a possessive mentality and implies the doctrine of self-ownership and thus soul-body dualism. A simple analogy should suffice to show the deficiency of this line of argument. Within the context of justice, rights and duties (or obligations) are parallel concepts. If the language of "having rights" implies self-ownership, then the language of "having duties" implies the same. Yet no one objects to the language of "having" obligations or "having" duties, and no one would assert that such language implies the acceptance of the notion, characteristic of Liberal theories of rights, that an individual "owns" himself in the sense that he can dispose of himself as he pleases.[26]

Robert George responded to this argument in the following manner, framing his reply in the context of the right to life: "Nothing in the proposition that says that an unborn child has a right not to be aborted presupposes that an unborn child has, or that any of us has, a property of self-ownership. In fact, to get to the proposition that the unborn have a right to life, I think you have to deny person-body dualism, which is ex-

---

26. Nor is this the only way to view self-ownership or self-possession. Notable thinkers outside the Liberal tradition hold that the person possesses himself, without for that falling into soul-body dualism. Wojtyła, for instance, has written: "Only the one who has possession of himself and is simultaneously his own sole and exclusive possession can be a person. (In a different order of things, the person as a creature may be seen as 'belonging to God,' but this relation does not eliminate or overshadow that inner relation of self-possession or self-ownership which is essential for the person. It is not without reason that medieval philosophers expressed this relationship in the phrase, *persona est sui iuris*)" (*The Acting Person*, trans. Andrzej Potocki [Dordrecht, the Netherlands: D. Reidel, 1979], 105–6). Josef Pieper speaks of "dwelling in oneself" (citing Goethe's expression, "wohnen in sich selbst"). "The two together constitute spirit," Pieper continues, "not only the capacity to relate oneself to the whole of reality, to the whole world, but an unlimited capacity of living in oneself, the gift of self-reliance and independence that has always been regarded as the decisive element in personality in the philosophical tradition of Europe" (*Leisure: The Basis of Culture*, trans. Alexander Dru [Indianapolis: Liberty Fund, 1999], 90–91).

actly what's at stake."²⁷ In other words, the right to life, far from entailing dualistic self-ownership, is in fact antithetical to it.

Two examples illustrate the cogency of this logic. First, those who appeal to the right to life to defend an unborn person from abortion appeal to the same principle (the right to life) to *refute* a putative right to suicide, euthanasia, and assisted suicide. If self-ownership and unlimited liberty to dispose of one's person, as O'Donovan understands it, were implicit in the right to life, euthanasia and assisted suicide would be defensible by appealing to that principle. Absolute ownership of one's body would confer the freedom to destroy it, if one so chose, yet advocates of a right to life never reach this conclusion. Second, the right to life is defined as an inviolable right, which means that it cannot be violated even by the one who possesses it. The very concept of inviolable rights presupposes that there are certain rights that are nontransferable, or "unwaivable." No one can decline to "exercise" his right to life, because it is inviolable. Compare this to the right to property, which in Christian discourse is never described as inviolable. Since the person has ownership of his property, he may dispose of it as he pleases. He may give it to someone else, thereby relinquishing his ownership and his rights. This is unacceptable in the case of the right to life, precisely because Christian rights theory does not recognize self-ownership as unlimited freedom to dispose of oneself as one sees fit.

The second problematic facet of Liberal rights theory identified by O'Donovan, the trend toward civil rights as a substitute for natural rights, is substantially correct. The idea of the social contract, essential to Locke's political philosophy, introduced a sort of consensualism into political theory that placed great emphasis on the sovereign individual's free will. As a result, many today acknowledge only those rights that are created by law or by mutual consent through contract. Yet such theories, involving the "the pre-political natural equality of men, their primitive solitary existence, and the inauguration of society by a deliberate agreement among free individuals," take nothing away from the concept of natural rights as such. The absorption of natural rights into civil rights is an unfortunate phenomenon, and the attempt by Liberal theorists to identify specific natural rights was flawed by their understanding of human na-

---

27. George, "A Response to Joan Lockwood O'Donovan," 164.

ture and the "natural state of man." Nevertheless, the fundamental idea of the human person's deserving certain goods in justice simply by being human remains intact and valid.

Much of the confusion flows from a modern tendency to equate society with the state and moral obligation with legal obligation. As O'Donovan has noted, "In contemporary contractarian liberalism, all communal obligations are derived from contract."[28] To many moderns, an obligation with no foundation in law (and thus an unenforceable obligation) is really no obligation at all. Such reasoning is tantamount to the denial of any nonlegal obligation, whether or not it happens to be a natural right. This error goes with the modern Liberal mentality per se and must be considered separately from the foundational human rights question.

The final objection springs from O'Donovan's discomfort with the pedigree of rights. Just as in the past persons born out of wedlock were viewed as unsuitable for certain posts in society because of their illegitimacy, so too, implies O'Donovan, should Christians be wary of adopting "a child of such questionable parentage as the concept of human rights." Knowing the origin of a given term or concept provides invaluable help in understanding its use and in assessing its aptness for assimilation into Christian moral discourse. But is bad birth alone sufficient to permanently disqualify words from our moral vocabulary?

A first response addresses O'Donovan's implication that rights theory grew exclusively within the Liberal tradition. Though, as she points out, a certain natural rights theory flourished in that tradition, its roots go back further than Hobbes and Locke. In reality, two parallel theories of natural rights exist,[29] one that grounds rights on Christian anthropology and the status of the human person as worthy of a certain sort of treatment and the other rooted in British Enlightenment anthropology, which posited a natural state of antagonism among individuals and a natural right to self-preservation, from which other rights emerged. In fact, a rights theory rooted in the Christian view of the human person grew out of the University of Salamanca a full century before Hobbes's *Leviathan*.

28. O'Donovan, "The Concept of Rights in Christian Moral Discourse," 153.

29. Possenti affirms that "two traditions exist regarding the rights of man, which certainly exhibit commonalities, but which differ both in the list and order of rights claims as well as in their justification: one tradition emerging in 1789 and the other older tradition proceeding from the bosom of Christianity and Mediterranean culture" ("Diritti umani e natura umana," 251; author's translation).

Through his studies of the way the *indios* were being treated in the recently discovered New World, the celebrated legal theorist Francisco de Vitoria (1480–1546) developed a teaching on natural rights based on a scholastic theological anthropology and ethics. None of Liberalism's atomistic and individualistic presuppositions about man, or of a supposed "natural state of man" prior to society, appears in Vitoria's writings. This absence would be inexplicable if, as O'Donovan suggests, rights theory depended on these elements. Though O'Donovan briefly acknowledges that rights theorizing was going on at Salamanca, she treats this development as a mere precursor to the Liberal school rather than as the parallel tradition it is.

Moreover, even if rights theory had developed exclusively under the aegis of Liberal thinking, no mere historical connection proves that those who reject Liberal individualism cannot now deploy the language of rights without thereby importing into their thought features of that philosophy antithetical to the value of community and other important human goods. Historical ties to Liberalism can put one on guard against dimensions of Liberal theory that run contrary to Christian and classical ethics, but they remain at the level of the circumstantial rather than the essential. A person brought up by negligent parents and surrounded by bad friends will likely pick up many of the unsavory qualities of those companions, but such influences do not necessarily corrupt absolutely. Guilt by association, both in criminal law and in philosophy, is never sufficient in and of itself to pronounce a verdict.

Fresh, clear springs can well up from the muddy earth, and sensible ideas can sometimes arise from contaminated philosophies. The task of Christian thinkers—in fact the task of all thinkers—is to ascertain the truth. Most serious thinkers do not reject a priori the concept of human rights simply because it lacks the proper genealogy.[30] Far more important

30. In an earlier essay I made a similar case with regard to the use of the word "values," against the arguments of Allan Bloom who, in his 1987 work, *The Closing of the American Mind*, advocates the banishment of the word "values" from social discourse, because of its unseemly origins in the relativistic philosophy of Friedrich Nietzsche and his followers. "The proposal to jettison 'values' from philosophical and ethical lexicon reflects an erroneous understanding of the nature and role of words. All words run the risk of being manipulated, but they can also be redeemed. In culture wars, as in philosophical debate, words are often like towns along the battle front: they offer a strategic position and must be fought for and defended, and not relinquished as soon as the enemy advances" (Thomas D. Williams, "Values, Virtues, and John Paul II," *First Things* 72 [April 1997]: 30).

than the origins of rights are their intrinsic consistency with the message of the Gospel—and specifically the Christian understanding of the human person and society. The content of a proposition carries much greater weight than its authorship.

The Second Vatican Council speaks of the Church's responsibility to read the signs of the times and interpret them in the light of the Gospel: "In language intelligible to every generation, she should be able to answer the ever recurring questions which men ask about the meaning of this present life and of the life to come, and how one is related to the other."[31] This concern for expressing unchanging truth in "language intelligible to every generation" reflects a spirit of adaptability to semantic evolution rather than a strict adherence to a static canon of terms. As Francis Canavan has written, the

Popes "can also draw, at least indirectly, upon the thought of thinkers outside the Church, but only insofar as they find it capable of being incorporated into the Catholic tradition."[32] The criterion is compatibility, that is, whether a particular idea or affirmation squares with the rest of Catholic teaching, which is always seen as a coordinated whole.

O'Donovan's aversion to the language of rights leads her to make problematic statements. Again, in her debate with Robert George on the right to life of the unborn, she states: "It's correct to say that it is wrong to kill unborn fetuses, that it is unjust to kill unborn fetuses, that Christ commands you not to kill unborn fetuses, and that it's against the law of God to kill unborn fetuses, but not that fetuses have rights."[33]

One must ask exactly what is wrong with such killing. One answer would be that it contravenes the divine law. The two propositions "Christ commands you" not to kill fetuses and "it's against the law of God" to kill fetuses are normative assertions of positive divine law. They are valid in their own right for anyone who accepts Christian revelation. From a natural law perspective, however, these two claims will be dismissed—not as false, but as outside the competence of natural law theory and, coincidentally, of civil discourse bearing on legislation in a pluralist society. O'Donovan's propositions, "it is unjust" to kill fetuses and "fetuses have rights," are the only two that fall within the ambit of natural law,

---

31. *GS*, 4.
32. Canavan, "The Image of Man in Catholic Thought," 15.
33. O'Donovan, "The Concept of Rights in Christian Moral Discourse," 163.

and they are mutually implicational. If it is correct to say "It is unjust to kill a fetus," then it is equally correct to say "The fetus has a right to life," unless one wishes to step outside the concept of justice held by the classical tradition. According to that tradition, justice is the stable disposition to render others their due. If it is naturally knowable that killing an unborn person is unjust, that can only be because respect for his life is *due* to him in justice, or he *deserves* such respect. Deserving something in justice does not differ from having a right to something.

In sum, O'Donovans arguments provide helpful information for understanding the evolution of rights theory in the Liberal tradition but do not succeed in undermining the legitimacy of all uses of rights language. Though she sets out to offer theological grounds for objecting to rights language, O'Donovan never shows any incompatibility between human rights and Christian theology; she only clearly shows that some thinkers who espoused a non-Christian view of the human person also contributed to the development of a certain theory of rights. Here, too, the fundamental concept of human rights remains intact.

6. THE ACCUSATION OF INNOVATION

A THIRD ARGUMENT against rights comes from Ernest L. Fortin (1923– 2002), a Straussian who for years taught Catholic theology and political theory at Boston College, where he also codirected the Institute for the Study of Politics and Religion. As a theologian and political philosopher, Fortin saw "a number of tensions inherent in the Church's current position on social matters," many of which are linked directly with the Church's endorsement of human rights.[1]

As a classicist, Fortin was particularly concerned by the innovation of rights theory vis-à-vis traditional ethical theory. In his many essays on the topic, he argues that the Church's traditional social teaching, which "presented itself as first and foremost a doctrine of duties and hence of virtue or dedication to the common good," has assimilated ideas issuing from the natural rights doctrine developed by Thomas Hobbes and his successors in which rights, rather than duties, are "paramount"—without, however, discarding the language of virtue and duty. As a result of this ethical hodgepodge, Fortin suggests, the Church's social teaching combines traditional Christian ideas with "ideas that were once and may still be fundamentally antithetical to it" and consequently "suffers from a latent bifocalism that puts it at odds with itself and thereby weakens it to a considerable extent."[2]

Though in the end Fortin does not recommend that the bishops completely abandon their defense of rights, especially since "the pseudomorphic collapse of Neo-Thomism in the wake of Vatican II has left them without any alternative on which to fall back," he does contend that the

---

1. Ernest L. Fortin, "The Trouble with Catholic Social Thought," in *Human Rights, Virtue, and the Common Good,* 303.
2. Ibid., 304.

adoption of rights language has given rise to problems without any clear solution. "[T]he Church is having to pay a price for espousing the principles of the Enlightenment along with their hidden premise, the ideology of progress."[3]

Fortin brings into play a number of interconnected critical arguments of greater or lesser importance. I have attempted to select the most relevant among them and have grouped them together loosely under three headings: (1) the substitution of rights for duty and virtue as the axis of moral theory; (2) the self-centered mentality inherent in this substitution; and (3) the prudential argument against the use of rights language.

OBJECTIONS

Rights Have Replaced Duty and Virtue

This first argument comprises two subthemes. In the first place, Fortin asserts, the rise of Liberalism occasioned a shift in the popular understanding of morality. Where morality used to be a question of duty and virtue, under Liberalism it became a question of individual rights. Natural rights likewise replaced natural law. Second, the Liberal theory of natural rights rested on a new understanding of the human person. Rights, which arose as part of a matrix of ideas, embody an atomistic anthropology that is incompatible with the classical "premodern" understanding of man as naturally social and political. After Hobbes and Locke, man is seen as a solitary individual with no clear good to which he tends.

Like O'Donovan, Fortin discerns a major shift in emphasis from the classical understanding of justice to a newer understanding of justice that has its origins in the Enlightenment. Rights—understood as inhering in each human being by reason of the fact that he is a human being—represent an innovation in moral thought. "Nowhere in the older tradition," writes Fortin, "does one run across anything like a theory of natural rights."[4] This is true both of the classical tradition and Christian theology where, until very recently, "rights" were mentioned "only sparingly." Even the Bible, "which shares to some degree the perspective of classical philosophy on this point, does not . . . promulgate a Bill or Rights, of which it

3. Ibid., 311, 308.
4. Ernest L. Fortin, "Human Rights and the Common Good," in *Human Rights, Virtue, and the Common Good,* 20.

knows nothing; instead, it issues a set of commandments."[5] The Enlightenment theory of rights not only brought new elements into the moral equation, therefore; it fundamentally changed the rules by which human actions are to be evaluated.

Moreover, natural rights were not simply integrated into the existing natural law theory, they replaced it. "The passage from natural law to natural rights and later (once 'nature' had fallen into disrepute) to 'human' rights represents a major shift, indeed, *the* paradigm shift in our understanding of justice and moral phenomena generally."[6] For Fortin, natural rights are not an integral part of natural law theory—indeed, they are antagonistic to it. The two cannot coexist. Thus the passage from natural law to natural rights entailed a shift in our understanding of justice and morality.

The same phenomenon has occurred in the case of Catholic theology. "For centuries," Fortin avers, "the cornerstone of Catholic moral theology was not the natural or human *rights* doctrine but something quite different, called the natural *law*." Rights, to the extent that they were mentioned. at least by implication, were peripheral and contingent on the fulfillment of prior duties. "Simply stated," Fortin concludes, "what the church taught and tried to inculcate was an ethic of virtue as distinct from an ethic of rights."[7]

This major change in focus did not occur by chance or through a natural development over time. In speaking of the evolution of natural law theory through the centuries, Fortin turns to "the seventeenth-century founders of modern liberalism, especially Hobbes and Locke, who broke decisively with the previous tradition and sought to establish the whole of political thought on a new and supposedly more solid foundation." This break issued from a change in the understanding of the human person. "Human beings were no longer said to be naturally political and social. They are solitary individuals who once existed in a prepolitical 'state of nature.' . . . Individual rights, conferred by nature, replace duties as the primordial moral phenomenon."[8]

---

5. Fortin, "The Trouble with Catholic Social Thought," 304–5.
6. Fortin, "Human Rights and the Common Good," 20.
7. Fortin, "The Trouble with Catholic Social Thought," 305.
8. Ernest L. Fortin, "Natural Law," in *Human Rights, Virtue, and the Common Good*, 161–62.

According to Fortin, then, the rights-based moral scheme is incompatible with genuine community, because it embodies Liberalism's view of man as essentially independent and individualistic. Unlike the classical theory, which held that human beings are interdependent and find their perfection in society, the modern theory "views them instead as atoms that are complete in themselves and hence not dependent on others for the achievement of their perfection." Fortin expresses his doubts whether this "narcissistic atomization of individuals can coexist with genuine community—whether any society is likely to endure, let alone prosper, without a shared notion of the good life."[9] The true good for which morality aims is no longer the common good but the good of the individual.

But the differences don't end there. The new understanding of the human person as essentially solitary led to a nonteleological understanding of human life that ran counter to Christian moral philosophy. Rights doctrine

emerged by way of a reaction against premodern thought and signals a radical departure from it. Its underlying premise is that, contrary to what had been previously assumed, human beings are not intrinsically ordered to a natural end, in the attainment of which they find their happiness or perfection. In Hobbes's own words, "there is no *finis ultimus,* utmost aim, nor *summum bonum,* greatest good, as is spoken of in the books of the old moral philosophers."[10]

Fortin acknowledges that contemporary ethicists, as well as the pastors of the Catholic Church, have not simply accepted Hobbes's theory wholesale. Rather, "they are vastly more influenced by Kant and his latter-day disciples, who managed to give the original rights theory a more exalted status by grounding it, not in a selfish passion, but in practical reason or the dignity of the individual person as an autonomous moral agent." Yet even this more noble grounding does not save rights from their dubious philosophical baggage because, in the final analysis, "Kant's theory is still only a modification of the Hobbesian theory, whose nonteleological orientation it preserves and with which it has more in common than it does with classical moral philosophy."[11]

---

9. Fortin, "Human Rights and the Common Good," 23.
10. Fortin, "The Trouble with Catholic Social Thought," 305, citing Thomas Hobbes, *Leviathan,* ch. ii, init.
11. Ibid.

The Exaltation of Selfishness

The substitution of rights for duties meant that people began thinking about what they *deserved* rather than what they *owed* to others, and the focus on the individual meant a decline in interest for the common good. Fortin writes: "What once presented itself as first and foremost a doctrine of duties and hence of virtue or dedication to the common good of one's society now takes its bearings, not from what human beings owe to their fellow human beings, but from what they can claim for themselves."[12] This was not an unintended side effect but part of the Liberal project to create a new type of man. Under the new vision of man and society, the exaltation of selfishness was seen as a means to achieve the common good. Rights were developed to encourage this selfishness, replacing virtue, which demanded self-sacrifice for the common good.

The question arises as to whether the "substitution" of rights for duties and virtue is really as radical as Fortin suggests. Fortin acknowledges that many do not view rights as inconsistent with natural law, duties, or virtue. "At first glance," he writes, "the difference between the two views might be looked upon as one of approach rather than of genuine substance." He cites the case of Christianity's adoption first of Plato, and later of Aristotle, for expounding Christian philosophy, noting that no one would "describe the two groups as being at loggerheads with each other."[13]

Such is not always the case, however. In the Liberal project, it wasn't long before the new focus on the individual good over and above the common good grew into the focus on *my* good rather than that of *others*. Fortin sees human rights doctrine as a natural extension of the Lockean Liberalism, which thought to secure public benefit by encouraging selfishness, a political theory that finds its economic counterpart in Adam Smith's theory of capitalism. Encouraging people to think about individual rights dovetailed perfectly with the quest for a self-centered populace.

Thus Fortin notes an important difference in the case of the concept of human rights that distinguishes it from the Christian assimilation of other theoretical systems such as Platonism or Aristotelianism. "If one's method of procedure has been deliberately chosen with a view to a differ-

12. Ibid., 304.
13. Ibid.

ent end, rather than as a different means to the same end, its employment is bound to have an impact on what is accomplished."[14] In other words, the difference between a rights-based morality and a duty-based morality is substantial, not merely circumstantial, because rights doctrine was formulated not as a means to achieve a virtuous populace but as a means to create a selfish populace motivated by self-interest.

Fortin states that the easiest way to understand Locke's political philosophy is to contrast it with that of his predecessors. For the bulk of the classical tradition, "there is no preestablished harmony between the individual and the civil society to which he belongs or between self-interest and the common good." The premodern theory held that self-interest had to be overcome for the sake of the common good. It was necessary to forge moral virtue, which requires a "painful conversion" from the concern with worldly goods to a concern with the good of the soul. Only through such a conversion does the individual come to look upon the good of society as his own good. All that changed, however, with the modern theory. "Locke for his part," Fortin suggests, "claims to have found a safer way to achieve a similar result. The trick consists in using private vice or selfishness to procure public benefits."[15] Thus though its engineers were motivated by "the laudable desire to put an end to the evils that had always plagued society and that had become particularly acute in the wake of the wars of religion that were then ravaging Europe," this shift in moral framework rested on the abandonment of virtue and the untrammeled pursuit of private material well-being. "Pursuing one's selfish interest, it was decided, was the best way to serve others."[16] Rights, then, are wrapped up in a complex political philosophy whereby the selfishness of the individual works to bring about benefit to all. Encouraging people to think about their own subjective rights would facilitate this selfishness and the public good that attends it.

According to Fortin, even in contemporary thought, the underlying political philosophy of rights places more importance on good social and juridical structures than on individual virtue which, "although desirable, is not essential to the scheme, and one need not acquire it in order to

---

14. Ibid.
15. Ernest L. Fortin, "Thoughts on Modernity," in *Human Rights, Virtue, and the Common Good,* 149.
16. Fortin, "Human Rights and the Common Good," 23.

reap its benefits." Rather, according to current rights theories, heavily influenced by Kant, the key to the proper functioning of the just society "is not genuine moral virtue, on which one can rarely depend, but enlightened self-interest."[17]

Fortin acknowledges that many consider rights and duties to be two correlative, rather than antagonistic, principles. He summarizes this viewpoint: "As correlatives, rights and duties imply each other. If I have the duty to do something, I must have the right to do it."[18] Fortin recognizes a prima facie plausibility to this argument but asserts that it merely scratches the surface of the problem. "At first hearing," he notes, "the objection sounds unimpeachable, but it does not get to the heart of the matter inasmuch as it fails to address the question of the priority of duties over rights or vice versa. . . . All indications point to the fact that in the premodern view the duty came first."[19]

Not so in modern moral theory, says Fortin, even as espoused by the Catholic Church. In speaking of the U.S. bishops' pastoral letter on the economy, Fortin asserts that though the text begins with a discussion of duties, it is clear that "these duties are rooted in pre-existing rights which everyone is obliged in conscience to honor and which must, therefore, be regarded as the primary moral phenomenon."[20] As Fortin sees it, either rights must proceed from duties or duties must proceed from rights, and the difference is not immaterial.

To illustrate the primacy of duties over rights as ethical principles, Fortin asks: "Did Socrates have the right to defend himself or was it his duty to do so? Which of the two is the primary moral counter and takes precedence over the other in the event of a conflict between them?"[21] The implication is that a truly virtuous citizenry can come only from a society that encourages duty rather than rights.

If, however, we look not to *our* rights but to the rights of *others,* we still misdirect our attention, says Fortin. Morality is chiefly a question of the goodness or evil of free acts, and these acts affect the character of the moral agent much more than the receiver of the action. "In the final

17. Fortin, "The Trouble with Catholic Social Thought," 306.
18. Fortin, "Human Rights and the Common Good," 21. See also Fortin, "The Trouble with Catholic Social Thought," 304.
19. Fortin, "Human Rights and the Common Good," 21.
20. Fortin, "The Trouble with Catholic Social Thought," 304.
21. Fortin, "Human Rights and the Common Good," 21.

analysis," he affirms, "we are confronted with two vastly different conceptions of morality, one that looks at it from the point of view of what a given action does to the person who performs it, and the other from the point of view of what it does to the recipient."[22] Rights will always be the rights of the recipient of human actions rather than the agent. Duty, on the other hand, correctly places emphasis on the center of morality: the moral agent. Fortin illustrates this principle by citing the English mystery writer Agatha Christie:

The problem has not escaped the great Hercule Poirot, who, when asked one day by that impossible woman, Mrs. Ariadne Oliver, whether he did not think that some people "ought" to be murdered, had the good sense to reply: "Quite possibly, madam, but you do not comprehend. It is not the victim who concerns me so much; it is the effect on the character of the slayer." This is not to say that what happens to the victim is unimportant, but only that it is not the primary consideration and the one through which the nature of the moral act reveals itself most profoundly.[23]

We find an example of this shift in focus from the acting person to the person acted upon in the case of abortion, where the rights of the unborn are often invoked as the basis for outlawing the practice. "Earlier theologians," Fortin affirms, "would have begun by asking, not what abortion does to the foetus, but what it does to the person who performs it or undergoes it. Duties took precedence over rights and determined the conduct that was appropriate in a given set of circumstances."[24]

The Prudential Question

Besides theoretical arguments that advise against rights, Fortin also brings into play practical or prudential arguments that would lead to the same conclusion. Actually, all or nearly all of his arguments contain a prudential edge; that is, they question the suitability of rights language as a vehicle of ethical discourse, independent of theoretical considerations.

As a specific example of the inopportuneness of rights, Fortin cites the difficulty of adjudicating between rival rights claims, a problem he argues existed only in a much mitigated form in the older tradition of moral reasoning. He offers two concrete examples. The first is again that of abor-

---

22. Ibid., 22.
23. Ibid.
24. Fortin, "The Trouble with Catholic Social Thought," 307.

tion. Earlier theologians, Fortin tells us, had an easier time judging such cases since virtue-based morality allowed for greater leeway in the exercise of prudence. "The more complex the case, the more it called for deliberation in the light of certain general principles which remain the same at all times but whose degree of applicability varies greatly from one instance to another." This left considerable room for the exercise of prudence, through which one could hope to arrive at a sensible decision. The same cannot always be said of the argument from rights, says Fortin, "which deprives us of the ability to determine in a principled way which of the two supposedly unconditional rights, that of the mother or that of the unborn child, has the green light when they come into conflict with each other."[25] The difference, as Fortin sees it, is that previously moral theologians relied on immutable general principles whose varying application allowed for a broad exercise of the virtue of prudence, whereas nowadays conflicting claims of unconditional rights allow for no such moral maneuvering to come to a suitable conclusion.

A second example of such conflict is the Church's efforts to deal with theologians who dissent from its official teaching. Since the Church insists on human rights and the dignity of conscience, how can it rebuke theologians with heterodox opinions who invoke the same principle? "Having endorsed the principle of freedom of conscience and freedom of expression," Fortin writes, "the bishops have been hard pressed to defend the sanctions imposed by Rome on some of the dissenters. One cannot publicly proclaim the rights of the individual conscience and then take action against the person who exercises them and thus appears to have justice on his side."[26] Here, as in the case of abortion, Fortin believes that moral reasoning based on human rights leads to gridlock, as neither absolute claim will bend before the other.

RESPONSE

Rights Have Replaced Duty and Virtue

One hastens to recognize the immense amount of truth in Fortin's arguments on this issue. Today there is undoubtedly much more stress laid on rights than on duties and responsibilities, and a more atomistic, non-

---

25. Ibid.
26. Ibid., 308.

teleological view of man has become the reigning model in much of the Western world.

As in the case of Joan Lockwood O'Donovan, much of Fortin's argument rests on historical association, and there is no need to repeat here the last chapter's rebuttal of the insufficiency of these circumstantial arguments. It is important to note, however, that myriad other social factors have contributed to the changes Fortin mentions, and thus even historically his arguments are debatable. It would seem, for instance, that abandonment of talk of duty and responsibility in favor of rights reached its peak not in the period of the Enlightenment but in the last fifty years, beginning in the postwar period of unprecedented material prosperity and facilitated by the sexual revolution. Talk of duty and responsibility abounded in the 1940s and early 1950s, despite the fact that the Enlightenment had come and gone nearly two centuries earlier. Similarly, it could be argued that developments in the social sciences with roots in the philosophies of Auguste Comte and Friedrich Nietzsche, especially psychological schools originating in the second half of the nineteenth century and the first three-quarters of the twentieth, have contributed immensely to the contemporary understanding of man as atomistic and nonteleological.[27] These brief examples are adduced simply to show that historical phenomena, especially of the sweeping nature of those proposed by Fortin, almost always involve the interplay of numerous factors and can rarely be attributed to a single cause.

From certain expressions employed by Fortin, one also senses that his understanding of human rights is limited to the rationale offered by Liberalism. True to his mentor, Leo Strauss, he often seems to be taking issue more with Liberalism than with the idea of human rights per se, at least as these are understood by the Catholic Church. For example, one wonders how else Fortin's description of the Christian God as one who "did not command hatred between nations and make it a duty to detest foreigners but taught that all human beings were entitled to the same gentle and benevolent treatment" can be squared with his denouncement of hu-

---

27. For helpful critiques of the role of psychology in promoting this individualistic view of man with its attendant focus on the self, see Philip Rieff, *The Triumph of the Therapeutic* (New York: Harper & Row, 1966); Christopher Lasch, *The Culture of Narcissism: American Life in an Age of Diminishing Expectations* (New York: Norton, 1978); D. G. Meyers, *The Inflated Self* (New York: Seabury, 1981); Paul C. Vitz, *Psychology as Religion: The Cult of Self-Worship*, 2nd ed. (Grand Rapids, Mich.: William B. Eerdmans, 1994).

man rights.[28] What is the core of human rights in the Christian tradition if not that "all human beings were entitled to the same gentle and benevolent treatment"? Down to the keyword "entitled," Fortin (unwittingly) encapsulates human rights theory as understood by Catholic social teaching in describing the novelty of Christianity as compared to all religions that came before it.

This fundamental misunderstanding of the nature of rights may also account for Fortin's pitting natural rights against natural law. Fortin sees the two concepts as essentially antagonistic, whereby the passage from natural law to natural rights represents *the* paradigm shift in our understanding of justice. In the Catholic tradition, however, natural law refers to man's ability to discern moral truth by the light of human reason. Natural law does not preclude natural rights, it embraces them. As Pope John Paul has written, "the natural law expresses the dignity of the human person and lays down the foundation for his fundamental rights and duties."[29]

Fortin likewise asserts that the focal shift from duties to rights represents a fundamental sea change in moral theory. Whereas previously rights were seen as deriving from duties, now duties are seen as springing from rights. Where does the truth lie? It is no doubt correct, as Fortin puts it, that if I have the duty to perform a certain action, then I also have a fortiori the right to do so.[30] In the case of religious freedom, for instance, the Second Vatican Council affirmed: "Everybody has the duty and *consequently* the right to seek the truth in religious matters."[31] In this sense, at least, rights can be said to truly proceed from duties.

In another sense as well it is true to say that rights depend on duties, insofar as all people have the duty to pursue their integral good and hence the right to those things that are essential to this pursuit. Pope Paul VI went so far as to assert that man "is responsible for his fulfillment as he is for his salvation."[32] The preservation of life, the development of

---

28. Ernest L. Fortin, "The Regime of Separatism: Theoretical Considerations on the Separation of Church and State," in *Human Rights, Virtue, and the Common Good*, 3.

29. *VS*, 51.

30. See also George Weigel's assertion that "rights exist so that we can fulfill our obligations" (*Soul of the World: Notes on the Future of Public Catholicism* [Grand Rapids, Mich.: Ethics and Public Policy Center/William B. Eerdmans, 1996], 132).

31. *DH*, 3; emphasis added.

32. Paul VI, *Populorum Progressio*, 15. In the following number the Pope states: "Just as the

one's talents and qualities, and the search for truth are not morally indifferent but truly binding. The Belgian philosopher Joseph de Finance summarizes this thought as follows:

> [T]here is an obligation on the human person to respect the movement towards a continued and ever deepening existence which is essential to his nature: the conservation of his life, of his physical integrity, of his liberty insofar as it is the condition for genuinely human activity, the effort to attain a certain level of cultured development and, in general, the conditions of life in default of which human existence degenerates—all these will constitute inevitable and universal obligations, even though on certain points, such as the last-mentioned obligation, the manner in which they are applicable can vary considerably.
>
> In brief, there is a certain obligation to strive after the values which we have called infra-moral, insofar as these values correspond to certain human tendencies; and the more human these tendencies are, the greater will be the obligation.[33]

Yet an understanding of rights as deriving from duties poses certain problems. In the first place, while rights are at times a subset of duties, this model does not exhaust all possibilities. It is true that if something is *commanded,* then it is also necessarily *permitted.* But are there not many things that are permitted that are not commanded? People surely have rights to things that they are under no strict moral obligation to pursue. To take a simple example, the right to migration does not proceed from a duty to move about. Man has natural rights to a range of activities that help to realize him as a human person, but in many cases there is no strict obligation to pursue any one of these activities, only his integral fulfillment as a whole. A one-to-one correlation of rights to duties at this level cannot therefore be said to exist. At best, we could say that man's general obligation to pursue his integral human fulfillment corresponds to a span of rights to activities that make such fulfillment possible.

Second, we have the case of human persons who have no moral duties,

---

whole of creation is ordained to its Creator, so spiritual beings should of their own accord orientate their lives to God, the first truth and the supreme good. *Thus it is that human fulfillment constitutes, as it were, a summary of our duties.* But there is much more: this harmonious enrichment of nature by personal and responsible effort is ordered to a future perfection. By reason of his union with Christ, the source of life, man attains to new fulfillment of himself, to a transcendent humanism which gives him his greatest possible perfection: this is the highest goal of personal development" (emphasis added).

33. de Finance, *An Ethical Inquiry,* § 185, p. 320.

strictly speaking, since they are unable to exercise their freedom. Such would be the case of the unborn, infants prior to the age of reason, and severely mentally handicapped persons. As human persons, do not these individuals possess human rights such as the right to life despite the absence of moral obligation? We could speak of a latent obligation to self-fulfillment even in such cases as these, but to do so seems to stretch the idea of moral obligation to the breaking point. There must be another, deeper foundation to rights than duty.

Returning to Fortin's argument, a further problem lies with his predicating rights and duties only of the selfsame moral agent. Justice is an interrelational cardinal virtue, involving at least two moral subjects. Correlating one's rights to others' duties and one's duties to others' rights makes more sense than trying to construct a causal relation between the rights and duties of the same human subject. In an interpersonal relationship of justice, a true one-to-one correspondence between rights and duties exists that is absent when correlating one's rights to one's own duties.

The Exaltation of Selfishness

The question of whose rights and whose duties are being considered ties directly into Fortin's argument that rights encourage a self-centered morality. Fortin claims that rights were concocted according to the political theory that enlightened self-interest was the best possible means of bringing about the greatest good for the greatest number. Whereas according to premodern moral thought, the individual was called upon to subject private interest to the common good—an operation that required virtue and self-sacrifice—the new school endeavored to achieve the same effect by encouraging selfishness. Enlightened self-interest held the key to securing the public weal. Therefore, the shift from duty to rights naturally entailed a shift in emphasis from what I *owe* others to what I can *claim* from them.

Rights language is indeed a two-edged sword. The same principle can be used in radically different ways. It is clear that it can and often is used to justify selfishness, but can it not also be used to promote greater justice? Can focusing on what others deserve of us serve to create a greater awareness of the requirements of justice? By insisting on rights, the Catholic Church clearly does not intend to issue an invitation to egotism or to the exclusive consideration of what one is owed by others; the

Church intends to foster true justice and charity, inviting the faithful to look to the good of neighbor, to recognize his rights, and to work to satisfy them.

Fortin claims that the shift from law to rights signaled a de-emphasis of the common good in favor of personal, private good. Certainly the Church's engagement with the human rights movement in the twentieth century did come about, at least in part, as a reaction to a distorted understanding of the common good (seen as the good of the abstract collectivity) into which individual human persons were subsumed as expendable component parts. Where injustices occurred under the rationale of the individual's subordination to the collectivity, the Church was swift to reaffirm the inviolable dignity of the individual person. According to the Catholic conception of the common good, however, the particular good of individuals and the common good of the community are not in opposition—they complement each other.

The concept of rights is not intrinsically selfish any more than the concept of justice is intrinsically selfish. The language of justice and duty, like that of rights, can be employed in selfish ways. One can plead for justice or proclaim others' duties to oneself as easily as one proclaims one's own rights. On the other hand, by focusing on the *content* of justice (what is, in fact *due*), the language of rights helps in the analysis of what is just and unjust in the various realms of human affairs.

There is undoubtedly a danger in framing the moral question only in terms of "my rights" or "my duties." The question is not exhausted by these two possibilities. They cover only half the field. Along with "my rights" are "others' rights," and along with "my duties" are "others' duties." When a person insists on his own rights he is simultaneously insisting on others' duties to himself, and when he emphasizes his duties to others, he also has in mind—at least implicitly—the rights of others. The basic question is not whether we frame our morality in terms of rights or duties but rather whether we frame our morality in terms of ourselves or others.[34]

---

34. Servais Pinckaers attributes this shift in emphasis to the influence of fourteenth-century nominalism. "The modern era is characterized by its subjective conception of rights as formulated by fourteenth-century nominalism. From that time on rights refer not to what I owe others, but to what others, and society, owe me. Rights have changed hands: I think now in terms of my own rights, not those of others" (*The Sources of Christian Ethics*, 38).

Yet even if we look not to our rights but to the rights of others, we still misdirect our attention, insists Fortin. The moral question always deals with the goodness or evil of the moral agent, which proceeds from his free choices, and the language of duty and responsibility correctly places emphasis on the moral agent. Rights language, on the contrary, mistakenly places the attention on the recipient of the action. This is a valid point. A moral evaluation is made not of the net material good or evil done but of the disposition of the will of the moral agent and the conformity or unconformity to the moral law of his deliberate choices. It is true that in analyzing a moral action *post factum* we are aware above all of the effects it has on the moral state of the one performing it rather than on the one suffering it. The victim has lost only his life, the criminal may lose his soul. The moral evil of the agent can be far more serious than the physical evil resulting from his act.

Nevertheless, three distinct dimensions of the moral act are in play here. First, Fortin rightly underscores the consequences of the action on the moral agent. He fears that undue attention on the rights of others will draw attention away from the real matter at hand: the effects of deliberate choices on the character and moral status of the agent.

Second, however, one notes that the primary source of the goodness or badness of the action in itself stems from its conformity with right reason or the moral law. This is commonly referred to as the *object* of the moral act, i.e., *what* is being chosen by the moral agent.[35] One can ascertain the effects of an action on the moral agent only by considering *what* he is freely choosing to do. In the abortion example, the effects of an abortion on the person who performs it depend on what an abortion does to the foetus and who the foetus is. If a human foetus were not the sort of being that deserves respect, its elimination would do nothing to the moral state of the person performing the elimination.

Third, the goodness of the action also depends on the intention and motivation of the moral agent. Moral people don't act only for the personal benefit of becoming good but for the sake of the other. Here it is essential to bear in mind that what is most important as an *effect* (i.e., consequences on the moral character of the agent) is not necessarily what should be at the forefront of the *intention* of the acting person. In living out the supreme commandment of love, for instance, what should be

---

35. See, inter alia, *VS,* 78; *S. Th.* I-II, 18, 6; *CCC,* 1751.

first and foremost in one's intention: one's own moral perfection or the good of the recipient of our actions? Moral motivations can be framed with the emphasis on the first person: *I* have to love my neighbor and in so doing *I* will become a just and righteous person, or in the second person: *You* deserve my love. True moral goodness comes as a side effect when the moral agent seeks not his own moral good in the first place but the other's good.

An example may help. If I see a boy who has fallen through the frozen surface of a pond screaming for help, my first consideration should be the good of that fellow human being in need, not how helping him will affect my moral character. What is directly *intended* in my choice is the good of the other, not my own moral good. Thus it would seem that when the moral agent is deciding how to conduct himself, his primary concern and motivation ought not be how his action will affect his own moral status but rather how it affects the person he is acting upon. By genuinely seeking the good of the other, his own moral stature increases as a corollary, because the value of our actions grows with the disinterestedness of our motivation. If the moral agent's primary concern is with his own righteousness, he has knocked his morality down a peg and ends up *using* the other person for his own benefit, albeit his moral benefit. The more he acts purely for the good of the other and for love of God, the more meritorious and less mercenary his action, and, paradoxically, the better he becomes.

The Prudential Question

Fortin's third objection deals with the suitability of rights language for moral discourse. This immensely important question deals not with the truth or interior logic of human rights language but its advisability on the practical level. The prudential question of whether it is better—in the sense of yielding more favorable consequences—to formulate ethical theory and propositions in terms of human rights or to avoid rights language occupies the attention of numerous moral theologians, philosophers, lawyers, and social commentators. Despite its practical nature, this concern also serves as the impetus behind much theoretical opposition to rights discourse. Though the intention of this study is to engage the question of the foundation of rights on the theoretical plane, it is impossible to keep the two spheres—the theoretical and the prudential—completely separated. Several tangentially practical questions have already presented themselves along the way. Furthermore, because of the importance of the prudential question and its influence even on theoretical considerations, it cannot be passed over altogether. Therefore, this final section will address these concerns sufficiently to adumbrate the main arguments in favor of the use of rights language without seeking to offer a comprehensive reply.

Although rights cannot be roundly discarded in principle, the question remains whether rights language is a helpful vehicle in moral discourse. Regardless of whether the concept of rights is intrinsically linked to Liberalism, wouldn't the frequent misuse of the term counsel against its employment? In other words, even if rights can be defended in *theory*, should they be defended in *practice*? Shouldn't more conventional ethical language be adopted?

Rights language is clearly dispensable. After all, humanity got along reasonably well without it for centuries. This fact alone proves that the use of rights talk cannot be a logical necessity of moral theory, unless those centuries of rights-free moral discourse are to be dismissed as fatally inadequate.

On the other hand, though the language of human rights is relatively new, the phenomenon of rights as principles of justice is not. The evolution of language toward greater precision and flexibility should not be summarily rejected unless strong arguments make such a course of action necessary. Fortin thinks he has such an argument: the difficulty in adjudicating between the claims of rival rights.

Unlike traditional moral theory whose principles permitted the exercise of the virtue of prudence to resolve dilemmas, argues Fortin, a rights-based ethics results in a moral impasse.

As Fortin rightly points out, evaluating complex moral situations often requires the ability to juggle several principles at once and to determine for each case which principle (or principles) is to be applied and how. Nonetheless, he falsely attributes to human rights an unconditional nature that necessarily results in moral logjams. No serious moral philosopher or theologian attributes to every right an absolute character any more than they would attribute an absolute character to every general moral precept. Very few human rights bear the quality of inviolability, just as few moral injunctions deserve this title. Catholic moral theology starts from a simple principle: the truth is one. Therefore, while different goods and principles may come into play in a given moral problem, there is always a moral solution (i.e., a solution according to right reason, that pleases God, and does not involve sin). One must distinguish, as the Church does, between absolute rights and relative rights and up to what point they are applicable. Very few rights indeed are absolute rights, and these imply a corresponding absolute moral obligation.

To respond to the first of Fortin's two examples, abortion, in reality, from the perspective of Catholic moral theology, the case of abortion generally poses no moral dilemma either to those who reason from rights or to those who reason from duties. It is unclear what problem Fortin sees with abortion, other than that it supposedly pits the right of the mother against the rights of the child. The right to life of both is absolute, and that is why voluntary abortion (the direct, intentional killing of the child) is systematically excluded as a moral possibility, just as the direct, intentional killing of the mother to save the child's life is also ruled out. Even in the case where the mother's life is at stake, the Church has consistently taught that direct abortion is not a moral option.

Concerning Fortin's example of theological dissent, the right to freedom of conscience is not an open-ended right to teach private opinion in the name of the Church. The inviolability of conscience cannot be cavalierly stretched to include teaching in the name of the Church but in a way contrary to Church doctrine.[36] In both cases a good dose of pru-

---

36. According to the Congregation for the Doctrine of the Faith, discussing the case of the theologian who might have serious difficulties in accepting a nonirreformable magisterial teaching: "Such a disagreement could not be justified if it were based solely upon the fact that the validity of the given teaching is not evident or upon the opinion that the opposite position would be the more probable. Nor, furthermore, would the judgment of the subjective conscience of the theologian justify it because conscience does not constitute an autonomous and exclusive authority for deciding the truth of a doctrine" (*Instruction on the Ecclesial Vocation of the Theologian,* May 24, 1990, § 28). "Finally, argumentation appealing to the obligation to follow one's own conscience cannot legitimate dissent. This is true, first of all, because conscience illumines the practical judgment about a decision to make, while here we are concerned with the truth of a doctrinal pronouncement. This is furthermore the case because while the theologian, like every believer, must follow his conscience, he is also obliged to form it. Conscience is not an independent and infallible faculty. It is an act of moral judgment regarding a responsible choice. A right conscience is one duly illumined by faith and by the objective moral law and it presupposes, as well, the uprightness of the will in the pursuit of the true good. The right conscience of the Catholic theologian presumes not only faith in the Word of God whose riches he must explore, but also love for the Church from whom he receives his mission, and

dence is necessary to correctly apply rights to situations, a practice whose feasibility Fortin seems unwilling to accept. Yet it is no more difficult to adjudicate among rival rights claims than it is to adjudicate among apparently conflicting duties or among apparently contradictory ethical principles, all of which can be appealed to. There is no simple, all-embracing rule that will clear up every case by its mere application. Prudence must be used both in reasoning from rights and in reasoning from moral obligations or precepts.

Finally, it should be noted that Fortin creates an artificial opposition between rights and duties. Moral theologians need not opt *for* rights and *against* duties or vice versa. A good moral evaluation of a case usually involves the application of several principles together. Rights and duties support and complement each other; they can be and are easily employed together.

Further Thoughts on the Prudential Question

The fact that rights language is not inherently more problematic than the language of duties for resolving moral dilemmas does not in and of itself provide sufficient cause to employ such language, given the many real problems occasioned by rights talk. What are, then, the reasons that offer positive support for the adoption of rights language?

In his work *Natural Law and Natural Rights*, John Finnis sketches a summary of three advantages of rights talk:

> [I]f its logic and its place in practical reasonableness about human flourishing are kept in mind, the modern usage of claims of right as the principal counter in political discourse should be recognized (despite its dubious seventeenth-century origins and its abuse by fanatics, adventurers, and self-interested persons from the eighteenth century until today) as a valuable addition to the received vocabulary of practical reasonableness (i.e. to the tradition of "natural law doctrine"). For first, the modern usage of rights-talk rightly emphasizes equality, the truth that every human being is a locus of human flourishing which is to be considered with favour in him as much as in anybody else. In other words, rights-talk keeps justice in the foreground of our considerations. Secondly, it tends to un-

---

respect for her divinely assisted Magisterium. Setting up a supreme magisterium of conscience in opposition to the magisterium of the Church means adopting a principle of free examination incompatible with the economy of Revelation and its transmission in the Church and thus also with a correct understanding of theology and the role of the theologian" (ibid., § 38).

dercut the attractions of the "calculations" of the consequentialists.... Thirdly, since rights must be and are referred to by name, modern rights-talk amplifies the undifferentiated reference to "the common good" by providing a usefully detailed listing of the various aspects of human flourishing and fundamental components of the way of life in community that tends to favour such flourishing in all.[37]

In the first place Finnis observes that rights language emphasizes equality, the understanding that all persons are essentially equal and valuable, and therefore equally merit a certain sort of treatment. No distinction between persons can be made, as if some were inherently inferior, less deserving, or at the disposition of others. Such an emphasis on equality, it can be argued, is especially necessary today when a utilitarian mentality threatens to evaluate persons according to their productivity rather than their essential worth. Despite its abundant abuses, the language of rights underscores the primacy of the person, forcing us to look hard at the good of the individual person, which is untransferable and universal, down to the "least" of our brethren.

Second, Finnis notes that rights talk tends to undercut the "calculations" of the consequentialists. Especially in the case of certain inviolable or inalienable rights, determined actions can *never* morally be undertaken with regard to persons, even when the overall calculus of results would seem to yield a net positive.[38] In other words, inviolable rights make possible exceptionless moral norms, since the person by nature is inviolable. The good of an individual person can never be sacrificed as a mere means so that others, even many others, may benefit.[39] The very fact that the revival of the human rights movement in this century took its impetus

---

37. Finnis, *Natural Law and Natural Rights*, 221.

38. Spaemann observes that "it is possible to establish a bottom-line. There are some actions which always harm human dignity and which always violate the person as an end-in-himself. These actions cannot be justified by appeal to any so-called higher or more comprehensive duties.... It follows quite obviously from this that the direct and intentional killing of another human being, torture, rape or the exploitation of sexuality as a means to certain ends is always bad. Also it is not possible to justify lying to a person who has placed his full trust in us" (*Basic Moral Concepts*, 75).

39. Finnis writes elsewhere: "The precepts protecting fundamental aspects of human personal good are guides to human choice; they guide by excluding options inconsistent with love of the very person whom the logic of our choosing makes our nearest neighbor" (*Moral Absolutes: Tradition, Revision, and Truth* [Washington, D.C.: Catholic University of America Press, 1991], 11).

from the abuses of totalitarian states against individual persons shows how one of the primary social consequences of rights language is the defense of the individual against tyranny.[40]

In the third place, Finnis asserts that the denomination of specific rights contributes to an understanding of the common good by providing a detailed listing of the various aspects of human flourishing. The common good is not an abstract concept but the good of real, concrete persons. Rights, by pointing to specific goods of the human person, point the way to a just ordering of society. When the state and individuals order their existence in such a way that the rights of all are respected and promoted, the common good is advanced.

Indicating the various elements of human flourishing in turn helps to shift emphasis in the moral life from legal prohibitions to the goods pursued when one acts in accord with right reason. Many hold that moral theology before the Second Vatican Council placed an excessive emphasis on obligation while neglecting the corresponding natural and supernatural goods that form its foundation.[41] In response to the Council Fathers' call for a renewal of moral theology, especially as regards its scriptural grounding and focus on man's vocation to holiness,[42] numerous writers have elaborated new treatises in this vein. Pope John Paul II himself has given a decisive push to this trend.[43] Rights talk throws light on the posi-

---

40. "The eighteenth-century 'rights of man,' like modern 'human rights,' all mark a stand against the abuse and arbitrary exercise of power. They are landmarks in the recognition of the dignity of the individual human person and of our potential to be free and self-determining" (Glendon, *Rights Talk*, 11).

41. This is one of the central theses of Servais Pinckaers, who links the exaggerated stress on obligation to the influence of medieval nominalism, especially William of Ockham. "Ockham," Pinckaers writes, "established the idea of obligation at the center of his moral theory so definitively that even charity was subsidiary to it. Love of God no longer had a directly and essentially moral value for him" (*The Sources of Christian Ethics*, 248). Pinckaers asserts that a new morality of obligation supplanted the Christian and classical ethical structure, which gave pride of place not to obligation but to happiness or beatitude (see ibid., especially 18–22, 262, 267–68).

42. The conciliar document *Optatam Totius*, for example, states in a well-known passage: "Special care must be given to the perfecting of moral theology. Its scientific exposition, nourished more on the teaching of the Bible, should shed light on the loftiness of the calling of the faithful in Christ and the obligation that is theirs of bearing fruit in charity for the life of the world" (16).

43. As George Sim Johnston notes, "John Paul's way of presenting unchanging truth is light years ahead of the alienating legalism that handicapped Catholic teaching a generation ago. And he starts with a simple proposition: behind every 'No' in the moral commandments there

tive side of negatively formulated injunctions like the Ten Commandments and reminds Christians that the Church, like her Founder, is essentially affirmative, all refusal being nothing more than the other side of a positive affirmation.

Furthermore, as seen earlier in this chapter, from the point of view of ethics or moral theology, a change in focus from personal righteousness to the good of the other can contribute to an increase in true morality, especially from the perspective of the commandment to love, which Christ describes as the summary of the Law and the prophets. When one seeks the other's good in the first place, rather than one's own moral good, one grows as a moral subject.

Matthew Berke, in considering Pope John Paul's assertion of the rights of children to live in a united family and in a healthy moral environment, suggests that "in the boldness of its formulation and in its emphasis on the needs of children over those of adults, it presents us with a wholesome way to rethink some of our social problems."[44] In what way could this new way of formulating social problems be "wholesome"? What does it contribute to social and ethical discourse? Mary Ann Glendon notes: "Legally enforceable rights can assist citizens in a large, heterogeneous country to live together in a reasonable peaceful way. They have given minorities a way to articulate claims that majorities often respect, and have assisted the weakest members of society in making their voice heard."[45] And while "legally enforceable rights" clearly produce empirical results in society, it is to be reasonably hoped that the insistent proclamation of *moral* rights likewise produces a change, especially as regards the reigning ethical mentality.[46] Learning to see all other persons as deserving of basic human goods and ourselves as somehow responsible for assuring

---

is an even greater 'Yes'" ("JPII's Personalism Speaks to a Post-Christian World," *National Catholic Register* 73/40 [October 5–11, 1997], 7).

44. John Paul made this assertion in *CA*, 47. Berke, "A Jewish Appreciation of Catholic Social Teaching," 247.

45. Glendon, *Rights Talk*, 15.

46. While acknowledging the vital importance of legal protection for rights, we must recognize that in practice, a change in the reigning ethic is often of equal or even greater importance than juridical structures concerning rights. A case in point is the ex–Soviet Union, whose written constitution was a model in human rights rhetoric both in the civil-political and economic-social arenas but whose practice was notoriously defective. "In the last analysis a nation's deepest convictions as to human worth will be far more important than its particular constitutional mechanisms" (Montgomery, *Human Rights and Human Dignity*, 53–54).

that they have access to them pushes society in the direction of creating a civilization of justice and love.

Back in 1966 Joel Feinberg went further still in his assertions regarding the appropriateness of rights language, maintaining that "human rights are indispensably valuable possessions. A world without [them], no matter how full of devotion to benevolence and duty, would suffer an immense moral impoverishment." Feinberg's arguments are intriguing and compelling. The absence of rights would make purely civil behavior and basic decency toward others an act of gratuitous charity, and the poor and needy would find themselves in the humiliating situation of begging for favors they in no way deserve. "Persons would no longer hope for decent treatment from others on the ground of desert or rightful claim," Feinberg writes. "Indeed, they would come to think of themselves as having no special claim to kindness or consideration from others, so that whenever even minimally decent treatment is forthcoming they would think themselves lucky rather than inherently deserving, and their benefactors extraordinarily virtuous and worthy of great gratitude." In fact, Feinberg concludes, a world with rights claims "is one in which all persons, as actual or potential claimants, are dignified objects of respect, both in their own eyes and in the view of others. No amount of love and compassion, or obedience to higher authority, or *noblesse oblige,* can substitute for those values."[47]

Though some may remain unconvinced of the appropriateness of rights talk, at very least it may be accepted that there are serious arguments in favor of it; it is an issue on which reasonable people may disagree. What is clear by now is that the fundamental case against rights, from the perspective of arguments of nonexistence, inseparability, or innovation, falls short of its goal. The ethical category of rights comes through these accusations unscathed, though still badly in need of a foundation. This foundation is marvelously provided by Thomistic personalism.

47. Joel Feinberg, "Duties, Rights, and Claims," *American Philosophical Quarterly* 3/2 (1966): 8.

PART THREE

A NEW SOLUTION TO AN OLD PROBLEM
Thomistic Personalism

A solid theory of human rights demands more than the ability to parry contrary arguments. After the *pars destruens* comes the more essential *pars construens*. And since sound moral theory depends on a sound philosophical anthropology, rights theory will stand or fall with its understanding of the human person. With these points in mind, personalism appears as a particularly well-suited candidate for the role of building up a cogent human rights ethics.

Several steps are involved in this process. First, an adequate grasp of personalistic theory is necessary in order to understand why Thomistic personalism, rooted in the metaphysics and anthropology of Thomas Aquinas and enriched by contemporary personalistic thought, furnishes the best raw material for laying the groundwork for human rights. This will be the subject matter of chapter 7.

Second, personalistic anthropology offers a unique and richly textured idea of the human person as both the subject and object of moral action, which has a vital bearing on rights theory and shows how rights do not depend on an individualistic notion of man but rather on his essentially relational and transcendent character. We will explore this in chapter 8.

Third, a clarification of the idea of human dignity as a bridge between anthropology and ethics will set the stage for the actual founding of human rights from a theological and philosophical perspective. The dignity of the human person is often cited as the foundation of human rights without the necessary effort to describe exactly how comes to be. An understanding of the human person as fundamentally deserving of a certain sort of treatment is implicit in most theories of justice but needs to be drawn out and justified in a coherent way, as chapter 9 does.

Fourth, personalism's claim that every human person by his very nature deserves to be loved, i.e., treated as an end and never merely a means, must be squared with Aquinas's conception of love. Is the personalistic definition of love adequate, and how does this love differ from other loves? Moreover, how does Wojtyła's assertion that all human dealing with reality can be broken down into two mutually exhaustive categories, using and loving, stand up to a classical understanding of human behavior? Chapter 10 will discuss these themes.

Fifth, love, as the radical human right, proves to be the source of the specific ethical requirements termed human rights, which in turn relate to particular human goods. Christ's commandment to love corresponds to the person's dignity, while the commandments of the Decalogue correspond to the person's natural rights. Such is the study of chapter 11.

Sixth, the Trinitarian and Christological foundations of human dignity throw additional light on Christian human rights theory. Far from espousing the Hobbesian conception of a hypothetical state of nature where man is at war with his fellows, Christ reveals the exalted human vocation to divine filiation and consequently to interpersonal communion. The dignity of the human person created in the image of God and redeemed by Christ not only summons individuals to live in a way worthy of their status, it also conditions what it means to treat others justly, as we discuss in chapter 12.

7. A PERSONALISM PRIMER

THE TITLE "personalism" can legitimately be applied to any school of thought or intellectual movement that focuses on the reality of the person (human, angelic, divine) and on his unique dignity, insisting on the radical distinction between persons and all other beings (nonpersons).[1] As a philosophical school, personalism draws its foundations from human reason and experience, though historically personalism has nearly always been attached to Biblical theism.[2]

Maritain hastens to point out that personalism represents a big tent under which many different lines of thought take refuge. Far from being a single school, personalism splits into multiform manifestations, each with its own particular emphases, such that it is more proper to speak of "personalisms" than personalism.[3] Unlike most intellectual currents that find their inspiration in a single work or thinker, diverse forms of person-

---

1. Personalism, though generally considered a philosophical school, can be applied as well to other branches of speculative thought, yielding such titles as theological personalism, economic personalism, and psychological personalism (along with their inversions: personalistic theology, personalistic economics, personalistic psychology, and so forth).

2. As Hans Urs von Balthasar observes, the "history of the initially Jewish and Christian personalism has been described often enough, and its essential elements may be presupposed as familiar. Without the biblical background it is inconceivable: its forerunners (Pascal, Kierkegaard, Jacobi, Maine de Biran, Renouvier) and its main representatives (the late Cohen, Buber, Ebner, Guardini, and the strongest of them Franz Rosenzweig)—they all live from their biblical inspiration" ("On the Concept of Person" trans. Peter Verhalen, *Communio: International Catholic Review* 13 [Spring 1986]: 24).

3. Maritain asserts that "nothing can be more remote from the facts than the belief that 'personalism' is one school or one doctrine. It is rather a phenomenon of reaction against two opposite errors [totalitarianism and individualism], which inevitably contains elements of very unequal merits." He adds that there are at least "a dozen personalist doctrines, which at times have nothing more in common that the word 'person'" (*The Person and the Common Good*, trans. John J. Fitzgerald [Notre Dame, Ind.: University of Notre Dame Press, *1985*], *12–13*).

alism emerged in a relatively short space of time in different sites with many different exponents.

Rigobello groups the many strains of personalism into two fundamental categories: personalism in a strict sense and personalism in a broader sense.[4] Strict personalism places the person at the center of a philosophical system that originates from an "intuition" of the person himself and then goes on to analyze the personal experience that is the object of this intuition. The method of this strict personalism draws extensively from phenomenology and existentialism, departing from traditional metaphysics and constituting a separate philosophical system. The original intuition is really that of self-awareness by which one grasps values and essential meanings through unmediated experience. The knowledge produced by reflecting on this experience is nothing more than a development of the original intuition, which in turn generates an awareness of a framework for moral action. The intuition of the person as the center of values and meaning is not exhausted, however, in phenomenological or existential analyses. These analyses point beyond themselves, indicating a constitutive transcendence of the person himself, irreducible either to its specific manifestations or to the sum total of those manifestations.

In its broader sense, personalism inserts a particular anthropology into a global philosophical perspective. Here the person is not considered as the object of an original intuition, nor does philosophical research begin with an analysis of the personal context. Rather, in the scope of a general metaphysics the person manifests his singular value and essential role. Thus the person occupies the central place in philosophical discourse, but this discourse is not reduced to a development of an original intuition of the person. In this context, the person does not justify metaphysics but rather metaphysics justifies the person and his various operations. More than an autonomous metaphysics, personalism in the broad sense offers an anthropological-ontological shift in perspective within an existing metaphysics and draws out the ethical consequences of this shift.[5] This broader sort of personalism will form the basis of the following discussion of human dignity and rights.

4. Armando Rigobello, "Personalismo," in *Dizionario teologico interdisciplinare*, vol. 2 (Torino: Marietti Editori, 1977), 726–30.

5. As Wojtyła points out, "Personalism is not primarily a theory of the person or a theoretical science of the person. Its meaning is largely practical and ethical" ("Thomistic Personal-

Perhaps the best-known strain of personalism in the broad sense is so-called Thomistic personalism, which is of prime importance for the present study. Represented by such figures as Jacques Maritain, Yves Simon, Étienne Gilson, Robert Spaemann, and Karol Wojtyła, Thomistic personalism draws on principles of Thomas Aquinas's philosophical and theological anthropology to formulate a coherent development of inchoate elements of Thomas's thought. As Wojtyła puts it, St. Thomas was not as familiar with personalism as he was with the concept of the person, but since he presented the problem of the person so clearly, "he also provided at least a point of departure for personalism in general."[6] With his rigorous metaphysics and clear theological-philosophical anthropology, Aquinas provided fertile soil in which personalistic theory could take root.

THE HISTORY OF PERSONALISM

Nothing is born in a vacuum. Personalism grew out of a specific historical and philosophical context, as a reaction to trends that were perceived as dehumanizing. Nineteenth-century philosophy was marked by determinism and materialism. Enamored of the scientific method, some followers of Isaac Newton posited theories of human nature that blurred or cancelled the distinction between man and the rest of nature, robbing him of his spiritual character and free will. The philosophical positivism of Auguste Comte (1798–1857), forerunner to modern sociology, affirmed as a historical law that every science (and the human race itself) passes through three successive stages—the theological, the metaphysical, and the positive, each superior to the last—as it sloughs off the vestiges of superstition, with positive science representing the perfection of human knowledge.[7] The absolute idealism of G. W. F. Hegel (1770–1831) held that Kant's noumenal reality is not an unknowable substratum of appearances but a dynamic process, which in thought and in reality passes from thesis to antithesis and finally resolves itself in synthesis. This process is absolute mind, the state, religion, philosophy. Hegelianism in turn

---

ism," a paper presented on February 17, 1961 at the Fourth Annual Philosophy Week at the Catholic University of Lublin, printed in Woznicki, *Person and Community,* 165.

6. Ibid., 165. See also Maritain, *The Person and the Common Good,* 13.

7. Comte "insists so much on the reality and predominance of society that this becomes for him the true subject, while the individual is regarded as an abstraction" (de Finance, *An Ethical Inquiry,* § 76, p. 142).

opened the door to the evolutionism of Charles Darwin (1809–1882), to the dialectical materialism of Karl Marx (1818–1883), and to the eternal return of Friedrich Nietzsche (1844–1900). In this intellectual environment, man came to be seen as a mere phenomenal being, easily assimilated into the collectivities of the family, the community, and the state.[8] He was a product of external forces, an insignificant piece in a cosmic puzzle, without dignity, freedom, or responsibility. Darwinism, in particular, uprooted the classical understanding of man as essentially superior to the rest of creation by offering a theory whereby man would be simply the most advanced life form along an unbroken continuum, and the difference between man and irrational animals would be merely in degree, not in kind. Meanwhile, in the arena of psychology, Sigmund Freud (1856–1939) proposed another sort of determinism, that of unconscious and instinctive sexual forces (libido) located in that part of the psyche known as the *id*.

Contemporaneous with the rise of Hegelian determinisms came another form of subjection of the individual: the industrial revolution and its philosophical underpinnings in Liberalism. Paradoxically, Liberalism, both in its atomistic anthropology and laissez-faire economic theory, grounds itself in an extreme individualism, yet this individualism more closely resembles Darwin's survival of the fittest than a Christian understanding of the inviolable dignity and worth of the human person. Based on a Hobbesian concept of man's asocial nature and instinctive hostility to his fellows *(homo homini lupus)*,[9] Liberalism encouraged each man to look for his own welfare with the assurance that such "enlightened self-interest" would guarantee the best outcome for all. Despite their many differences, both Hobbes and Locke had posited their philosophies on a presocial natural state of man, contrary to the classical and Christian understanding of the person as naturally social.

This ideological context spawned protests that reacted to materialism, evolutionism, and idealism by seeking to rescue the human person from absorption into larger determining forces. Central to this response was the

---

8. Hegel's idealism saw history as an unfolding of absolute spirit through a necessary dialectical process (thesis, antithesis, synthesis), and this scheme left no room for the freedom of persons or the importance of the individual. His determinist teaching profoundly influenced political leaders of twentieth-century totalitarianism, both on the left (Communism, through Marx) and on the right (National Socialism, through Nietzsche).

9. According to Hobbes, in his natural condition, "every man is enemy to every man" (Leviathan, 89; citing Plautus, *Asinaria*, II, 4, 88).

existentialist movement, especially through the work of the Danish pastor and philosopher Søren Kierkegaard (1813–1855). Contrary to impersonal Hegelian idealism, Kierkegaard underscored the value of the individual person, both for philosophy and for life in general. He accused idealism of emptying life of meaning by neglecting the reality of human existence.

Whereas Kierkegaard and later existentialists (Marcel, Sartre, Camus, Blondel) focused on issues central to the meaning of human existence (love, marriage, death, faith, morality, etc.), other thinkers began to engage in exploration of the meaning and nature of the person himself. Contrary to Hegelian collectivism and the fierce individualism of Nietzsche's superman, these thinkers, who would become known as personalists, stressed the inviolable dignity of the individual person and at the same time his social nature and vocation to communion.[10] In the twentieth century these personalists gathered especially around three European centers of higher learning: Paris, Munich, and Lublin.[11]

Until recently, the best known and most prolific of these three schools was the Parisian group. Between the First and Second World Wars the

---

10. So much was personalism a reaction to dehumanizing forces that personalist Jean Lacroix has declared personalism to be an "anti-ideology" more than a true philosophy. For Lacroix, personalism is an attitude, a speculative aspiration, and an intentional direction of thought awoken by social and political situations that are alienating to the human person. In the face of such forces, personalism reaffirms the absolute dignity and interrelationality of the human person (see *Le personalisme comme anti-idéologie* [Paris, 1972]).

The term "personalism" used to designate a particular philosophical current was coined by Renouvier in 1903 to describe his philosophy. It also appears in American literature from the early part of the twentieth century, such as in B. P. Bowne's *Personalism,* published in 1908. Whereas it is generally acknowledged that personalism as a movement arose in the nineteenth century, some authors speak of a Christian personalism in referring to the Middle Ages. Étienne Gilson, for instance, observes that where Plato locates the center of reality on ideas, with concrete instantiations of these being merely accidental, and Aristotle places emphasis not on numerical individuals but on the universal specific form, Thomas Aquinas sees the individual person as unique among beings because of reason and self-mastery (see *L'esprit de la philosophie médiévale* [Paris: Librairie Philosophique J. Vrin, 1932], ch. 10, "Le personnalisme chrétien," 195–215). St. Thomas writes that "in a more special and perfect way, the particular and the individual are found in the rational substances which have dominion over their own actions; and which are not only made to act, like others; but which can act of themselves; for actions belong to singulars. Therefore also the individuals of the rational nature have a special name even among other substances; and this name is 'person'" (*S. Th.*, I, 29, 1).

11. In addition to these three European centers, the personalist movement spread to Italy, Asia, North America, and Latin America. Italian personalism grew through the academy, especially as a result of the work of Luigi Stefanini (1891–1956), university professor in Padua in the decisive–post World War II years. American personalism, represented by such figures as B. P.

French personalistic movement revolved around a monthly journal, *Ésprit,* founded by Emmanuel Mounier (1905–1950) and a group of friends in 1932. In the face of economic collapse and political and moral disorientation, the French personalists proposed the human person as the criterion according to which a solution to the crisis was to be fashioned. The new, irreducible key to thought, especially regarding social organization, was to be the human person. And though personalism was indeed a reaction against dehumanizing forces, from the outset Mounier distanced himself from simplistic reactionaries who would enter into tactical alliance with the corrupt bourgeois for the sake of revolution. In his programmatic essay "Refaire la Renaissance," which appeared in the first issue of *Ésprit,* Mounier proposed the need to disassociate the spiritual world from the reactionary world. The real revolution was to be the creation of a new humanism, where the bourgeois ideal of "having" would yield to Christian "being," a being in communion with others.

The spiritual revolution envisioned by Mounier was to be above all the work of committed witnesses to the truth, who through their own interior renewal and living faith would galvanize the masses into a new communal structure. Such a revolution entailed a triple commitment: denunciation, meditation, and technical planning. Underlying this program was Mounier's bold conception of Christian experience, an experience of "tragic optimism," colored both by the drama of Christian existence and by the certainty of eschatological victory. The Christian's most important virtue is that of the heroic witness, far from the evasiveness or sentimentality of other, eviscerated strains of Christianity. Thus Mounier's idea of the Christian as the watchful athlete engaged in spiritual combat provided a stark response to Nietzsche's criticism of Christianity as a religion of the weak. His assertion that there is no true progress without the dimension of transcendence countered the Marxist search for an earthly paradise through class struggle. His acceptance of the importance of psychology while reemphasizing man's freedom and responsibility furnished an answer to Freud's instinct-centered psychoanalysis.

Bowne (1814–1910), G. H. Howison (1834–1916), and A. C. Knudson (1873–1954), takes a different tack from continental European personalism in that instead of a reaction to idealism, it is often actually a form of idealism, wherein being is defined as personal consciousness. Similar to European personalism of the stricter sort, American personalism takes the person as its point of departure for understanding the world and draws all moral truth from the absolute value of the person.

Mounier's work attracted the attention of important French thinkers such as Gabriel Marcel, Denis de Rougemont, and Jacques Maritain, who through their research, lectures, and writings helped develop French personalistic thought. Maritain, who worked with Mounier for a number of years, was responsible for bringing personalism to the United States and also played a role in drafting the 1948 United Nations Universal Declaration of Human Rights. Like other Thomistic personalists, Maritain criticized the frailty of certain widespread strains of Scholasticism and appealed to the important role of intuitive experience in philosophy.[12]

Personalism in Germany was closely wedded to another philosophical school, phenomenology, developed by Austrian-born Edmund Husserl (1859–1938). Like existentialism and French personalism, phenomenological realism was a response to German idealism, though it bore a distinctive focus on epistemological questions. Husserl's *Logische Untersuchungen*, published in 1900, laid out his phenomenological method and suppositions. The distinguishing characteristic of phenomenology is methodological, not doctrinal. Seeking to avoid the imposition of preconceived notions or structures on reality, phenomenology goes "back to the thing" *(zurück zum Gegenstand)* by bracketing *(epoché)* all philosophical presuppositions about the world, man, and the rest of reality. This direct observation and consultation of reality eschews the problems of deductive reasoning by focusing on the intellectual act of intuition, or direct apprehension of reality. The eidetic reduction focuses on the essential structures of what appears (phenomenon), so that one is dealing not only with empirical observation, or with a description of Platonic forms, but with the phenomenon's meaning. Phenomenologists identified the object of intuition as the essences of things and in so doing sought to overcome the Kantian noumenon/phenomenom dichotomy as well as the errors of positivism and nominalism.

Though in his later life Husserl leaned toward philosophical idealism,

---

12. "The misfortune of ordinary scholastic teaching, and above all that of the manuals, is in practice to neglect this essential intuitive element and to replace it with a pseudo-dialectic of concepts and formulas. There is nothing doing so long as the intellect does not see, so long as the philosopher or student philosopher do not have an intellectual intuition of essence" (Jacques Maritain, *"Lettera sulla filosofia nell'ora del Concilio,"* cited in Rocco Buttiglione, *Karol Wojtyła: The Thought of the Man Who Became Pope John Paul II*, trans. Paolo Guietti and Francesca Murphy [Grand Rapids, Mich.: William B. Eerdmans, 1997], 36–37).

earlier and in *Logical Investigations* he embraced philosophical realism.[13] A realist phenomenology, like Thomistic personalism, stresses phenomenology's contribution to perennial philosophy and seeks to explore through experience the ultimate structures of being. By going back to the thing itself, phenomenology aims at eluding both the Scylla of empiricism (which reduces reality to the measurable) and the Charybdis of idealism (which rarefies reality into abstraction and subjectivism). Among Husserl's students were Catholic converts Max Scheler (1874–1928), Dietrich von Hildebrand (1889–1977), and Edith Stein (1891–1942). These, together with Roman Ingarden, came to believe that the later thought of Husserl abandoned his original commitment to reconnect philosophical reflection and objective reality. They therefore struck out on their own, each creating an original body of work in pursuit of Husserl's original intention. Stein, for instance, looked to phenomenological method as a complement to Thomism, and von Hildebrand introduced phenomenology into ethics in a personalistic synthesis.

The third and youngest of the three centers of personalistic thought grew up around the Catholic University of Lublin. Roman Ingarden (1893–1970), took phenomenology and interest in personalistic topics back to his native Poland in the early 1940s, and there he met a young priest by the name of Karol Wojtyła, whom he encouraged to read Max Scheler. Wojtyła became interested in Scheler's phenomenology; he did his 1953 doctoral dissertation on Scheler's ethics of values.[14] "I wrote on the contribution which Scheler's phenomenological type of ethical system can make to the development of moral theology. This research benefited me greatly. My previous Aristotelian-Thomistic formation was enriched by the phenomenological method."[15] Wojtyła developed a creative

---

13. "Husserl's later turn to Idealism, which came about in the '20s, precipitated a break with not only Ingarden himself, but with Max Scheler, Martin Heidegger, Nikolai Hartmann, Oskar Becker, and Hedwig Conrad-Martius" (Buttiglione, *Karol Wojtyła*, 54–55).

14. Karol Wojtysła, *Ocena możliwości zbudowania etyki chrześsijańskiej przy założeniach systemu Maksu Schelera* (An Evaluation of the Possibility of Constructing a Christian Ethics on the Basis of the System of Max Scheler) (Lublin: Towarzystwo Naukowe KUL, 1959).

15. John Paul II, *Gift and Mystery* (Nairobi: Paulines Publications Africa, 1996), 108. Wojtyła is careful to distinguish phenomenology from Kantian phenomenalism. He writes that "phenomenology—despite the similarity of its name—differs decisively from Kantian phenomenalism. Phenomenalism assumes that the essence of a thing is unknowable; phenomenology, on the other hand, accepts the essence of a thing just as it appears to us in immediate experience" ("The Separation of Experience from the Act in Ethics: In the Philosophy of Immanuel Kant and Max Scheler," in Woznicki, *Person and Community,* 32.

and original personalistic synthesis, enhancing Thomistic metaphysics and anthropology with insights from phenomenology.[16]

In 1956 Wojtyła became professor of ethics at Lublin's Catholic University, where he founded the Polish personalistic school.[17] Wojtyła, who was also influenced by the writings of another of Husserl's disciples, Dietrich von Hildebrand, produced two significant texts in personalistic studies, *Love and Responsibility* (1960) and *The Acting Person* (1962), as well as numerous essays, lectures, and articles. Wojtyła's personalistic arguments prove an especially useful source for vital principles with which to ground human rights.

The development of Wojtyła's personalism was influenced by his experience of Hegelian totalitarianisms in his native Poland, both of Nietzschean (National Socialism) and Marxist (Leninist Communism) stamp. In his 1994 work *Crossing the Threshold of Hope*, Pope John Paul narrates how interest in man and in his dignity became the main themes of the polemic against Marxism, and this because the Marxists themselves had made the question of man the center of their arguments. This polemic at first took the form of natural philosophy under the tutelage of the noted intellectual Fr. Kazimierz Kłósak, who in his scholarly writings challenged the Marxists' dialectical materialism. The Pope observed that this kind of controversy was short lived. "It soon came about that man himself—and his moral life—was the *central problem under discussion.*"[18] At the same time this initial seed burgeoned into a personal "mission" when Wojtyła found his calling. His concern for "the acting person," as he says, arose not from the disputes with Marxism but rather from his deep personal interest in man. In describing his own calling, John Paul writes that "when I discovered my priestly vocation, man became the *central theme of my pastoral work.*"[19]

From the above, one can anticipate the anthropological slant that Wojtyła's work later took. The centrality of the human person in moral theology represents a shift of emphasis from a more nomothetic framework

---

16. The net results, writes George Weigel, "would be what Wojtyła would call, years later, a way of doing philosophy that 'synthesized both approaches': the metaphysical realism of Aristotle and Thomas Aquinas and the sensitivity to human experience of Max Scheler's phenomenology" (Weigel, *Witness to Hope*, 128).

17. See John Paul II, *Gift and Mystery*, 108.

18. John Paul II, *Crossing the Threshold of Hope*, 199; emphasis in original.

19. Ibid.; emphasis in original.

to an ethics based on philosophical and theological anthropology. In an address to the Congregation for the Doctrine of the Faith, Pope John Paul II underscored the need for a return to Christology and anthropology in order to renew moral theology. "The weighty problems calling . . . for an answer in accordance with truth and goodness can find a genuine solution only if the anthropological and Christological foundation of the Christian moral life is recovered."[20] At the same time, Wojtyła sought to incorporate into Aquinas's objectivistic anthropology of the person a more dynamic, personalistic approach.

Karol Wojtyła's personalistic theory, laid out in 1960, did not constitute for him a phase in a process of philosophical development but came rather to form a enduring pillar of both his philosophy and his theology. As Pope he has continued to employ personalistic arguments in his magisterial teaching. In a sense he has conferred on personalism a certain authority that raises it above the level of a mere philosophical position. John Paul clearly sees personalism as coalescing with revealed truths about the human person and therefore as a contribution to theological reflection and renewal. He speaks of "regret" that the Second Vatican Council's doctrine of the dignity of the human person, who is united through the Covenant to Christ, the Creator and Redeemer, "has still not been introduced into theology nor has it been well applied."[21] From this, John Paul identifies "the *need for theological renewal based on the personalistic nature of man:* that is, a real defense of the fundamental rights which are the consequence of that dignity."[22] He likewise explicitly invokes the personalistic argument in his encyclical letters *Laborem Exercens* and *Ut Unum Sint* as well as his 1994 *Letter to Families*.[23]

CHARACTERISTICS OF PERSONALISTIC THOUGHT

Though personalism as a philosophical and theological movement suffers from a lack of systematic development, several key features set it

---

20. "Address to the Congregation for the Doctrine of the Faith," October 24, 1997, *L'Osservatore Romano,* English edition, October 29, 1997, 2.

21. John Paul II, "Address to the International Theological Commission," December 5, 1983, in *Human Rights in the Teaching of the Church: From John XXIII to John Paul II,* ed. George Filibeck (Vatican City: Libreria Editrice Vaticana, 1994), 40.

22. Ibid; emphasis added.

23. *Laborem Exercens,* 15; *Ut Unum Sint,* 28 (http://www.vatican.va/edocs/ENG0221/_P7.

apart from other philosophical and theological schools.[24] For the present study it is essential to grasp personalism's specific contribution in order to see how it differs from traditional Thomism and in what way these differences are vital to grounding human rights. The distinctive characteristics of personalism include an insistence on the radical difference between persons and nonpersons, an affirmation of the dignity of persons, a concern for the person's subjectivity, attention to the person as object of human action to be treated as an end and never as a mere means, and particular regard for the social (relational) nature of the person. Each of these principles will be explored in greater depth a little further on, yet a brief comment on each can help to indicate the overall direction of the discussion.

Personalists stress the uniqueness of persons vis-à-vis all other entities and designate the essential dividing line of reality as that which separates personal and nonpersonal being. Dealings with persons, therefore, require a completely different paradigm from that used to describe dealings with nonpersonal realities. The "rules" of dealing with nonpersonal reality do not stand up when dealing with persons and vice versa. This radical dichotomy between persons and nonpersons is essentially ontological but produces immediate consequences on the ethical level.

At the center of personalism stands an affirmation of the dignity of the person, which is the quality that constitutes the unique excellence of personhood and gives rise to specific moral requirements.[25] Dignity refers to the inherent value[26] of the person, as a "someone" and not merely "something," and this confers an absoluteness not found in other beings. Every person without exception, therefore, is of inestimable worth, and no one

---

HTM); Letter to Families, 14 (http://www.vatican. va/holy_father/john_paul_ii/ letters/documents/hf_jp-ii_let_02021994_families_en.html).

24. Many major philosophical and theological schools have at their core one particular thinker, or even one central work, from which development has emerged as spokes jutting out from a hub. A typical case in point is Scholasticism, which has constant recourse to Thomas Aquinas and to the *Summa Theologiae* in particular. Personalism has been a more diffused movement, and by its very emphasis on the subjectivity of the person and its ties to phenomenology and existentialism, it has not lent itself particularly to systematic treatises.

25. "Every human person is first an individual, but he is much more than an individual, since one only speaks of a person, as of a personage, in the case that the individual substance under consideration possesses in his own right a certain dignity" (Gilson, *L'esprit de la philosophie médiévale*, 207; author's translation).

26. Various arguments can be made for avoiding the term "value" when speaking of persons. Robert Spaemann asserts that the term "dignity" is more precise than "value" when

is dispensable or interchangeable. The person can never be lost or assimilated fully into the collectivity, because despite his interrelatedness he possesses a unique, irreplaceable value. Attributing a unique dignity or worth to the human person shores up Christian ethical theory and particularly the cardinal virtue of justice. Rendering "to each his due" hinges on one's understanding of what each deserves, which cannot be correctly ascertained without comprehension of the worth of the individual person and all persons, by the very fact of their personhood. The person's absolute character likewise provides for the possibility of absolute moral norms when dealing with persons.

Personalists assert that only persons are truly "subjects." This is not to say that in the syntactic sense other entities do not "act" or "produce" or "cause," but properly speaking they do not possess "subjectivity," which depends on interiority, freedom, and personal autonomy. In other words, though nonpersonal beings may "act" in the syntactic sense, they are not truly subjects of action since the cause of their action is extrinsic to them. Personal subjectivity embraces different dimensions, such as the moral and religious, that are part and parcel of the person's nature as an intelligent, free, willing subject in relation with God and others. Furthermore, as free, thinking subjects, persons exercise creativity through their thought and action, a creativity that affects both the surrounding world and the person himself. As regards the ethical question, not only are persons free and responsible moral subjects, their subjectivity also conditions others' ethical responsibility toward them.

Personalists therefore lay special stress on what persons deserve by the very fact of their personhood, and thus on the difference between acting toward a person and acting toward any other reality. When the person is the object of one's action, a whole ethical structure enters into play that is absent when the object of one's action is a thing. How persons should be

---

speaking of the human person. "That is why Kant said that human beings do not have value, but dignity. This is because all values are commensurable. One value can be measured against others. 'Dignity' on the other hand is the name we give to the characteristic which leads us to rule out the possibility of involving another being in this sort of trade-off" (*Basic Moral Concepts*, 73). Likewise, since the term "value" often connotes the self-referential *bonum mihi*, it can cause ambiguity when used to refer to the human person, who ought never be treated in the first place as a *bonum mihi* but always as a *bonum a se*. Unlike "value," "dignity" underscores the person's specific identity as an end. Nevertheless, a case can be made for the incommensurability of values, and when speaking of the person's "inherent value" the objective, singular worth of the person vis-à-vis things is clearly evidenced.

treated forms an independent ethical category, separate in essence and not only in degree from how nonpersons (things) are to be treated. Whereas traditional ethical systems stress the internal mechanisms of the moral agent (conscience, obligation, sin, virtue, etc.) and the effect that free actions have on moral character, personalists add to this a particular concern for the transcendent character of human action and the dignity of the one being acted upon.

Finally, personalists delve into the ontological and ethical repercussions of the person's nature as a social being. The person never exists in isolation, and moreover he finds his human perfection only in communion with other persons. Interpersonal relations, consequently, are never superfluous or optional to the person, they are constitutive of his inherent makeup and vocation. By underscoring the person's vocation to communion, personalists endeavor to overcome the polarization of individualism on the one hand and collectivism on the other.[27]

THE MEANING OF 'PERSON'

Personalism, then, comprises a system of thought that highlights the centrality of the person and the essential distinction between persons and all other beings. Before turning to the specific contribution of personalism to ethics, some metaphysical and anthropological considerations are in order. The centrality accorded to the person by personalism is not an arbitrary choice; it derives from the ontological status of persons. Likewise, the decision to focus on the person as the key to understanding all of creation, and indeed as the pinnacle of that creation,[28] responds to the demands of intellectual integrity rather than subjective preference. Since Thomistic personalism draws out the ramifications of Thomas's philosophical and theological anthropology, personalistic considerations of the

---

27. Wojtyła characterizes these two extremes in the following way: "On the one hand, persons may easily place their own individual good above the common good of the collectivity, attempting to subordinate the collectivity to themselves and use it for their individual good. This is the error of individualism, which gave rise to liberalism in modern history and to capitalism in economics. On the other hand, society, in aiming at the alleged good of the whole, may attempt to subordinate persons to itself in such a way that the true good of persons is excluded and they themselves fall prey to the collectivity. This is the error of totalitarianism, which in modern times has borne the worst possible fruit" ("Thomistic Personalism," 174).

28. And not only of creation but of all being, since personalists recognize the personal nature of uncreated being (God), in whose image created persons were made.

essence of personhood will benefit significantly from a Thomistic understanding of the person.

The term "person" comes from the Latin *persona,* whose origins are traceable to Greek drama, where the *prosopon,* or mask, became identified with the role assumed by an actor.[29] The thrust of the word into the mainstream of intellectual parlance, however, came with theological discourse during the patristic period, notably the attempts to clarify or define central truths of the Christian faith. These discussions focused primarily on two doctrines: the mystery of the Blessed Trinity and the mystery of the Incarnation of the second Person of the Trinity, which in turn involves the hypostatic union of two natures, divine and human. Confusion marred these discussions because of ambiguities in the various theological terms, such that, for example, Sabellius advanced the thesis that in God there was one *hypostasis* and three *prosopa,* where *hypostasis* conveyed the meaning of "person," and *prosopa* bore the sense of "roles" or "modes" of being. In order to present these mysteries with precision, the concept of person and the relationship of person to nature needed clarification. The debates culminated in the First Council of Nicaea (325), the First Council of Constantinople (381), and in the drafting and propagation of the Nicene-Constantinopolitan creed.

Though the concept of "person" as understood today developed in a theological context, it has been assumed into the patrimony of human thought, even outside theology. "Philosophy," writes von Balthasar, "can in some way appropriate for the human person the dignity bestowed on *person* by trinitarian doctrine and christology, whether the concept of the human person as such influences theology or seeks to make itself completely independent."[30]

Thus despite its theological origins, the word "person" assumed its enduring philosophical definition from Boethius (ca. 480–524): "Persona est naturae rationalis individua substantia."[31] Thomas Aquinas adopted and defended this Boethian definition and had frequent recourse to it in

---

29. *Prosopon* is thought by some to proceed, in turn, from the Etruscan *phersu,* meaning mask. Such usage is carried over today in the word "persona," referring to characters in fictional literature or drama or to the second identities that people adopt for behavior in given social contexts.

30. Balthasar, "On the Concept of Person," 19–20.

31. Boethius, *De Persona et Duabus Naturis,* ch. III, PL 64:1345. Cited by St. Bonaventure, *In I Sent.,* dist. 5, art. 2, q. 1; and by Thomas Aquinas, *S. Th.,* I, 29, ad 1.

his theological speculations on the Trinity and the hypostatic union.[32] Personalists also make reference to this definition, but Wojtyła characteristically offers a more dynamic description as well, describing the person as "a subsistent subject of existence and action."[33]

Boethius's definition consists fundamentally of two parts. The essential starting point is a subsistent individual: a singular, existing *suppositum* or hypostasis.[34] Nevertheless, hypostasis is not identical with person, since a person is a certain kind of hypostasis, namely one of rational nature.[35] Therefore, the second element of the definition—*naturae rationalis*—qualifies the notion of individual: the person is an individual possessing a *rational nature*. It is precisely this rational, spiritual nature that gives rise to the different qualities that distinguish the person, qualities to which personalists attach great importance.

Indeed, man's dignity is rooted in his rational nature, which separates him from the rest of visible creation and wherein chiefly lies his resemblance to God. No matter what other elements are emphasized—the person's freedom, his creativity, his action, his self-consciousness, his interiority, his sociability, and so forth—they all have their objective base in an intellectual, and thus a spiritual, nature.[36] According to Thomistic theology and philosophy, the distinguishing characteristic of the person is precisely his rational nature, from which his unique dignity derives.[37]

Thomas's objectivistic view of the person and his faculties is essential to understanding who the person is and how he is able to act as he does.

---

32. For example: *Summa Contra Gentiles*, trans. English Dominicans (London: Burns, Oates, and Washbourne, 1934; hereafter *CG*), bk. 4, chs. 38, 41, 48, 63; *S. Th.*, I, 29, 1–4; I, 30, 1; I, 34, 3; I, 40, 2; III, 2, 2–3; III, 16, 12; *De Potentia*, 9, arts. 1, 2, 4; 10, art. 5; *Compendium Theologiae*, I, 210. Thomas confronts the objection that in the case of the persons of the Trinity Boethius's definition is inadequate, since the divine intelligence is not rational (discursive) but rather intuitive. Thomas replies that "rational" can be taken to mean, in a broad sense, an intelligent nature (see *S. Th.*, I, 29, 3, ad 4).

33. Wojtyła, "Thomistic Personalism," 167.

34. Hypostasis refers to a first substance and thus includes the adjective "individual" and distinguishes such an existing substance from common or second substance (see Aquinas, *De Potentia*, 9, 2, ad 7; *S. Th.*, I, 29, *resp.* and ad 2).

35. "If we observe the difference between hypostasis and person, we shall see that they do not differ altogether; in fact, person is a kind of hypostasis, since it is a hypostasis of a particular nature, namely rational" (*CG*, bk. IV, ch. 38).

36. "The perfection of the person is undeniably the result of its rational, and thus spiritual, nature, which finds its natural complement in freedom" (Wojtyła, "Thomistic Personalism," 167).

37. *S. Th.*, I, 29, 3, ad 2.

A purely subjectivistic approach to understanding the person, so characteristic of modern philosophy, risks losing the objective base that makes human subjectivity and lived experience possible. This is where a broader personalism, and particularly Thomistic personalism, ensconced as it is in an objective metaphysics, offers surer footing for anthropology and ethics than a strict personalism that endeavors to reinvent metaphysics on the basis of man's self-consciousness.[38] For Thomas, consciousness and self-consciousness derive from the rational nature that subsists in the person; they are not subsistent in themselves.[39] Thus as Wojtyła notes, if consciousness and self-consciousness characterize the person, "then they do so only in the accidental order, as derived from the rational nature on the basis of which the person acts."[40]

At the same time, the essentially objectivistic approach adopted by Thomas may be incomplete, especially when dealing with questions of primary importance for the modern mindset, in that it offers all the raw material for understanding personal existence but goes no further in actually exploring man's subjectivity.[41] Thomas develops much of his philo-

---

38. Wojtyła presents a critique of this modern view of the person, which "proceeds by way of an analysis of the consciousness, and particularly the self-consciousness, that belongs to the human being." According to Wojtyła, the most characteristic feature of such a philosophy is its subjectivism, "its absolutizing of the subjective element, namely, lived experience, together with consciousness as a permanent component of such experience." According to this modern understanding of man, the person "is not a substance, an objective being with its own proper subsistence—subsistence in a rational nature" but rather "a certain property of lived experiences," so that "consciousness and self-consciousness constitute the essence of the person" ("Thomistic Personalism," 170). For Wojtyła's understanding of the difference between "subjectivity" and "subjectivism," see Wojtyła, *The Acting Person*, 58–59.

39. This consciousness, which is an aspect of man's rational nature, also reveals man's spirituality. Wojtyła remarks that "consciousness opens the way to the emergence of the spiritual enactment of the human being and gives us an insight into it. The spiritual aspect of man's acts and actions manifests itself in consciousness, which allows us to undergo the experiential innerness of our being and acting" (*The Acting Person*, 47).

40. Wojtyła, "Thomistic Personalism," 170. Nevertheless, Wojtyła also stresses that consciousness "constitutes a specific and unique aspect in human action." Whereas in the Scholastic approach the aspect of consciousness was, "as it were, hidden in 'rationality'" and "contained in the will," Wojtyła notes the need to "go farther and to exhibit consciousness as an *intrinsic and constitutive aspect of the dynamic structure,* that is, *of the acting person*" (*The Acting Person,* 30–31; emphasis in original).

41. Wojtyła observes that "the Boethian definition mainly marked out the 'metaphysical terrain'—the dimension of being—in which personal human subjectivity is realized, creating, in a sense, a condition for 'building upon' this terrain on the basis of experience" ("Subjectivity and the Irreducible in the Human Being," a paper sent to an international conference in Paris, June 13–14, 1975, in Woznicki, *Person and Community,* 212).

sophical and theological anthropology in the context of man as a part of creation, albeit the most exalted part.[42] His analyses of the concept of "person," on the contrary, take place primarily in his theological considerations of the Trinity and the Incarnation and bear the mark of patristic speculative theology. The idea of the person is all but absent in Thomas's considerations of man. Thomas's objectivism is perhaps his greatest strength, but it can also be a limitation. As Wojtyła remarks:

> For St. Thomas, the person is, of course, a subject—a very distinct subject of existence and activity—because the person has subsistence in a rational nature, and this is what makes the person capable of consciousness and self-consciousness. On the other hand, when it comes to analyzing consciousness and self-consciousness—which is what chiefly interested modern philosophy and psychology—there seems to be no place for it in Thomas' objectivistic view of reality. In any case, that in which the person's subjectivity is most apparent is presented by St. Thomas in an exclusively—or almost exclusively—objective way. He shows us the particular faculties, both spiritual and sensory, thanks to which the whole of human consciousness and self-consciousness—the whole human personality in the psychological and moral sense—takes shape, but that is also where he stops.[43]

The great value of personalistic thought is that, in a sense, it picks up where Thomas leaves off. While acknowledging the objective properties of the person that form the natural basis of his unique dignity, Thomistic personalism goes beyond the objective analysis to complement it with a subjective, experiential reading of the person. With Thomas as a point of departure and permanent reference point,[44] personalism offers a specific contribution to Thomas's doctrine on the person, which facilitates the passage from Thomas's anthropology to human rights.

---

42. Aquinas asserts that in the whole of creation the person is the highest perfection—*id quod est perfectissimum in tota natura.* See *S. Th.*, I, 29, 3.

43. Wojtyła, "Thomistic Personalism," 170–71.

44. "We find in this system not just a point of departure, but also a whole series of additional constitutive elements that allow us to examine the problem of personalism in the categories of St. Thomas' philosophy and theology" (Wojtyła, "Thomistic Personalism," 165).

8. THE PERSON ACCORDING TO PERSONALISM

PERSONALISM IS NOT in the first place a theory of the person or a theoretical science of the person. It focuses rather on the person as subject and object of activity and thus deals fundamentally with practical and ethical questions. Nonetheless, since every ethical theory depends on its underlying suppositions about the person, a proper anthropology is essential.

Thomistic personalism elaborates on the constitutive elements of Thomas's understanding of the person and draws from them the key insight that will make possible a satisfactory grounding of human rights, namely, that persons are unique not only as rational *subjects* of action but also as rational *objects* of action. Awareness of this uniqueness of persons as objects of action emerges from the personalists' new take on Thomas's hierarchy of being.

MAN DISTINGUISHED FROM OTHER CREATURES

Thomas clearly maintained the human person's primacy over the rest of created reality, but he envisioned that primacy as the peak of an ontological continuum. All infra-mundane beings inhabit a specific place on this continuum, and human beings, because of their rational nature, occupy the highest place. Nevertheless, Thomas's approach emphasizes how the entire continuum occupies the same metaphysical plane, that of created being. Thus rather than accentuate man's similarity to God and dissimilarity to the rest of creation by reason of man's personhood, Thomas chose to focus on man's place among created beings.

The personalists' phenomenological reflections on the manifestations of man's rational nature led them to a different conception. Instead of a creaturely ladder with persons occupying the top rung, created reality includes a fundamental separation between personal and nonpersonal being. The rationality of personhood actually opens up a gulf between man and all other creatures.

According to the personalist conception, the fundamental classification of all beings, created and uncreated, is the distinction between persons and nonpersons.[1] In the words of Jacques Maritain: "Whenever we say that man is a person, we mean that he is more than a mere parcel of matter, more than an individual element in nature, such as is an atom, a blade of grass, a fly or an elephant. . . . Man is an animal and an individual, but unlike other animals or individuals."[2]

What makes man "unlike" other animals is different from what makes a baboon unlike a giraffe or even from what makes a baboon unlike a rock.[3] Traditional Aristotelian anthropology defines man as a rational animal, thereby fulfilling Aristotle's requirement for defining a species in terms of its proximate genus (animal) and specific difference (rational).[4] Yet as Wojtyła observes, such a construction "excludes—when taken simply and directly—the possibility of accentuating the irreducible in the human being. It implies—at least at first glance—a belief in the reducibility of the human being to the world."[5] This objective, cosmological view of man as an animal with the distinguishing feature of reason, by which man is primarily an object alongside other objects in the world to which he physically belongs,[6] is valid but insufficient, according to Thomistic personalism. In an effort to interpret the subjectivity that is

---

1. For an excellent exposé on the difference between persons and things, see Robert Spaemann, *Personen: Versuche über den Unterschied zwischen "etwas" und "jemand"* (Stuttgart: Klett-Cotta, 1996), especially ch. 18, "Sind alle Menschen Personen?" 252–64.

2. Jacques Maritain, *The Rights of Man and Natural Law* (Glasgow: Robert Maclehose/University Press, 1945), 5–6.

3. "Man is, to be sure, an animal, but an animal of a superior kind, much farther removed from all other animals than the different kinds of animals are from one another" (Grotius, *De Iure Belli ac Pacis*, prolegomena, 11).

4. Aristotle, *Hist. Anim.*, I, 1:488a7; *Nichomachean Ethics* I, 5:1097b11; VIII, 12:1162a16; IX, 9:1169b18; *Politics*, I, 2:1253a3.

5. Wojtyła, "Subjectivity and the Irreducible in the Human Being," 210–11.

6. As an example, when Thomas ponders the distinction among created things, he observes that "in natural things species seem to be arranged in degrees; as the mixed things are more perfect than the elements, and plants than minerals, and animals than plants, and men than other animals; and in each of these one species is more perfect than others" (*S. Th.*, I, 47, 2).

proper to the person, personalism expresses "a *belief in the primordial uniqueness of the human being, and thus in the basic irreducibility of the human being to the natural world.*"[7]

Wojtyła speaks of a "great gulf that separates the world of persons from the world of things."[8] Man deals with all other realities as objects (something related intentionally to a subject), but there is a substantive difference between the human person and all other objects.[9] "As an object a man is 'somebody'—and this sets him apart from every other entity in the visible world."[10] Only the human person is simultaneously object and subject. This is true for all persons, irrespective of age, intelligence, qualities, etc. If the objectivity of persons as created beings is, in Thomas's conception, connected to the general assumption of the reducibility of the human being to the world, subjectivity proclaims "that the human being's proper essence cannot be reduced to and explained by the proximate genus and specific difference. *Subjectivity is, then, a kind of synonym for the irreducible in the human being.*"[11]

Grounded as it is in metaphysical realism, Thomistic personalism posits the essential difference between man and all other objects on man's ability to reason, which "differentiates a person from the whole world of objective entities."[12] It is precisely his intellectual nature that makes subjectivity possible, and in this sense we can say that "the subjectivity of the human person is also something objective."[13] Yet man's subjectivity, which is derivative of his rational nature, manifests still more clearly his separation from nonpersonal beings. The person differs from even the most advanced animals by "a specific inner self, an inner life" that revolves around truth and goodness.[14] This inner or "spiritual" life gener-

---

7. Wojtyła, "Subjectivity and the Irreducible in the Human Being," 211; emphasis in original.

8. Karol Wojtyła, *Love and Responsibility*, trans. H. T. Willetts (New York: Farrar, Straus, & Giroux, 1995), 21.

9. In distinguishing the world of persons from the world of things, Wojtyła includes animals in the latter category. Although we would hesitate to call an animal a "thing," he writes, nonetheless "no one can speak with any conviction about an animal as a person" (ibid.).

10. Ibid.

11. Wojtyła, "Subjectivity and the Irreducible in the Human Being," 211; emphasis in original.

12. Wojtyła, *Love and Responsibility*, 22.

13. Wojtyła, "Subjectivity and the Irreducible in the Human Being," 211.

14. Or, as Maritain would have it, "Man is an individual who holds himself in hand by his

ates in man numerous questions, of which Wojtyła identifies two as central. The first engages cognition (What is the ultimate cause of everything?) and the second aspiration (How can one be good and possess goodness at its fullest?).[15] A further indication of the person's singularity in the created world is his intimate involvement and communication the invisible, not merely the visible, world—most importantly, with God.

This rich conception of personhood as a unique kind of subjectivity in the midst of objective reality not only redimensions the Thomistic understanding of the hierarchy of being, it also throws into sharp relief another aspect of personhood, the aspect that makes possible a grounding of human rights. Understanding reality as delineated by the essentially distinct categories of personhood and nonpersonhood enabled the personalists to reflect on persons not only as subjects but also as unique, rational objects of action. The quality of that uniqueness, which personalists refer to as human dignity, will prove to be the bedrock of human rights.

THE PERSONALISTIC ITINERARY

Personalism arrived at this new, bipartite conception of infra-mundane reality through its phenomenological examination of the different dimensions of personal experience. This reflection started from Thomas's clear perception of rationality as the distinctive trait of the person and frequently returned to it as a sure reference point, but personalism gradually enriched that basic concept by developing a more nuanced and robust vision of the constitutive elements of personhood: subjectivity, creativity, self-determination, freedom, and interpersonal relationality. A full appreciation of the personalistic vision of the person as rational subject as well as rational object, so essential for the grounding of human rights, can emerge only by following the itinerary of reflection that produced it—a necessarily phenomenological itinerary, synthesized in the remainder of this chapter.

---

intelligence and his will. He exists not merely physically; there is in him a richer and nobler existence; he has spiritual superexistence through knowledge and through love" (*The Rights of Man*, 6).

15. See Wojtyła, *Love and Responsibility*, 23.

Individuals or Persons?

In recent decades, much stress has been laid on the difference between the concept of "person" and that of "individual." The major distinction is that an individual represents a single unit in a homogenous set, interchangeable with any other member of the set,[16] whereas a person is characterized by his uniqueness and irreplaceability. Von Balthasar, for example, writes: "Few words have as many layers of meaning as *person*. On the surface it means just any human being, any countable individual. Its deeper senses, however, point to the individual's uniqueness which cannot be interchanged and therefore cannot be counted."[17] In this deeper sense persons cannot, properly speaking, be counted, because a single person is not merely one in a series within which each member is identical to the rest, for all practical purposes, and thus exchangeable for any other. One can count apples, because one apple is as good as another (i.e., what matters is not that it is *this* apple, but simply that it is *an* apple), but one cannot count *persons* in this way.[18] One could count human beings, as individuals of the same species, but the word *person* emphasizes the uniqueness of each member of the human species, his incommunicability.[19]

---

16. This understanding can be traced to the doctrine of hylomorphism, whereby any individual of a species of being is essentially indistinguishable (and thus interchangeable) from any other individual in the species, the defining difference of "individuation" being provided by prime matter "quantitate signata." Thus Thomas says: "A twofold distinction is found in things; one is a formal distinction as regards things differing specifically; the other is a material distinction as regards things differing numerically only" (*S. Th.*, I, 47, 3). See also Aquinas, *De Trinitate*, 4, 2; *Sent.* II, 3, 1, 4; *CG*, bk. IV, chs. 63–64; *S. Th.*, I, 76, 2 ad 3; *De Potentia*, 9, 2, ad 1.

17. Balthasar, "On the Concept of Person," 18.

18. Aquinas brings out this same distinction. Whereas all individuals are created for the good of the species, in the case of persons (rational creatures), God directs their actions "not only in the point of their belonging to the species, but also inasmuch as they are personal," since only the person is governed and cared for by God "on its own account" (*CG*, bk. III, ch. 113).

19. Von Balthasar goes on to say: "If one distinguishes between *individual* and *person* (and we should for the sake of clarity), then a special dignity is ascribed to the person, which the individual as such does not possess. We see this in the animal kingdom where there are many individuals but no persons. Carrying the distinction over to the realm of human beings, we will speak in the same sense of 'individuals' when primarily concerned with the identity of human nature, to which, of course, a certain dignity cannot be denied insofar as all human beings are spiritual subjects. We will speak of a 'person,' however, when considering the uniqueness, the

As valid as these distinctions are philosophically, "human person" and "human individual" are synonymous in everyday language and have the same referent. Some thinkers have proposed a real distinction between a human person and a human individual. From their perspective, personhood would be an acquired "extra" for a human being, a status reached not simply by being an individual of the species but by entering into relationships with other persons in a conscious, intentional way. In other words, while all human persons would be human individuals, the reverse would not be true.

This argument has an apparent plausibility, since the requisites here laid down for personhood correspond roughly to the qualities one generally associates with persons. Deeper exploration reveals the flaws in this reasoning, however. The crux of the debate centers on whether personhood consists in the *exercise* or in the *possession* of certain powers: reason, free will, and self-awareness. Those who speak of personhood as an acquired quality do so on the grounds that one is a person only through the *exercise* of reason or the acquisition of a determined degree of self-consciousness. Those who insist that any human being is, by the very fact of being human, a person, base their arguments on the *possession* of those faculties that distinguish humans from all other creatures.

Such arguments often come to the fore in disputes over abortion. The judgment of whether the unborn child has personhood or lacks it determines whether the individual is considered eligible for protection as a subject of constitutional and moral rights—particularly, the right to life. In his book *Rethinking Life and Death,* the Australian ethicist Peter Singer cites recent discussions in bioethics, concluding that a person is "a being with certain characteristics such as rationality and self-awareness."[20] Personhood, Singer claims, should not be attributed to every member of the human species but only to those members who display such characteristics. Likewise, members of other species should not be randomly excluded from the category of personhood. "There are other persons on this planet. The evidence for personhood is at present most conclusive for the

---

incomparability and therefore irreplaceability of the individual" ("On the Concept of Person," 18).

20. Peter Singer, *Rethinking Life and Death: The Collapse of Our Traditional Ethics* (Oxford: Oxford University Press, 1994), 180. See also Singer, *Practical Ethics* (New York: Cambridge University Press, 1993), 110–11.

great apes, but whales, dolphins, elephants, monkeys, dogs, pigs and other animals may eventually also be shown to be aware of their own existence over time and capable of reasoning." And since Singer judges these characteristics by their exercise and not their possession, he can query: "Why should we treat the life of an anencephalic human child as sacrosanct, and feel free to kill healthy baboons in order to take their organs?"[21]

Though in a more nuanced way, similar arguments appear in John Rawls's *A Theory of Justice,* first published in 1971.[22] Rawls separates human beings into two categories: "moral persons" and others. Moral persons are distinguishable by two traits: "first they are capable of having (and are assumed to have) a conception of their good (as expressed by a rational plan of life); and second they are capable of having (and are assumed to acquire) a sense of justice."[23] Rawls dismisses the problematic nature of moral personality as the necessary attribute for the possession of rights. "I assume," he writes, "that the capacity for the sense of justice is possessed by the overwhelming majority of mankind, and therefore this question does not raise a serious practical problem."[24]

Yet this issue could and often does present real problems. Rawls himself has to backpedal and acknowledge that a distinction may be made between capacity and exercise.[25] In fact, only by recognizing person-

---

21. Singer, *Rethinking Life and Death,* 182, 183.

22. In the present work, all quotations from *A Theory of Justice* have been taken from the revised edition (John Rawls, *A Theory of Justice,* rev. ed. [Oxford: Oxford University Press, 1999]).

23. Rawls, *A Theory of Justice,* 442.

24. Ibid., 443. Rawls refrains from pronouncing on whether moral personality is necessary as well as sufficient for being entitled to equal justice and recommends against denying justice to those persons who may lack it. In making it the fundamental criterion for entitlement to justice, however, Rawls unmistakably sets the groundwork for withholding justice from those who do not satisfy the condition.

25. Rawls provides for the possession of rights by children and some others who do not actually have a "rational plan of life" by distinguishing between capacity and exercise of powers. "I have said that the minimal requirements defining moral personality refer to a capacity and not to the realization of it. A being that has this capacity, whether or not it is yet developed, is to receive the full protection of the principles of justice. Since infants and children are thought to have basic rights (normally exercised on their behalf by parents and guardians), this interpretation of the requisite conditions seems necessary to match our considered judgments" (ibid., 445–46). Nonetheless, the allowance that some "scattered individuals" (443) of the human race do not possess this capacity opens the door to excluding some human beings from the principles of justice, based on the judgment that these human beings are somehow not moral persons.

hood's roots in human nature and by distinguishing the possession of certain attributes from their exercise can this hurdle by cleared. In this regard, Finnis posits the basis of human equality and equal rights on the fact that

> each living human being possesses, *actually and not merely potentially,* the *radical capacity* to reason, laugh, love, repent, and choose *as this unique, personal individual,* a capacity that is not some abstract characteristic of a species but rather consists in the unique, individual, organic functioning of the organism that comes into existence as a new substance at the conception of that human being and subsists until his or her death, whether ninety minutes, ninety days, or ninety years later; a capacity, individuality, and personhood that subsists as real and precious even while its operations come and go with many changing factors such as immaturity, injury, sleep, and senility.[26]

Though the Church's Magisterium offers no philosophical definition of "person," it makes clear that such a distinction between human beings and persons is foreign to a Christian understanding of humanity: regardless of the label applied, all human beings are equal in dignity and must be treated as persons.[27] In the 1987 declaration *Donum Vitae* of the Congregation for the Doctrine of the Faith, the topic is broached in the form of a rhetorical question: How could a human individual not be a human person?[28] The document goes on to conclude that the "human being is to be respected and treated as a person from the moment of concep-

---

26. John Finnis, "Abortion, Natural Law, and Public Reason," in *Natural Law and Public Reason,* ed. Robert P. George and Christopher Wolfe (Washington, D.C.: Georgetown University Press, 2000), 91.

27. Wojtyła writes that "a child, even an unborn child, cannot be denied personality in its most objective ontological sense, although it is true that it has yet to acquire, step by step, many of the traits which will make it psychologically and ethically a distinct personality" (*Love and Responsibility,* 26).

28. "Certainly no experimental datum can be in itself sufficient to bring us to the recognition of a spiritual soul; nevertheless, the conclusions of science regarding the human embryo provide a valuable indication for discerning by the use of reason a personal presence at the moment of this first appearance of a human life: how could a human individual not be a human person? The Magisterium has not expressly committed itself to an affirmation of a philosophical nature, but it constantly reaffirms the moral condemnation of any kind of procured abortion. This teaching has not been changed and is unchangeable (Cf. Pope Paul VI, Discourse to participants in the Twenty-third National Congress of Italian Catholic Jurists, December 9, 1972: *AAS* 64 [1972], 777)" (Congregation for the Doctrine of the Faith, *Donum Vitae,* I, 1).

tion," which in turn carries with it the corollary that "from that same moment his rights as a person must be recognized, among which in the first place is the inviolable right of every innocent human being to life."[29]

Interiority and Subjectivity

All created things can be examined and known from the outside, as *objects*. In a sense, they stand in front of us, they present themselves to us—but always as outside of us. They can be described, qualified, and classified. It is legitimate, and even necessary, to know man in this way. From this objective viewpoint one discerns the superiority of the human being to the rest of created reality. Yet in the case of the human person, a thoroughly unique dimension presents itself, a dimension not found in the rest of created reality.[30] Human persons experience themselves first of all not as *objects* but as *subjects*, not from the *outside* but from the *inside*, and thus they are *present to themselves* in a way that no other reality can be present to them.[31] This self-presence is the interiority of the human per-

---

29. "Thus the fruit of human generation, from the first moment of its existence, that is to say from the moment the zygote has formed, demands the unconditional respect that is morally due to the human being in his bodily and spiritual totality. The human being is to be respected and treated as a person from the moment of conception; and therefore from that same moment his rights as a person must be recognized, among which in the first place is the inviolable right of every innocent human being to life" (ibid.).

30. Peter Singer asserts that there is solid evidence that some animals are self-conscious. The evidence he adduces, however, is less than compelling. According to Singer, a chimpanzee by the name of Washoe "does not hesitate, when shown her own image in a mirror and asked 'Who is that?' to reply: 'Me, Washoe'" (*Practical Ethics*, 111). Self-awareness, however, is surely more than self-identification, which is inherently indistinct from recognition of another. The ability to acknowledge a label for oneself does not demonstrate any sort of self-presence.

31. "The human being holds a position superior to the whole of nature and stands above everything else in the visible world. This conviction is rooted in experience.... Our distinctiveness and superiority as human beings in relation to other creatures is constantly verified by each of us.... It is also verified by the whole of humanity in its ongoing experience: in the experience of history, culture, technology, creativity, and production.... A being that continually transforms nature, raising it in some sense to that being's own level, must feel higher than nature—and must *be* higher than it" (Wojtyła, "On the Dignity of the Human Person," 178). "When we speak of the human person, we are not just thinking of superiority, which involves a relation to other creatures, but we are thinking above all of what—or rather *who*—the human being essentially is. Who the human being essentially is derives essentially from within that being" (ibid.).

son,[32] and it is so central to the meaning of person that Maritain can say that personality "signifies interiority to self."[33]

Metaphysics in the classical tradition identifies matter as the individuating principle in composite beings. This accounts for the existence of individuals in any species and the possibility of a multiplicity of instantiations of a given essence. In the case of the human person, however, this distinction among individuals does not nearly do justice to the irreplaceability and incommunicability of each human being in his personal uniqueness. The human being, writes Wojtyła, is "given to us not merely as a being defined according to species, but as a concrete self, a self-experiencing subject. Our own subjective being and the existence proper to it (that of a *suppositum*) appear to us in experience precisely as a self-experiencing subject."[34] Because of the person's subjectivity, he is capable of acting from within, from the core of his own subjectivity, not merely of being acted upon and moved by external forces. Since he is the author of his actions, he possesses an identity of his own making that cannot be reduced to objective analysis and thus resists definition. This resistance to definition, this "irreducibility," does not mean that the person's subjectivity and lived experience is unknowable, but rather that we must come to know it differently, by a method that merely reveals and discloses its essence. *"In my lived experience of self-possession and self-governance, I experience that I am a person and that I am a subject."*[35]

The lived experience of the human person, as a conscious and self-conscious being, discloses not only *actions* but also inner *happenings* that depend upon the self. These experiences, lived in a conscious way, go into the makeup and uniqueness of the person as well. Thus the experience of the human being "cannot be derived by way of cosmological reduction; we must pause at the irreducible, at that which is unique and unrepeat-

---

32. Animal rights activists often seek to make subjectivity a function of sentience. Thus Peter Singer invites readers to put themselves in the place of a suffering animal with the question: "What is it like to be a possum drowning?" And he logically concludes that the most precise answer is "It must be horrible" (*Practical Ethics*, 277). His conclusion is logical because when we put *ourselves* in the place of the possum, we cannot help but *personalize* the animal. We cannot help but project our own personality—the condition for the possibility of such lived experience—into the animal's situation.

33. Maritain, *The Person and the Common Good*, 41.

34. Wojtyła, "Subjectivity and the Irreducible in the Human Being," 213.

35. Ibid., 214; emphasis in original.

able in each human being, by virtue of which he or she is not just *a particular human being*—an individual of a certain species—but *a personal subject*."[36] This is the only way to come to a true understanding of the human being. Obviously, the framework of the irreducible is not exhaustive of the human condition, and such an understanding must be supplemented by a cosmological perspective. Nevertheless, it is impossible to come to a true understanding of the person while neglecting his subjectivity.

Here the influence and value of the phenomenological method is apparent. Phenomenology explores the essence of the person as an intuition from the inside, rather than as a deduction from a system of thought or through strict empirical observation. In 1975 Wojtyła wrote: "With all the phenomenological analyses in the realm of that assumed subject (pure consciousness) now at our disposal, we can no longer go on treating the human being exclusively as an objective being, but we must also somehow treat the human being as a subject in the dimension in which the specifically human subjectivity of the human being is determined by consciousness."[37] This contribution does not replace earlier, more objectivist notions of man, it complements them.

Self-determination

Man's intellectual nature, which according to Boethius is the distinguishing characteristic of personhood, is also the font of freedom, subjectivity, immortality, and man's cognitive and moral life.[38] Because the person possesses a spiritual nature, the source of personal action is internal to the person and not extrinsic.[39] Ethicists draw an important distinction between human action involving the efficient, creative agency of the person *(actus humanus)* and acts of man where such agency is absent *(actus hominis)*.[40] Human action in the present context refers to human acts in

---

36. Ibid.; emphasis in original. 37. Ibid., 210.

38. For a full treatment on the personal structure of self-determination, see Wojtyła, *The Acting Person*, 105–48. Gilson notes that "it is as a rational being, and therefore as a person, that the individual can distinguish true from false, i.e., have a science, and distinguish good from evil, i.e., have a morality" (*L'esprit de la philosophie médiévale*, 210; author's translation).

39. For St. Thomas action is proper to singulars, and therefore among all individual substances persons bear a special title, since rational substances "have dominion over their own actions" and thus are not only made to act, like others, but can act of themselves (*S. Th.*, I, 29, 1).

40. See *S. Th.*, I-II, 1, 1. Wojtyła prefers the term *actus voluntarius* to *actus humanus* in that

the proper sense, meaning those acts that proceed from a deliberate will.[41] Nonpersonal beings are not truly subjects of action since the principle of their acts is extrinsic to them.[42] The importance of this characteristic of personhood should not be undervalued, since it forms the basis of personal freedom and also conditions the way both God and other men deal with the person. Unlike those of irrational creatures, the human person's ends are not predetermined for him but are subject to his free choice.[43] As Caffarra observes, "God's decision to create is a decision to call others to participate in his Being. To decide that these others will be *persons* is to decide that they will determine themselves with reference to this participation; otherwise they determine nothing but simply *are determined.*"[44]

Thus in his contact with the world, the human person acts not in a purely mechanical or deterministic way;, he acts from the inner self, as a subjective "I," with the power of self-determination. Possession of free will means that the human person is his own master *(sui iuris)*.[45] Self-mastery is another name for freedom, and freedom characterizes personal beings.[46] The person's power of self-determination explains the nontransferable *(alteri incommunicabilis)* nature of personality. His incommunicability does not refer only to the person's uniqueness and unrepeatability,

---

it manifests with greater precision man's potentiality as the source of acting by pointing directly "to the power that serves as the dynamic basis in conscious acting, the basis of action. The power in question is free will" (*The Acting Person,* 26).

41. See *S. Th.,* I-II, 1, 1.

42. St. Thomas affirms that "man differs from irrational animals in this, that he is master of his actions" (*S. Th.,* I-II, 1, 1), and he further explains that "if a thing has no knowledge of the end, even though it have an intrinsic principle of action or movement, nevertheless the principle of acting or being moved for an end is not in that thing, but in something else, by which the principle of its action towards an end is not in that thing, but in something else, by which the principle of its action towards an end is imprinted on it." Irrational animals may apprehend the end of their acts "without knowing it under the aspect of end or the relationship of an act to the end." In this sense, nonrational creatures do not have within themselves the principle of their action (see *S. Th.,* I-II, 6, 1–2).

43. "It was he who created man in the beginning, and he left him in the power of his own inclination. If you will, you can keep the commandments, and to act faithfully is a matter of your own choice. He has placed before you fire and water: stretch out your hand for whichever you wish" (Sirach 15:14–16).

44. Caffarra, *Living in Christ,* 141.

45. See, for instance, *S. Th.,* I, 29, 3, ad 4; I, 30, 4, obj. 2.

46. "To designate the individuality proper to a free being, one says that it is a person" (Gilson, *L'esprit de la philosophie médiévale,* 208; author's translation).

which is common to all entities. What is incommunicable or inalienable in a person "is intrinsic to that person's inner self, to the power of self determination, free will.... No one can substitute his act of will for mine."[47] This self-determination sets the human person above all other created beings, as the summit of creation.[48]

In what does self-determination consist? Wojtyła explains that the distinction between human acts and so-called "acts of man," between something that "happens" in the subject and an "action" of the subject allows us "to identify an element in the comprehensive experience of the human being that decisively distinguishes the activity or action of a person from all that merely happens in the person."[49] This element Wojtyła terms self-determination. Self-determination involves a sense of efficacy on the part of the acting subject, who recognizes that "'I act' means that 'I am the efficient cause' of my action and of my self-actualization as a subject," which is not the case when something merely happens to me. One's sense of efficacy as an acting person in relation to the action performed is in turn closely connected to one's sense of responsibility for the activity.[50] This experience, on the phenomenological level, draws attention to the will as the person's power of self-determination while at the same time making clear that self-determination is a property of the person himself, and not just of the will.[51]

Self-determination is not limited to the concept of efficacy, however. In acting, the person not only directs himself toward a value, he determines himself as well.[52] He is the efficient cause of his actions, but he is

---

47. Wojtyła, *Love and Responsibility*, 24.

48. Wojtyła, citing *Gaudium et Spes* (40), wrote later as Pope: "Among all other earthly beings, only a man or a woman is a 'person,' a conscious and free being and, precisely for this reason, the 'center and summit' of all that exists on the earth" (John Paul II, apostolic exhortation *Christifideles Laici* [Rome: Libreria Editrice Vaticana, 1988], 37; hereafter *CL*).

49. Karol Wojtyła, "The Personal Structure of Self-Determination," in Woznicki, *Person and Community*, 189.

50. The idea of dignity is therefore closely linked with that of conscience. The very concept of conscience, as Spaemann notes, "implies the idea of human dignity.... It is because of the presence of the universal, the objective, the absolute, in the individual person, that we talk of human dignity; there is no other reason" (*Basic Moral Concepts*, 58–59).

51. Thus "it is the person's freedom, and not just the will's freedom, although it is undeniably the person's freedom through the will" (Wojtyła, "The Personal Structure of Self-Determination," 190).

52. "[I]f we pay very close attention to the experience of our freedom, we will observe that what moves me to choose *this* good rather than *that* one is my decision that this good is a good,

also in some sense the creator of himself, especially his moral self. By choosing to carry out good or bad actions, man makes himself a morally good or bad human being.[53] When a person acts, he acts intentionally toward an object, a value that attracts the will to itself. At the same time, self-determination "points as though inward—towards the subject, which, by willing this value, by choosing it, simultaneously defines itself as a value."[54] As a result of this, the human being is capable of existing and acting "for itself," or is "capable of a certain *autoteleology*, which means capable not only of determining its own ends but also of becoming an end for itself."[55] In this way, the person is not only responsible for his actions, he is also responsible for himself, for his moral identity.[56]

Man's freedom and self-determination bear a close relation to another characteristic of his spiritual nature: creativity. Freedom as a property of the person or an attribute of the will allows the person to create through thought and action. The will is not simply the executor of the intellect's reasoned conclusions. The intellect presents a variety of goods to be realized, none of which imposes itself in such a way as to be necessarily desired or chosen above the others. The will itself decides "spontaneously," "freely," and thus constitutes the moral value and identity of the person. "This particular good has value for me according to the me that I freely desire and choose to be." This creativity, so characteristic of the person, takes place both outside and inside the person. As Wojtyła has written:

> We are by nature creators, not just consumers. We are creators because we think. And because our thought (our rational nature) is also the basis of our personalities, one could say that we are creators because we are persons. Creativity is real-

---

a value for *myself*. This is the good for me, for the *me* that I now want, that I now decide to be" (Caffarra, *Living in Christ*, 137).

53. "Action accompanies becoming; moreover, action is organically linked to becoming. Self-determination, therefore, and not just the efficacy of the personal self, explains the reality of moral values: it explains the reality that by my actions I become 'good' or 'bad,' and that then I am also 'good' or 'bad' as a human being" (Wojtyła, "The Personal Structure of Self-Determination," 190).

54. Ibid., 192.

55. Karol Wojtyła, "The Family as a Community of Persons," in Woznicki, *Person and Community*, 317. "I call the finality that is proper to the person *autoteleology*: self-fulfillment, like self-possession and self-governance, is proper to the person" (321).

56. "The dynamic structure of self-determination reveals to me that I am given to myself and assigned to myself" (Wojtyła, "Subjectivity and the Irreducible in the Human Being," 214).

ized in action. When we act in a manner proper to a person, we always create something: we create something either outside ourselves in the surrounding world or within ourselves—or outside and within ourselves at the same time. Creating as derived from thinking is so characteristic of a person that it is always an infallible sign of a person, a proof of a person's existence or presence.[57]

Relation

As much as he may strive for independence, the human person necessarily relies on others.[58] In the first place, he depends radically on God as the source of his being. Moreover, from the moment of conception he depends on other persons for his survival and development, and this interdependence is a hallmark of human existence. The human person tends toward society as a basic human value. Thus Aristotle, when considering the good of self-sufficiency, hastens to add that such a term is not employed with reference "to oneself alone, living a life of isolation, but also to one's parents and children and wife, and one's friends and fellow citizens in general, since man is by nature a social being."[59]

Thomas observes that "of all things that may be useful to man, other men hold the first place, since man is by nature a social animal: for he needs many things that cannot be provided by one man alone." And, quoting Ecclesiastes, he goes on to praise the benefits of human companionship: "It is better . . . that two should be together, than one: for they have the advantage of their society: if one fall he shall be supported by the other. Woe to him that is alone, for when he falleth, he hath none to lift him up. And if two lie together, they shall warm one another; how shall one alone be warmed? And if a man prevail against one, two shall withstand him (Eccles. iv. 9–12)."[60]

Such society is not only a matter of utility or convenience, however, it reflects an innate tendency of the person to seek out his fellows and enter into association with them. Grotius notes that "among the traits characteristic of man is an impelling desire for society, that is, for the social life—not any kind and every sort, but peaceful, and organized according to the measure of his intelligence, with those who are of his own kind;

---

57. Wojtyła, "Thomistic Personalism," 171.
58. See Alasdair C. MacIntyre, *Dependent Rational Animals* (Chicago: Open Court, 1999).
59. Aristotle, *Nichomachean Ethics*, I, 7:1097b13–15.
60. *CG,* bk. III, ch. 128.

this social trend the Stoics called 'sociableness.'"[61] This trait of sociableness has been observed since the earliest philosophers. It reflects, on the one hand, man's dependence on other people for his subsistence and development and on the other, his vocation to communion.

Relation, in fact, is proper to the person, as Thomas notes.[62] Personalism in particular has endeavored to highlight this aspect of personhood. Since personalism arose as a reaction against both collectivism and individualism, it is understandable that the person's vocation to communion has assumed a central position in personalist thought. In the words of Pope John Paul II, the human being is a "'being for others' in interpersonal communion. Today, to think of the person in his self-giving dimension is becoming a matter of principle."[63] From this perspective, then, relationship is not an optional accessory for the human person, it is essential to his personhood.[64] He is a being-for-relation.[65]

Nonetheless, it must be noted that man's social nature and his vocation to interpersonal communion are not the same thing, though they are clearly not opposed to one another.[66] Rather, they complement each other, since one of the things that makes human beings social beings is precisely their capacity for rational community and friendship. The person's capacity for *communio,* however, is deeper than sociability and "is far more indicative of the personal and interpersonal dimension of all social systems."[67] "Society," in fact, is sometimes analogously applied to nonpersonal beings that live and interact as a group rather than in isolation from one another (and thus some animals are considered more "so-

61. Grotius, *De Iure Belli ac Pacis,* prolegomena, 11.
62. *S. Th.,* I, 29, 4.
63. John Paul II, General Audience of Wednesday, November 24, 1999, *L'Osservatore Romano,* English edition, December 1, 1999, 11.
64. The Second Vatican Council teaches that "by their innermost nature human beings are social beings, and unless they relate to others they can neither live nor develop their potential" (*GS,* 12).
65. Pope John Paul likewise draws this principle from Scripture and observes that "biblical man discovered that he could understand himself only as 'being in relation'—with himself, with people, with the world and with God" (John Paul II, encyclical letter *Fides et Ratio* [Rome: Libreria Editrice Vaticana, 1998], 21; hereafter *FR*).
66. Wojtyła observes that "there is a certain difference between saying, on the one hand, that the human being, who is a person, also has a social nature and, on the other, that the human being as a person has the capacity for rational community as *communion*" ("The Family as a Community of Persons," 319).
67. Ibid.

cial" than others), whereas the word *communio* could never be understood in this way. *Communio,* as understood by Wojtyła, refers to "a mode of being and acting [in common] through which the persons involved mutually confirm and affirm one another, a mode of being and acting that promotes the personal fulfillment of each of them by virtue of their mutual relationship."[68] This mode of being and acting is an exclusive property of persons. Though the person's vocation to interpersonal communion is discernible to human reason, it finds its deepest explanation in revelation, especially in that man was created in the image and likeness of God, who is himself *communio personarum.*

The human person's vocation to communion once again finds its ontological basis in rational nature, through the person's subjectivity and self-determination. Far from closing the person in on himself, these characteristics of man's spiritual nature make him capable of and dispose him toward communication with other persons. Thus as Maritain observes, the "subjectivity of the person has nothing in common with the isolated unity, without doors or windows, of the Leibnitzian monad. It requires the communications of knowledge and love. By the very fact that each of us is a person and expresses himself to himself, each of us requires communication with *other* and *the others* in the order of knowledge and love. Personality, in its essence, requires a dialogue in which souls really communicate."[69]

This communication, in turn, depends on the person's self-determination with its distinctive structure of self-possession and self-governance. As a free, willing subject, the person cannot be possessed by another, unless he chooses to make a gift of himself to another.[70]

It is often remarked nowadays that a fundamental error of modern rights discourse is the assumption that a person somehow "belongs to himself." This would be a result of body-soul dualism, the proverbial Cartesian "ghost in a machine," where man identifies with his soul or spirit, which is free to dispose of the body as he pleases. Though this con-

---

68. Ibid., 321.
69. Maritain, *The Person and the Common Good,* 41–42.
70. "Through his voluntary activity, his free choice, the person subsists in himself, in a specific independence . . . from the world and his environment. From the person's subsistence in himself through free action we derive the conclusion that he is independent, that he can be possessed by no one, unless it is he who makes a gift of himself" (Caffarra, *Living in Christ,* 134).

cern is legitimate, in the sense that man's body is not a piece of property owned by his soul, man does in a real way belong to himself, without the need to posit soul-body dualism. The person belongs to himself, in fact, in a way that no other thing or animal can.[71] In this respect, Aquinas wrote: "A person is free when he belongs to himself; a slave, on the contrary, belongs to his master. In the same way, he acts freely who acts spontaneously, while he who receives his impulse from another does not act freely."[72]

Self-possession in no way implies isolationism. On the contrary, writes Wojtyła, "both self-possession and self-governance imply a special disposition to make 'a gift of oneself,' and this a 'disinterested' gift. Only if one possesses oneself can one give oneself and do this in a disinterested way. And only if one governs oneself can one make a gift of oneself, and this again a disinterested gift." This vocation to self-giving is so essential to the constitution of the person that "it is precisely when one becomes a gift for others that one most fully becomes oneself."[73] Consequently, what Wojtyła terms "the law of the gift" is inscribed deeply within the dynamic structure of the person. Without a disinterested gift of self, man cannot achieve the finality proper to a human being by virtue of being a person, or, as the Council puts it, cannot "fully discover his true self."[74]

This "law of the gift" shows that the communion of which the person alone is capable, and which is necessary for his realization as a person, consists not only in association but in love. It consists in a love that gives and gives itself, that receives not only things but other persons as well. Only persons can give love and only persons can receive love. Love has as its true object other persons—not things or even qualities, but persons themselves.[75]

---

71. "To bestow oneself, one must first exist; not indeed, as a sound, which passes through the air, or an idea, which crosses the mind, but as a thing, which subsists and exercises existence for itself. Such a being must exist not only as other things do, but eminently, in self-possession, holding itself in hand, master of itself. In short, it must be endowed with a spiritual existence, capable of containing itself thanks to the operations of the intellect and freedom, capable of super-existing by way of knowledge and love" (Maritain, *The Person and the Common Good*, 39–40).

72. Thomas Aquinas, *Commentary on 2 Cor 3*, lesson 3. From here we receive Thomas's dictum that "liber est, qui est causa sui."

73. Wojtyła, "The Personal Structure of Self-Determination," 194.

74. *GS*, 24.

75. Thus Maritain writes: "Love is not concerned with qualities. They are not the object of

Whereas individualism seeks the self above all and views others as means to one's own profit, love seeks to make of the self a gift to another.[76] Where individualism hopes to find personal realization in self-interest, love knows that, in the words of the Council, "man can fully discover his true self only in a sincere giving of himself."[77] Here the antagonism between individualism and personalism manifests itself. Pope John Paul II has written forcefully in this regard:

> Love, the civilization of love, is bound up with personalism. Why with personalism? And why does individualism threaten the civilization of love? We find a key to answering this in the council's expression, a "sincere gift." Individualism presupposes a use of freedom in which the subject does what he wants, in which he himself is the one to "establish the truth" of whatever he finds pleasing or useful. He does not tolerate the fact that someone else "wants" or demands something from him in the name of an objective truth. He does not want to "give" to another on the basis of truth; he does not want to become a "sincere gift." Individualism thus remains egocentric and selfish. The real antithesis between individualism and personalism emerges not only on the level of theory, but even more on that of ethos. The ethos of personalism is altruistic: It moves the person to become a gift for others and to discover joy in giving himself. This is the joy about which Christ speaks (cf. Jn. 15:11; 16:20, 22).[78]

The Person as Object of Human Action

This chapter began with the assertion that personalism's key insight with regard to grounding human rights concerns persons' uniqueness not only as rational *subjects* of action but also as rational *objects* of action. This is, in fact, a distinctive trait of personalism as compared with traditional ethical theory, which concentrated heavily on the duties of the

---

our love. We love the deepest, most substantial and hidden, the most *existing* reality of the beloved being.... This is a center inexhaustible, so to speak, of existence, bounty and action; capable of giving and of *giving itself;* capable of receiving not only this or that gift bestowed by another, but even another self as gift, and other self which bestows itself" (*The Person and the Common Good,* 39).

76. "Thus, if the first condition of individualism is the centralization of the individual in himself, the first condition of personalism is his decentralization, in order to set him in the open perspectives of personal life" (Emmanuel Mounier, *Personalism,* trans. Philip Mairet [Notre Dame, Ind.: University of Notre Dame Press, 1952], 19).

77. *GS,* 24.

78. John Paul II, *Letter to Families,* 14.

moral agent, saying little about the rights of the recipient of action. The radical difference between persons and nonpersons affects not only the operations of each but also the moral coloring of situations where the object of one's acts is a person.[79] The ontological difference between person-

---

79. Other strains of personalism, such as that of the Jewish personalist Martin Buber, pay less attention to the difference between persons and nonpersons and underscore instead the way one relates to all of reality. Like Wojtyła, Buber separates the way of dealing with other realities into two, which he terms "I-Thou" and "I-It" relationships, the first reflecting a fundamental openness to the reality of the other and the latter reflecting an objectivization and subordination of the other to oneself. Wojtyła says that we either treat other beings as ends or as means; that is, we either *use* them or *love* them. Buber says that we engage others either as an *It*, forming an *I-It* primary word, or as a *Thou*, forming the *I-Thou* primary word. Yet whereas Wojtyła (as we will have occasion to see further on) would assert that such an *I-Thou* relationship is the only appropriate way of dealing with persons and the *I-It* relationship the only appropriate way of dealing with things, Buber seems to present the *I-Thou* relationship as the ideal for the human person's dealing with all reality, personal and nonpersonal alike. And though this *I-Thou* relation will take on different characteristics according to the sphere in which the world of relation arises (nature, men, spiritual beings), for Buber the fundamental difference lies within the human person himself and in the attitude with which he engages reality.

In 1957 Buber published a postscript to *I and Thou* in which he publicly answered queries posed to him by readers over the intervening three and a half decades. One key area of doubt refers to the nature and possibility of an *I-Thou* relation with beings other than men. How is mutuality possible with nonpersonal beings and in what does it consist? Buber here distinguishes between animals and other beings. In the case of animals, a certain reciprocity exists, as exhibited in "taming." Man, writes Buber, "draws animals into his atmosphere and moves them to accept him, the stranger, in an elemental way, and to respond to him. He wins from them an often astonishingly active response to his approach, to his addressing them, and moreover a response which in general is stronger and directer in proportion as his attitude is a genuine saying of *Thou*" (157).

But what of animals as "initiators" or "speakers" of these two primary words? Buber offers no clear indication. "An animal is not, like man, twofold," he writes (158). At the same time Buber says that "there is here a latent twofoldness. That is why we may call this sphere, in respect of our saying of *Thou* out towards the creature, the threshold of mutuality" (158). Now mutuality means equal from both sides, "having the same relation each toward the other." In other words, a relationship where one party initiates, speaks, and engages, while the other party receives, accepts, and listens, is not a mutual relationship. It is a complementary relationship. In Buber's terminology, it would seem that mutuality would require the *I-Thou* primary word to be reciprocated by another *I-Thou* primary word initiated by the other.

The fundamental problem with the formulation of this problem lies in the assumption that the animal stands as an *I* before reality, and that the animal can therefore "speak" the primary word. An *I* supposes a self-conscious subject. For a being to be an *I*, that is, for a being to utter the word *I*, requires a personal subjectivity, a personal identity, or a self-concept.

For Buber, even in the case of plants mutuality is not totally lacking. "It is part of our concept of a plant," Buber writes, "that it cannot react to our action towards it: it cannot 'respond.' Yet that does not mean that here we are given no reciprocity at all. . . . there is a reciprocity of

al and nonpersonal being, therefore, explains the difference between acting toward a person and acting toward any other reality.[80] When the object of one's action is a person, another dimension comes into play—an ethical dimension.

This is intuitively clear. It is not the same to throw a stone into a lake and to throw your neighbor into the lake. It is not the same to shut the dog out for the night and to shut your little sister out. The ontological difference between personal and nonpersonal being, therefore, justifies the difference between acting toward a person and acting toward any other reality.

But why? What reality founds the truth of that intuition? *Why* can't I treat a person in the same way that I treat a nonperson? What is it about the ontology of personhood that not only makes persons free, creative, interpersonal subjects themselves but also makes them morally demanding objects of other persons' actions? The answer to that question can be summed up in one word: dignity. Because of the unique structure of human dignity, it bridges the gap between metaphysics and ethics, laying bare the ultimate foundation of human rights.

---

the being itself, a reciprocity which is nothing but being in its course" (158). See Martin Buber, *I and Thou,* 2nd ed., trans. Ronald Gregor Smith (Edinburgh: T & T Clark, 1987).

80. "A person's dignity is grounded in the fact that he is not just one aspect of reality amongst others, but that he is urged by his conscience to deal justly with reality. As a potentially moral being, a person deserves unconditional respect" (Spaemann, *Basic Moral Concepts,* 73).

9. DIGNITY AND ITS DUE

WHEN THE OBJECT of one's action is a person, an ethical structure enters into play that is absent when the object of one's action is a thing. Thus without ignoring the immanence of human action and its effects on the character of the moral agent, personalists lay special emphasis on the transitive nature of human acts and the dignity of the one being acted upon, i.e., the reason why this ethical dimension emerges. The fundamental question personalists ask in this regard is: How is the human person to be treated?

The question of human rights is, in the final analysis, a question of what is due to the human person. In other words, it is a question of justice. Grounding human rights requires coming to an understanding of how the person is to be treated and, above all, why he must be treated in that way and not in another. Though he deals extensively with the topic of justice, Thomas fails to single out what the person has a right to by the mere fact of being a person. He establishes that each should be rendered his due and that a certain equilibrium must be maintained, but he does not identify the content of this moral due. Thomistic personalism, and in a particularly apt and succinct way the personalism principle as formulated by Karol Wojtyła, does provide this content, both on a general level and in its concrete instantiations.

As opposed to the Humean idea that an "ought" can never proceed from an "is," Thomistic personalism asserts that it is precisely the metaphysical "is" that furnishes the only possible foundation for an ethical "ought." Any other "ought" can only be a conventional obligation, extrinsic to the person and therefore not in and of itself ethical. The person, by the very fact of being a person, is owed certain things, which are his right. This is personalism's primordial claim. Examining its inner dynamics will uncover the true foundation of human rights.

MAKING THE TRANSITION

Pope John XXIII asserted that because "every human being is a person, that is, his nature is endowed with intelligence and free will . . . he has rights and obligations flowing directly and simultaneously from his very nature. And as these rights and obligations are universal and inviolable so they cannot in any way be surrendered."[1] How does this progression from personhood to rights come about? By linking two key personalistic arguments.

First, the key mediating concept between personhood and rights, the notion of personal dignity, must be shown to be a bridge between anthropology and ethics. Only if human dignity is able to span the abyss between what is and what should be will it succeed as a mediating concept. Second, Karol Wojtyła has claimed that all our dealings with reality can be broken into two types, depending on whether the object of those dealings has personal dignity or not: using as a means and loving as an end. Wojtyła further claims that the only proper way to deal with a person is to love the person as an end. These claims, and the ethical consequences that flow from them, must be carefully weighed and evaluated. If they are true, then love will present itself as a sort of original human right from which all other rights derive, and the New Testament commandment of love will be seen as a requirement not just of positive revealed law but of the natural moral law itself.

DIGNITY

"Dignity" in the Papal Magisterium

Emphasis on the dignity of the human person in papal magisterial teaching, with the moral consequences it engenders, has been growing steadily since before the Second Vatican Council.[2] The Council itself

---

1. *PT,* 9.
2. During the course of the council itself, Karol Wojtyła wrote that the council and the Church "regard the call concerning the dignity of the human person as the most important voice of our age" (Wojtyła, "On the Dignity of the Human Person," 179).

stressed human dignity especially in the Decree on Religious Freedom *(Dignitatis Humanae)* and the Pastoral Constitution on the Church in the Modern World *(Gaudium et Spes)*. Particularly during the pontificate of Pope John Paul II, one notes a marked emphasis on the centrality of human dignity in the Church's social doctrine, an emphasis that John Paul openly encourages.[3] John Paul goes so far as to place the promotion of the dignity of the person at the heart of the Church's mission. In his 1988 apostolic exhortation, *Christifideles Laici,* the Pope writes:

> To rediscover and make others rediscover the inviolable dignity of every human person makes up an essential task, in a certain sense, the central and unifying task of the service which the Church and the lay faithful in her are called to render to the human family.[4]

According to magisterial teaching, dignity forms the basis of rights.[5] Michael Perry has written that the idea of human rights consists of two parts. According to the first, "each and every human being is sacred—each and every human being is 'inviolable,' has an inherent 'dignity and worth,' is 'an end in himself,' or the like." According to the second, *because* every human being has an inherent dignity, "certain choices should be made and other choices rejected; in particular, certain things ought not to be done to any human being and certain other things ought to be done for every human being."[6]

The Deconstruction of Dignity

Recent experience, however, shows that a generic appeal to "human dignity" as a grounding for human rights is insufficient. Groups with different ideas of human good have sought, with varying degrees of success, to co-opt the term "dignity" and put it at the service of supposed human "rights" that are in fact nothing of the sort.

---

3. "The sense of the dignity of the human person must be pondered and reaffirmed in stronger terms. A beneficial trend is advancing and permeating all peoples of the earth, making them ever more aware of the dignity of the individual: the person is not at all a 'thing' or an 'object' to be used, but primarily a responsible 'subject,' one endowed with conscience and freedom; called to live responsibly in society and history; and oriented towards spiritual and religious values" (ibid., 5).

4. *CL,* 37.

5. See, as a sample, *CCC,* 1930, 1935, 1944, 1945, 1956, 1978, 2203, 2407, 2414.

6. Michael J. Perry, *The Idea of Human Rights: Four Inquiries* (New York: Oxford University Press, 1998), 4–5.

Take for example the appeal pro-euthanasia organizations make to a so-called death with dignity. The philosophy behind this expression equates human dignity with absolute autonomy and decision-making power over one's existence, especially over the moment and manner in which one dies. A well-known homosexual advocacy group in the United States goes by the name of "Dignity," lobbying under this banner for a greater acceptance and approval of the homosexual lifestyle. Here again, dignity implies the freedom to live as one pleases, without so much as moral disapproval from others. More and more animal rights groups assert the dignity of primates, or mammals, or all sentient life, blurring the distinction between irrational animals and man in order to gain legal protection for the "rights" of the former.

Such variant uses of the term "dignity" are not a strictly modern phenomenon. In the sixteenth century the British philosopher Thomas Hobbes expounded a thoroughly utilitarian concept of dignity as a value set by society rather than the intrinsic worth of a person. "The *Value* or WORTH of a man," wrote Hobbes, "is as of all other things, his Price; that is to say, so much as would be given for the use of his Power: and therefore is not absolute; but a thing dependent on the need and judgement of another." Furthermore, "[t]he publique worth of a man, which is the Value set on him by the Common-wealth, is that which men commonly call DIGNITY."[7] According to this mindset, dignity is a mere function of a person's productivity or usefulness to others rather than an innate quality underlying man's equality with his fellows.

With these examples in mind, it is evident that mere recourse to the term "dignity" as the foundation of rights is inadequate. Personal dignity must be sufficiently well defined to distinguish it from these alternative uses. Moreover, dignity must possess certain characteristics if it is to ground universal human rights. In the first place, it must be capable of drawing ethical requirements from man's nature; second, it must be universally predicated of all human beings; and third, it must be distinctive of the human person. Only if dignity possesses these traits can it be said to ground universal human rights.

---

7. Thomas Hobbes, *Leviathan* (1651), ed. Richard Tuck (Cambridge: Cambridge University Press, 1991), 63.

Drawing an "Ought" from an "Is"

The Latin *dignitas,* from the root *dignus* (worthy, deserving), means both worth, worthiness, or desert and the grandeur, greatness, or excellence that causes such worth.[8] This double meaning has been carried over into English, where dignity denotes "an excellence deserving esteem or respect."[9] Thus a person of high rank or position is said to possess a dignity, an excellence that merits special regard.[10] In the case of rank, dignity is superadded to the notion of personhood and distinguishes one person from another. There is, however, a dignity proper to the human person as such. It results from the excellence of his very personhood and makes all people worthy of a particular respect not due to nonpersonal creatures. Embodying both "excellence" and "worth," dignity forms a sort of bridge concept that spans the gap from the metaphysical/anthropological sphere of what man *is* to the ethical sphere of how man *should* therefore *be treated.*

Two and a half centuries ago, the Scottish Enlightenment philosopher David Hume argued that ethical principles can never be extrapolated from metaphysical realities. An "is," argued Hume, can never give rise to an "ought."[11] This is true, of course, on the level of logical discourse. Premises in the indicative mode can never logically yield an imperative for a conclusion. An imperative premise is required for an imperative conclusion, which implies that if moral imperatives exist at all, there must be an imperative axiom that functions as a premise and that is not derived from any other principle. Yet as will be shown, this strictly linguistic limitation does not apply to the causal relationship between metaphysical realities and ethical obligations.

The link between "is" and "ought" can be examined in two ways, either from the perspective of the person as moral agent or from the per-

---

8. "During the Roman Republic, *dignitas* was a term of praise for the high and mighty, primarily for the patrician senators and others holding political office or inherited status" (Virginia Black, "What Dignity Means," in *Common Truths: New Perspectives on Natural Law,* ed. Edward B. McLean [Wilmington, Del.: ISI Books, 2000], 127).

9. The *Oxford English Dictionary* defines dignity as "1. The quality of being worthy or honourable; worthiness, worth, nobleness, excellence"; as also "The quality of being worthy of something; desert, merit."

10. Inherent dignity arises from an objective excellence and hence is not something bestowed on or subjectively attributed to a person, as Hobbes would have it.

11. David Hume, *A Treatise of Human Nature,* ed. L. A. Selby-Bigge (Oxford: Clarendon Press, 1896), III.i.1, pp. 455–70.

spective of the person as object of human action. These two perspectives are encapsulated in the well-known statement from *Gaudium et Spes,* that "man is the only creature on earth that God has wanted for its own sake" and therefore "man can fully discover his true self only in a sincere giving of himself."[12]

From the angle of the person as moral agent, the "ought" derives from man's teleological nature. Metaphysically speaking, all things naturally tend toward their perfection, which is simply the fullness of their mode of being. While irrational creatures spontaneously and necessarily tend to their proper end, if a man wishes to perfect himself he must exercise his liberty in such a way as to freely conform his choices to his true end, an end that brings him into interpersonal communion with absolute being, and therefore possesses an obligatory character.[13]

Applying Aristotle's categories of act and potency, man not only "is," he is also "becoming," and it is not a matter of indifference what he becomes. Because the human person has an end or telos, his free choices bring him either closer to this end or farther away from it.[14] In fact, as a rational being, man has the possibility of entering into personal communion with transcendent being (the source of all contingent goodness and truth), and precisely because that possibility is transcendent, or absolute, it is also obligatory—it "should be" achieved. Now, to achieve it and thereby become fully himself (i.e., what he is meant to be, what he is obliged to be), man must make certain choices. Thus man's dignity (his excellence, which demands respect) springs from his rational nature, which gives him both a spiritual/transcendent purpose and the capacity of freedom and self-determination. He "ought" to do certain things, and avoid other things, simply because he is a human being, a creature in a

---

12. *GS,* 24.

13. In this regard the council cites Ecclesiasticus, recalling that "God willed that man should 'be left in the hand of his own counsel' (Cf. Eccl. 15:14) so that he might of his own accord seek his creator and freely attain his full and blessed perfection by cleaving to him" (*GS,* 16).

14. Aristotle expresses this as a rhetorical question: "Are we then to suppose that, while the carpenter and the shoemaker have definite functions or businesses belonging to them, man as such has none, and is not designed by nature to fulfill any function? Must we not rather assume that, just as the eye, the hand, the foot and each of the various members of the body manifestly has a certain function of its own, so a human being also has a certain function over and above all the functions of his particular members?" (Aristotle, *Nichomachean Ethics,* I, 1097b.29–34).

self-propelled process of becoming, of entering into interpersonal communion with absolute being. Certain choices perfect him (when he chooses true goods) and other choices hinder his attainment of his integral good. In the words of the Council, he must learn to make a "sincere gift" of himself.

Alasdair MacIntyre argues that to deny the possibility of extrapolating an "ought" conclusion from an "is" premise assumes that no moral arguments involve what he calls "functional concepts," i.e., concepts defined in terms of the function or purpose they serve. And as MacIntyre points out, moral arguments within the classical Aristotelian tradition "involve at least one central functional concept, the concept of *man* understood as having an essential nature and an essential purpose or function.... That is to say, 'man' stands to 'good man' as 'watch' stands to 'good watch' or 'farmer' to 'good farmer' within the classical tradition."[15]

In presenting dignity as the foundation of rights, however, personalism focuses especially on the ethical dynamics of situations where man is the *object* of human action or, in other words, how a human being should *be treated* simply because he is a human being. From this perspective, the specific "ought" deriving from man's "is" involves what should be done to or for another human person and what never should be done to or for another human person. Human experience testifies to the truth of this reasoning. Every child knows it is not the same to beat a stick upon the ground and to beat someone's head with it. The quality of these two moral acts is radically different, though the physical motion is the same. The ground has no "dignity" that appeals for a certain treatment, whereas the person does. Morality has to do with our way of dealing with reality (and realities): God, others, ourselves, other creatures. There is a correct way and an incorrect way to deal with these realities which, according to Christian tradition, can be naturally known.

In his concise apologia for the objectivity of moral value, *The Abolition of Man,* C. S. Lewis refers to a quality possessed by things or persons that requires us to treat them in a certain way. Drawing from universal natural law, which Lewis likes to call "the *Tao*" (the Chinese word for "the Way"), he refutes radical subjectivism and lays a basis for morality. "It [the *'Tao'*] is the doctrine of objective value," and those who know it "recognize a quality [in persons] which *demands* a certain response from

---

15. MacIntyre, *After Virtue,* 58.

us whether we make it or not."¹⁶ To say that persons are to be treated in a certain way, then, is not an expression of a philanthropic sentiment to which others may or may not subscribe, it is a statement about the true nature of things. Human dignity is "a quality which *demands* a certain response from us."

The Universality of Human Dignity

If this dignity inheres in man's nature as a free and intelligent being, it can be predicated equally of all members of the human race. In order to be universal, personal dignity could not be a function of intelligence, abilities, accomplishments, moral worth, or baptism, for these factors vary from person to person. It must rather be a function of the human being simply by virtue of his humanity, of his personhood, a natural quality that cannot be acquired or lost.¹⁷ The very expression "human dignity" implies that dignity resides in human nature itself and thus ensures a fundamental ontological equality among all persons.¹⁸

Not everyone agrees with this. Ernest L. Fortin has expressed serious misgivings with "John Paul II's unprecedented insistence on the more or less Kantian notion of the 'dignity' that is said to accrue to the human being, not because of any actual conformity with the moral law, but for no other reason than that he is an 'autonomous subject of moral decision' (*CA*, 13)."¹⁹ The "more usual view," for which Fortin manifests evident

---

16. C. S. Lewis, *The Abolition of Man: How Education Develops Man's Sense of Morality* (New York: Macmillan, 1947), 29; emphasis in original.

17. "It is this idea of inherent moral worth with which we have to come to terms. It carries with it the notion of universality; moral necessity demands that we ascribe or impute inherent dignity to all persons as equals because reasoning recognizes our common capacity for moral agency and moral responsibility.... treating others humanely rests minimally on something we cannot deny. This is our common nature" (Black, "What Dignity Means," 131).

18. As Anne Mette Maria Lebech observes, Christian universalism (through St. Thomas) overcomes Aristotelian elitism, being broadened to attribute dignity to all men, whereas Aristotle accorded full human status only to free Athenian men. Aquinas's appropriation of Boethius's definition of person accounts for two important ideas: "that the dignity of the human being depends on human nature, which is *intrinsic* to the individual, and that *all* human beings possess this dignity equally, precisely because it is inherent in their nature. Equality and inherent dignity are two aspects of the same idea" ("Clarification of the Notion of Dignity," in *The Dignity of the Dying Person: Proceedings of the Fifth Assembly of the Pontifical Academy for Life*, ed. Juan Vial Correa and Elio Sgreccia [Vatican City: Libreria Editrice Vaticana, 2000], 445n11).

19. Fortin, "From *Rerum Novarum* to *Centesimus Annus*," 229. The phrase Fortin cites is

nostalgia, "is that one's dignity as a rational and free being is contingent on the fulfillment of prior duties." The dignity of which Fortin speaks "was meant to be achieved" and "could be forfeited." In other words, before the arrival of the Rousseauian and Kantian notion of the sovereign individual, "to be and to be good were two different things." Thus dignity would not be universally enjoyed by human beings, nor would it be an enduring quality. Fortin's objections would seem to square with certain expressions in the Vatican II pastoral constitution *Gaudium et Spes,* where dignity is tied to obedience to moral conscience,[20] is gained when man freely chooses the good,[21] and can be lost through the willful corruption of conscience.[22]

Fortin disparagingly describes the idea of universal human dignity as a "Kantian notion." Though Kant offered invaluable insights into human dignity, the idea itself was no invention of Kant's and enjoys a venerable, albeit limited, place in perennial Christian anthropology.[23] Thomas Aquinas, for example, dealt with this question and in fact directly bound the idea of *dignity* to the idea of *person.*

For as famous men were represented in comedies and tragedies, the name "person" was given to signify those who held high dignity. Hence those who held high rank in the Church came to be called "persons." Thence by some the definition of person is given as "hypostasis distinct by reason of dignity." And because

---

actually not tied to human dignity in the context of *CA,* 13 and is misleading when taken by itself. John Paul offers a vigorous critique of theories of moral autonomy in *VS,* 35–41.

20. "For man has in his heart a law written by God; to obey it is the very dignity of man; according to it he will be judged" (*GS,* 16).

21. "Man's dignity, therefore, requires him to act out of conscious and free choice, as moved and drawn in a personal way from within, and not by blind impulses in himself or by mere external constraint. Man gains such dignity when, ridding himself of all slavery to the passions, he presses forward towards his goal by freely choosing what is good, and, by his diligence and skill, effectively secures for himself the means suited to this end" (ibid., 17).

22. The council affirms that conscience sometimes goes astray through unavoidable ignorance "without thereby losing its dignity," whereas this "cannot be said of the man who takes little trouble to find out what is true and good, or when conscience is by degrees almost blinded through the habit of committing sin" (ibid., 16).

23. "The idea of the dignity of the human person, it is true, had long been a foundational element in the Church's anthropology. What spurs the far-reaching development in the Church's social teaching that crystallizes in the Conciliar documents, however, is a new emphasis on man's personhood, and a new and deeper understanding of the dignity this implies and of its implications for the organization of social and political life" (Grasso, "Beyond Liberalism," 35).

subsistence in a rational nature is of high dignity, therefore every individual of the rational nature is called a "person."²⁴

For Aquinas, then, man's basic dignity flows from his personhood, from the fact that he is endowed with a rational nature. Moreover, dignity is seen by Aquinas to be the distinguishing characteristic of personhood.²⁵ It is the dignity of a rational nature that qualifies man as a person, and thus dignity is grounded in the metaphysical reality of the person as "subsistence in a rational nature."²⁶

The great Franciscan theologian and contemporary of Aquinas, Saint Bonaventure, wrote similar things concerning dignity in his famous commentary on the Sentences. Like Aquinas, Bonaventure conceived of dignity as the characteristic mark of personhood. A person is, in Bonaventure's words, a distinct substance possessing dignity.²⁷ Clearly, for these two doctors of the Church, dignity is not an addendum pasted onto personhood—it is essential to the very concept of personhood.

To Kant, on the other hand, goes the credit for distinguishing between price and dignity, whereby price is a measure of one's value to another and dignity the measure of one's intrinsic worth. "In the realm of ends," he writes, "everything has either a *price* or a *dignity*. Something that has a price can be exchanged for something else of *equal value*; whereas that which exceeds all price and therefore admits of no equivalent, has a dignity."²⁸ Dignity he defines as intrinsic value *(innern Werth)*. For Kant, morality has dignity since it is the condition by which man is an end to himself. Furthermore, "*autonomy* is the foundation of the dignity of human nature and of every rational nature."²⁹ Kant's conception of personal autonomy is problematic, since values and moral norms do

---

24. *S. Th.*, I, 29, 3, ad 2.

25. Elsewhere Thomas reiterates that person "is expressive of dignity" (*S. Th.*, II-II, 32, 5), that "person implies dignity" (I, 32, 3, ad 4), and that person adds "a distinguishing property of dignity" to hypostasis (I, 40, 3, ad 1).

26. Pope John Paul II has written, "[I]t is metaphysics which makes it possible to ground the concept of personal dignity in virtue of [the person's] spiritual nature" (*FR,* 83).

27. "Persona de sui ratione dicit suppositum distinctum proprietate ad dignitatem pertinente... ideo persona dicitur suppositum distinctum habens dignitatem, et ratione huius dignitatis, cum deberet per naturam vocabuli dici persona, penultima correpta, dicitur persona, penultima producta" (St. Bonaventure, *In I sent.,* dist. 23, art. 1, q. 1, Resp.).

28. Immanuel Kant, *Grundlegung zur Metaphysik der Sitten* (1785), BA 77 (Darmstadt: Wissenschaftliche Buchgesellschaft), 68; author's translation.

29. Ibid., (BA 79), 69.

not have their ultimate source in practical reason but in God, mediated by the natural law and revelation.[30] Nonetheless, his efforts to overcome a utilitarian ethic by appealing to man's personal dignity rooted in freedom deserves acknowledgment, and his distinction between price (one's utility to others) and dignity (one's intrinsic worth) is especially helpful. Thomistic personalism draws on these intuitions about human dignity and establishes them firmly on a realist metaphysics of the person.

What answer can be given, then, to Fortin's objections, which seem to find an echo in the words of the Council? The key to a response lies in distinguishing between an *ontological* dignity, common to all human beings by reason of their nature, and a *moral* dignity, which reflects the consistency with which a person lives according to moral truth.[31] Moral probity, which undoubtedly merits a particular regard, varies from person to person and even in the context of the same person at different moments. The fundamental human dignity that undergirds universal human rights, however, is connatural to all men and exists as a binary reality. One either possesses or does not possess this dignity and the rights that accrue to it, just as one is, or is not, a person. Whereas moral dignity can be acquired and also forfeited, ontological dignity remains constant, since the rational nature on which it rests endures independent of moral choices.

In his 1980 encyclical letter on God's mercy, *Dives in Misericordia*, Pope John Paul II takes the parable of the Prodigal Son (Luke 15:14–32) as a starting point for reflection on the relationship of sin, dignity, and mercy. When the son in the parable comes to his senses, he realizes what he has lost, and his lament over lost goods conceals a deeper loss, which the Pope calls "the tragedy of lost dignity, the awareness of squandered sonship."[32] The Pope points out that indeed, in strict justice, the son no

---

30. See *VS*, 40.

31. Grisez and Boyle distinguish between two ways of looking at human dignity, which they term "elitist" and "universalist." According to the elitist perspective, dignity signifies the excellence of those who distinguish themselves as superior to others by rank, birth, ability, and so forth. The second way of looking at dignity has its roots in Christian thought and is based on man's creation in God's image and likeness. See Germain Grisez and Joseph Boyle, Jr., eds., *Life and Death with Liberty and Justice: A Contribution to the Euthanasia Debate* (Notre Dame, Ind.: University of Notre Dame Press, 1979). Anne Lebech also takes up this theme, distinguishing between "extrinsic" dignity, inherited or acquired through one's effort, and "intrinsic" dignity, belonging to man's nature and equal in all (see ("Clarification of the Notion of Dignity," 444–45).

32. John Paul II, encyclical letter *Dives in Misericordia* (Rome: Libreria Editrice Vaticana, 1980), 5; hereafter *DM*.

longer deserves a filial place; he "no longer has any right except to be an employee in his father's house." Here love proves superior to justice, since "love is transformed into mercy when it is necessary to go beyond the precise norm of justice—precise and often too narrow." Thus a certain dignity is indeed a function of man's faithfulness to God's law.

And yet, paradoxically, despite his lost moral dignity, the son continues to be the son. That is, while moral dignity was truly lost through sin, there is another more rudimentary, ontological dignity that remains. The Pope considers that from the father's perspective, "it was his own son who was involved, and such a relationship *could never be altered or destroyed by any sort of behavior.*"³³ In short, a certain dignity is lost through sin, yet another essential dignity cannot be lost. Or, as John Paul expresses it, the father's joy on receiving his son back "indicates a good that has remained intact: even if he is a prodigal, a son does not cease to be truly his father's son; it also indicates a good that has been found again, which in the case of the prodigal son was his return to the truth about himself."³⁴ These two "goods"—one that remains intact despite sin, and the other that is lost—manifest the two levels of human dignity corresponding to man's nature and his moral character. Although man can deprive himself of the moral dignity that depends on his deliberate choices, he retains the inherent, ontological dignity of a human person.³⁵

Conflating these two levels of dignity leads to irresolvable difficulties, and arguments that human dignity can be acquired and forfeited run aground on ethical shoals as well. If human dignity depended on moral merit, a child before the age of reason, for example, would have no dignity, and hence no rights, until he had made his first moral choice. Moreover, on committing a mortal sin persons would lose their human dignity and thus all their rights. They could rightly be dealt with as one deals with irrational animals.³⁶ Therefore, from the perspective not only of

---

33. *DM*, 5; emphasis added.   34. Ibid., 6.

35. Wherefore Thomas teaches that "sinners do not cease to be men, for sin does not destroy nature. Therefore we ought to love sinners out of charity" (*S. Th.*, II-II, 25, 6). If sinners do not cease to be men, then anything that depends on human nature (such as human dignity and rights) must perdure in sinners. Thus, too, Pope John XXIII wrote: "A man who has fallen into error does not cease to be a man. He never forfeits his personal dignity; and that is something that must always be taken into account" (*PT,* 158). Similarly, Pope John Paul II has written: "Not even a murderer loses his personal dignity, and God himself pledges to guarantee this" (*EV,* 9).

36. This is effectively what Aquinas argues. "By sinning man departs from the order of

philosophical and theological anthropology but also from the perspective of ethics, it is clear that dignity must be predicated universally of all human beings, and just as this dignity is connatural to the human person and was not acquired, neither can it be forfeited.

TWO WAYS TO TREAT REALITY

This dignity, which bridges the gap between the metaphysical and ethical realms, gives rise to particular moral obligations. Dignity is an excellence that calls for special regard, but what form does this special regard take?[37] To answer this question, Karol Wojtyła has laid out a particularly relevant road map in his 1960 work on sexual ethics, *Love and Responsibility*.

Wojtyła examines the meaning of the verb "to use" and then contrasts it with "to love." As a thinking and willing subject, according to Wojtyła, man deals with all other beings in one of two ways: either as a means or as an end. In other words, whenever man deals with reality, he either incorporates the other into his own purposes as a means or recognizes and

---

reason, and consequently falls away from the dignity of his manhood, in so far as he is naturally free, and exists for himself, and he falls into the slavish state of the beasts, by being disposed of according as he is useful to others.... Hence, although it be evil in itself to kill a man so long as he preserve his dignity, yet it may be good to kill a man who has sinned, even as it is to kill a beast. For a bad man is worse than a beast, and is more harmful, as the Philosopher states (Polit. i, 1 and Ethic. vii, 6)" (*S. Th.*, II-II, 64, 2, ad 3).

In 1998 I examined this argument in the context of capital punishment, arguing that sin does not destroy man's inherent resemblance to his Creator nor his personhood. "If things were otherwise we could rightly treat anyone in a state of sin (which, in any event, we can never ascertain with certainty) with the same impunity with which we treat animals. Not only would murderers be liable to the death penalty, but under the right conditions, so would adulterers, heretics, fornicators, and those who willfully miss Mass on Sunday. Moreover there could be no further talk of 'humane' punishment for such perpetrators; they could be dispatched like a lame horse or a blind dog. Punishment itself, in fact, would lose all retributive meaning, since the very concept implies a free and willing wrongdoer, and consequently personal dignity" (Thomas D. Williams, "Capital Punishment and the Just Society," *Catholic Dossier* 4/5 [September–October 1998]: 30).

37. "The dignity of the human person? The expression means nothing if it does not signify that ... the human person has the right to be respected, is the subject of rights, possesses rights. These are the things that are owed to man because of the very fact that he is a man" (Maritain, *The Rights of Man*, 37). Pope John Paul II likewise affirms: "In situations strongly influenced by ideology, in which polarization obscured the awareness of a human dignity common to all, the Church affirmed clearly and forcefully that every individual—whatever his or her personal convictions—bears the image of God and therefore deserves respect" (*CA*, 22).

affirms the other as having its own independent and equally valuable purpose.³⁸ To treat an object as a means is denoted by the verb "to use."³⁹ To treat an object as an end, which means recognizing it as another *subject* that possesses its own independent purpose, is designated "love." Intrinsic to the concept of using is the *subordination* of the means to the end and to some extent, also the subordination of the means to the agent. Thus as Wojtyła puts it, "the means serves both the end and the subject."⁴⁰

Whereas man's relationship to *things* is and must be of this kind, a problem arises when the object of one's actions is another *person*. Is it permissible to regard a person as a means to an end and to use a person in that capacity?

Wojtyła concludes that the very nature of personhood as already discussed—as a thinking and willing subject, capable of making decisions—means that a person must never be used *merely* as the means to an end for another person.⁴¹ This is not an arbitrary precept; it flows directly from man's nature. Wojtyła goes still further. "Anyone who treats a person as a means to an end does violence to the very essence of the other, to what constitutes its natural right."⁴² In other words, if the person deserves to be treated as an end-in-himself, he has a right to such treatment, and using the other person as a means violates this basic natural right.⁴³ Person-

---

38. All human actions are for an end (See *S. Th.* I-II, 1, 1). In all that he freely chooses, man pursues a known good, either as a value for himself or as an end in itself (see *S. Th.* I, 5, 1; I-II, 26, 4).

39. Wojtyła defines the verb "to use" as "to employ some object of action as a means to an end" (*Love and Responsibility*, 25). See also *S. Th.*, I-II, 16, 3.

40. Wojtyła, *Love and Responsibility*, 25.

41. St. Thomas offers the same fundamental distinction when speaking of the order of creation. Irrational creatures were created as means, to be used for the good of rational creatures, while the rational creature alone God treats as an end. The rational creature, by reason of its freedom, "requires that the care of providence should be bestowed on it for its own sake," whereas irrational creatures "are cared for, not for their own sake, but as being directed to other things." Thomas compares irrational creatures, the source of whose action is extrinsic to them, to "instruments" and observes that "an instrument is required, not for its own sake, but that the principal agent may use it." Thus, concludes Thomas, God "makes provision for the intellectual creature for its own sake, but for other creatures for the sake of the intellectual creature" (*CG*, bk. III, ch. 112).

42. *Love and Responsibility*, 27.

43. De Finance observes that "any attempt to treat a human being as if he were no more than a thing, to use him as a mere means or as an instrument, is contrary to right reason and is, as such, objectively evil and unjust" (*An Ethical Inquiry*, § 213, pp. 376–7). This also corresponds to what Aquinas adumbrates in his explanation of the effects of sin: "By sinning man

al dignity would demand that the human being always be treated as an end and never subordinated to another as a mere means. Wojtyła extends the prohibition of using persons even to the Creator. "Nobody can use a person as a means towards an end, no human being, nor yet God the Creator."[44] In the case of God, it would in fact be out of the question, since God Himself created man as a thinking and willing subject, thereby ordaining that each person choose for himself the ends of his activity.[45]

The Personalistic Principle

Wojtyła encapsulates this thought in a maxim that he alternately terms the "personalistic principle" or the "personalistic norm."[46] This principle, which springs from human dignity, furnishes the groundwork for personalistic ethics and for human rights. From his reflections on "using" and "loving," Wojtyła arrives at the conclusion that a person, unlike nonpersonal objects, may never be a mere instrument of action.[47] Wojtyła designates this truth an inherent component of the natural moral order, by which the natural order itself acquires personalistic attributes. Kant had already formulated this basic principle of the moral order as an impera-

---

departs from the order of reason, and consequently falls away from the dignity of his manhood, in so far as he is naturally free, and exists for himself, and he falls into the slavish state of the beasts, by being disposed of according as he is useful to others" (*S. Th.*, II-II, 64, 2, ad 3).

44. Wojtyła, *Love and Responsibility*, 27.

45. Wojtyła writes that God, by giving man an intelligent and free nature, "has thereby ordained that each man alone will decide for himself the ends of his activity, and not be a blind tool for someone else's ends. Therefore, if God intends to direct man towards certain goals, he allows him to begin with to know those goals, so that he may make them his own and strive towards them independently" (ibid.).

46. "And it is precisely from a pastoral point of view that, in *Love and Responsibility*, I formulated the concept of a *personalistic principle*. This principle is an attempt to translate the commandment of love into the language of philosophical ethics. *The person is a being for whom the only suitable dimension is love*. We are just to a person if we love him. This is as true for God as it is for man. Love for a person *excludes the possibility of treating him as an object of pleasure*. This is a principle of Kantian ethics and constitutes his so-called second imperative. This imperative, however, does not exhaust the entire content of the commandment of love. . . . It requires more; it requires the *affirmation of the person as a person*" (John Paul II, *Crossing the Threshold of Hope*, 200–1; emphasis in original).

47. This is a recurring theme in John Paul's Papal Magisterium. For example, in the apostolic exhortation *Christifideles Laici*, the Pope writes, "In virtue of a personal dignity, the human being is always a value as an individual, and as such demands being considered and treated as a person and never, on the contrary, considered and treated as an object to be used or as a means or as a thing" (37).

tive: Act always in such a way that the other person is an end and not merely the instrument of your action.⁴⁸ In the light of his preceding reflections on personhood, Wojtyła restates this personalistic principle: "Whenever a person is the object of your activity, remember that you may not treat that person as only the means to an end, as an instrument, but must allow for the fact that he or she, too, has, or at least should have, distinct personal ends." In this positive formulation, the personalistic principle not only excludes treating another person as a means, it "bids us show 'loving kindness,' and treat a person in a manner appropriate to his or her essential nature." Thus the personalistic principle is "the demand for the affirmation of the person."⁴⁹

Wojtyła considers three situations in which it would seem that this principle fails to hold, that is, where persons are appropriately treated as means: (1) the organization of labor in a factory; (2) the relationship between a commanding officer and his soldiers; and (3) the relationship between parents and children in a family. Doesn't an employer use a worker for his own ends? Doesn't a commanding officer use the soldiers under him to attain ends he himself has planned and often known only by him? And don't even parents in a sense regard their children as a means to ends of their own, since the children do not understand those ends or consciously strive for them?

Wojtyła responds that even in these cases, in order for the relationship to be morally correct, the person—worker, soldier, or child—must never be treated *merely* as a means for another. The very nature of personhood—what a person *is*—*precludes* treating a person merely as a means for another.⁵⁰ The adverb "merely" is essential to this principle, because

---

48. See Kant, *Grundlegung zur Metaphysik der Sitten* (BA 66–67), 61. Spaemann explains this as follows: "The question remains as to whether there is such a thing as a responsibility which every human being has simply through being human, a responsibility which all human beings have. There is also the question as to whether there are certain actions which deny this responsibility. Kant formulated this universal demand by saying that we should never act in such a way as to use ourselves or others merely as a means. It is possible to object that in fact we always need each other as means to certain ends, that the whole common life of humanity depends on this. But of course Kant was well aware of this. What he meant was that we should only ever use each other partially as means. We may indeed profit from the capacities and achievements of others, but at the same time we should remain aware of the fact that the other person is also an end-in-himself and also has the right to claim certain services from his fellow human beings" (*Basic Moral Concepts*, 55–56).

49. Wojtyła, *Love and Responsibility*, 28, 211, 290n4.

50. Wojtyła later enlarges this principle still further: "[A] human being cannot be solely or

clearly persons are often a means for other persons, such as in the above cases. Yet even here the person must be regarded first and foremost as a free and intelligent subject with his own ends and only secondarily as a means to the ends of another.

How does this personalistic principle square with traditional Christian doctrine? Doesn't Christianity teach that man is created not as an end in himself but for God? A prima facie juxtaposition of the personalist assertion with St. Augustine's teaching as expounded in *De Doctrina Christiana* reveals an apparent contradiction. Augustine poses the same question as Wojtyła and his answer is diametrically opposed to Wojtyła's. Like Wojtyła, Augustine distinguishes between use and enjoyment *(uti* and *frui)*. He reflects that "to enjoy a thing is to rest with satisfaction in it for its own sake. To use, on the other hand, is to employ whatever means are at one's disposal to obtain what one desires."[51] After considering that the things of the world must be used, not enjoyed, Augustine arrives at the case of man himself:

> And so it becomes an important question, whether men ought to enjoy, or to use, themselves, or to do both. For we are commanded to love one another: but it is a question of whether man is to be loved by man for his own sake, or for the sake of something else. If it is for his own sake, we enjoy him; if it is for the sake of something else, we use him. It seems to me, then, that he is to be used for the sake of something else. For if a thing is to be loved for its own sake, then in the enjoyment of it consists a happy life.... But a curse is pronounced on him who places his hope in man (Jer. 17:5).[52]

It would seem, then, that for Augustine man is not to be treated as an end but as a means to loving God, whereas in Wojtyła's view, it is the other way around. Does Wojtyła deliberately reject Augustine's conclusion? If not, how can these two opinions be reconciled? The key factor to be considered is what the two thinkers mean by the term "end." In the cited work, Augustine is considering man's final end. In other words, Augustine is asking if one man can constitute the final end for another man,

---

mainly an object to be used, for this reason, that the role of a blind tool or the means to an end determined by a different subject is contrary to the nature of a person" (*Love and Responsibility*, 28).

51. St. Augustine, *De Doctrina Christiana*, bk. I, ch. 4, no. 4, p. 523.
52. Ibid., bk. I, ch. 22, no. 20, p. 527.

thus allowing one to rest in another as his consummate good and satisfaction. Can a person treat another man as *his* end? The answer is no. Wojtyła, on the other hand, says that one must recognize in each other person a subject with his *own* ends (and whose final end is God), and therefore it is illicit to use another person merely as a means to one's own ends without taking into account that the other too has ends and is, as a self-determining subject, an end to himself.

In this vein, the 1983 declaration by the International Theological Commission provides a helpful clarification. In analyzing the Church's teaching on the dignity of the human person and human rights, the commission noted that in the Gospel "man appears not as an object and instrument to be used but as an intermediate end in himself, whose welfare both personal and ultimately as a being for God must be our aim."[53] The human person is, therefore, an *intermediate end in himself,* and also a *being for God,* his ultimate end.[54] In other words, man has a true and inviolable end in himself and must be treated as an end; on the other hand, one person cannot constitute the final end for another, or for himself, since man is made to find his total fulfillment in union with God.

John Paul himself addresses this point of possible misunderstanding in his 1994 *Letter to Families.* The Pope asks, "Does affirming man's ultimate destiny not conflict with the statement that God wills man for his own sake? If he has been created for divine life, can man truly exist for his own sake?" This is a critical question for modern man, who often understands freedom precisely as a total autonomy, even from the Creator. In responding, John Paul appeals to Augustine himself:

> St. Augustine provides us with the answer in his celebrated phrase: "Our heart is restless until it rests in you." This "restless heart" serves to point out that between the one finality and the other there is in fact no contradiction, but rather a relationship, a complementarity, a unity. By his very genealogy, the person created in the image and likeness of God exists for his own sake and reaches fulfillment precisely by sharing in God's life.[55]

---

53. International Theological Commission, "Propositions on the Dignity and Rights of the Human Person," in *International Theological Commission: Texts and Documents, 1969–1985,* ed. Michael Sharkey (San Francisco: Ignatius Press, 1989), 255.

54. And, as St. Thomas observes: "The proximate end does not exclude the ultimate end" (*S. Th.,* I, 65, 2, ad 2).

55. John Paul II, *Letter to Families,* 9.

Another way to approach this dilemma takes as its point of departure the expression that man is made "for the glory of God," a truth often misunderstood. One may easily imagine a great, egotistical deity, a divine despot who creates subjects to attend to his needs and pay him homage. If this were the case, God would clearly be "using" man, rather than loving him. In reality, the glory of God is the manifestation of His surpassing love and the outpouring of His goodness and mercy. In his 1996 *Holy Thursday Letter to Priests,* John Paul once again touches on this theme:

Gloria Dei vivens homo. These words of St. Irenaeus[56] profoundly link *the glory of God and man's self-realization.* . . . What does *vivens homo* mean? It means *man in the fullness of his truth:* man created by God in his image and likeness; man to whom God has entrusted the earth in order that he might have dominion over it; man marked by the rich variety of nature and grace; man freed from the slavery of sin and raised to the dignity of an adopted child of God.[57]

Since God willed man to be eternally happy in Him, it is in man's attainment of his own integral good that God Himself is glorified. When man turns away from God, God does not feel "cheated" out of homage that is due to Him. He wills man's return simply because He loves man and knows that man can never achieve his true and lasting good apart from Him.

The personalistic principle does not merely forbid using a person solely as a means to an end (which "does violence to the very essence of the other"). The personalistic principle "has a dual content: a positive content ('Thou shalt love!') and a negative content ('Thou shalt not use!')."[58] Once Wojtyła has excluded the ethical possibility of treating the human person as a mere means to an end, since that would be contrary to the nature of a person, he proceeds to explore the ethical alternative ("the only clear alternative")to such instrumentalization.[59] If man is made to be loved, then love not only constitutes the fundamental content of what is "due" to human dignity, it also mediates between dignity and particular human rights.

---

56. See St. Irenaeus, *Adversus Haereses,* IV, 20, 7; Sch. 100/2, 648–649.
57. John Paul II, *Holy Thursday Letter to Priests* (Rome: Libreria Editrice Vaticana, 1997), §§ 6–7, pp. 11–13.
58. Wojtyła, *Love and Responsibility,* 171.
59. Ibid., 28.

10. THE TWO LOVES

WOJTYŁA DIVIDES ALL FREE HUMAN ACTION into using (incorporating other realities into one's own ends) and loving (affirming others as an end in themselves). He furthermore defines love as treating others as an end and never as a mere means. The truth of these two claims is not immediately self-evident. If the psychological sciences have taught us anything, it is that human behavior is an extremely complex and knotty business. Can all transitive human action really be broken into use and love? Second, in the many definitions of love on the market, treating others as an end seldom appears. By "love" some mean passion, others friendship, and others romantic attachment, among many other possible definitions. C. S. Lewis famously wrote about "four loves" in a work by that title and none was of affirming others as an end in themselves.[1] Is Wojtyła's definition of love defensible? How do these claims stand up, for instance, to a Thomistic understanding of love and of human action?

In the *Summa Theologiae*, Aquinas treats of love first as a passion and second as a virtue (charity).[2] As a passion, the object of love is the good, and thus love—properly speaking—pertains to the concupiscible appetite (desire).[3] Just as the appetite exists on different levels (natural ap-

---

1. C. S. Lewis, *The Four Loves* (London: Harper Collins, 1960).
2. See *S. Th.*, I-II, 26–28; II-II, 23–46. Thomas defines charity as friendship with God (and love of neighbor for God's sake) and repeats his distinction between love of concupiscence and love of friendship, defining the virtue of charity as a love of the second type.
3. Thomas says that "good causes, in the appetitive power, a certain inclination, aptitude or connaturalness in respect of good: and this belongs to the passion of 'love'" (ibid., I-II, 23, 4). Love is a passion in the proper sense when we are speaking of the natural or sensitive appetites; it is called a passion in a broader sense of the term when referring to the will (see ibid., I-II, 26, 2).

petite, sensitive appetite, intellectual appetite), so there are different loves corresponding to these appetites (natural love, sensitive love, intellectual or rational love). In each case, love is the principal movement toward the end loved, though free will is operative only on the level of intellectual love, which is the movement of the intellectual appetite or will. The appetite is moved by the good, first as complacency (attraction), then as desire (movement toward), and finally by joy (resting in the good).[4]

In *Love and Responsibility,* Wojtyła follows this latter tripartite division, to wit: love as attraction *(amor complacentiae),* as desire *(amor concupiscentiae),* and as goodwill *(amor benevolentiae).*[5] These three elements correspond not to different types of love but to moments or dimensions of love. Wojtyła asserts that while the first two elements are indeed charac-

---

4. "Prima ergo immutatio appetitus ab appetibili vocatur amor, qui nihil est aliud quam complacentia appetibilis; et ex hac complacentia sequitur motus in appetibile, qui est desiderium; et ultimo quies, quae est gaudium" (ibid., I-II, 26, 2). Elsewhere Thomas distinguishes these three as separate passions. Love is the passion operated on the soul by a good, desire is produced by a good not yet possessed, and joy is produced in the soul by resting in a good obtained (see ibid., I-II, 23, 4).

5. See Wojtyła, *Love and Responsibility,* 74–84. This division roughly follows Thomas's distinction of love according to its presence or absence and kind. For instance, when speaking of the mutual indwelling caused by love, Thomas writes that "the object loved is said to be in the lover, inasmuch as it is in his affections, by a kind of complacency *(complacentiam):* causing him either to take pleasure in it, or in its good, when present; or, in the absence of the object loved, by his longing, to tend towards it with the love of concupiscence *(amorem concupiscentiae),* or towards the good that he wills to the beloved, with the love of friendship *(amorem amicitiae)*" *(S. Th.,* I-II, 28, 2). On attraction, Wojtyła states, for example, that it "is of the essence of love and in some sense is indeed love, although love is not merely attraction" *(Love and Responsibility,* 76). It should noted here that Wojtyła sees this attraction, or "liking," to go beyond the emotional reaction to a perceived good proper to the passions. He refers to the nature of attraction as "to be regarded as a good" (ibid., 74), and in its truest form, it has as its object not just particular values or qualities but "a person, and its source is the whole person" (ibid., 76). Since emotional-affective reactions may equally well further or hinder an attraction to a true good (see ibid., 77), they must be integrated with the truth about the person who is their object to ensure that love be genuine (see ibid., 78). Therefore, attraction to a person will always differ from attraction to a thing, since "the person, as an entity, and hence as a good, is different from all that is not a person" (ibid., 79).

Wojtyła asserts that desire "is of the essence of love" (Wojtyła, *Love and Responsibility,* 80). He adds, however, that there is a "profound difference" between love as desire *(amor concupiscentiae)* and desire itself *(concupiscentia)* (see ibid., 81), and this love is felt as a longing for the person as such: "I want you because you are a good for me" (ibid.). Desire must be integrated into true love so it may not dominate, since "it is that aspect of love in which attitudes close to the utilitarian can most easily find a home" (ibid., 82). Therefore, Wojtyła asserts that a love between man and woman "would be evil, or at least incomplete, if it went no farther than love as desire" (ibid., 83).

teristic of love, the third is most distinctive of true love, because without benevolence, love (for a person) is not love at all, but egoism.[6] Wojtyła argues that love as goodwill—the purest form of love—"is the same as selflessness in love: not 'I love you as a good' but 'I long for your good,' 'I long for that which is good for you.'"[7] All true love for persons, therefore, is necessarily benevolent, since goodwill "brings us as close to the 'pure essence' of love as it is possible to get."[8] This benevolent love equates to treating others as an end, never as a mere means.

Thomas asserts that there are essentially two types of love, the love of desire *(amor concupiscentiae)* and the love of friendship *(amor amicitiae)*.[9] Appropriating Aristotle's definition, Thomas states that "to love is to wish good to someone."[10] Therefore, he continues, "the movement of love has a twofold tendency: towards the good which a man wishes to someone (to himself or to another) and towards that to which he wishes some good."[11] The latter of these tendencies (love of friendship) Thomas denotes as "primary" and the former (love of desire) as "secondary," in that "that which is loved with the love of friendship is loved simply and for it-

---

6. See ibid., 83. The genuineness of love is determined by its appropriateness to the object loved. A person is to be loved in one way and things in another. To love persons as things (means) is to love falsely and to fall necessarily into egoism. At the same time, Wojtyła does not identify *amor complacentiae* and *amor concupiscentiae* with "using" and *amor benevolentiae* with "loving." The first two forms of love are aspects of true love and are brought to perfection when integrated with *amor benevolentiae*. Without this latter, the other two forms would easily degenerate into a utilitarian attitude. When lived well and informed by the personalistic principle, *amor complacentiae* and *amor concupiscentiae* are attraction toward and desire for the person as a person, as personal good distinct from all other goods, even when perceived as a good for the one who loves.

7. Ibid., 83. It is evident here how closely this description of love coincides with the personalistic principle. Love, to be true, must seek the good of the other as an end, for the sake of the beloved.

8. Ibid., 84.

9. See *S. Th.*, I-II, 26, 4. A little further along, Thomas writes: "Now love being twofold, viz. love of concupiscence and love of friendship; each of these arises from a kind of apprehension of the oneness of the thing loved with the lover. For when we love a thing, by desiring it, we apprehend it as belonging to our well-being. In like manner when a man loves another with the love of friendship, he wills good to him, just as he wills good to himself: wherefore he apprehends him as his other self, in so far, to wit, as he wills good to him as to himself" (ibid., I-II, 28, 1).

10. Aristotle, *Rhetoric*, ii, 4; *S. Th.*, I-II, 26, 4. Elsewhere Thomas repeats that "to love is, properly speaking, to will good to someone" (*Commentary on St. John*, vol. 1, trans. James A. Weisheipl and F. R. Larcher [Albany, N.Y.: Magi Books, 1980], ch. 3, lecture 3, 477).

11. *S. Th.*, I-II, 26, 4.

self; whereas that which is loved with the love of concupiscence, is loved, not simply and for itself, but for something else." Thomas ties this twofold manner of loving to the metaphysical foundation (object) of love, which is goodness. What is good *in itself* is loved simply and for itself, whereas that which is good *for another* is a relative good. Here once again, one perceives the essential difference between personal good and nonpersonal good. Nonpersonal good is good relative to another, as ordered to the person, whereas personal good is good in itself, for its own sake. Consequently, Thomas concludes, "the love with which a thing is loved, that it may have some good, is love simply; while the love, with which a thing is loved, that it may be another's good, is relative love."

The fundamental trait of the love of friendship is benevolence, or goodwill. Aquinas states that "not every love has the character of friendship, but that love which is together with benevolence, when, to wit, we love someone so as to wish good to him. If, however, we do not wish good to what we love, but wish its good for ourselves, (thus we are said to love wine, or a horse, or the like), it is love not of friendship, but of a kind of concupiscence."[12]

Thomas's separation of love into love of desire and love of friendship corresponds closely to Wojtyła's classification of using and loving. Since according to Thomas what is loved with a love of desire is loved "for something else," it is loved only insofar as it is useful (including here the use of pleasure) for that person, be it oneself or someone else. Man loves a *thing* (for himself or for another) only in a relative, instrumental way: for the profit or pleasure it affords him.[13] The thing loved is a *means* to the good of the one to whom it is directed and is, in fact, desirable only because of its instrumental value. Thus if wine goes sour, one will discard it because it has no value in and of itself (is not loved for its own sake) but only inasmuch as it affords pleasure to its owner. The person (friend), on the contrary, is loved for his own sake, as an end. Consequently, though he lose his instrumental utility (for example, if he is incapacitated), he is still loved, since he is loved not for his value to the lover but for himself.

---

12. Ibid., II-II, 23, 1. Aquinas further notes that "it would be absurd to speak of having friendship for wine or for a horse." Not only is the reciprocity proper to friendship impossible, but as we observed earlier, we cannot wish wine or a horse well for their own sake.

13. Thomas asserts that "in the love of concupiscence, the lover, properly speaking, loves himself, in willing the good that he desires" (*S. Th.*, I-II, 27, 3).

But what of Wojtyła's assertion that man necessarily deals with reality in one of these two ways, by use or by love? In Thomistic language, this would correspond to the affirmation that man always deals with reality out of love, whether love of desire or love of friendship. It would seem perhaps inaccurate to reduce all man's dealings with reality to love. Yet in a certain sense man does indeed always act out of love, of one sort or another, since he always acts in pursuit of some perceived good (or to avoid a perceived evil). Wherefore Thomas says that "every agent, whatever it be, does every action from love of some kind."[14] Thomas asserts that all activity is toward an end. Furthermore, "in each of these appetites, the name 'love' is given to the principle movement towards the end loved."[15] All movement toward the good, whether it takes its origin from the sensitive appetite (the passions)[16] or the intellectual appetite (the will), is a form of love, and thus man always tends toward the good. Now, he may pursue the good either for his own benefit or for the sake of the beloved. The first type of love, which Aquinas defines as a kind of concupiscence, corresponds closely to what Wojtyła refers to as "using," and the second type, the love of benevolence or friendship, is what Wojtyła calls "loving."[17]

These two forms of "loving" are different, since *amor complacentiae* and *amor concupiscentiae* are sufficient when loving things (and in this case are identified with "use"), yet when persons are loved in this way, this love is "evil or at least incomplete" without *amor benevolentiae*.[18] Here, "using" means that something is not chosen for *itself*, for *its own sake*, but

14. Ibid., I-II, 28, 6.
15. Ibid., I-II, 26, 1.
16. For this reason Thomas says that love is at the base of all the other passions, and "there is no other passion of the soul that does not presuppose love of some kind" (ibid., I-II, 27, 4).
17. Wojtyła distinguishes between two meanings of the word "use." The first refers to the straightforwardly utilitarian use of applying means to attain an end. A second sort of "use" refers to "enjoyment," where something is sought for its own sake and not for the purpose of obtaining something else, such as the contemplation of a sunset. Here, "its own sake" means that it is immediately valuable to the moral agent in and of itself as a source of pleasure or delight. While such a good is valued in and of itself, it is valued *for* the one who is acting. In essence, then, "use" as enjoyment represents "a particular variant of 'use' in its first meaning" (Wojtyła, *Love and Responsibility*, 33). When the object of one's enjoyment is a person, therefore, the same principles apply as in the first sort of use. Wojtyła asserts that the belief that the human being is a person "leads to the acceptance of the postulate that enjoyment must be subordinated to love. 'Use,' not only in the first, broader, and more objective, meaning, but also in the second, narrower, and more subjective meaning . . . can be raised to the level appropriate to an interpersonal relationship only by love" (ibid., 34).
18. Ibid., 83.

for the sake of obtaining something else or simply for the sake of the one who is acting. Loving things for oneself *(amor complacentiae* and *amor concupiscentiae)* and loving persons *not* for oneself, but for *their* sake *(amor benevolentiae)* are not the same thing. Although we use the same word, "love" *(amor),* the human activities or dispositions described are different.

Not all believe this difference is so fundamental. Germain Grisez, for instance, has written:

> Abstract as it may seem to call love a disposition toward a fulfilling good, we do use the word this way: People "love" steak and they "love" truth. Even more often we speak of loving people, ourselves and others. But the two things, loving something and loving somebody, are not separate; they are different aspects of the same thing. Thus to be disposed to a fulfilling good is to be disposed to the person fulfilled by that good. St. Thomas distinguishes between these two aspects of love, calling the disposition to that which is good "love of concupiscence" and the disposition to the person "love of friendship." This terminology misleads if it is mistaken to mean two different kinds of love—for example selfish love and love which is altruistic.[19]

When man pursues a perfective good, he seeks the end of his own fulfillment, toward which he—like all imperfect beings—naturally tends. In this context, the end for which the subject acts is the subject himself. This is morally correct and cannot be termed egotistical, rather "what is here in question is a natural structure, which is not in our power to alter and so cannot be in any way the measure of our moral worth."[20] Nonetheless, when taken by itself, such a love is unjust in the case of other persons.[21] Whereas all the rest of reality is ordered to man's perfection and is rightly incorporated into his quest for self-realization, other persons exist for their own sakes and must be loved in an essentially different way.[22]

In his critique of the "new natural law theory," Russell Hittinger takes

---

19. Grisez, *Christian Moral Principles,* 24.A.5, p. 575.
20. de Finance, *An Ethical Inquiry,* § 141, p. 235.
21. It is unjust precisely because it does not render the person his "due," which is to be treated as a "person," as an end in himself and not merely a means to another's fulfillment.
22. Thus whereas love of things as perfective goods of the self is not egoistic but correct, since created things serve this purpose, loving persons in this way (as mere objects of desire or as a means to one's perfection) is a false love. A false love, writes Wojtyła, "is one which is directed towards a specious good, or, most often, to a genuine good in a way which does not cor-

issue with Grisez's smoothing over differences between these two loves. "Grisez is correct in saying that, for Aquinas, the *amor concupiscentiae* is not necessarily morally bad, in the sense of being selfish. However, Aquinas *does* argue that the *amor concupiscentiae* is morally deficient if the object of one's love is a being of equal or greater ontological rank than oneself. To love another person, or God, in such a way that one principally loves one's own delight rather than the other for his or her own sake is morally deficient."[23]

Yet not only is loving another person solely as a means to one's personal flourishing morally deficient, it fundamentally thwarts the aim of the one who engages in it. True human flourishing is possible only when one goes beyond seeking goods for oneself and learns to make of oneself a gift. That is why the pursuit of basic human goods is by itself an insufficient program for human fulfillment. Within this framework there are shallower activities[24] (such as devoting oneself to "play" throughout life), but even humanly more valuable pursuits (such as science or medicine), when engaged in purely or principally for motives of self-fulfillment without true love, do not permit a person to reach full human stature.[25] Paradoxically, to reach integral human flourishing one must leave oneself aside, since love refuses to be a means toward anything, even so noble a goal as this. This is surely one sense of Christ's words: "For anyone who wants to save his life will lose it; but anyone who loses his life for my sake will find it" (see Matt. 16:25; Mark 8:35; Luke 9:24). Love *(amor benevolentiae)*, therefore, falls outside the framework of basic human goods, since it means pursuing the good of another and by its very nature it cannot be chosen as a means of personal fulfillment.

Hittinger expresses concern that Grisez's axiology, in not distinguishing sufficiently between different kinds of love corresponding to the differences between persons and things (either of which may be fulfilling in

---

respond to but is contrary to its nature. . . . It is not enough to love a person as a good for oneself, one must also, and above all, long for that person's good" (*Love and Responsibility*, 83).

23. Russell Hittinger, *A Critique of the New Natural Law Theory* (Notre Dame, Ind.: University of Notre Dame Press, 1987), 54.

24. In calling such activities "shallow," I do not wish to imply that they are immoral but only that they occupy a lower tier on a true hierarchy of human values and are less humanly fulfilling than other pursuits.

25. Thus Wojtyła can assert that "Freedom exists for the sake of love" (*Love and Responsibility*, 135). Since man's vocation is to love, when he does not reach the point of loving truly and disinterestedly, he remains essentially stunted in his moral life.

some respect or another), "thereby becomes one-dimensional, with the emphasis weighted toward goods characterized simply as one or another *bonum mihi*."[26] This danger lies at the level of intentionality when one conceives of the moral life principally in terms of self-fulfillment.

In the personalist framework, love for persons cannot be defined as a disposition toward a fulfilling good.[27] While friendship and benevolence do undoubtedly redound to the moral benefit of the one who practices them, they are not *sought* chiefly as self-perfecting goods.[28] One does not set out to "practice the virtue of friendship" but to love the other as a friend. The self-perfecting virtue of friendship *results from* loving the other principally for his own sake and not for one's own benefit. Finnis, a sharer in Grisez's theory of basic human goods, acknowledges this when he states that for A to be B's friend, "A must act (at least in substantial part) for the sake of B's well-being, and must value B's well-being for the sake of B. A must treat B's well-being as an aspect of his (A's) own well-being."[29]

Finally, a distinction should be made between friendship in the Aristotelian sense[30] and the habitual disposition to love all other persons for

---

26. Hittinger, *A Critique of the New Natural Law Theory*, 54.

27. On this note Hittinger makes an important point. For Aquinas, though either mode of love can be fulfilling in one way or another, "the issue is not merely the good as objectively fulfilling, but rather the morally appropriate kind of love with regard to various kinds of entities being loved. The appropriateness of love with regard to its objects sets the criteria for what is appropriately fulfilling, and, by nature, what is most fulfilling. In short, right reason requires attention not only to a good as it promises to fulfill the self, but also to the status of the beloved" (ibid.).

28. Gilbert Meilaender lodges a similar complaint with Alasdair MacIntyre's ethical framework. "In part the problem is that concern for others has from the outset been set within the context of one's own flourishing. Not, to be sure, as if one's own good constituted the reason for helping others. Still, for MacIntyre, moral action is set within a framework of self-realization. The teleological starting point requires it. In making others' good my good, I flourish—I realize my nature as a human being" ("Still Waiting for Benedict," *First Things* 96 [October 1999], 54).

29. Finnis, *Natural Law and Natural Rights*, 142–43.

30. "In the fullest sense of 'friendship', A is the friend of B when (i) A acts (or is willing to act) for B's well-being, for the sake of B, while (ii) B acts (or is willing to act) for A's well-being, for the sake of A, (iii) each of them knows of the other's activity and willingness and of the other's knowledge, and (iv) each of them co-ordinates (at least some of) his activity with the activity (including acts of friendship) of the other so that there is a sharing, community, mutuality, and reciprocity not only of knowledge but also of activity (and thus, normally, of enjoyment and satisfaction). And when we say that A and B act 'for the sake of each other,' we mean that the concern of each for the other is founded, not in devotion to some principle according to

their own sakes, as described by Wojtyła *(amor benevolentiae).*³¹ At least three differences can be noted. First, while justice requires that every person be treated as an end, it would be nonsensical to assert that justice requires friendship with every person. Aquinas states that "neither does well-wishing suffice for friendship, for a certain mutual love is requisite, since friendship is between friend and friend."³² Justice clearly cannot require this aspect of mutuality, since it lies outside the free choice of the moral agent. One can choose to be friendly toward others, but one cannot guarantee that they will respond in kind; or, in Gospel terms, in loving one's enemies one does not thus become their friend.³³

Second, the habitual loving disposition toward all persons proper to *amor benevolentiae* precludes another essential aspect of Aristotelian friendship, namely that one's "feeling of goodwill must be known to its object."³⁴ In order for there to be reciprocal affection, both parties must be aware of the other's regard. Wojtyła posits a need to love even when knowledge of the other and, a fortiori, affection for the other, is impossible, and when the other has no knowledge of being so loved. For Wojtyła, it is enough to know that the other is, in fact, a person.

A third difference between Wojtyła's *amor benevolentiae* and friendship

---

which the other (as member of a class picked out by that principle) is entitled to concern, but in regard or affection for that individual person as such" (ibid., 142).

31. Though Thomas uses the term "amor amicitiae," he states that the defining characteristic of such love is benevolence. Furthermore, Thomas carefully points out that love is not divided into friendship and concupiscence but *love of* friendship and *love of* concupiscence (see *S. Th.,* I-II, 27, 4, *ad* 1). Wojtyła prefers the term "amor benevolentiae," which eschews the problem of attributing all the characteristics of friendship to the love of persons.

32. *S. Th.,* II-II, 23, 1. Aristotle likewise asserts that "persons who wish another good for his own sake, if the feeling is not reciprocated, are merely said to feel goodwill for him: only when mutual is such goodwill termed friendship" (*Nichomachean Ethics,* VIII, 1155b32–34).

33. Aquinas addresses the need for reciprocity in love of friendship when considering whether charity can be characterized as love of friendship. The objection reads: "Further, there is no friendship without return of love (Ethic. VIII, 2). But charity extends even to one's enemies, according to Matt. 5:44: 'Love your enemies.' Therefore charity is not friendship" (*S. Th.,* II-II, 23, 1, *ob.* 2). To this Aquinas replies, "Friendship extends to a person in two ways: first in respect of himself, and in this way friendship never extends but to one's friends: secondly, it extends to someone in respect of another, as, when a man has friendship for a certain person, for his sake he loves all belonging to him, be they children, servants, or connected with him in any way. Indeed so much do we love our friends, that for their sake we love all who belong to them, even if they hurt or hate us; so that, in this way, the friendship of charity extends even to our enemies, whom we love out of charity in relation to God, to Whom the friendship of charity is chiefly directed" (ibid., II-II, 23, 1, ad 2).

34. Aristotle, *Nichomachean Ethics,* VIII, 1155b34–35.

in the Aristotelian sense is the dimension of shared, or common, activity. Aristotle posits shared activity as an essential characteristic of friendship, but such activity is impossible except with a limited number of persons, unless one broadens the definition of activity to include the common activity of human existence itself.

Despite these essential differences, the universal love proposed by Wojtyła and Aristotelian friendship share a common core: a certain disinterestedness or *benevolentia*.[35] This *amor benevolentiae* is a naturally disinterested love, by the very fact that it affirms the other not as a means but as an end, a good in himself. "An act of love, as an act of affirmation of the person to whom it is directed, is in respect for that person's dignity of its very nature a disinterested act."[36] In the light of the Aristotelian tripartite relational model (relationships of utility, relationships of pleasure, true friendship),[37] Wojtyła would affirm that *all* of these relationships must develop in the presence of an enduring disposition to seek the good of the other as an end. For Wojtyła, a relationship of pure utility or of pleasure lacking the underlying disposition of disinterested love is an immoral relationship.

THE COMMON GOOD

How is such a love possible, if man naturally acts for his own good? How can human love be truly disinterested? It would indeed be impossible if a man were alone in the world surrounded only by "things," which one can only desire for one's own sake. Disinterestedness is possible only through the discovery of other persons as other selves, made not for one's sake but for their own sake. When the other is discovered as a good in himself, a good to be prized not for his usefulness but for his own sake, a whole new horizon of human activity opens up. Man is able to desire the good of the other for the other's sake, and thus the good of the other becomes his own good. This good is no longer exclusive to the moral agent but becomes a shared good, a common good. As an effect, such disinter-

---

35. Aristotle distinguishes among different forms of friendship with their characteristic marks and locates in the first place the definition of a friend as "one who wishes, and promotes by action, the real or apparent good of another for that other's sake" (ibid., IX, 1166a3–4).

36. Wojtyła, *Love and Responsibility*, 305n55. See also Wojtyła, "The Personal Structure of Self-Determination," 194.

37. Aristotle, *Nichomachean Ethics*, VIII, 1156a5–1156b33.

ested love is perfective of the moral agent, but it is perfective by the very fact of its disinterestedness and thus cannot be chosen for the sake of its perfective value, but for the good of the other.[38]

The love Wojtyła refers to is a bond produced between two people when they consciously choose a common aim.[39] Then they are no longer merely two individuals who seek the same good, they are two individuals united by the bond of a *common good*. This bond, according to Wojtyła, "constitutes the essential core around which any love must grow."[40] The common good sought by both persons places them on a footing of equality and precludes the subordination of one to the other. The formation of this bond entails the passage from "I" to "we" as a necessary component of love. Thus charity necessarily gives rise to communion.[41] Recognizing each human person as my neighbor and my brother or sister allows me to speak of "us" in reference to all persons united in a single family with a common origin and destiny. Here, too, one catches a foretaste of Pope John Paul II's later insistence on the social principle of solidarity. "Man's capacity for love depends on his willingness consciously to seek a good together with others, and to subordinate himself to that good for the sake of others, or to others for the sake of that good."[42]

Returning to his prior examples of apparently instrumental human relationships (employer/employee, officer/soldier, parent/child), Wojtyła shows that, though the utilitarian attitude is always a danger, it can be avoided by emphasizing the joint pursuit of a common good. This common good unites the persons in a bond of love and eliminates the possibility of subordinating one person to the other. Employers must therefore be attuned to the good of employees, officers to that of the soldiers under their command, and parents to the needs of their children.

---

38. Man is an imperfect being, and even in his disinterested love he seeks his own perfection, that is, he simultaneously seeks his own good and the good of the other. Paradoxically, however, the more he is able to love without seeking himself or his own good, the more that action perfects him.

39. Later Wojtyła remarks that there may be more than two people tied to a common end. Since he treats here specifically the love between a man and a woman, he uses the number two.

40. Wojtyła, *Love and Responsibility*, 28.

41. Caffarra, *Living in Christ*, 224.

42. "In and through charity, in fact, the person enters into a deep spiritual communion with his neighbor, a communion that brings him to want the other in and for himself and to internalize the other's desire to exist fully according to the truth of his vocation" (Wojtyła, *Love and Responsibility*, 29).

A case in point, and one to which Pope John Paul II has devoted extensive attention, is the relationship between labor and management. In his encyclical letter *Laborem Exercens,* he dedicates a chapter to "The Personalist Argument," emphasizing the absolute priority of labor over capital. To prevent the possibility that the worker should be "used" as a mere instrument of production, management must recognize him as a "subject of work," with his own ends. "When man works . . . he wishes to be able to take part in the work process as a sharer in responsibility and creativity at the workbench to which he applies himself."[43] Thus "the person who works desires not only due remuneration for his work; he also wishes that, within the production process, provision be made for him to know that in his work . . . he is working 'for himself.'" John Paul refers to these provisions as "specific rights of workers," which spring from the personalist argument.

Expanding this argument to all human relations, the content of the *common good* is identified not with any particular project but with the good of the person as such. Wojtyła frames this responsibility to safeguard the good of the person in absolute terms, affirming that "everyone must always, with all possible consciousness and with a feeling of total responsibility, make his concern that basic good for each of us and for all of us together which is, quite simply, 'humanity,' or if you like, the assertion of the value of the human person."[44] As Wojtyła widens the scope of the common good, universalizing it to extend to all human persons, the link between the personalistic principle and the question of human rights (as the affirmation of specific human goods) becomes clearer.[45]

Yet this understanding of the nature of benevolent love as a transfer of good is not specific to Christianity; it is an observable phenomenon of any true human love. Aristotle, in his *Nichomachean Ethics,* writes that

> when men wish the good of those they love for their own sakes, their goodwill depends not on emotion but on a fixed disposition. And in loving their friend they love their own good, for the good man in becoming dear to another be-

---

43. *LE,* 15. Along this same line, Maritain wrote fifteen years earlier, "What is involved in all this is the sense of the dignity of work, . . . the feeling for the rights of the human person in the worker, the rights in the name of which the worker stands before his employer in a relationship of justice and as an adult person, not as a child or as a servant" (*The Rights of Man,* 53).

44. Wojtyła, *Love and Responsibility,* 31.

45. In his 1994 *Letter to Families,* Pope John Paul elaborates still further on this theme. He asserts that *"the common good of the whole of society dwells in man."* And shortly thereafter,

comes that other's good. Each party therefore both loves his own good and also makes an equivalent return by wishing the other's good.⁴⁶

At the same time, such benevolent love requires a certain disinterestedness in the intention of the moral agent. Once the person is loved merely for the good of the moral agent, rather than for his own sake, love is vitiated and slides into concupiscence.

How does this understanding of the common good square with the definition of the same principle in Catholic social teaching? Strictly speaking, a common good is a good held in common. Catholic social teaching, on the other hand, speaks of the common good as a set of conditions that permit persons to reach their integral fulfillment. The *Catechism* states that the "common good of society consists in the sum total of those conditions of social life which enable men to achieve a fuller measure of perfection with greater ease."⁴⁷ As applied to society as a whole, then, the good sought for all and held in common is a just and peaceful social order that offers conditions necessary for members of the community to flourish. Efforts to achieve an environment conducive to human flourishing entail an understanding of the nature of this flourishing. In other words, one cannot work for conditions that "enable men to achieve a fuller measure of perfection with greater ease" unless one has a prior notion of human perfection. A skewed vision of human perfective good gives rises to a reductive view of the common good.

In this regard, the German philosopher Josef Pieper reflects on the need to overcome a modern tendency to conceive the *bonum commune* as the sum total of society's *material* production, a conception that springs from a technical mindset that believes that everything can be manufactured. For Pieper, the primary meaning of the *bonum commune* refers to "the good," as the essence of all the different goods that together form a community's reason for existing and that a commonwealth would have to achieve in order to realize its full potential. For Pieper, then, to "render to each and all their due" means "to make sure that the individual members of the population are given the opportunity to add their contribution to

---

"*Man is a common good:* a good of the family and of humanity, of individual groups and of different communities" (11; emphasis in original).

46. Aristotle, *Nichomachean Ethics*, VIII, 1157b32–36.

47. *CCC,* 1906. See also *DH,* 6; *MM,* May 15, 1961, in *AAS* 53 (1961): 417; *PT,* April 11, 1963, in *AAS* 55 (1963): 273.

the realization of the *bonum commune*. . . . This points to a further aspect: the 'good of a commonwealth' includes the inborn human talents, qualities and potentials, and part of the *iustitia distributiva* is the obligation to protect, preserve and foster these capacities."[48]

Critics of rights theories often cite as a flaw the abandonment of the common good in favor of the good of the individual. Behind these criticisms one often discerns an understanding of the common good as somehow fundamentally separate from the notion of individual good. It is true that the common good is contrary to *individualism* and to *egotism*, but it is not contrary to the true good of the individual. From the personalistic viewpoint, and indeed from the traditional Christian viewpoint, this radical separation does not exist. Because the person tends to communion with other, those goods he shares with others form an essential part of his own good. John Finnis rightly notes that

> the common good is fundamentally the good of individuals (an aspect of whose good is friendship in community). The common good, which is the object of all justice and which all reasonable life in community must respect and favour, is not to be confused with the common stock, or the common enterprise, that are among the means of realizing the common good. . . . talk about benefitting "the community" is no more than a shorthand (not without dangers) for benefitting the members of that community.[49]

The common good must in fact be assimilated as a true good for each member of society, or it will cease to be a "common good" and will become rather a "foreign good," a burden, the dues individuals are expected to pay in order to access the benefits of the commonwealth. Keys observes that "the common good is not an alien good but the 'proper good' *(bonum proprium)* of those who share in it. . . . The good sought by any being is necessarily its own good *(bonum suum)*, whether it be a particular good or the common good, for which it has an even greater natural love."[50] Hence there is no intrinsic antagonism between rights (which are ethical restatements of personal good) and the common good, since the

---

48. Josef Pieper, "The 'Common Good' and What It Means," in *Josef Pieper: An Anthology*, trans. Lothar Krauth (San Francisco: Ignatius Press, 1989), 66.

49. Finnis, *Natural Law and Natural Rights*, 168.

50. Mary M. Keys, "Personal Dignity and the Common Good: A Twentieth-Century Thomistic Dialogue," in *Catholicism, Liberalism, and Communitarianism: The Catholic Intellectual Tradition and the Moral Foundations of Democracy*, ed. Kenneth L. Grasso, Gerard V. Bradley, and Robert P. Hunt (Lanham, Md.: Rowman & Littlefield, 1995), 179.

latter is intimately related to the former. Personal good necessarily comprises the common good, just as there can be no common good without the personal goods that make it up.

Nor is the common good an annihilation or absorption of the individual person. Since man—every man—was made for communion as part of his intimate structure, to speak of the common good is to speak of the good of persons, not the good of an abstract collectivity or state.[51] Consequently, when it is said that the person is a "part" of society, this does not mean that he is subordinated to society. In fact, "the human being is a 'part' of society in the sense that his or her fulfillment requires participating in or partaking of goods that transcend the purely private sphere of individuality. The person is not 'part' of the community as the hand is part of the body, nor even . . . as discovering his or her identity in a collective subjectivity, the only true repository of moral agency."[52] It is precisely the irreducibility of the human being as person that excludes the possibility of being merely a part of anything, since such a relationship entails the subordination of the part to the whole. Thus though the person is *ordered* to society, he also stands *prior* to it.

The harmony that exists between individual good and common good is best understood by considering the anthropological principles developed earlier in the light of Thomistic personalism. Unlike other creatures, man is essentially social and made for interrelationship.[53] The divine observation that "it is not good for man to be alone" (Gen. 2:18) summarizes the anthropological truth that man is ordered to society with other men. Not only does man naturally tend to society, his personal good is intimately bound up with it. As Rommen observes:

Sociality is just as constitutive of the essential nature of man as is his rationality. Sociality, indeed, so pertains to man that a definition which omits this constitu-

---

51. In speaking of the limits of public authority over the physical being of citizens, Pope Pius XII distinguished between a physical organism, which "has a unity subsisting in itself," and whose members have no sense or finality outside the whole organism, and the moral community, which "is not a physical unity subsisting in itself and its individual members are not integral parts of it" (*Address to the First International Congress of Histopathology of the Nervous System,* September 14, 1952, in *AAS* 14 [1952]: 786–87).

52. Keys, "Personal Dignity and the Common Good," 179.

53. In this regard, Thomas Dubay notes: "A cabbage needs no companions to be a perfect cabbage, but men desperately require all sorts of other people if they are to achieve their aims in life: parents, siblings, friends, teachers, writers, musicians" (*The Evidential Power of Beauty: Science and Theology Meet* [San Francisco: Ignatius Press, 1999], 19).

tive element must be considered incomplete. It is therefore nothing superadded; it is equally original. The individual person and the community are ontologically so related to each other that they can have no existence independently of each other. Even though the individual person may always have a genuine self-subsistence and hence a unique kind of being, he has at the same time a limited existence that does not yet perfectly realize the idea of man. For man is perfected only in the community.[54]

Yet man is not ordered only to society and to interaction with his fellows. He is ordered very specifically to love and to communion. Man is made for love: to give it and receive it.[55] The commandment to love, therefore, far from being an "unnatural" prescription, confirms by divine mandate man's greatest good and ultimate realization as a creature made to love and be loved. When a person loves, he not only acts justly by giving the other his due, he also fulfills himself as a creature whose perfection is wrapped up in love. Herein lies the logic of the Council in saying that man is in fact "the only creature on earth which God willed for itself" and at the same time he cannot "fully find himself except through a sincere gift of himself."[56] Therefore, these two aspects—self-affirmation and the sincere gift of self—"not only do not exclude each other, they mutually confirm and complete each other. *Man affirms himself most completely by giving of himself.*"[57]

Selfishness—the quest for one's individual good even at the expense of the good of others—will always be a temptation for man. Dedication to the common good requires sacrifice; "enlightened self-interest"—in this case the certainty that one's happiness lies in pursuing the common good—is insufficient. By bridling selfish individualism and making oneself a gift for others, man truly finds himself. He must be brought to realize that by

> partaking in the common good, and indeed building it together with others on the practical planes of family, intermediate association and politics, the person achieves his end, i.e. attains perfection and finds happiness. Paradoxical as it may

---

54. Heinrich A. Rommen, *The Natural Law: A Study in Legal and Social History and Philosophy*, trans. Thomas R. Hanley (Indianapolis: Liberty Fund, 1998), 209–10.

55. "Man cannot live without love. He remains a being that is incomprehensible for himself, his life is senseless, if love is not revealed to him, if he does not encounter love, if he does not experience it and make it his own, if he does not participate intimately in it" (*RH*, 10).

56. *GS*, 24.

57. John Paul II, *Crossing the Threshold of Hope*, 202–3; emphasis in original.

seem, it is by subordinating private goods to serve and partake of the common good that man achieves his truest and most complete *personal good.*[58]

In a sense, then, the inherent tension between *amor concupiscentiae* and *amor benevolentiae,* or between "using" for one's own good and "loving" the other for his own sake, is not fully resolvable when the object of one's action is a person. All persons are "called," interiorly impelled by their rational nature, to reach their own personal fulfillment; yet that personal fulfillment necessarily involves sincerely putting oneself at the service of other persons' fulfillment. In other words, these two types of love are not mutually exclusive, and both are legitimately present in interpersonal relations as long as benevolent love takes precedence. This benevolent love purifies and sublimates the love of desire so that one desires the other not as a mere object for one's gratification but precisely as a person. To search for an "integral human flourishing" without recognizing the essential and central place of benevolent love in such a search can only lead to failure. Nevertheless, the bipartite division of personal action into using and loving stands: persons treat reality either as objects to be subordinated to one's own pursuits or as objects to be loved and respected as acting subjects themselves, even though that respect also contributes to one's own fulfillment.

58. Keys, "Personal Dignity and the Common Good," 178–79; emphasis in original.

11. FROM LOVE TO HUMAN RIGHTS

THE FOREGOING EXPOSITION, especially as regards Wojtyła's personalistic principle, offers the elements needed to determine the fundamental content of the "special regard" to which human persons are entitled by reason of their dignity. Human dignity gives rise to a primordial right from which other rights flow.[1] Each and every human being is to be treated as a person, that is, loved as an end and never merely used as a means. In this sense, love—to be treated as an acting subject with a transcendental purpose and never as a mere means—constitutes the content of the regard due to human dignity. The fundamental right, the "Ur-right," of the human person is the right to be loved.

Christians are accustomed to hearing that love is at the heart of morality. To love God and neighbor is, after all, Jesus' summary of the moral law. It forms the essence of his teaching and of the Gospel message itself. Yet man's duty to love does not issue arbitrarily from God's commandment; God commands it because man's personal nature demands it. Love is the only ethical option when dealing with persons. This bold assertion requires justification. Is love the "new commandment" or a requirement of natural law? Or are two different sorts of love in play?

JUSTIFYING THE GREAT COMMANDMENT

In *Love and Responsibility*, Karol Wojtyła makes an audacious proposal. He puts forward the personalistic principle as a *justification* for the New Testament commandment to love persons—God and others.[2] So, while

---

[1]. "Moreover, does not the spiritual subject possess a dignity . . . which immediately demands that it be respected? Does it not constitute a radical and innate 'right'?" (de Finance, *An Ethical Inquiry*, § 203, p. 358).

[2]. "The personalist norm does, as we have seen, provide a justification for the New Testa-

the commandment to love "does not put in so many words the principle on the basis of which love between persons is to be practised," such a basis is implicitly contained in the command.[3] Thus "if the commandment to love, and the love which is the object of this commandment, are to have any meaning,[4] we must find a basis for them. . . . This can only be the personalist principle and the personalist norm."[5] Wojtyła here posits a necessary link between the personalistic principle and the commandment to love. He later wrote that essentially the personalistic principle "is an attempt to translate the commandment of love into the language of philosophical ethics" and that, conversely, the command to love is "an embodiment of the personalistic norm."[6] The commandment to love, therefore, while not identical with the personalistic principle or norm, "derives from this norm," and the norm in turn provides "an appropriate foundation for the commandment to love."[7] The command becomes an imperative restatement of the foundation, since "the commandment says: 'Love persons,' and the personalistic norm says: 'A person is an entity of a sort to which the only proper and adequate way to relate is love.'" In other words, the personalistic norm makes a statement about the human person that necessarily gives rise to an imperative in dealing with human beings.

The idea of "justifying" the commandment to love would seem to imply that this commandment, like the Decalogue,[8] forms a part of natural law and is therefore comprehensible by human reason. Biblical revelation of the commandment to love would thus remind and confirm, but not unveil as something otherwise unknowable, how man is to treat his fel-

---

ment commandment" (Wojtyła, *Love and Responsibility*, 41). Here Wojtyła refers explicitly to the commandment to love God and neighbor. When asked which of the commandments is the greatest, Jesus replied, "'You shall love the Lord your God with all your heart, and with all your soul, and with all your mind.' This is the greatest and first commandment. And the second is like it: 'You shall love your neighbor as yourself.' On these two commandments hang all the law and the prophets" (Matt 22:37–40; Mark 12:29–31; Luke 10:27–28). These two commandments are taken from the Old Testament injunctions found in Deut. 6:5 and Lev. 19:18, and thus can be distinguished from Jesus' "new commandment" (John 13:34), where Jesus adds the phrase "as I have loved you."

3. Ibid., 40.

4. Wojtyła obviously does not mean to impugn the authority of the Gospel as sufficient basis for the meaning and force of the commandment to love but rather seeks to discover the anthropological foundation for the love that is commanded.

5. Wojtyła, *Love and Responsibility*, 41.

6. John Paul II, *Crossing the Threshold of Hope*, 200–1; Wojtyła, *Love and Responsibility*, 213.

7. Wojtyła, *Love and Responsibility*, 41.

8. "The Decalogue contains a privileged expression of the natural law" (*CCC*, 2070).

lows.⁹ Love, Joseph Ratzinger has written, "is not an arbitrary choice; love is the substance of being: love and truth. . . . [Therefore] being itself has a moral content, and the commandments translate the language of being and of nature into human language."¹⁰

The assertion that being has a moral content forms the indispensable basis for any affirmation of the natural law. God has written meaning into creation, a meaning that is accessible to man's reason. Love, for Ratzinger as well as Wojtyła, is the fundamental discovery of moral reason in relation with other persons and thus *the fundamental content of justice*. The commandment to love, says Wojtyła, "defines and recommends a certain way of relating to God and to people, a certain attitude towards them."¹¹ This attitude and way of dealing with others, in turn, "is in agreement with what the person is, with the value which the person represents, and therefore it is fair." To be fair with reality means to treat all things according to the nature of their being, and in the case of persons love is the only fair attitude.

LOVE AND JUSTICE

Any attempt to "justify" the commandment to love places love within the scope of natural law and thereby leads to further questions, chiefly regarding the relationship between justice and love. By the very fact of offering a justification of the commandment to love, one implicitly locates love within the realm of justice.¹² It therefore becomes just to love and unjust not to love. Wojtyła has written that:

to be just always means giving others what is rightly due to them. A person's rightful due is to be treated as an object of love, not as an object for use. In a

---

9. Actually, Wojtyła carefully attenuates this deduction, speaking of the personalistic principle as the "natural content" of the commandment to love. "The commandment to love, as it occurs in the Gospels, is more than the 'personalistic norm,' it also embodies the basic law of the whole supernatural order, of the supernatural relationship between God and man. Nevertheless, the personalistic norm is most certainly inherent in it—it is the 'natural' content of the commandment to love, that part of it which we can equally well understand without faith and by reason alone" (Wojtyła, *Love and Responsibility*, 213).

10. Joseph Ratzinger, *Journey towards Easter*, trans. Dame Mary Groves (Slough, England: St. Paul Publications, 1987), 40.

11. Wojtyła, *Love and Responsibility*, 42.

12. Wojtyła states that "the basis of this norm (which enjoins on us the love of the person) is justice" (ibid., 246).

sense it can be said that love is a requirement of justice, just as using a person as a means to an end would conflict with justice. In fact the order of justice is more fundamental than the order of love—and in a sense the first embraces the second inasmuch as love can be a requirement of justice.[13]

According to the personalistic principle, the only adequate relation and attitude toward the person is love. Hence love, as what is rightly due *(ius)*, is a requirement of justice. Persons, in a sense, have a right to be loved.[14] Anything short of love is injustice, because it offers less than what is "rightfully due." For Wojtyła, there are only two ways to deal with an object: use (means) and love (end). Whatever is not love must be use and, in the case of persons, is therefore unjust.[15]

Such an assertion would seem to coincide with a familiar text from St. Paul: "Pay to all what is due them—taxes to whom taxes are due, revenue to whom revenue is due, respect to whom respect is due, honor to whom honor is due. Owe no one anything, except to love one another; for the one who loves another has fulfilled the law" (Rom. 13:7–10). Paul lays down the traditional understanding of justice as rendering to all their due. In this context of strict justice he advises Christians to stay out of debt, except the inescapable debt of love, which is due to all. He seems to place love as a universal duty from which no one is exempted. This same thought is neatly summed up by Wojtyła: "Man's duty is to love."[16]

Can such an affirmation stand up to rigorous analysis? Can love truly be a requirement of justice? Is it not a reduction of love to make it a right?

Wojtyła does not, in fact, reduce love to justice or make love a subset of justice. While justice is more "fundamental" (i.e., more basic, foundational) than love, it does not entirely encompass love. Wojtyła speaks, rather, of the "interpenetration of love and justice in the personalistic

---

13. Ibid., 42.

14. De Finance, on the contrary, argues that "one cannot speak of a right to be loved; this would be to detract from the generosity and gratuitousness that are proper to love" (*An Ethical Inquiry*, § 203, pp. 358–59). Yet de Finance would readily admit that we have a duty to love, since we are commanded by Christ to do so. How is it that acting in obedience to a commandment entails greater "spontaneity and gratuitousness" than loving a person because he deserves to be loved?

15. As we have seen, in saying that the person is always to be treated as an end does not mean that the person becomes the final end of the agent ("my end"), since the person's final end is God alone, but rather is recognized as having his own ends.

16. Wojtyła, *Love and Responsibility*, 160.

norm."[17] Seen in this light, justice and love form two complementary and closely united principles.[18] In comparing and contrasting justice and love, Wojtyła adopts a stance consonant with the Biblical understanding of justice and love. In Scripture, as Pinckaers points out, "justice has none of the impersonal, juridical, and legal overtones we associate with it today." Far from being a cold minimalism at odds with love, justice "runs as deep as love, since the first two commandments, love of God and love of neighbor, are at its origin and source. Justice and love form one unique entity: justice emphasizes the righteousness of love, while love stresses the profound spontaneity that attracts people to one another. Seen in this light, justice becomes the supreme moral quality in Scripture, as wisdom is for the Greeks."[19]

How can this paradox be explained? How can love be a requirement of justice and yet surpass justice? If justice encompasses love, how is it that justice alone is not sufficient?[20] The dilemma may be resolved by assigning to justice a self-transcendent, self-surpassing quality. Spaemann hints at justice's self-transcendence when he writes: "Dealing justly with people and with reality goes beyond mere justice."[21] Yet how can justice go beyond justice? A further distinction is needed.

Justice and love, while closely related and interdependent, operate at distinct levels. Justice, Wojtyła writes, concerns itself with things (material or moral goods) in relation to persons, while love is concerned directly and immediately with persons.[22] Justice deals specifically with particular goods as relating (belonging, or being due) to another person, whereas love affirms the good of the person as such. Thus justice renders "what is

---

17. Ibid., 43.
18. The Congregation for the Doctrine of the Faith affirmed the same in confronting the issue of Christian liberation. "There is no gap between love of neighbour and desire for justice. To contrast the two is to distort both love and justice. Indeed, the meaning of mercy completes the meaning of justice by preventing justice from shutting itself up within the circle of revenge" (*Instruction on Christian Freedom and Liberation* [March 22, 1986], 57).
19. Pinckaers, *The Sources of Christian Ethics*, 36.
20. In his encyclical letter *Dives in Misericordia* John Paul II returns to this point of the insufficiency of justice. He writes: "The experience of the past and of our own time demonstrates that justice alone is not enough, that it can even lead to the negation and destruction of itself, if that deeper power, which is love, is not allowed to shape human life in its various dimensions" (12).
21. Spaemann, *Basic Moral Concepts*, 47.
22. Thus St. Thomas writes that "justice is about certain external operations. . . . These

due" to the person, while love affirms the person himself. On the other hand, evidently there can be no love (affirmation of the person himself) without justice (affirmation of those goods that contribute to the person's fulfillment). Justice is necessarily included in love. Wojtyła writes:

> At the same time love—if we are to consider its very essence—is something beyond and above justice; the essence of love is simply different from the essence of justice. Justice concerns itself with things (material goods or moral goods, as for instance one's good name) in relation to persons, and hence with persons rather indirectly, whereas love is concerned with persons directly and immediately: affirmation of the value of the person as such is of its essence. Although we can correctly say that whoever loves a person is for that very reason just to that person,[23] it would be quite untrue to assert that love for a person consists merely in being just.[24]

The dynamic relationship between justice and love, however, is irreducible to the mere distinction between their objects (things vs. people). Justice draws interpersonal relationships into the realm of love, since persons deserve not only the things that help them reach fulfillment (justice) but also the affirmation of their personhood (love). But then love in turn lifts interpersonal relationships above the strict demands of justice. In other words, justice reveals that the person deserves love, and love in turn elevates the interpersonal discourse beyond the question "What is due to this person?" to ask "What is the highest good for this person?" Justice could never claim, for instance, that a person "deserves" mercy, but love often insists that mercy would indeed be "good" for him. In this way, then, true justice transcends itself and blossoms into love, much as the soil transcends its inanimate nature by drawing into itself and nourishing the seed of a flower.

---

consist in the use of certain externals, whether things, persons or even works: of things, as when one man takes from or restores to another that which is his; of persons, as when a man does an injury to the very person of another, for instance by striking or insulting him, or even by showing respect for him; and of works, as when one man justly exacts the work of another, or does a work for him" (*S. Th.*, II-II, 61, 3).

23. Aristotle states that "if men are friends, there is no need of justice between them; whereas merely to be just is not enough—a feeling of friendship is also necessary. Indeed the highest form of justice seems to have an element of friendly feeling in it" (Aristotle, *Nichomachean Ethics*, VIII, 1155a27–30).

24. Wojtyła, *Love and Responsibility*, 42.

Justice toward God

The interplay between justice and love manifests itself in a preeminent way in man's relationship with God. The supreme personal being, from whom both personhood and being proceed, is God Himself. If love is the right of all persons by reason of their personhood, it is eminently the right of the Creator. Thus not only love for man but also—and especially—love for God is based on justice. "We are just to a person if we love him," writes Wojtyła, and this is "as true for God as it is for man."[25] Furthermore, in agreement with Aquinas, Wojtyła states that true religion "consists in justice towards God so understood, or as St. Thomas puts it, the virtue of religion constitutes *pars potentialis justitiae*."[26] In other words, God deserves our love; it is a requirement of justice:

> To be just means rendering to another person all that rightly belongs to that person. God is the Creator, the unfailing source of the existence of every creature. . . . This being so, the rights of the Creator over the creature are very extensive: it is entirely the property of the Creator, for even beings who have themselves "created" depend upon existence: if the creature did not exist its own creative activity would be impossible. If a man considers all the implications of this for justice to the Creator he must reach the following conclusion: if I want to be completely just to God the Creator, I must offer him all that is in me, my whole being, for he has the first claim on all of it.[27]

Nonetheless, the love-justice paradox reveals itself again. Though religion is indeed a "potential part" of the virtue of justice, justice alone is insufficient in dealing with God to an even greater degree than it is insufficient in dealing with other human beings. Indeed, a "relationship with God, a religion, based on justice alone, is of necessity incomplete and flawed, since the relationship of man to God is in principle one in which justice cannot be done."[28] No matter what man gives to God, it will always be infinitely inadequate. Man cannot surrender all he has to God, imagining that by so doing he has paid his debt in full. Not only is man's gift always insufficient, God is not interested principally in those "things"

---

25. John Paul II, *Crossing the Threshold of Hope*, 200–1.
26. Wojtyła, *Love and Responsibility*, 246.
27. Ibid., 249–50.
28. Ibid., 250.

that man can render Him, since heaven and earth and all they contain are His. Rather, He desires man's heart, his freely given love. Thus man must surrender to God not his property but his very *self*, and this self-giving is rooted not only in justice but in love.[29] And this is where the paradox grows more complicated still. Love is not satisfied with merely receiving or giving what is "due" but necessarily seeks union with the beloved.[30] Thus religion as taught by Christ "makes straight the way from person to person, and from man to God (without evading the problem of a debtor's obligation to pay his debt)."[31] In other words, while including the demands of justice, true religion surpasses it, since "love raises man's relations with God to a higher level than mere justice could. Justice is not at all concerned with the unification of persons, whereas love aims precisely at this."

On the one hand love is a requirement of justice, and on the other hand that justice in and of itself is insufficient as a foundation for religion. This paradox can be better understood in the light of the second half of the commandment to love.

Self-Love as the Measure of Love for Others

Jesus was asked which of the commandments was the greatest. His answer was not one but two commandments. After he had replied that loving God with all one's self constitutes the supreme commandment, he immediately added a complementary precept. These two precepts are so closely bound together that one cannot truly fulfill the first without fulfilling the second.[32] The second is "like the first": Love your neighbor as

---

29. "If a man should leave his home, still, it is little, and if having left all things he should surrender to love, then he begins to understand what love is worth" (Marciel Maciel, *Salterio de mis días* [Rome: Ediciones CES, 1991], Psalm IV, § 2, p. 32; author's translation). "What more do I require of you, than that you try to fully submit yourself to me? Whatsoever you give Me outside of yourself does not interest me; for I do not seek your gift, but I seek you. As it would not suffice you if you had all things except me, so neither can it please me, whatever you give, if you do not give yourself to Me" (Thomas à Kempis, *The Imitation of Christ*, trans. the Daughters of St. Paul [Boston: St. Paul Editions, 1983], bk. IV, ch. 8, p. 394).

30. As St. Thomas observes, citing Dionysius: "It belongs to love to seek union" (*CG*, bk. I, ch. 91). See also *S. Th.*, I-II, 28, 1.

31. Wojtyła, *Love and Responsibility*, 250.

32. Thus St. John declares: "Those who say, 'I love God,' and hate their brothers or sisters, are liars; for those who do not love a brother or sister whom they have seen, cannot love God

you love yourself. As has often been noted, Jesus places these two commandments at the heart of the entire moral order, as its summit and consummation: "On these two commandments hang all the law and the prophets" (Matt. 22:40).

This second great commandment in turn has two parts. We are not only obliged to love our neighbor, we are to do so in a certain way. When Jesus enjoins his followers to love one another, he chooses self-love as the standard of measure: "Love your neighbor *as you love yourself*" (Matt. 19:19; Matt. 22:39; Mark 12:31; Luke 10:27; see also Lev. 19:18; Rom. 13:9; Gal. 5:14; James 2:8). This comparison—"as you love yourself"—is often assumed to be a measure of the intensity, degree, or magnitude of love. Seen in this way, the "second great commandment" could be restated as "Love your neighbor *as much as* you love yourself."[33] A better interpretation, however, and one more in accord with Christian personalism, does not take the comparative "as" quantitatively, to signify "as much as," but rather qualitatively: "in the same way as." Thus reformulated, the precept would read: "Love your neighbor *in the same way as* you love yourself." Here earlier distinctions between different *sorts* or *modes* of love prove useful once again. Though one may honestly love pizza or a pet iguana, one may not love these nonpersons in the same way as one love persons. Nor may one love his neighbor the way he loves pizza. This is not a question of intensity of love, but rather of *kind*.

But why would Christ use "oneself" as the point of reference for personal love? By nature, humans cannot love themselves except as persons, that is, as an *end*, as someone with a transcendent good as his inherent purpose. Since man naturally seeks his own transcendent good, he is structurally unable to instrumentalize himself the way he could be tempted to instrumentalize others. While he may be drawn to subordinate others to his own ends, he will never subordinate himself to others' ends (unless he identifies their ends as a good for himself). He cannot view himself as a means to something else; he necessarily relates to himself as a being with an inherent, transcendent purpose.

Thomas Aquinas offers a similar analysis of Christ's commandment to

---

whom they have not seen. The commandment we have from him is this: those who love God must love their brothers and sisters also" (1 John 4:20–21).

33. Spaemann, for instance, interprets Christ's saying as follows: "'Love your neighbour as yourself' does not mean 'Love him as something more important than anything else,' but that

love others as oneself.[34] Man must love his neighbor in like manner to himself in three ways, designated by the adjectives "holy," "righteous," and "true." If man loves his neighbor for God's sake, his love will be "holy." If he loves his neighbor by willing for him only truly good things, his love will be "righteous." Finally, his love for his neighbor will be "true" if he loves him not for personal profit or pleasure but for his neighbor's good. It is the latter characteristic, "truth" in love, that is underscored by personalism.

Moreover, this third characteristic most truly captures the meaning of Christ's words, since Christ is holding up for imitation a natural model of love. Metaphors and similes are devices used to illuminate what is unknown by means of something known. In making such a comparison, Christ presents a "known" (how we necessarily love ourselves) to illustrate an "unknown" (how we should love others). In order for such a pedagogical device to work, the known must be universal or natural. Man's love for himself is not naturally "holy," since he does not necessarily love himself for God's sake. It is often not even "righteous," since he frequently pursues merely apparent goods for himself and for others[35] and must constantly be on guard to ensure that his aims correspond to his authentic good. On the other hand, man naturally loves himself "truly"—for his own sake, in order to propel himself to the achievement of his own transcendent purpose—and cannot do otherwise. This is the most distinctive trait of a person's natural love for himself.

In the light of this reasoning, the suitability of the personalistic principle as a basis for Christ's commandment to love neighbor as oneself be-

---

when it comes to willing the good, you should make no difference between yourself and your neighbour" (*Basic Moral Concepts*, 71).

34. "The mode of love is indicated in the words 'as thyself.' This does not mean that a man must love his neighbor equally as himself, but in like manner as himself, and this in three ways. First, as regards the end, namely, that he should love his neighbor for God's sake, even as he loves himself for God's sake, so that his love for his neighbor is a 'holy' love. Secondly, as regards the rule of love, namely, that a man should not give way to his neighbor in evil, but only in good things, even as he ought to gratify his will in good things alone, so that his love for his neighbor may be a 'righteous' love. Thirdly, as regards the reason for loving, namely, that a man should love his neighbor, not for his own profit, or pleasure, but in the sense of wishing his neighbor well, even as he wishes himself well, so that his love for his neighbor may be a 'true' love: since when a man loves his neighbor for his own profit or pleasure, he does not love his neighbor truly, but loves himself" (*S. Th.*, II-II, 44, 7, *resp.*).

35. See, for example, *S. Th.*, I-II, 8, 1; II-II, 23, 7.

comes abundantly clear. Loving others as oneself excludes the possibility of "using" others as means, requiring that they be loved for their own sake.

FROM ONE RIGHT TO MANY

The essential content of human dignity as the right to be loved as an end and never merely used as a means must somehow be reflected in more specific ethical considerations, since persons fulfill themselves gradually in the context of changing circumstances and needs. If personal dignity is to ground concrete human rights, such as the right to life or religious freedom, it must pass from the general right to be loved to specific rights to concrete human goods. What is the relationship between these two levels?

Love Means Affirming Good and Goods

Love, which Wojtyła defines as "an ambition to ensure the true good of another person," means affirming not only the *good* of the person as such but also affirming the particular *goods* of the person.[36] Since man is a composite being, made up of body and soul, his "good" is not simple and indivisible—it comprises a bundle of elements, all of which must be promoted for there to be true promotion of the person himself. Therefore, love, in order to be true, must be just; that is, it must extend to willing for the person those goods that lead to his perfection or integral fulfillment.[37] If the human person has a right to be loved, to have the fulfillment of his being affirmed, he likewise has a right to those particular goods whose promotion forms the content of love. Thus in asserting that the person must not be an object to be used but only an object of love, one is led to conclude, with Wojtyła, that "the personalistic norm lays down the rights of the person."[38]

In other words, the personalistic concept of love, in its affirmation of

---

36. Wojtyła, *Love and Responsibility,* 272. "Willed love expresses itself above all in the desire of what is good for the beloved person" (ibid., 136–37).

37. Love that affirms the general value of the person, but neglects those particular goods that the person needs, is unjust. "It is precisely here that the main task is the elaboration of a concept of love which is just to the person, or if you like a love prepared to concede to each human being that which he or she can rightfully claim by virtue of being a person" (ibid., 43).

38. Ibid., 245.

the value of the person as such, is prepared to grant the person such "things" *(suum)* as are ordered to the good of the person. This consideration casts still more light on the relationship between justice and love. The first step of justice—the recognition of the presence of a person who deserves respect—already contains the seeds of love, since affirming that the person deserves something implicitly affirms that his existence itself is worthwhile.[39] In this sense, justice presupposes a rudimentary kind of love as its underlying force, an affirmation of the *existence* of a person, a being with a distinct, human dignity. This naturally opens into a more mature love, that will affirm the *value* of that existence, that it is good for that person to exist. It is precisely this "ambition to ensure the true good of another person" that impels one to grant the other his due. To affirm the value of the other is to will the integral good, that is, the perfection of the other. For its part, perfection is linked to the nature and end of the person. Thus love means willing the perfection of the person according to his nature and end, by means of those particular perfective goods that are conducive to this end. The affirmation of the value of the person, which is love, therefore implies a disposition to grant a person his rights, those things that are necessary for his integral fulfillment as a human being. That is why these basic human rights are said to be inalienable, in that they necessarily belong to the human person, and inviolable, since their violation would be incompatible with an attitude of love.[40]

Love, if it is true, cannot remain at the level of a vague sentiment of benevolence. It must be ready to express itself in acts.[41] *Benevolentia* must manifest itself in *beneficentia*.[42] Love, consequently, is more than emo-

---

39. John Paul relates St. Augustine's reflection: "Does love bring about the keeping of the commandments, or does the keeping of the commandments bring about love?" with the corresponding reply: "But who can doubt that love comes first? For the one who does not love has no reason for keeping the commandments" (St. Augustine, *In Ioannis Evangelium Tractatus*, 82, 3: CCL 36, 533; cited in John Paul II, *VS*, 22).

40. Thus Spaemann writes that "there are certain actions which are, regardless of the circumstances, bad, at all times and in all places, because by their very nature they deny the quality of a person as an end-in-him- or -herself, that is to say, they deny a person's dignity. With such actions there is no more room for calculating consequences" (*Basic Moral Concepts,* 56).

41. "If a brother or sister is naked and lacks daily food, and one of you says to them, 'Go in peace; keep warm and eat your fill,' and yet you do not supply their bodily needs, what is the good of that?" (James 2:15–16). "How does God's love abide in anyone who has the world's goods and sees a brother or sister in need and yet refuses help? Little children, let us love, not in word or speech, but in truth and action" (1 John 3:17–18).

42. "The sort of love we are talking about here is not the same as sympathy. . . . Love is

tional goodwill, the affective desire for the person to "be well" or flourish.[43] It entails an objective affirmation of those *true* goods that are perfective of the person according to his nature and vocation.[44] Wojtyła has written:

> It is, of course, not enough just to *want* to affirm the other person for the consequent act (of goodwill) to become also an act of love. It is necessary in addition for the action undertaken with the intention of affirming another person to be objectively suited to the role which the agent's intention assigns to it. Whether it is or is not suitable is decided by the objective structure of the person affected by the action. Only success in understanding the other person and allowing when acting for that person's specific traits ensures that the act will be recognizable as a genuine act of love. An imperfect understanding of the structure of the object person must, in consequence, become the source of (inadvertent and hence involuntary) action to the detriment of that person.[45]

At the same time, such active willing of good things for another requires knowledge of the good. Without knowledge of the objective, intelligible good of the other, and hence of his "objective structure," love either remains at the level of a feeling of goodwill devoid of content or, worse still, expresses itself through random gestures unrelated to the person's true good. It may of course be expressed subjectively, in terms such as "I wish the best for you" or "I hope you attain whatever it is you seek," but it cannot be transferred to any universal framework with effective expression. In fact, even an expression of love such as "I hope you attain whatever it is you seek" implies a notion of the good—in this case that

---

more like goodwill, willing that others should come to have whatever is good for them" (Spaemann, *Basic Moral Concepts*, 47). "The personalistic norm relates in the first place to the attitude of the subject *(benevolentia)*: the subject must take steps to ensure the good of the other person, its objects, and is certainly not free to subordinate the other entirely to its own ends. In putting this postulate into practice *(beneficentia)* we cannot affirm the object in any way without assuring for that person pre-moral goods which are not in themselves moral goods (life, health, etc.), which have value to the extent that they serve the person" (Wojtyła, *Love and Responsibility*, 307n61).

43. "Now the will carries into effect if possible, the things it wills, so that, consequently, the result of an act of love is that a man is beneficent to his friend" (*S. Th.*, II-II, 31, 1).

44. "To recognize the human person as such means to recognize him as the inviolable subject of rights, that is, as a subject possessing faculties sanctioned not only (and not principally) by human conventions dictated by utilitarian expedience, but by moral norms, and thus ultimately by creative wisdom itself. This is the recognition that goods—every good necessary for integral growth—are inviolably ordered to the human person" (Caffarra, *Living in Christ*, 215).

45. Wojtyła, *Love and Responsibility*, 292n11.

what is good is for each person to attain what he seeks. This relationship between love and knowledge of human good has far-reaching consequences for rights theory. If no good can be posited of man as man, then the quality of universality can never be predicated of any right. Natural rights must have as their content true particular goods of the person.

A notion of love as willing particular, temporal goods to one's neighbor may give rise to other theoretical difficulties. Christians readily understand how love means willing eternal salvation to one's neighbor. If there exists a hierarchy of goods for man, love will seek the highest good for another, the same way it seeks the highest good for self. But what of temporal, and hence relative, goods? These do not infallibly lead to man's greatest, eternal good. How then can there be absolute rights to relative goods?

Furthermore, if eternal salvation is the only thing that really matters in the end, why should a Christian devote time and energy to satisfying his neighbor's material needs? Everything pales in relation to this one eternal good. It was Jesus himself, after all, who rhetorically asked what it profits a man to gain the whole world and lose his soul. Love means desiring what is best for the other. From a spiritual viewpoint, what is best does not always coincide with what is most pleasant. As Ernest Fortin has written, "if the poor are really closer to God, I suppose one should think twice before robbing them of their poverty."[46] If abnegation, poverty, and destitution win God's favor and assistance, will relieving these needs really be in our neighbor's best interest? Contrariwise, securing for our neighbor all he needs to live a satisfying life from a purely temporal perspective, while failing to lead him to God, could be likened to fattening him up for hell. Surely the witch's offerings of sugared adornments from her gingerbread house were no act of charity toward Hansel and Gretel.

The answer to this objection is threefold. In the first place, though the human person is made for God and only in Him attains his true, everlasting good, this does not mean that God, his *summum bonum* and *finis ultimus*, is his *only* good *(bonum unicum)*. In the case of the human person, teleology implies a hierarchy of ends and of goods, but even the intermediate goods are true goods. Willing the good of the person as such means willing his integral good, which comprises all particular goods and not just his final good.

46. Fortin, "The Trouble with Catholic Social Thought," 309.

Second, though on certain occasions particular goods may act to hinder a person's moral or spiritual life, these goods are not obstacles in themselves—they become obstacles only through misuse. In reality, any partial good can become an obstacle to man's greatest good, because any good can be treated as man's final good, as an "idol." It is impossible to know with certainty when a particular good may pose an obstacle to a person's ultimate good. If I save a person's life, will he subsequently become a saint or a great sinner? If this child receives an education, will she grow proud and self-sufficient and turn her back on God? The answer does not fall within the scope of human knowledge. Even if it did, however, it would not affect the person's rights. The person is a free subject, and the task of a Christian is not to force people into heaven but to assist them in their free conformity to God's will and free cooperation with His saving grace. Whereas love prohibits willingly placing obstacles in another's path, it enjoins providing him with basic goods, which in turn he may use for good or for evil. Moreover, natural rights have as their matter what is most basic to a person's integral human good (life, education, religion, employment, etc.); natural rights do not imply the necessity of an abundance, wherein most often lies the more serious impediments to spiritual growth. The right to food does not mean a right to mountains of chocolate any more than the right to shelter means a right to a Beverly Hills mansion.

A third response reflects a more properly personalistic approach. If man's greatest good is friendship with God, love will desire this above all things for one's neighbor. The greatest good for man, and in fact the only true and lasting good, is to achieve salvation through faith and love.[47] Love must therefore will this above all other things for all persons. But how does a person come to faith and love? How does a person achieve the freedom to make of himself a gift and by so doing discover who he is?[48] The only way he can do this is by first having experienced unconditional love, God's fatherly, providential love, in his own life. Only when a person has experienced the love of God can he begin to love, since human

---

47. Jesus graphically presents the relativity of temporal goods to eternal life: "If your right eye causes you to sin, tear it out and throw it away; it is better for you to lose one of your members than for your whole body to be thrown into hell. And if your right hand causes you to sin, cut it off and throw it away; it is better for you to lose one of your members than for your whole body to go into hell" (Matt. 5:29–30).

48. See *GS*, 24.

love has its origins in a response to God's love.[49] Yet he must be able to perceive this love naturally. In other words, it must be manifested *in a way readily accessible to him*. God's love can be revealed in a variety of ways, but preaching the love of God to another while denying him basic human goods would hardly be convincing. Rather, to reveal God's love, one must "witness" to his love by helping others to see God's loving hand in their lives and in the world. By promoting the temporal well-being of neighbor, one also witnesses to the provident love of God and thereby assists his neighbor in turning to God, his greatest good.

A Hierarchy of Goods and Hence of Rights

The foregoing reflections only hint at an answer to how a relative good can ground an absolute right. Of course, not all rights are absolute, nor do they all bear the same moral weight. Rights, like the goods they protect, are ordered according to a hierarchy.[50]

The commandment to love is absolute, so anything incompatible with love is absolutely prohibited. At the same time, it does not follow that all rights are absolute. Since love is open-ended (in the positive sense, one can always do more for neighbor and love him more perfectly), there are clearly many expressions of love that cannot be mandated, only openly indicated as an ideal. The more closely a particular good is bound up with a person's integral human fulfillment, the more stringent is the right that "protects" such a good.[51] Other goods, which may contribute to a person's integral perfection but are in no way necessary to his fundamental good, carry a lesser moral obligation.[52] A "hierarchy" exists among human rights, such that some are fundamental, and therefore absolute, and

---

49. "We love because he first loved us" (1 John 4:19).

50. In chapter 2 this idea of a hierarchy among rights was discussed in the context of "absolute" vs. "relative" rights. These present reflections build on earlier considerations in the light of personalism's unique contribution.

51. "The necessity of a particular good in relation to this actualization destines this good to the human person: it is what is absolutely and unconditionally *owed* him by every other person" (Caffarra, *Living in Christ,* 220).

52. Jean Porter writes, "The more basic such an inclination is, the more stringent the claims that it generates, over against both the community as a whole and other members of that community, presumably because one who is frustrated in pursuing one of the more basic inclinations will have much less, or no, opportunity to pursue the more distinctively human inclinations" (*The Recovery of Virtue: The Relevance of Aquinas for Christian Ethics* [Louisville: Westminster/John Knox Press, 1990], 136).

others are more collateral, conditioned by particular circumstances. In this regard Wojtyła has written:

> The way in which goods other than moral goods are bound up with the good of the person reveals to us a hierarchy of goods, which is constant to the extent that human nature is constant. Effective affirmation of the object-person demands, on the part of the subject, conscientious effort to determine the relative importance of the pre-moral goods involved in any situation. Respect for goods which are vitally bound up with the good and the development of the person is a test which shows how far the attitude of the subject is really one of love.[53]

The International Theological Commission addressed the question of the hierarchy among human rights in its 1983 document on the subject. The commission outlines a three-tiered division among rights according to their relationship to the dignity of the person. Of the first tier, the commission notes: "Certain rights are so 'fundamental' that they can never be gainsaid without belittling the dignity of human persons."[54] This level comprises rights that can never be put aside, such as the inherent right to life, the dignity of the physical person, the fundamental equality of persons, freedom of conscience and religion. The rights of this first level can be termed "inviolable" or "inalienable," which expresses their quality of absoluteness.

On the second tier are found "other rights of a lesser nature but also basically essential." These include civil, political, economic, social, and cultural rights concerned with more particular situations. Many times such rights will appear as "contingent consequences of fundamental rights," and thus in concrete circumstances could be likewise inviolable. In other situations, the commission suggests, these basically essential rights "may present themselves as less immune, especially in difficult circumstances."[55]

On the third tier are "other human rights that are not requisites of the rights of nations or strictly obligatory norms but postulates of an ideal of progress toward a universal 'humanization.'"[56] Though not "inviolable," these true rights point to the integral human fulfillment of human per-

---

53. Wojtyła, *Love and Responsibility,* 307n61.
54. International Theological Commission, "Propositions on the Dignity and Rights of the Human Person," 252.
55. Ibid.
56. Ibid.

sons and thus constitute a requirement of love, though subject in practice to particular circumstances and realities. Though the commission offers no specific examples of such rights, one infers that they represent access to human goods that are not strictly necessary to the fulfillment of the person but would be desirable. For example, some cultural or artistic goods to which only a few have access could well form part of a category of an ideal of progress toward a universal humanization. As such goods become more and more accessible to all, they could well pass into the second category of rights.

Returning to the question of how a relative good—such as human life, which is necessarily temporal—can be the matter of an absolute right, the answer lies once again in the dignity of the human person. The subject of rights is the human person, with a spiritual as well as a corporal dimension. A sharp distinction cannot be drawn between temporal "goods for the body" and eternal "goods for the soul" without falling into Cartesian dualism. A good for the body, like a good for the soul, is a good for the human person. The person's enduring spiritual nature endows certain rights with an absolute character. Thus there can be absolute rights to relative goods because the right is ordained not to the good first, but to the person. The primordial right to be loved is absolute and inviolable, and all the rights that spring from it derive their degree of obligation from their importance to love. And since love affirms the good of the person, the more closely a particular good is tied to the good of the person as such, the more binding the right that protects it.

Love and the Commandments

A final matter of inquiry concerns the relationship between rights and the Decalogue. Natural rights are concrete expressions of the general right to be loved, as manifested in the personalistic principle. All of the Ten Commandments are concrete expressions of the specific commandments to love God and to love one's neighbor as oneself. Thus a parallel exists between the personalistic principle and rights, on the one hand, and the commandment to love and the Ten Commandments, on the other. The personalistic principle, which proclaims the person's right to be loved, gives rise to a series of rights corresponding to particular human goods. The great commandment to love one's neighbor as oneself similarly gives rise to and sums up the commandments of the Decalogue, which in turn protect human goods.[57] The personalistic principle and rights refer to the human person as the *object* of action, whereas the commandment to love and the Decalogue address the human person as *subject* of action. The personalistic principle (embodying "dignity") and specific human rights proclaim the moral right of persons to general and particular goods, while the commandment to love and the Decalogue mandate love of the person as such and respect for his particular goods.[58] From different angles, both the commandments and human rights proclaim the good of the person.[59] Consequently, the personalistic analysis that Wojtyła conducts with the commandment to love could likewise be conducted with the Ten Commandments, especially the so-called second tablet of the law dealing with other human persons.[60] As the commandment to love finds its justification in the dignity (general good) of the human person, so the different precepts of the Decalogue find their justification in the particular goods of the person. This correlation can be displayed graphically as in Diagram A.

Rights, like the precepts of the Decalogue, provide a minimum level of just treatment of neighbor. They lay out what is prohibited in relation to others, but in so doing, they also reveal the underlying good of the other to be defended and promoted. The precepts of the Decalogue, which receive their authority from the dignity of the human person confirmed by God's revelation, offer a minimum rule that safeguards the rights of other persons but also points to a richer, positive affirmation of the human person.[61] As Pope John Paul II has written:

---

57. St. Paul asserts that "the one who loves another has fulfilled the law. The commandments, 'You shall not commit adultery; You shall not murder; You shall not steal; You shall not covet'; and any other commandment, are summed up in this word, 'Love your neighbor as yourself.' Love does no wrong to a neighbor; therefore, love is the fulfilling of the law" (Rom. 13:7–10). "For the whole law is summed up in a single commandment, 'You shall love your neighbor as yourself'" (Gal. 5:14).

58. "The Ten Commandments ... teach us the true humanity of man. They bring to light the essential duties, and therefore, indirectly, the fundamental rights inherent in the nature of the human person" (*CCC*, 2070).

59. "The rightness of action is always intelligibly related to human good, indeed to the good of particular individuals or groups of individual persons. The upright heart, the will, the choice, is always a choice, will, heart which does and pursues that good and avoids what harms that good" (Finnis, *Moral Absolutes*, 11).

60. Thus each precept of the Decalogue could be reformulated as a specific personalist norm. "Thou shalt not kill" would become "The person is the sort of being whose life must be protected and defended."

61. "Jesus shows that the commandments must not be understood as a minimum limit not

DIAGRAM A

Person	General good	→	Specific goods
As OBJECT *of action*	Personalistic principle (right to be loved)	→	Human rights (rights to particular goods)
As SUBJECT *of action*	Commandment to love	→	Commandments of the Decalogue

The different commandments of the Decalogue are really only so many reflections of the one commandment about the good of the person, at the level of the many different goods which characterize his identity as a spiritual and bodily being in relationship with God, with his neighbor and with the material world. . . . The commandments . . . are meant to safeguard the good of the person, the image of God, by protecting his goods. "You shall not murder; You shall not commit adultery; You shall not steal; You shall not bear false witness" are moral rules formulated in terms of prohibitions. These negative precepts express with particular force the ever urgent need to protect human life, the communion of persons in marriage, private property, truthfulness and people's good name.[62]

Based on natural law and comprehensible to human reason, the commandments forbid actions that violate fundamental human goods.[63] They apply the commandment to love to specific human goods as instantiations of the general good of the person himself. In this way the com-

---

to be gone beyond, but rather as a path involving a moral and spiritual journey towards perfection, at the heart of which is love (cf. Col 3:14). Thus the commandment 'You shall not murder' becomes a call to an attentive love which protects and promotes the life of one's neighbor. The precept prohibiting adultery becomes an invitation to a pure way of looking at others, capable of respecting the spousal meaning of the body" (*VS*, 15).

62. Ibid., 13.

63. "The link between the Decalogue and human fulfillment is no mere construction of early theologians. It is intrinsic. . . . Each of the precepts of the second table of the Decalogue protects some aspects of human persons in some fundamental aspect of their individual reality" (Finnis, *Moral Absolutes*, 10).

mandments manifest the natural order of love, as directed to the person himself and to the various aspects of personal good that contribute to his integral perfection.[64] This natural order of love in turn provides a guide for all human activity, as the Council teaches.[65] From the standpoint of Thomistic personalism, the commandments rule out actions that do not respect the dignity of the person, that is, actions that do not treat the person as an end in himself—as someone propelled from within toward a transcendent purpose—but rather as a mere means.[66] In this way they indicate the path of love by pointing out specific goods to be protected and by excluding actions that cannot be reconciled with an attitude of love.[67]

Expressed as moral imperatives, the commandments embody both duties and rights. The commandment "Thou shalt not kill [a person]" could variously be restated as "It is not right to kill a person" or "The person has a right not to be killed" without doing violence to the commandment's intrinsic meaning. Only the form and point of reference change. Thus just as the commandment to love one's neighbor as oneself reveals the implicit dignity of the human person and his intrinsic "lovableness," so the specifications of the commandment to love, such as the injunctions of the second tablet of the Decalogue, reveal particulars of that dignity—which are natural human rights.

Love, then, as the primordial "Ur-right" of every human person, gives rise to other, more specific human rights, ordered in a hierarchy based on the requirements of human nature. The mutually clarifying relationship

---

64. "The Ten Commandments are thus the fundamental requirements of charity: they express its necessary order. And they therefore correspond to the two fundamental precepts of charity, being divided into two tablets or parts: the requirements of charity toward God and the requirement of charity toward man (oneself and others)" (Caffarra, *Living in Christ*, 209–10).

65. "The norm of human activity is this: that in accord with the divine plan and will, it should harmonize with the genuine good of humankind, and allow men as individuals and members of society to pursue and fulfill their integral vocation" (*GS*, 35).

66. "There are some actions which always harm human dignity and which always violate the person as an end-in-himself. These actions cannot be justified by appeal to any so-called higher or more comprehensive duties.... It follows quite obviously from this that the direct and intentional killing of another human being, torture, rape or the exploitation of sexuality as a means to certain ends is always bad. Also it is not possible to justify lying to a person who has placed his full trust in us" (Spaemann, *Basic Moral Concepts*, 75).

67. "The precepts protecting fundamental aspects of human personal good are guides to human choice; they guide by excluding options inconsistent with love of the very person whom the logic of our choosing makes our nearest neighbor" (Finnis, *Moral Absolutes*, 11).

of the personalistic principle and the commandment to love reveals how Christ's commandment coheres with the demands of human nature. In a sense, therefore, just as the classical tradition places the content of the Ten Commandments within the realm of the natural law, the personalistic vision also helps confirm and consolidate what man can naturally glean about the requirements of interpersonal relations. Christ's commandment to love does more than confirm reason's conclusions, however; it reveals the lovableness of every human person, even where such lovableness would not be immediately evident. In this way Christian revelation provides a precious and irreplaceable resource for understanding the deeper theological grounding of human dignity. This grounding will round out and complete Thomistic personalism's contribution to a theory of natural rights.

12. CHRIST AND HUMAN DIGNITY

PHILOSOPHY DOES NOT have the final word on natural rights. A personalistic analysis of human rights takes place fundamentally on the level of natural law, since natural rights as such are comprehensible as principles of justice.[1] Nonetheless, divine revelation adds much to the discussion and both confirms and exceeds what human reason alone can grasp. Christian personalism—Thomistic personalism in particular—benefits greatly from revelation for its understanding of the human person and his vocation to communion with God and is thereby able to offer even surer footing for human rights than can be provided by a personalism that relies on reason alone.

Sacred Scripture reveals many truths to which the unaided light of reason alone can also attain, but this neither makes Scripture superfluous nor invalidates the knowledge acquired by reason.[2] As the First Vatican Council teaches, the truth attained by philosophy and the truth of revelation are neither identical nor mutually exclusive. There exists, rather, "a twofold order of knowledge," one order being that of natural reason, the other divine faith.[3] Since, however, original sin weakened man's intelligence, so that only with difficulty does he arrive at certain truths, theology provides an invaluable assistance to philosophical research.[4]

---

1. Thus Hamel notes: "The rights of man are inherent in the person as such and belong in themselves to the domain of reason and not of faith" ("Fondement théologique des droits de l'homme," 309; author's translation).

2. Thus the *Catechism* states: "The precepts of natural law are not perceived by everyone clearly and immediately. In the present situation sinful man needs grace and revelation so moral and religious truths may be known 'by everyone with facility, with firm certainty and with no admixture of error' (Pius XII, *Humani Generis:* DS 3876; cf. *Dei Filius* 2: DS 3005)" (*CCC*, 1960).

3. See Dogmatic Constitution on the Catholic Faith *Dei Filius,* IV: DS 3015.

4. "Of spiritual punishments, the principal is weakness of reason, the result being that

In a well-known text Aquinas considers whether it is fitting that truths accessible to reason should be proposed to man as an object of belief.[5] Aquinas enumerates three disadvantages that would result if certain truths were left solely to the inquiry of human intelligence. First, few people would arrive at these truths, either because of a natural indisposition to speculative thought, or laziness, or a lack of time to devote to such pursuits. Second, these truths would be reached only after a long time because of their complexity and depth, the need for previous knowledge of many things, and the fact that youth do not possess the calm and prudence needed to reach the knowledge of sublime truths. Third, much falsehood is mingled into the knowledge acquired by human reason, especially on more difficult topics, and given that many people considered wise teach contrary opinions regarding these issues. These same arguments, which Aquinas adduces regarding the revelation of divine truths such as the existence of God, apply equally well to principles of natural law.[6]

Revelation provides an especially useful service by shoring up natural ethics with certain principles regarding the nature of the human person and what he deserves in justice. "Numerous are the philosophical errors concerning the nature of justice and rights," explains Ashley, "which require to be corrected in the light of God's Word. For example, the materialists deny the difference between human beings and brute animals, and hence either deny both any rights, or (more recently) claim that animals have the same rights as humans."[7] Thus, for example, though human reason is capable of discerning the essential difference between persons and nonpersons, many do not arrive at this truth, so Scripture's attestations concerning the uniqueness of the human person made in God's image

---

man encounters difficulty in acquiring knowledge of the truth, and easily falls into error" (*CG*, bk. IV, ch. 52).

5. See ibid., I, 4. See also Pius XII, *Humani Generis:* H. Denzinger and A. Schönmetzer, eds., *Enchiridion Symbolorum,* 33rd ed. (Freiburg, 1965), 3876 (hereafter DS); *Dei Filius,* II: DS 3005.

6. Speaking of the difference between a purely natural ethics and Christian ethics, C. Henry Peschke asserts: "There is only a difference in the knowledge and understanding of human nature, of the ultimate end, and by that of the moral law; a difference, certainly, which is still important and which is not to be slighted. Christian faith imparts to man an insight into human nature, the final goal and the moral order which is much deeper, fuller, and more to the point than the insight gained by reason alone" (*A Presentation of General Moral Theology in the Light of Vatican II* [Dublin: C. Goodliffe Neale, 1977], 104).

7. Ashley, *Living the Truth in Love,* 277.

and likeness and redeemed by Christ play a vital role in bringing it to light or confirming it.[8]

As the Second Vatican Council declares, without the assistance of revelation, "man remains a question to himself, one that is dimly perceived and left unanswered."[9] "Only divine revelation—by simultaneously throwing 'a new light on all things' (*GS* 11), and opening up 'new horizons closed to human reason' (*GS* 24)—can enable us to perceive 'his dignity . . . and vocation . . . in their true light' (*GS* 12)."[10]

Divine revelation and the theological elaboration of key anthropological and ethical principles make two especially important contributions to the foregoing arguments regarding the dignity and rights of the human person. First, man's creation in God's image—*imago Dei*—forms the bedrock of Christian anthropology and therefore of Thomistic personalism's understanding of human dignity.[11] Second, the Christ-event represents the completion not only of God's self-revelation but also of his revelation of man to man himself, in terms of both his nature and his destiny.

'IMAGO DEI' AS THE SOURCE OF HUMAN DIGNITY

From the Judeo-Christian perspective, human dignity derives from man's being created in the image and likeness of his Creator.[12] If man's dignity and certain rights proper to it bear an absolute character, it can only be because the human person participates in the absoluteness of

---

8. "*The Gospel is the fullest confirmation of all of human rights.* Without it we can easily find ourselves far from the truth about man. The Gospel, in fact, confirms the divine rule which upholds the moral order of the universe and confirms it, particularly through the Incarnation itself. . . . *The Redeemer confirms human rights* simply by restoring the fullness of the dignity man received when God created him in His image and likeness" (John Paul II, *Crossing the Threshold of Hope*, 197; emphasis in original).

9. *GS*, 21.

10. Grasso, "Beyond Liberalism," 36.

11. "The Old Testament already contains the principles and the values which require conduct in full conformity with the dignity of the human person, created 'in the image of God' (Gn. 1:27). Through the revelation of God's love that comes in Christ, the New Testament sheds the fullest light upon these principles and values" (Pontifical Biblical Commission, *The Interpretation of the Bible in the Church* [Rome: Libreria Editrice Vaticana, 1994], III.D.3).

12. After citing from the first chapter of Genesis, Rabbi Yaakov Menken writes: "The Torah teaches that we, as human beings, are entirely unlike any other creature on the planet. We are created in the likeness of G-d, with a Soul of Life uniquely close to our Creator—in a Kabbalistic sense, a 'part' of G-d's essence. He breathed into man a unique soul, rendering every hu-

God.[13] Maritain writes that "the deepest layer of the human person's dignity consists in its property of resembling God—not in a general way, but in a *proper* way. It is the *image of God.*"[14] Though all creatures bear a likeness to God by the fact that they participate in Being, only man is said to be made to his *image*. Or, as Thomas would have it, "man surpasses other things, not in the fact that God Himself made man . . . but in this, that man is made to God's image."[15]

To insist that human dignity finds its origin in man's creation to God's image and likeness is to underscore man's *similarity* to God and his *dissimilarity* to nonpersonal creatures.[16] Whereas the experimental and human sciences, often weighed down by materialist philosophical presuppositions and the constraints of their objectivist methodology, tend ever more to emphasize the continuity between man and other creatures, divine revelation provides a sure confirmation that man is not mistaken when he sees himself as radically distinct from and superior to the rest of the created world.[17]

Levels of Dignity

The doctrine of man's creation in God's image and likeness permits a deeper understanding of how different levels of dignity can exist, and how a certain sort of dignity can be lost while another may remain.

---

man being precious. This fundamental truth applies to every human life, and at every moment" ("Valuing Life," in *Jewish World Review,* Internet edition, October 8, 1999).

13. "The rights of man find their ultimate foundation in God the Creator and are only absolute in the measure that they participate in the Absolute of God. In creating man in his image, God confers on him an inalienable value" (Hamel, "Fondement théologique des droits de l'homme," 312; author's translation).

14. Maritain, *The Person and the Common Good,* 42.

15. *S. Th.,* I, 91, 4, ad 1.

16. "The whole world of created persons derives its distinctness from and its natural superiority over the world of things (non-persons) from a very particular resemblance to God" (Wojtyła, *Love and Responsibility,* 40). Or as Aquinas writes: "Man is said to be after the image of God, not as regards his body, but *as regards that whereby he excels other animals.* Hence, when it is said, 'Let us make man to our image and likeness,' it is added, 'And let him have dominion over the fishes of the sea' (Gn. 1:26). Now man excels all animals by his reason and intelligence; hence it is according to his intelligence and reason, which are incorporeal, that man is said to be according to the image of God" (*S. Th.,* I, 3, 1, ad 2; emphasis added). Or again, St. Augustine: "Man's excellence consists in the fact that God made him to His own image by giving him an intellectual soul, which *raises him above the beasts of the field*" (St. Augustine, *Gen. ad lit.* vi, 12; emphasis added).

17. "Man is not deceived when he regards himself as superior to bodily things and more

Aquinas distinguishes four levels of similitude to God. First, the similitude of irrational creatures to God exists "by reason only of a trace." Second, man, the rational creature, enjoys a particular similitude "by reason of the likeness of His image." Third, "of others He is the Father by similitude of grace, and these are also called adoptive sons." And last, God is the Father of others "by similitude of glory, forasmuch as they have obtained possession of the heritage of glory."[18]

According to Aquinas, then, resemblance or likeness to God has four distinct levels: (1) that common to all creatures, by the very fact that they "are" and thus resemble God, who "is"; (2) that enjoyed by rational creatures, which confers on them not only "likeness" but also the "image" of God *(imago Dei)*; (3) that of rational creatures elevated to adoptive sonship by grace, which includes all the baptized; and (4) that of the souls in heaven, united perfectly to God in glory.[19]

Of these four levels of likeness to God, the one that corresponds to the dignity proper to all men lies at the second level, that of *image*. That which properly separates man from all nonpersonal created beings is his particular resemblance to God. God has impressed his image in man's nature as a spiritual, rational being. The excellence of man, by the very fact of his being made in God's image and likeness, surpasses the excellence of all of creation.

There is also a dignity that corresponds to the third level, a dignity of adopted sonship that a person *acquires* through baptism.[20] At baptism the

---

than just a speck of nature or a nameless unit in the city of man. For by his power to know himself in the depths of his being he rises above the whole universe of mere objects" (*GS*, 14).

18. *S. Th.*, I, 33, 3.

19. Thomas elsewhere affirms that the image of God is in every man, with the following distinction. "Since man is said to be the image of God by reason of his intellectual nature, he is the most perfectly like God according to that in which he can best imitate God in his intellectual nature. Now the intellectual nature imitates God chiefly in this, that God understands and loves Himself. Wherefore we see that the image of God is in man in three ways. First, inasmuch as man possesses a natural aptitude for understanding and loving God; and this aptitude consists in the very nature of the mind, which is common to all men. Secondly, inasmuch as man actually and habitually knows and loves God, though imperfectly; and this image consists in the conformity of grace. Thirdly, inasmuch as man knows and loves God perfectly; and this image consists in the likeness of glory. Wherefore on the words, 'The light of Thy countenance, O Lord, is signed upon us' (Ps. 4:7), the gloss distinguishes a threefold image of 'creation,' of 're-creation,' and of 'likeness.' The first is found in all men, the second only in the just, the third only in the blessed" (ibid., I, 93, 4).

20. The council states that "there is a common dignity of members deriving from their re-

person becomes a child of God and a temple of the Blessed Trinity through the indwelling of the three divine Persons.[21] By the very fact that it is acquired, this dignity is not shared by all; it is exclusive to baptized Christians. It is also the source of new rights.[22] Christians are called to love in a new and more perfect way—as Christ loved us. This dignity, however, builds on and elevates basic human dignity rather than superseding it.

A still more exalted dignity corresponds to the fourth level of similarity with God, which is enjoyed by the glorified in heaven, who are perfectly united to God and "see Him as He is" (1 Cor. 13:12). Dignity derives from man's conformity to Christ, perfect image of the invisible God, and it is through grace that we "are being transformed into the same image from one degree of glory to another" (2 Cor. 3:18). Still, the fundamental dignity enjoyed by all human beings by reason of their nature is that which corresponds to the second level, that of "image."

Image and Likeness

Though the terms "image" and "likeness" appear almost synonymous, Aquinas's differentiation of different levels of likeness underscores the unique quality of image. For Thomas, "likeness" refers to any similarity, whereas "image" expresses a particular sort of similarity. Thus "image" includes the idea of "likeness," but "likeness" does not imply "image."[23] It is precisely this sort of likeness that makes man a person and confers on him the dignity of one who exists for his own sake, as an end (a person with an inherent, transcendent purpose) and never merely a means.

---

birth in Christ" and thus "a true equality between all with regard to the dignity and to the activity which is common to all the faithful in the building up of the Body of Christ" (Second Vatican Council, Dogmatic Constitution on the Church *Lumen Gentium*, 32).

21. "Baptism not only purifies from all sins, but also makes the neophyte 'a new creature,' an adopted son of God, who has become a 'partaker of the divine nature,' (2 Cor 5:17; 2 Pt 1:4; cf. Gal 4:5–7) member of Christ and co-heir with him, (Cf. 1 Cor 6:15; 12:27; Rom 8:17) and a temple of the Holy Spirit (Cf. 1 Cor 6:19)" (*CCC,* 1265).

22. The *Code of Canon Law* speaks of rights accruing to Christ's faithful by reason of their baptism. See especially *Codex Iuris Canonicis* (hereafter *CIC)*, cann. 208–23. *The Catechism of the Catholic Church* specifies that "the baptised person also enjoys rights within the Church: to receive the sacraments, to be nourished with the Word of God and to be sustained by the other spiritual helps of the Church" (*CCC,* 1269). See also *Lumen Gentium,* 37.

23. "Where an image exists, there forthwith is likeness; but where there is likeness, there is not necessarily an image" (*S. Th.,* I, 93, 1). See also ibid., I, 35, 1.

Several qualities not necessarily found in "similarity" are proper to the idea of "image." In the first place, an image must be *copied* from something else.[24] To be an image, it is not enough for one thing to be circumstantially like another, it must in some way be taken from it, such as a reflection in a mirror or a sculpture of a model. In the case of the human person, God created man with Himself as exemplar or model. Scripture highlights the innovation of man's creation as compared with the creation of the other beings. In creating the fish and sea creatures, God says: "Let the waters bring forth swarms of living creatures" (Gen. 1:20) and likewise for the land animals: "Let the earth bring forth living creatures of every kind" (Gen. 1:24). Yet when creating man, God looks neither to the earth nor to the waters but to Himself and says: "Let us make humankind in our image, according to our likeness" (Gen. 1:26).

In this biblical text another characteristic of "image" appears, namely that of *origin*. For the rest of creation God issues commands as passive imperatives: "Let there be light," "Let there be a dome," "Let the earth put forth vegetation," "Let the waters bring forth swarms of living creatures." In the case of man, however, God announces his intention[25] and speaks of his own active making: "Let us make," as if He were more personally "involved" in the creation of man than in the rest of creation.[26] Though man, too, is made from the mud of the earth, still, God does not say: "Let the earth put forth human beings" but rather "*Let us make humankind* in our own image, according to our likeness."[27] Though God is

---

24. Aquinas further remarks that "an image adds something to likeness—namely, that it is copied from something else. For an 'image' is so called because it is produced as an imitation of something else" (ibid., I, 93, 1).

25. "Both the Meshech Chochma, Rabbi Meir Simcha of Dvinsk, and Rabbi Shamson Raphael Hirsch, note that unlike the Creation of the birds or animals, G-d precedes the Creation of Man by announcing what He is about to do: 'let us create Man in our form, in our likeness.' They explained that this is because Man is to rule over the creatures of the world, as is explained in the verse. Man is the apex of Creation, and all the world exists for our benefit" (Menken, "Valuing Life").

26. "In the biblical narrative, the difference between man and other creatures is shown above all by the fact that only the creation of man is presented as the result of a special decision on the part of God, a deliberation to establish a particular and specific bond with the Creator: 'Let us make man in our image, after our likeness' (Gen. 1:26). *The life* which God offers to man is a gift by which God shares something of himself with his creature" (*EV,* 34).

27. In referring to this passage, Richard J. Clifford and Ronald E. Murphy observe: "The origin of human beings is not simply from the waters on the earth like the plants, fishes/birds, and animals; it is 'in our image, according to our likeness'" ("Genesis," in *The New Jerome Bib-*

the first cause of all things, man proceeds from God in a way that the rest of creation does not. Such is also the origin of man's personhood. Aquinas writes that "for a true image it is required that one proceeds from another like to it in species, or at least in specific sign. Now whatever imports procession or origin in God, belongs to the persons. Hence the name 'Image' is a personal name."[28]

The second Biblical narrative of man's creation sheds important light on another aspect of man's personhood: the idea of being made for relation and for communion.[29] The Genesis chapter two account of creation relates that once God had created man, he placed him in the garden of Eden to till it and keep it. But on contemplating Adam, God found him in some way incomplete and observed (as He had not done in the case of the other creatures): "It is not good for man to be alone. I will make him a helper as his partner" (Gen. 2:18). All that God created He found to be good, but unlike the other creatures God created, man was, in a sense, "imperfect" as a sole individual. Solitude was not good for man, since man's perfection consists precisely in his communion with other persons and preeminently with God, the supreme personal Being.

Trinitarian theology reveals that man's vocation to communion is not something extrinsic or additional to his existence, it is constitutive of his creation in the image and likeness of God, who is One and Three.[30] "Human beings," writes Wojtyła, "are like unto God not only by reason of their spiritual nature, which accounts for their existence as persons, but also by reason of their *capacity for community with other persons.*"[31] From the perspective of divine revelation, then, the human person's relational dimension derives from his creation in the image and likeness of God, who is the first *communio personarum*.[32] The Father communicates his

---

lical Commentary, ed. Raymond E. Brown, Joseph A. Fitzmyer, and Roland E. Murphy [London: Geoffrey Chapman, 1989], 9).

28. *S. Th.*, I, 35, 1.

29. "Today it is more necessary than ever to present the biblical anthropology of relationality, which helps us genuinely understand the human being's identity in his relationship to others.... In the human person considered in his 'relationality,' we find a vestige of God's own mystery revealed in Christ as a substantial unity in the communion of three divine Persons" (John Paul II, General Audience of Wednesday, November 24, 1999, 11).

30. "The divine image is present in every man. It shines forth in the communion of persons, in the likeness of the union of the divine persons among themselves" (*CCC*, 1702).

31. Wojtyła, "The Family as a Community of Persons," 318.

32. "Indeed, the Lord Jesus, when He prayed to the Father, 'that all may be one . . . as we

entire self to the Son, such that "all he has is mine, and all I have is his" (see John 17:10). The three-way communication among Father, Son, and Holy Spirit begets a perfect communion, which in turn is the exemplar of all human interpersonal relations. Like God, who is love, man is made for love and for communion with God and with his fellows.[33] To say that man was created in God's image and likeness is to attribute to man personality and the vocation to communion.

Reflecting on the God of the Bible as "a God-in-relationship," Joseph Ratzinger remarks that the concept of person "has become for us the fundamental concept of the analogy between God and man, the very center of philosophical thought."[34] Since God is described as a Trinitarian set of relations, as *relatio subsistens,* when "we say that man is the image of God, it means that he is being designed for relationship; it means that, in and through all his relationships, he seeks that relation which is the ground of his existence."[35] Man cannot fulfill his vocation or reach the plenitude of his personal existence except in communion with other persons and ultimately with his Creator.[36]

CHRIST'S REVELATION OF MAN'S TRUE DIGNITY

This understanding of man's creation in God's image remains fundamentally incomplete unless one considers its Christological dimension.

---

are one' (John 17:21 22) opened up vistas closed to human reason, for He implied a certain likeness between the union of the divine Persons, and the unity of God's sons in truth and charity" (*GS,* 24).

33. "These considerations also bring to light the significance of the *imago Dei.* Man is like God in that he is capable of love and truth" (Joseph Ratzinger, *Gospel, Catechesis, Catechism: Sidelights on the Catechism of the Catholic Church* [San Francisco: Ignatius Press, 1997], 16). "*The true personalistic interpretation of the commandment of love is found in the words of the Council:* 'When the Lord Jesus prays to the Father so that "they may be one" (John 17:22), He places before us new horizons impervious to human reason and implies a similarity between the union of the divine persons and the union of the children of God in truth and charity'. . . . In this sense *the person is realized through love*" (John Paul II, *Crossing the Threshold of Hope,* 202; emphasis in original).

34. Joseph Ratzinger, *Many Religions—One Covenant: Israel, the Church, and the World,* trans. Graham Harrison (San Francisco: Ignatius Press, 1999), 75, 76.

35. Ibid., 76–77.

36. "All men are called to the same end: God himself. There is a certain resemblance between the union of the divine persons and the fraternity that men are to establish among themselves in truth and love. (Cf. *GS,* 24)" (*CCC,* 1878).

Christ the Son is the true image of the Father, and all sonship, and hence all imagery of the Father, takes place in and through Him. As Thomas teaches, the idea of "image" is related directly to filiation, such that even the Holy Spirit is the image only of the Son, not of the Father, since "the Holy Ghost, although by His procession He receives the nature of the Father, as the Son also receives it, nevertheless is not said to be 'born.'"[37] Man images God inasmuch as he is made to participate in Christ's sonship (see Rom. 8:15, 23; Gal. 4:5; Eph. 1:4–5).

Christ alone is the Image of the Father (see 2 Cor. 4:4; Col. 1:15). For this reason it is more proper to speak of man having been made "to the image" of God, which expresses a tendency or "movement toward."[38] Toward what does man tend? Toward the Son. Man is made "to the image" of God, and that perfect image *is* the Son. Thus Christ is "the image of the invisible God," and all men are "predestined to be conformed to the image of his Son, in order that he might be the firstborn within a large family" (Rom. 8:29).[39] This text brings to light the significance of the Council's statements: "He who is the 'image of the invisible God' (Col 1:15), is himself the perfect man," and therefore "it is only in the mystery of the Word made flesh that the mystery of man truly becomes clear." It is Christ the Lord, Christ the new Adam who "fully reveals man to him-

---

37. *S. Th.*, I, 35, 2.

38. Aquinas writes that "in order to express the imperfect character of the divine image in man, man is not simply called the image, but 'to the image,' whereby is expressed a certain movement of tendency to perfection. But it cannot be said that the Son of God is 'to the image,' because He is the perfect Image of the Father" (*S. Th.*, I, 35, 2, ad 3).

39. Here we will not enter into the thorny question of predestination and whether all are called to adoptive sonship. Indeed, however, Scripture attests that Christ's coming was news of great joy to "all people" (Luke 2:10), the life in him was the light of "all people" (John 1:4), when lifted up from the earth Christ would draw "all men" to himself (John 12:32), and St. Paul calls God "the savior of all people, especially those who believe" (1 Tim. 4:10), affirming that God's grace "has made salvation possible for the whole human race" (Titus 2:11) since he "died for all" (2 Cor. 15), and that "God desires all men to be saved" (1 Tim. 2:4). St. John notes that Christ is the atoning sacrifice not only for our sins "but also for the sins of the whole world" (1 John 2:2). The Council of Arles, moreover, condemned the proposal that "some are destined to death and others predestined to life" or that "those who perish do so by God's will" (DS 160a). The Second Vatican Council, too, declared that "since Christ died for all, and since all men are in fact called to the same destiny, which is divine, we must hold that the Holy Spirit offers to all the possibility of being made partners, in a way known to God, in the paschal mystery" (*GS,* 22). These texts and others suggest that salvation in Christ is possible, and indeed willed by God, for all, and that none is excluded a priori from salvation. Sundry other texts could be adduced to the contrary, but these suffice to allow for openness on the matter.

self and brings to light his most high calling."⁴⁰ Every human person, in fact, has been redeemed by Christ, called to participate in his own divine sonship, and destined for eternal happiness in heaven.⁴¹

From what has been said it becomes evident that revelation performs an invaluable service in putting into relief the greatness of man's nature and therefore his exalted dignity.⁴² Through Christ's revelation of man to himself, we come to know *who* man is and consequently how he should be treated.

Philosophical reflection on man's nature and dignity, both through objective study and through subjective experience, yields an understanding that man is the sort of being toward whom the only appropriate attitude is love. That understanding fits with the New Testament commandment to love one's neighbor as oneself. Yet if this approach of starting with reason and experience to confirm the truth of revelation *(intellego ut credam)* is valid and effective, the opposite approach *(credo ut intellegam)* is certainly no less so. Jesus' commandment to love one another reveals that the human person is fundamentally lovable. In actual fact, man's lovableness often remains so hidden that without the benefit of revelation few would arrive at this truth. Man's dignity and essential lovableness underlie the commandment to love and are thus prior to it, but one can also reason to what is prior from what is secondary.⁴³ In this way Jesus' com-

---

40. *GS*, 22.

41. "The dignity of the person is manifested in all its radiance when the person's origin and destiny are considered: created by God in his image and likeness as well as redeemed by the most precious blood of Christ, the person is called to be a 'child in the Son' and a living temple of the Spirit, destined for the eternal life of blessed communion with God. For this reason every violation of the personal dignity of the human being cries out in vengeance to God and is an offense against the Creator of the individual" (*CL*, 37).

42. In his first encyclical letter, Pope John Paul II observed that "in Christ and through Christ man has acquired full awareness of his dignity, of the heights to which he is raised, of the surpassing worth of his own humanity, and of the meaning of his existence" (*RH*, 11). And John XXIII wrote: "When, furthermore, we consider man's personal dignity from the standpoint of divine revelation, inevitably our estimate of it is incomparably increased. Men have been ransomed by the blood of Jesus Christ. Grace has made them sons and friends of God, and heirs to eternal glory" (*PT*, 10).

43. As MacIntyre has written: "It is a Cartesian error, fostered by a misunderstanding of Euclidian geometry, to suppose that first by an initial act of apprehension we can comprehend the full meaning of the premises of a deductive system and then only secondly proceed to inquire what follows from them. In fact it is only insofar as we understand what follows that we understand the premises themselves. . . . So in the construction of any demonstrative science we both argue *from* what we take, often rightly, to be subordinate truths *to* first principles ([Aquinas,] *Commentary on the Ethics* [I, lecture xii]) as well as from first principles *to* subordi-

mand to love all persons ratifies human dignity and the universal vocation to love and be loved.[44]

Revelation witnesses to man's dignity in a variety of ways. One of the most forceful testimonies to the dignity of the human person is the fact of revelation itself. That God holds man in such esteem as to judge him worthy of His self-revelation bears witness to the greatness of the person. As Wojtyła points out, the dignity of the human person "finds its full confirmation in the very fact of revelation, for this fact signifies the establishment of contact between God and the human being."[45] Thus in revealing Himself to man, "God confirms the personal dignity of the human being."

The most eloquent testimony to man's elevated dignity comes from the incarnation of the Second Person of the Trinity and his death on the cross for mankind. That "God so loved the world that he gave his only Son, so that everyone who believes in him may not perish but may have eternal life" (John 3:16) and that the Son "loved us and gave himself up for us" by dying on the cross bear witness to the worth that God attributes to man.[46] God so esteems man as to assume his humanity and give Himself up to death for him.[47]

It may be objected that since man clearly did not deserve the incarnation or the salvation that Christ won for him, such events actually tell us much about God's merciful love but very little about man's dignity.[48]

---

nate truths. . . . The moral life [is] a journey towards the discovery of first principles as an end, the full disclosure of which is, in both senses of 'end,' the end of that journey" (*Whose Justice? Which Rationality?* 174–75).

44. "Man cannot live without love. He remains a being that is incomprehensible for himself, his life is senseless, if love is not revealed to him, if he does not encounter love, if he does not experience it and make it his own, if he does not participate intimately in it. This . . . is why Christ the Redeemer 'fully reveals man to himself.' If we may use the expression, this is the human dimension of the mystery of the redemption. In this dimension man finds again the greatness, dignity and value that belong to his humanity" (*RH*, 10).

45. Wojtyła, "On the Dignity of the Human Person," 179.

46. "The Christian's distinctiveness begins and ends with the revelation that the infinite God loves the single human being infinitely; that is made known in the most exact fashion in the fact that he dies the redeemer's (i.e. the sinner's) death in human form for this beloved you" (Hans Urs von Balthasar, *Explorations in Theology: Spiritus Creator,* trans. Brian McNeil [San Francisco: Ignatius Press, 1993], 270).

47. "The 'price' of our redemption is likewise a further proof of the value that God himself sets on man and of our dignity in Christ" (*RH*, 20).

48. Thus St. Thomas writes: "Although God never acts contrary to justice, He sometimes does do something beyond justice. . . . if out of liberality one gives what is not deserved, this is

There is much truth to this, in that the disproportion between man's worth and God's gift is infinite. Yet at the same time God's wisdom permeates all He does. He would not give His life for a stick or for a worm, that is, for a being that was unable to receive the gift He offered. Though man did not deserve salvation, he was *capable of being saved* as well as being *capable of elevation to divine sonship.* Grace builds on nature but does not replace it.[49] Man is able to receive God's personal love because he was made, as a person, to love and be loved. Furthermore, God's love for man serves not only to manifest man's dignity, it also confers dignity on him. By loving man, God makes man lovable.

Revelation discloses not only *who* man is but to what he is *called.* By reason we can come to knowledge of the dignity that is proper to man by virtue of his nature, yet without divine revelation we could never have known his supernatural calling and the dignity that accompanies it. It is only in the light of man's exalted destiny to eternal communion with his Creator, in fact, that man's full dignity becomes apparent. "The dignity of man," the Council teaches, "rests above all on the fact that man is called to communion with God. The invitation to converse with God is addressed to man as soon as he comes into being." The full meaning of human life itself "can only be understood in reference to man's eternal destiny."[50]

If all of Christian morality is based on this fact of man's creation in God's image and his redemption by Jesus Christ, is there not a risk of positing two separate foundations for human rights, one based on revelation and the other on the natural law? In reality, revelation confirms and completes what natural law teaches in this regard. From human reason, unaided by the light of revelation, one discovers man's rational and hence spiritual nature as well as his subjectivity, his freedom, and his vocation to love and communion. This knowledge is confirmed, elevated, and perfected by the revelation that man is made in the image of his Creator. Human knowledge of man by reason and experience is true but imperfect, since it is only Christ who "fully reveals man to himself and brings to light his most high calling."[51]

---

not contrary to justice, but beyond it. Accordingly, when in this life God raises a human mind above its proper level, He does not act contrary to justice, but beyond it" (*De Veritate,* 13, 1, ad 4).

49. *S. Th.,* I, 1, 8, ad 2.   50. *GS,* 19, 51.
51. Ibid., 22.

PART FOUR

HUMAN RIGHTS AND CLASSICAL ETHICS

The firm theoretical grounding of human rights provided by Thomistic personalism harmonizes perfectly with traditional natural law theory, as many authors affirm.[1] The frequent accusations made to the contrary—such as those by William Edgar, professor of apologetics at Westminster Theological Seminary, who views an emphasis on natural rights as a "drift toward secularization" since rights themselves constitute "a secularization of natural law"[2]—stem either from an insufficient understanding of Thomistic personalism (already remedied in Part III), or from an insufficient grasp of classical natural law theory. An accurate and robust vision of that theory, in fact, has been one of the most unfortunate casualties of post-Enlightenment philosophical discourse. Recovering a clear, comprehensive theory of natural law will bring to light its consonance with Thomistic personalism's vision of human rights.

---

1. As just one example among many, Robert George states: "While talk of 'rights' does not figure prominently in the classical and medieval statements of that [traditional natural law] theory, its perfectionist concerns for human well-being provide ample grounds for the derivation of human rights by its modern exponents" (George, *Making Men Moral,* 92).

2. William Edgar, "The Reformed Tradition and Natural Law: A Response," in *A Preserv-*

Such a recovery requires a clear understanding of three major lines of argument. First, the key concepts having to do with natural moral law itself need a thorough explanation, which they are given in chapter 13. Second, an analysis of the virtue of justice, so crucial for classical natural law theory, shows how it implicitly includes the notion of natural, subjective rights. Such an analysis is undertaken in chapter 14. Finally, as chapter 15 shows, those rights, once they are seen as having only true human goods as their object and therefore as correlative to duties, can take a comfortable place within classical natural law theory, even while they make a serious contribution to its development.

---

ing Grace: Protestants, Catholics, and Natural Law, ed. Michael Cromartie (Grand Rapids, Mich.: Ethics and Public Policy Center/William B. Eerdmans, 1997), 118.

13. NATURAL LAW

THE FACT OF HUMAN FREE WILL—which entails the power to act or refrain from acting, to deliberate, evaluate, and choose among different courses of action—necessitates criteria from which to judge alternatives and arrive at practical decisions. Unlike irrational animals, the human person does not act out of necessity but may exercise free choice. When he acts, man naturally pursues some form of sensible or intelligible good.[1] At the same time, his evaluation of alternative actions goes beyond the categories of what is possible, useful, or pleasurable to include the moral categories of what is "right" and what is "wrong." A moral sense—the experience that some actions are proper, others permissible, others obligatory, and others prohibited—is common to all peoples in all times and places, though the practical instantiations of this sense vary widely.[2] In the end, the ideas expressed by the words "I ought," "I ought not," and "I may" are not foreign to any culture and are not reducible to other types of human experience.[3] Thus despite elabo-

---

1. See *S. Th.*, I, 80, 1, ad 2; I-II, 8, 1.

2. For the ancient Greeks, the notion of what is proper or improper was often expressed in terms of acting in a way worthy of a human being and was closely linked to the moral aesthetics of a desirable, beautiful life. Nonetheless, the pursuit of the good life was presented not as one possible course to follow but as the right course to follow, and a sense of moral obligation was not foreign to them. Plato, Aristotle, and the Stoics spoke of conduct that conformed to reason or was contrary to it, of what should be done or avoided.

3. In his book *The Problem of Pain*, C. S. Lewis expresses the singularity of this phenomenon: "All the human beings that history has heard of acknowledge some kind of morality; that is, they feel towards certain proposed actions the experiences expressed by the words 'I ought' or 'I ought not.' These experiences ... cannot be logically deduced from the environment and physical experience of the man who undergoes them. You can shuffle 'I want' and 'I am forced' and 'I shall be well advised' and 'I dare not' as long as you please without getting out of them the slightest hint of 'ought' and 'ought not.' ... Attempts to resolve the moral experience into something else always presuppose the very thing they are trying to explain" (*The Problem of Pain* [London: Fount, 1940], 8).

rate theories to the contrary, it may be affirmed with certainty that man is a moral animal.[4]

The moral experience does not take place as a solipsistic exercise, it embraces the person's relationship to realities external to himself: God, other people, things. Man's experience of personal freedom carries with it the knowledge that he is the author of his actions and thus is accountable for them, not only to himself but to others and, ultimately, to God. At the heart of the moral life is the call to act fairly with reality,[5] in the awareness that reality makes certain demands on man's freedom. Thus freedom entails responsibility, since as the author of his actions, man is accountable for them. Where there is no freedom, there is no praise or blame and, in the end, there is no accountability.

But how does the human person arrive at moral judgments? Whence do standards of moral good and evil proceed, and whence do they draw their authority? From an early age children are taught by parents and educators that some sorts of behavior are acceptable or praiseworthy, while other actions are unacceptable or blameworthy. A system of rewards and punishments communicates in a tangible way the approval or disapproval, praise or blame, attached to various forms of conduct.[6] An innate moral sense is thus reinforced by the approval, praise, acquiescence, scorn, or punishment accorded by the community for different types of behavior and by social mores that arise from the reigning ethical climate. Alongside the role of parents and teachers, the formative function of civil legislation on moral conscience must also be noted, since such legislation

---

4. Noteworthy among theories that deny moral sense are Freud's idea that moral consciousness represents a "sublimation" of elementary instincts such as the sexual libido, resulting from censorship by the superego (see especially *Totem und Tabu* [1913] and *Unbehagen in der Kultur* [1929]), and Nietzsche's condemnation of morality as a hypocrisy that conceals men's weakness and cowardice (especially in *Also sprach Zarathustra* [1883–1884], *Jenseits von Gut und Böse* [1886], and *Zur Genealogie der Moral* [1887]).

5. See Spaemann, *Basic Moral Concepts*, 72.

6. Many norms of conduct have a purely pragmatic genesis. In this way activities that produce undesirable results can be passed down as "to be avoided," though the original negative judgment proceeds from practical motives rather than moral impropriety. Thus distinctions between moral evil and inadvisability can be blurred, at least for a time. Take, for instance, the case of a child learning not to touch a hot stove top. When the child approaches the hot stove, his mother may correct him verbally or even slap his hand, and the child learns that approaching the stove is a practice "to be avoided." As his moral life matures he will learn to distinguish between actions to be avoided because of the negative practical consequences they occasion and actions to be avoided because they are morally wrong or unworthy in themselves.

represents an official declaration of what a particular society views as acceptable (legal) and unacceptable (illegal) behavior.

Nonetheless, the moral sense cannot be reduced to a desire to win praise and approval and avoid punishments and scorn. Nor can it be identified with the passive internalization of external norms of behavior that are inculcated by parents, educators, and the community. As a person matures, he does not merely internalize norms and precepts that have been passed on to him, he *questions* and *evaluates* them, *accepts* or *abandons* them.[7] He weighs them against his personal experience and what he observes around him. He comes to view certain choices as good and others as evil, not because of the punishment or rewards they may incur but because of their relationship to the truth of the world and his own existence. As he develops an understanding of his own identity as a person and the meaning of his life, he forms a judgment about what actions correspond to the truth of his being and destiny. He also comes to realize that his choices affect not only the single action at hand but his own character as a moral being. His personal (and vicarious) experience of having acted well or badly in the past, in a way worthy or unworthy of a human person, also influences his assessment of present and future possibilities.

The importance of personal experience and reflection does not preclude the need for external criteria in coming to an understanding of what is to be done and what is to be avoided. In every area of life a person must accept many truths on trust, and in so doing he places his belief in the competence and honesty of the authority that affirms them. This experience of trust does not dehumanize the person; rather, it constitutes an essentially human experience, which elevates him and creates bonds of communion with other persons.[8] Trust in others takes place in every

---

7. "Human beings are not made to live alone. They are born into a family and in a family they grow, eventually entering society through their activity. From birth, therefore, they are immersed in traditions which give them not only a language and a cultural formation but also a range of truths in which they believe almost instinctively. Yet personal growth and maturity imply that these same truths can be cast into doubt and evaluated through a process of critical enquiry. It may be that, after this time of transition, these truths are 'recovered' as a result of the experience of life or by dint of further reasoning. Nonetheless, there are in the life of a human being many more truths which are simply believed than truths which are acquired by way of personal verification. . . . This means that the human being—the one who seeks the truth— is also the one who lives by belief" (*FR*, 31).

8. "In believing, we entrust ourselves to the knowledge acquired by other people. This

sphere of human existence, including the moral sphere. Moral wisdom is handed on just as speculative wisdom or scientific knowledge are. In his process of maturation, then, the person not only assesses values and moral principles and decides which he will adopt as his own; he also decides in which authorities he will place his trust, confident that they will convey to him the truth about his existence and the way he is to live in order to be authentically human.

THE MORAL LAW

An indispensable aid to forming personal moral judgments comes from law.[9] According to the classical definition, law is "a rule of conduct enacted by competent authority for the sake of the common good."[10] Though one speaks of laws of nature (such as the law of gravity), properly speaking law refers to reason,[11] since law is not the efficient cause of order or a mere description of an existing order but a guide by which man himself is to measure and order his activity.

The Scholastic tradition subdivides law into the eternal law and temporal laws, the former being the plan in the mind of God according to which the whole universe is governed,[12] or simply divine wisdom, which directs all the activity of creatures,[13] and the latter being specific norms of

---

suggests an important tension. On the one hand, the knowledge acquired through belief can seem an imperfect form of knowledge, to be perfected gradually through personal accumulation of evidence; on the other hand, belief is often humanly richer than mere evidence, because it involves an interpersonal relationship and brings into play not only a person's capacity to know but also the deeper capacity to entrust oneself to others, to enter into a relationship with them which is intimate and enduring" (ibid., 32).

9. "Such, then, being the condition of human liberty, it necessarily stands in need of light and strength to direct its actions to good and to restrain them from evil. Without this, the freedom of our will would be our ruin. First of all, there must be law; that is, a fixed rule of teaching what is to be done and what is to be left undone" (Leo XIII, *Libertas Praestantissimum,* 7). Thomas speaks of three extrinsic principles of human acts: the devil, law, and grace. The devil incites man to evil, while God incites man to good through law and grace. See *S. Th.,* I-II, 90, preamble.

10. *CCC,* 1951. St. Thomas defines law as "a dictate of practical reason emanating from the ruler who governs a perfect community" (*S. Th.,* I-II, 91, 1) and "an ordinance of reason for the common good, made by him who has care of the community, and promulgated" (ibid., I-II, 90, 4).

11. See, for instance, *S. Th.* I-II, 90, 1 and I-II, 91, 2, ad 3.

12. Ibid., I-II, 91, 1.

13. Ibid., I-II, 93, 1.

human conduct. The eternal law is the ultimate source, in God, of all true law.[14] St. Augustine defined the eternal law as "the divine reason or will commanding that the natural order be preserved and forbidding that it be disturbed."[15] This law governs irrational creatures through physical and biological "laws" that direct their activity, and it governs man by providing him with principles of his activity to be freely chosen and adhered to.[16] The moral law, which "prescribes for man the ways, the rules of conduct that lead to the promised beatitude" and "proscribes the ways of evil which turn him away from God and his love," is "the work of divine Wisdom."[17]

Temporal laws may be divided into "positive laws," extrinsic to man, and "natural law,"[18] written on man's heart[19] and intrinsic to his rational nature.[20] Positive laws find their source in the reason and will of the legislator, and they induce to obedience either by the authority of the lawgiver or by the positive or negative sanctions attached to their observance.[21]

---

14. *CCC*, 1952.

15. St. Augustine, *Contra Faustum Manichaeum*, c. 22, n. 27; PL 42, col. 418.

16. As Tertullian wrote: "Alone among all animate beings, man can boast of having been counted worthy to receive a law from God: as an animal endowed with reason, capable of understanding and discernment, he is to govern his conduct by using his freedom and reason, in obedience to the One who has entrusted everything to him" (Tertullian, Ad. Marc, 2, 4: PL 2, 288–89).

17. *CCC*, 1950.

18. Thomas's division of law is somewhat different (eternal, natural, human, divine). But since he sees natural law as an expression of natural right (*S. Th.*, II-II, 57, 1, ad 2), we have taken his division of right into natural and positive (ibid., II-II, 57, 2), and applied them to law.

19. "When Gentiles, who do not possess the law, do instinctively what the law requires, these, though not having the law, are a law to themselves. They show that what the law requires is written on their hearts, to which their own conscience also bears witness; and their conflicting thoughts will accuse or perhaps excuse them" (Rom. 2:14–15).

20. There is considerable debate regarding whether the natural law is truly intrinsic to man's nature or rather extrinsic and internal. In other words, is the natural law part of man's nature or extrinsic to it? I understand the natural moral law to be "written into" and thus intrinsic to the fabric of man's nature. For the natural law to be an extrinsic principle, it would have to be somehow inserted into man in an act separate from his creation and abide in him as a sort of foreign occupant. For his part, Leo XIII declared that the natural law, written and engraved in the mind of every man, "is nothing but our reason, commanding us to do right and forbidding sin" (*Libertas Praestantissimum*, 8).

21. "Now the precepts refer to things which have to be done: and to their fulfilment man is induced by two considerations, viz. the authority of the lawgiver, and the benefit derived from the fulfilment, which benefit consists in the attainment of some good, useful, pleasurable or virtuous, or in the avoidance of some contrary evil" (*S. Th.*, I-II, 99, 5).

Positive laws are in turn further subdivided into positive divine law[22] revealed by God (the Old Covenant, or Mosaic Law, and the New Covenant, or Evangelical Law) and positive human laws (ecclesiastical or civil).[23] Positive divine laws serve to complement the natural law by determining what the natural law leaves indeterminate, by providing a sure guide of conduct that compensates for the uncertainty of human judgment, and by making possible the attainment of goals that could not be attained by the mere light of natural law.[24] Positive human laws, which derive from common accord or by the decree of the lawgiver, stipulate what is due to one and required of another.[25]

THE EXISTENCE OF NATURAL LAW

Countless volumes have been written on natural law theory. The idea of natural law, though expounded from antiquity, has always been fraught with controversy.[26] The important thing here is to grasp the received Christian understanding of natural law in order to explore its relationship to natural rights. The natural law has enjoyed a glorious but tumultuous history, which Maritain adequately sums up as follows:

The idea of a natural law is a heritage of Greek and Christian thought. It goes back not only to Grotius, who indeed began deforming it,[27] but, before him to

---

22. "[T]he Divine law is instituted chiefly in order to direct men to God; while human law is instituted chiefly in order to direct men in relation to one another" (ibid., I-II, 99, 3).
23. Thomas sees human laws as particular determinations deriving from the more general precepts of the natural law. See ibid., I-II, 91, 3.
24. See ibid., I-II, 91, 4. Here Thomas speaks specifically of the value of divine law.
25. See ibid., II-II, 57, 2.
26. "The doctrine of natural law is as old as philosophy" (Rommen, *The Natural Law*, 3). Fortin notes that "the notorious debates to which [natural law theory] gave rise and the variety of interpretations to which it was subjected suggest that its status always remained ambiguous." He adds: "It has been remarked more than once, usually by its defenders, that no single doctrine has so often risen from its ashes after having been repeatedly and solemnly pronounced dead. If these cycles of decline and rebirth are a sure sign of its abiding vitality, they also testify to a no less persistent vulnerability" ("Augustine, Thomas Aquinas, and the Problem of Natural Law," in *Classical Christianity and the Political Order*, 199).
27. It seems to me that much unmerited blame for the corruption of natural law theory has been placed on the shoulders of Grotius. His definition of the natural law, in fact, coincides almost exactly with that of the whole of Christian tradition: "The law of nature is a dictate of right reason, which points out that an act, according as it is or is not in conformity with rational nature, has in it a quality of moral baseness or moral necessity; and that, in consequence,

Suarez and Francisco de Vitoria; and further back to St. Thomas Aquinas (he alone grasped the matter in a wholly consistent doctrine, which unfortunately was expressed in an insufficiently clarified vocabulary, so that its deepest features were soon overlooked and disregarded); and still further back to St. Augustine and the Church Fathers and St. Paul (we remember St. Paul's saying: "When the Gentiles who have not the Law, *do by nature* the things contained in the Law, these, having not the Law, are a law unto themselves . . ." [Rom. 2:14]); and even further back to Cicero,[28] to the Stoics, to the great moralists of antiquity and its great poets, particularly Sophocles. Antigone, who was aware that in transgressing the human law and being crushed by it she was obeying a better commandment, the *unwritten and unchangeable laws,* is the eternal heroine of natural law: for, as she puts it, they were not, those unwritten laws, born out of today's or yesterday's sweet will, "but they live always and forever, and no man knows from where they have arisen."[29]

The existence of a natural law, though propounded in some form or another from the beginnings of civilization, has always been contested, and arguments against such a law are legion.[30] Sometimes the very proponents of natural law theory have been the cause of its fall from grace. Natural law theory has at times been presented in a simplistic way or made to do things it was never able to do, such that those of a more skeptical or critical mindset have had ample reason to doubt its existence.[31]

---

such an act is either forbidden or enjoined by the author of nature, God" (Grotius, *De Iure Belli ac Pacis,* bk. I, ch. I, X, 1, 38–39). Furthermore, against nominalism and voluntarism Grotius affirmed that God himself respects the order of the creation that is fruit of His wisdom. "The law of nature, again, is unchangeable—even in the sense that it cannot be changed by God. Measureless as is the power of God, nevertheless it can be said that there are certain things over which that power does not extend; for things of which this is said are spoken only, having no sense corresponding with reality and being mutually contradictory. Just as even God, then, cannot cause that two times two should not make four, so He cannot cause that that which is intrinsically evil not be evil" (ibid., bk. I, ch. I, X, 5, 40).

28. Cicero puts these words into the mouth of the righteous Laelius: "There is a true law, namely, right reason, which is in accordance with nature, applies to all men, and is unchangeable and eternal; by its commands it summons men to the performance of their duties, by its prohibitions it restrains them from doing wrong" (Cicero, *De Re Publica,* III.22.33, cited in Fortin, "Augustine, Thomas Aquinas, and the Problem of Natural Law," 203).

29. Maritain, *Man and the State,* 84–85.

30. I speak here of natural law in the broadest possible sense: as a moral standard for human behavior that is prior to positive law and discoverable by human reason. "The natural law expresses the original moral sense which enables man to discern by reason the good and the evil, the truth and the lie" (*CCC,* 1954).

31. "During the rationalist era jurists and philosophers have misused the notion of natural

Especially since the pontificate of Leo XIII, natural law doctrine has enjoyed acceptance as an established part of Church teaching, and from a theological perspective its existence is not in question.[32] Moreover, a worthy treatment of objections to natural law is outside the scope and intention of our study. Nonetheless, such arguments cannot be altogether passed over. The existence of natural rights depends on the existence of the natural moral law, and thus certain arguments against natural law must be dealt with. The following is in no wise an exhaustive presentation of objections to natural law theory. The five objections described here are, however, among the most notorious, and they offer a fair representation of the sort of criticisms voiced by opponents of natural law. The responses provided are meant only to indicate the direction a more thoroughgoing response could take.

A first, and perhaps the most typical, objection proposes that the wide variety of societal mores and ethical principles found in different cultures and historical periods excludes the possibility of a single, universal natural law. Were such a law in existence, critics say, one would observe greater ethical uniformity among peoples and cultures. Historicism and similar approaches seek to explain the assortment of moral codes by proposing that ethical norms are the product not of some abstract, immutable human nature, but of external conditioning forces, such as personal history, culture, and education. Some existentialists, in turn, deny the existence of human nature, asserting rather that existence precedes essence, and thus a natural law binding for all human beings is impossible.

A second objection rests on anthropological premises of a theological strain. The chief agents of the Protestant Reformation, whose accentuation on the corruption of human nature after the Fall cast doubt on reason's capability of furnishing trustworthy ethical criteria, by and large sidelined the natural law in favor of the law of the Gospel.[33] The ability

---

law to such a degree, either for conservative or for revolutionary purposes, they have put it forward in so oversimplified and so arbitrary a manner, that it is difficult to use it now without awakening distrust and suspicion in many of our contemporaries" (Maritain, *Man and the State*, 81).

32. Leo set forth the fundamental lines of the natural moral law especially in his encyclical *Libertas Praestantissimum* of June 20, 1888. This doctrine has been amply reiterated by Leo's successors and has been clearly formulated in the *Catechism of the Catholic Church*, §§ 1954–60, as well as in the encyclical letter *Veritatis Splendor*, especially §§ 40–60.

33. Among the reformers a variety of opinions existed. Calvin, for example, held that a sort of natural law is present in fallen man, and whereas his reason is sufficient to discern right from

of reason to ascertain moral truth was seen to be so limited as to be unreliable, and at any rate it was superseded by Christian revelation.[34]

A third objection typical of a modern scientific mentality questions the normative quality of human nature. Since man is called to subdue nature and harness it for his purposes, how can nature provide moral norms to which man must submit?

A fourth, more pragmatic objection would seek to deflect attention from foundational questions of moral justice in favor of practical consensus. If the goal of justice is social order and peace, consensus is to be preferred to principle since it goes straight to the heart of the matter without delving into theoretical considerations on which full agreement between peoples may never be reached, and which will therefore only stymie efforts to reach an accord.[35]

Fifth, and more recently, among moral theologians certain currents have sought to untether freedom from its mooring to theological and especially philosophical anthropology, which has resulted in a sweeping rejection of the natural law and its precepts.[36] Norms of morality would be

---

wrong, he is incapable of carrying out the good he sees. "There is imprinted on their hearts a discrimination and judgment by which they distinguish between what is just and unjust, between what is honest and dishonest . . . not of the power to fulfill the law, but of the knowledge of it" (John Calvin, *Commentary on Romans*, 2:15, cited by Daniel Westberg, "The Reformed Tradition and Natural Law," in *A Preserving Grace: Protestants, Catholics, and Natural Law*, ed. Michael Cromartie [Grand Rapids, Mich.: Ethics and Public Policy Center/William B. Eerdmans, 1997], 184n6). Martin Luther retained natural law in his theology, "though not without transforming its place and meaning within the framework of his overall understanding of the Gospel" (Carl E. Braaten, "A Response to Russell Hittinger," in *A Preserving Grace: Protestants, Catholics, and Natural Law*, ed. Michael Cromartie [Grand Rapids, Mich.: Ethics and Public Policy Center/William B. Eerdmans, 1997], 31).

34. De Finance notes that "Lutheran theology, in the measure in which it holds that human nature has been totally corrupted by original sin, so that human reason is now entirely incapable of grasping moral and religious truths, cannot but reject the notion of natural law. It is only revelation that can give people the knowledge of moral truths" (*An Ethical Inquiry*, § 182, p. 312).

35. For instance, as I noted earlier, Maritain observed that it was possible for the framers of the United Nations Universal Declaration of Human Rights to reach a consensus for the formulation of practical conclusions, despite the broad diversity of ideological allegiances, cultural backgrounds, and philosophical and religious traditions. Maritain states that "men mutually opposed in their theoretical conceptions can come to a merely practical agreement regarding a list of human rights" (*Man and the State*, 76).

36. "In fact, a new situation has come about *within the Christian community itself*, which has experienced the spread of numerous doubts and objections of a human and psychological, social and cultural, religious and even properly theological nature, with regard to the Church's

dictated by the autonomous moral conscience in its pursuit of the personal good, not by an objective moral code written into human nature.

A response to these objections could begin with the following considerations. In the first place, a distinction must be drawn between the existence of natural law and knowledge of the law. While cultural and historical circumstances undoubtedly influence one's grasp of moral principles, they do not negate such natural principles, nor do they dislodge the natural capacity of practical reason to discern moral truth. In studying the broad diversity of customs and moral norms operating in history and from culture to culture, one notes not only differences but also constants, which indicate commonality. To expect natural law to provide a detailed code of prescriptions immediately discernible to all is simply to demand too much from it.[37]

Second, Catholic anthropology differs from the Protestant view of man in that Catholics understand original sin to have wounded man's nature but not corrupted it beyond recognition. Though reason has been clouded and the will weakened, their operations remain substantially the same and thus man is still capable of knowing the truth—including moral truth—and adhering to it, albeit with difficulty.[38]

Third, as regards man's dominance over nature, care must be taken to avoid confusing different meanings of "nature." When we speak of man's dominance over "nature," the word refers to the physical world with its particular laws. When we speak of man's "nature" as the source of moral law, the word refers to a metaphysical principle: man's nature as a free, ra-

---

moral teachings. It is no longer a matter of limited and occasional dissent, but of an overall and systematic calling into question of traditional moral doctrine, on the basis of certain anthropological and ethical presuppositions. At the root of these presuppositions is the more or less obvious influence of currents of thought which end by detaching human freedom from its essential and constitutive relationship to truth. Thus the traditional doctrine regarding the natural law, and the universality and the permanent validity of its precepts, is rejected" (*VS*, 4).

37. "I think that one overstates the case to say that anything but the rudiments of moral law are known *naturaliter*" (Russell Hittinger, "Comments," in *A Preserving Grace: Protestants, Catholics, and Natural Law*, ed. Michael Cromartie [Grand Rapids, Mich.: Ethics and Public Policy Center/William B. Eerdmans, 1997], 42).

38. In his encyclical *Fides et Ratio*, Pope John Paul speaks of the censures delivered by the Magisterium to fideism and radical traditionalism "for their distrust of reason's natural capacities" (*FR*, 52). One of these, applied to Louis Bautain, reads as follows: "Although reason was weakened and darkened by original sin, yet sufficient clarity and strength remain in it to lead us with certainty to the knowledge of the existence of God" (Gregory XVI, *Theses a Ludovico Eugenio Bautain iussu sui Episcopi subscriptae* [September 8, 1840]: DS 2756).

tional being and incarnate spirit is what makes him what he is and distinguishes him from other sorts of beings. Moreover, even when we speak of nature in the sense of the physical world, man harnesses nature to his own purposes always through his understanding and application of nature's laws—not by flouting them. Through his understanding of gravity, for example, man is able to create a rocket that respects the law of gravity while allowing man to travel to the moon. Likewise, through man's knowledge of his own nature and end he is able to distinguish between activity that conforms to his true moral good and that which frustrates it.[39]

Fourth, concerning the superiority of pragmatic consensus to moral theorizing in political life, to employ the Latin maxim, here it is not a matter of *aut-aut* but *et-et;* that is, the two approaches are not mutually exclusive but complementary. The fact that consensus regarding practical action is often more expedient on a political plane does not preclude the need for study and discussion of the deeper foundational principles. What is consensus today can be changed in a single generation. Furthermore, even if for prudential reasons in a pluralist society pragmatic accords must be taken without insisting on agreement as to principle, it is essential to understand the deeper underpinnings of human moral principles to be able to distinguish them from false claims and to explain how they relate to true human fulfillment.

Finally, attempts to detach moral norms from an objective understanding of man and man's good cannot but lead to subjectivism or positivism, that is, either to the absence of objective moral norms or to moral principles grounded solely in the divine will and accessible only through revelation (or grounded in human will and dependent on civil legislation). Freedom seen as absolute independence is incompatible with natural law.[40]

---

39. Some falsely assert that natural law implies blind obedience to natural physiological processes rather than a law of reason. Thus Miranda explains that natural law is not, as some profess, "a series of moral conditions proceeding from physical nature, and specifically the corporal nature of man, as if the biological laws that govern bodily functions were in and of themselves morally binding on the conscience of the individual" (Gonzalo Miranda González de Echavarri, *Respuesta de amor: Manual de teología moral fundamental*, vol. 1 [Mexico City: Nueva Evangelización, 1998], 82; author's translation).

40. "If we understand human freedom in an entirely indeterministic way, as complete independence unlimited by anything whatsoever, then this concept, of course, already excludes all

This last point merits special consideration. Regardless of the specific content of natural law, to affirm its existence is to affirm that law cannot be reduced to positive law, and that positive law itself must submit to the rule of right reason.[41] Since natural and positive law are corporately exhaustive, the exclusion of natural law would leave positive law as the sole criterion of justice.[42] Right and wrong, just and unjust would become synonyms of legal and illegal. Hittinger asserts that "the most rudimentary form of natural law thinking arises in connection with the question of whether the *ius* is the mere artifice of positive law. Does this life, property, dignity, and status belong to me (him or them) exclusively by virtue of a contract or decree of the state or, for that matter, by the assertion of an individual?"[43]

The consequences of an affirmative reply are obvious. Without such a

---

natural law: natural law loses its meaning" (Wojtyła, "The Human Person and Natural Law," in Woznicki, *Person and Community*, 185).

41. In his Nichomachean Ethics, Aristotle notes this essential difference between positive and natural law, and emphasizes the stability of the natural law and the volatility of the positive. "Political justice is of two kinds, one natural and the other conventional. A rule of justice is natural that has the same validity everywhere, and does not depend on our accepting it or not. A rule is conventional that in the first instance may be settled in one way or the other indifferently" (V, 7: 1134b18–21).

It is our natural assumption that positive law mirrors and reinforces natural law, what is just in itself. MacIntyre writes: "We make laws providing penalties for performing certain types of action and for failing to perform others only if and when we believe that there are good reasons, prior to and independent of our lawmaking, for judging it to be good or right that such types of actions should be done or left undone. We also believe that those good reasons by themselves provide sufficient grounds for people in general to perform or to refrain from performing the relevant types of action. When by enacting laws we attach penalties to failure to perform or to refrain from performing, we provide additional grounds for those insufficiently motivated by such good reasons because of some deficiency of character. But our assumption is that anyone whose moral character was sufficiently educated would not need the motivation afforded by those additional sanctions for obeying the law" ("Theories of Natural Law in the Culture of Advanced Modernity," 99).

42. This holds true both for human law and divine law. Whereas nominalists beginning with Ockam asserted a divine voluntarism whereby God's commands are good *because* he commands them, Christian tradition has always maintained that God commands certain things because they are good. In other words, this tradition posits a harmony between the divine will and divine wisdom. Thus Thomas asks whether some human acts are right by nature, and not only because they are prescribed by law, and answers in the affirmative. The things, he writes, "prescribed by the divine law are right not only because they are prescribed by law, but also by their very nature" (*CG*, bk. III, ch. 129, 5).

43. Russell Hittinger, introduction to *The Natural Law: A Study in Legal and Social History and Philosophy*, by Heinrich A. Rommen (Indianapolis: Liberty Fund, 1998), xxix.

principle, human persons would be at the mercy of the whims of convention and legislatures (or, in their absence, reduced to anarchy). The majority could democratically enact laws subjugating minorities, and these latter could appeal to no higher standard than the democratic process, making way for a situation of tyranny of the strong over the weak.[44] Consensualism is a helpful political tool for ordering many aspects of human society, but it is seriously deficient as the final criterion of justice. Natural law refers to objective ethical principles that precede all legislation and by which legislation can be called to render an account and judged as just or unjust.[45] In 1953 Leo Strauss wrote that

> the need for natural right is as evident today as it has been for centuries and even millennia. To reject natural right is tantamount to saying that all right is positive right, and this means that what is right is determined exclusively by the legislators and the courts of the various countries. Now it is obviously meaningful, and sometimes even necessary, to speak of "unjust" laws or "unjust" decisions. In passing such judgments we imply that there is a standard of right and wrong independent of positive right and higher than positive right: a standard with which we are able to judge of positive right.[46]

Of course, a mere assertion of the desirability or even necessity of natural right or natural law does not prove its existence.[47] At the same time, every attempt to replace natural law with something else has fallen flat. Just as no speculative reasoning can be carried out without self-evident

---

44. Pope John Paul II has repeatedly cited the uncoupling of freedom from objective truth as the root of totalitarianism. "Totalitarianism arises out of a denial of truth in the objective sense. If there is no transcendent truth, in obedience to which man achieves his full identity, then there is no sure principle for guaranteeing just relations between people. Their self-interest as a class, group or nation would inevitably set them in opposition to one another. If one does not acknowledge transcendent truth, then the force of power takes over, and each person tends to make full use of the means at his disposal in order to impose his own interests or his own opinion, with no regard for the rights of others" (*VS,* 99; see also *CA,* 44, in *AAS* 83 [1991]: 848–49; Leo XIII, *Libertas Praestantissimum,* 224–26).

45. The same holds true concerning natural rights. "These rights are prior to society and must be recognized by it. They are the basis of the moral legitimacy of every authority: by flouting them, or refusing to recognize them in its positive legislation, a society undermines its own moral legitimacy" (*CCC,* 1939; see also *PT,* 65).

46. Leo Strauss, *Natural Right and History* (Chicago: University of Chicago Press, 1953), 2.

47. "Certainly, the seriousness of the need of natural right does not prove that the need can be satisfied. A wish is not a fact. Even by proving that a certain view is indispensable for living well, one proves merely that the view in question is a salutary myth: one does not prove it to be true. Utility and truth are two entirely different things" (ibid., 6).

principles, so too no practical reasoning can take place without self-evident first principles.[48] When natural law is discarded, positive law itself loses all authority except the power of force.

Perhaps the strongest argument in favor of the existence of natural law is that provided by common human experience. That right must proceed from some source other than (prior to) positive law is evidenced by the fact, as the quote from Strauss attests, that man habitually and spontaneously evaluates positive laws as just or unjust. Since history provides countless examples of unjust laws, it requires little imagination to come up with examples that bear this out. Laws that arbitrarily disadvantage individuals or groups grate against a sense of fairness that can be witnessed among all peoples in all eras. People spontaneously make judgments about both laws and human actions that reveal a sense of justice that stands independent of and above positive laws. Critics of natural law theory themselves, if they examine their own behavior and beliefs in an unbiased way, will discover that they cannot wholly refrain from evaluating human conduct in absolute terms of right and wrong, with no reference to positive law. Even little children, when playing together, will utter expressions such as "That's not fair!" which bear no relation to established rules but simply reflect a basic sense of right and wrong, just and unjust. The same principles of natural right or natural justice that allow us to evaluate actions as fair or unfair, good or evil, can be restated as precepts of law: Do this; avoid that.

THE IDEA OF NATURAL LAW

Though in itself law is an extrinsic principle of human activity,[49] God has written a law into man's nature. Thus "human acts can be regulated by the rule of human reason, which rule is derived from the created things that man knows naturally; and further still, from the rule of the Divine law."[50] Through His loving providence, God directs all of creation

---

48. "I draw the following conclusions. The thing which I have called for convenience the *Tao*, and which others may call Natural Law or Traditional Morality or the First Principles of Practical Reason or the First Platitudes, is not one among a series of possible systems of value. It is the sole source of all value judgements. If it is rejected, all value is rejected. If any value is retained, it is retained" (Lewis, *The Abolition of Man*, 56).

49. See *S. Th.*, I-II, 90, preamble.

50. Ibid., I-II, 74, 7.

to its proper end. Nevertheless, God provides for man differently from the way in which He provides for beings that are not persons, and natural law does not guide man to his proper end through coercion, as other laws do. Thus God "cares for man not 'from without,' through the laws of physical nature, but 'from within,' through reason, which, by its natural knowledge of God's eternal law, is consequently able to show man the right direction to take in his free actions."[51] Practical reason discovers precepts of right action written into created reality, which provide guidance to man's free will to choose good and avoid evil.[52] In this way God has made man a sharer in His own providence, since He desires to guide the world through man's reasonable and responsible care. The *natural law*, therefore, is the human expression of God's eternal law.[53]

Thus together with the body of positive moral norms and laws that come from without (so-called heteronomous precepts),[54] man also discovers internal normative principles of activity[55] to which he can reason independently and by which he can judge his own and others' actions.[56]

---

51. *VS*, 43. See also *S. Th.*, I-II, 90, 1, ad 1.

52. Thus Miranda defines the natural moral law as consisting of "a series of general moral principles that man's natural reason spontaneously formulates from his proper nature or way of being" (*Respuesta de amor*, 83; author's translation).

53. "Among all others, the rational creature is subject to divine providence in the most excellent way, insofar as it partakes of a share of providence, being provident both for itself and for others. Thus it has a share of the Eternal Reason, whereby it has a natural inclination to its proper act and end. This participation of the eternal law in the rational creature is called natural law" (*S. Th.*, I-II, 91, 2).

54. The divine positive law can be called heteronomous only in the sense of extrinsic, not in the sense of unrelated to man's true good. "Hence obedience to God is not, as some would believe, a *heteronomy*, as if the moral life were subject to the will of something all-powerful, absolute, extraneous to man and intolerant of his freedom. If in fact a heteronomy of morality were to mean a denial of man's self-determination or the imposition of norms unrelated to his good, this would be in contradiction to the Revelation of the Covenant and of the redemptive Incarnation. Such a heteronomy would be nothing but a form of alienation, contrary to divine wisdom and to the dignity of the human person" (*VS*, 41).

55. Hittinger holds that as a true law, the natural moral law is an extrinsic principle, but it is written into man's nature and thus governs his actions not by coercion but by appealing to his practical reason. "The natural law is extrinsic, but not external; whereas positive law is extrinsic and almost always external" ("Comments," 48).

56. Joseph Boyle sums up the traditional understanding of natural law as "a set of universal prescriptions whose prescriptive force is a function of the rationality which all human beings share in virtue of their common humanity" ("Natural Law and the Ethics of Traditions," in *Natural Law Theory: Contemporary Essays*, ed. Robert P. George [Oxford: Clarendon Press, 1995], 4).

These internal normative principles are traditionally referred to as "natural law," in that they pertain to man's nature as a free, rational being.[57] Natural moral law, then, can be defined as "that moral order which arises from the full reality of human nature and which can be recognized by man's reason, independent of positive revelation."[58] Indeed, man reasons that certain actions, though perhaps pleasurable or useful for attaining determined goods, are unworthy of him and degrade him as a human being, while other choices elevate him because they correspond to his true good, which his reason discerns. Man realizes, moreover, that his free choices constitute him as a moral subject, in that they make him into a particular sort of person: the sort of person who would avoid certain actions and perform others.[59] Therefore, whereas speculative reason leads man to understand what he *is*, practical reason leads him to understand what he *should be* and consequently what he *should do*.[60] It also discovers in other persons beings who *should be treated* in a certain way.

In his encyclical on the moral life, *Veritatis Splendor*, Pope John Paul II summarizes the Church's perennial teaching on natural law. According to this vision, the entire moral law finds its origin and its authority in God.[61] Nonetheless, on making man in His own image and endowing him with reason and free will, God wrote this law into man's nature, to be discovered and freely adhered to. For this reason, the natural law is a fully human law.[62] God created man and ordered him with wisdom and

---

57. A typical definition is that of Marcellinus Zalba: "The natural law is a necessary divine ordering of the rational creature to its natural final end, written into the selfsame nature and perceived by the natural light of reason" (*Theologiae Moralis Compendium I* [Madrid: BAC, 1958], § 316; author's translation). Wojtyła has written that "natural law is something that intimately corresponds to the person and that is proper to the person. For if the person is an 'individual substance of a rational nature,' it is hard to deny that an 'ordinance of reason' corresponds to and is proper to the person" ("The Human Person and the Natural Law," 184).

58. Peschke, *A Presentation of General Moral Theology*, 105.

59. For example, a man who deliberately chooses to lie not only chooses the act of lying, he also chooses to become a liar, since he chooses to be the sort of person who would lie. In this way, he both opts for conduct that is reprehensible and degrades himself as a moral subject.

60. "His reason, as 'speculative reason,' allows him to understand what is; and as 'practical reason' helps him to understand what he should be, and consequently, what he should do" (Miranda, *Respuesta de amor*, 36; author's translation).

61. Thus the Pope observes that "reason draws its own truth and authority from the eternal law, which is none other than divine wisdom itself. The moral law has its origin in God and always finds its source in him" (*VS*, 40).

62. John Paul adds that "at the same time, by virtue of natural reason, which derives from divine wisdom, it is a properly human law" (ibid.).

love to his final end, through the law that is inscribed in his heart (see Rom. 2:15), the "natural law." "[Natural law] 'is nothing other than the light of understanding infused in us by God, whereby we understand what must be done and what must be avoided. God gave this light and this law to man at creation.'"63

The obligatory character of natural law can be discussed from three different but complementary angles.64 In the first place, and most essentially, natural law can be viewed as the ordinance of the divine Lawgiver, reflected in man's nature. In this regard, Aquinas neatly sums up the natural law as "nothing else than the rational creature's participation of the eternal law."65 Hence the authority of the natural moral law—and its obligatory character—derives from the authority of God Himself.66 Second, natural law can be viewed as a function of man's nature. Man possesses an ontological structure that is a locus of intelligible necessities as well as of ends that correspond to his essential constitution. Furthermore, writes Maritain, "since man is endowed with intelligence and determines his own ends, it is up to him to put himself in tune with the ends necessarily demanded by his nature."67 Thus man can come to understand which actions correspond to his nature and true good, and which are unworthy of it. Third, natural law can be examined as an epistemological problem regarding man's cognitive grasp of the moral precepts written into his nature as a person. This means, continues Maritain, that "there is, by the very virtue of human nature, an order or a disposition which human reason can discover and according to which the human will must act in order to attune itself to the essential and necessary ends of the human being."68

---

63. John Paul II, *VS*, 12, citing St. Thomas Aquinas, *In duo praecepta caritatis et in decem legis praecepta. Prologus: Opuscula theologica,* II, no. 1129 (Paris: Ed. Taurinens, 1954), 245; see also *S. Th.*, I-II, 91, 2; *CCC*, 1955.

64. Russell Hittinger's treatment of the three foci of natural law discourse provides a clear summary of the theme. See "Natural Law and Catholic Moral Theology," in *A Preserving Grace: Protestants, Catholics, and Natural Law*, ed. Michael Cromartie, (Grand Rapids, Mich.: Ethics and Public Policy Center/William B. Eerdmans, 1997).

65. *S. Th.*, I-II, 91, 2.

66. The natural law "is written and engraved in the mind of every man; and this is nothing but our reason, commanding us to do right and forbidding sin. Nevertheless, all prescriptions of human reason can have force of law only inasmuch as they are the voice and the interpreters of some higher power on which our reason and liberty necessarily depend" (*Libertas Praestantissimum*, 8).

67. Maritain, *Man and the State*, 86.   68. Ibid.

THE UNIVERSALITY OF NATURAL LAW

These three complementary dimensions of the natural moral law provide an invaluable starting point for a discussion of the universality of the law. The first dimension deals with the origin of the natural moral law, the second with its impression on human nature, and the third with man's cognitive grasp of its precepts. As regards the first level, it is clear that the eternal law is one and is immutable and unchanging. Therefore, the *origin* of the natural moral law is universal, being the same for all. The question of the third level—the universality of man's *knowledge* of the natural law—will be left aside for the moment, since it merits a more in-depth treatment.

On the second level, the natural moral law shows itself to be written into man's nature not as an addition to that nature, but as constitutive and inherent to it. For this reason, it inheres in every individual who partakes of this nature, that is, in every human person. It is not a function of the degree of intelligence or any other quality that may vary from person to person, but simply of man's nature as a rational animal.[69] Because all human beings have a rational nature, all are subject to the same fundamental moral principles inherent in that nature.[70] This is why despite great cultural variance among peoples, the virtues (though perhaps not their concrete expressions) are the same for all, as are vices and sins.[71] Envy, lust, and treachery, just like courage, magnanimity, and loyalty, are universally intelligible moral categories, though their concrete expressions may differ.

The *Catechism*, in fact, stresses the universality and unchanging nature of the natural moral law, stating that the

> natural law is immutable and permanent throughout the variations of history (Cf. *GS,* 10); it subsists under the flux of ideas and customs and supports their

---

69. We speak of all men as intelligent, in the sense of having use of reason, but we do not speak of more intelligent persons as "more human." One either is, or is not, a human being. Thus humanity is a binary function. In the same way, the natural moral law inheres in all human beings by the fact of their humanity.

70. "The natural law, present in the heart of each man and established by reason, is universal in its precepts and its authority extends to all men" (*CCC,* 1956).

71. The *Catechism* points out that "in the diversity of cultures, the natural law remains as a rule that binds men among themselves and imposes on them, beyond the inevitable differences, common principles" (ibid., 1957).

progress. The rules that express it remain substantially valid. Even when it is rejected in its very principles, it cannot be destroyed or removed from the heart of man. It always rises again in the life of individuals.[72]

Just as those who deny basic axioms of speculative reason inevitably make use of the very principles they reject (think, for example, of Hume's denial of causality), so too, those who reject the basic precepts of the natural law end up appealing to them again and again, without calling them by name.

Maritain points out that since the natural moral law flows from first principles deriving from man's common nature, "the precepts of the unwritten law are in themselves or in the nature of things (I am not saying in man's knowledge of them) universal and invariable."[73] Because underlying human goods do not depend on man's preferences but rather on his unchanging nature, the precepts that enjoin the pursuit and protection of such goods and prohibit their violation are likewise universal. Practical reason, as Pope John Paul II observes, recognizes that it is "right and just, always and for everyone, to serve God, to render him the worship which is his due and to honor one's parents as they deserve."[74] Since these moral truths are accessible to human reason, the positive precepts that derive from them (the same truths, stated in the imperative, such as "Honor thy father and thy mother") "are universally binding; they are unchanging" and "unite in the same common good all people of every period of history, created for 'the same divine calling and destiny' (*GS*, 29)."[75]

In like manner, the *negative precepts* of the natural law are universally valid. "They oblige each and every individual, always and in every circumstance" because "the choice of this kind of behavior is in no case compatible with the goodness of the will of the acting person, with his vocation to life with God and to communion with his neighbor."[76]

---

72. Ibid., 1958. Thomas offers two distinctions regarding the immutability of the natural moral law. First, if one considers the change that is *addition* to the precepts of the natural law, there is nothing to hinder such change (though one could say that these superadded precepts are placed alongside the natural law, not added to its proper content). Second, there may be a certain mutability as regards the application of the natural law, whereby certain proper precepts may not be applicable in determined circumstances. Clearly, as regards the general principles of the natural moral law, no change is possible, since man's nature is constant and unchanging. See *S. Th.*, I-II, 94, 5.

73. Maritain, *The Rights of Man*, 39.
74. *VS*, 52.
75. Ibid.
76. Ibid.

One final distinction should be made concerning the universality of the natural moral law. Thomas notes that while it is indeed universal in its general precepts, as regards matters of detail—conclusions of these general precepts—the natural moral law holds in a "majority of cases."[77] Thomas takes the example of the common principle that goods taken in trust should be restored to their rightful owner on demand. He mentions the case of a person who would wish to use those goods to fight against his country (elsewhere he uses the example of a madman who demands restitution of his sword),[78] in which case the precept would not bind. Consequently, the natural moral law is universal in its general precepts, but since it deals with contingency of human action and a vast array of possible circumstances, in matters of detail it may occasionally vary.

THE CONTENT OF NATURAL LAW

What does the natural moral law in fact enjoin? Which specific moral precepts are included under the heading of the natural moral law? Here Aquinas's teaching can be especially helpful, though other reflections and considerations can complete his thought along the way.

The natural law deals primarily with first principles, with practical premises that cannot be reasoned to from other truths.[79] Thus Thomas teaches that "the precepts of the natural law are to the practical reason, what the first principles of demonstrations are to the speculative reason; because both are self-evident principles."[80] The quality of self-evidence is critical, since all discursive reasoning must begin with premises, both for speculative and practical reasoning. The compulsory character of particular moral norms likewise derives from the compulsory character of the general norm from which they originate. As Lewis says, "If nothing is self-evident, nothing can be proved. Similarly, if nothing is obligatory for

---

77. See *S. Th.*, I-II, 94, 4.
78. See ibid., II-II, 120, 1.
79. "The natural law states the first and essential precepts which govern the moral life" (*CCC*, 1955). "All the practical principles behind the Innovator's case for posterity, or society, or the species, are there from time immemorial in the *Tao*. But they are nowhere else. Unless you accept these without question as being to the world of action what axioms are to the world of theory, you can have no practical principles whatever. You cannot reach them as conclusions: they are premisses" (Lewis, *The Abolition of Man*, 52–53).
80. *S. Th.*, I-II, 94, 2.

its own sake, nothing is obligatory at all."[81] Insistence on the essence of natural law as dealing with first principles helps circumvent erroneous notions of natural law as a comprehensive code of detailed moral norms embracing every possible circumstance. Natural law deals with first principles, which must be instantiated in concrete circumstances by practical reason, perfected by the virtue of prudence.

Thomas continues with the analogy between speculative reason and practical reason in the search for a first principle. He states that speculative reason treats of being, and thus the first indemonstrable principle of speculative reasoning is the principle of noncontradiction, that "the same thing cannot be affirmed and denied at the same time" (based on the notion of "being" and "not-being"). From this principle, Thomas continues, all others are based.[82] But just as "being" is the first thing that falls under the apprehension simply, "so 'good' is the first thing that falls under the apprehension of the practical reason, which is directed to action: since every agent acts for an end under the aspect of good." Because in acting reasonably man always pursues the good, so the first principle of practical reason states that "good is that which all things seek after."[83] This principle likewise furnishes the first precept of law, that "good is to be done and pursued, and evil is to be avoided." A regression performed on any moral precept or ethical cause will ultimately arrive at this principle. Whether one advocates saving whales, advancing the cause of

81. Lewis, *The Abolition of Man*, 53.
82. *S. Th.*, I-II, 94, 2.
83. "It is easy to be confused by the Aristotelian tag that 'the good is what all things desire'—as if the goodness were consequential on the desires. But, as it applies to the human good and human desire, this tag was intended to affirm simply that (i) our primary use of the word 'good' (and related terms) is to express our practical thinking, i.e. our thinking, in terms of reasons for action, towards decision and action; and that (ii) we would not bother with such thinking, or such action, unless we were in fact interested in (*desirous* of . . .) whatever it is we are calling good. Those who use the tag were equally insistent that one's human desire is a pursuit of something in so far as it seems desirable, and that things seem desirable to one in so far as they (appear to) promise to make one better off (not necessarily 'materially,' or instrumentally)" (Finnis, *Natural Law and Natural Rights*, 70). Another way to express "to make one better off" would be to say that such a good "perfects" man or makes him not just "better off" but really "better." Now, to say that such a good perfects man means that it completes him, or makes him more truly what he is. This in turn implies some version of the Aristotelian concept of act and potency. Man is not fully actualized, and thus is susceptible to being improved or perfected. It likewise implies a teleology. Man is not only not fully what he is capable of being, he is also not fully what he is meant to be.

women, preserving Costa Rican rain forests, or feeding the poor, the ultimate grounds for justifying one's cause is that it is good, not in an instrumental but in an absolute way, and at least implicitly one acknowledges that *good is to be done and evil avoided.*

Therefore, just as all principles of speculative reason issue from the principle of noncontradiction, so too all natural moral law principles issue from the first principle of practical reason. This principle does not exhaust the natural law but forms its font and origin.[84] The natural moral law embraces the ensemble of moral principles that flow necessarily from this first essential principle.[85] How does this come about? Obviously from the precept that "good is to be done and evil avoided" nothing further can be logically deduced. It is only by adding further data about man's good that one can come to specific conclusions as to what is to be pursued and what avoided. Thus Thomas says that "whatever the practical reason naturally apprehends as man's good (or evil) belongs to the precepts of the natural law as something to be done or avoided."[86]

But here, too, data seems to be lacking. How does practical reason go about determining what is good? What criterion distinguished good from evil? Aquinas assigns this role in the first place to natural inclinations. "[A]ll those things to which man has a natural inclination, are naturally apprehended by reason as being good, and consequently as objects of pursuit, and their contraries as evil, and objects of avoidance.... Wherefore according to the order of natural inclinations, is the order of the precepts of the natural law."[87]

These inclinations Thomas arranges on three tiers. There is a good

---

84. Thus Thomas remarks that "the precepts of the natural law are many in themselves, but are based on one common foundation" (*S. Th.*, I-II, 94, 2, ad 2).

85. "The only practical knowledge all men have naturally and infallibly in common is that we must do good and avoid evil. This is the preamble and principle of natural law; it is not the law itself. Natural law is the ensemble of things to do and not to do which follow therefrom in *necessary* fashion, and *from the simple fact that man is man,* nothing else being taken into account" (Maritain, *The Rights of Man*, 36; emphasis in original). It should be noted that this "following from" in necessary fashion does not take the form of logical deduction, as if a whole string of moral precepts could be pulled from the sleeves of first practical principles. Rather, that which presents itself to the moral subject as good will present itself contemporaneously as "to be done," and that which the moral subject perceives as evil, he will likewise perceive as "to be avoided."

86. *S. Th.*, I-II, 94, 2.

87. Ibid.

pertaining to man's lower nature that he has in common with all other substances: the good of existence. Wherefore man, like other substances, naturally seeks the preservation of his being. Thomas concludes that "by reason of this inclination, whatever is a means of preserving human life, and of warding off its obstacles, belongs to the natural law." On the second tier Thomas places those goods that man shares with other animals, and again, by virtue of this inclination, those things are said to belong to the natural law, "which nature has taught to all animals, such as sexual intercourse, education of offspring and so forth." On the third tier one finds those goods that are proper to man "according to the nature of his reason," and thus man has a natural inclination to know the truth about God and to live in society. In this respect, Thomas concludes, whatever pertains to this higher inclination also belongs to the natural law, such as "to shun ignorance, to avoid offending those among whom one has to live, and other such things regarding the above inclination."[88]

Linking goods to inclinations sounds plausible but leaves problems in its wake. MacIntyre, for example, writes of

> the question of precisely which of our desires are to be acknowledged as legitimate guides to action, and which on the other hand are to be inhibited, frustrated or re-educated; and clearly this question cannot be answered by trying to use desires themselves as some sort of criterion. Just because all of us have, actually or potentially, numerous desires, many of them conflicting and mutually incompatible, we have to decide between the rival claims of rival desires.[89]

In other words, as a criterion for ascertaining man's good, natural inclinations do not seem to be sufficient. Left to themselves, man's natural tendencies pull in multiple directions, and due to the internal disorder that is the legacy of original sin, they do not always conform to man's true good. Some other coordinating principle must be invoked.

Thomas supplements his statements about human inclinations with teleological considerations regarding man's final end. Thomas teaches that "since everything desires its own perfection, a man desires for his ultimate end, that which he desires as his perfect and crowning good."[90]

---

88. Ibid.
89. MacIntyre, *After Virtue*, 48. It should be noted, however, that Thomas does not speak of momentary *desires* as guides to human action but rather of stable tendencies or inclinations as indicative of human goods.
90. *S. Th.*, I-II, 1, 5. See also ibid., I, 5, 1.

This perfect good, to which man naturally tends, is happiness. The natural moral law, in fact, is concerned chiefly with conducting man to his last end, which is beatitude. And so "the law must needs regard principally the relationship to happiness."[91] Far from an assault against man's happiness, the moral law finds its reason for being in this happiness, since it orders man's activities to attain it. It corresponds to his deepest desires and longings and leads him to the fullness of being.[92] Thomas notes that "as the intellect of necessity adheres to the first principles, the will must of necessity adhere to the last end, which is happiness."[93] Therefore, freedom is not exercised as regards the last end, which is "fixed." When man acts rationally, he necessarily seeks happiness in all he does. At the same time, he needs guidance concerning which means are to be chosen to reach his last end. Law, therefore, as a rule of action, teaches man to order his actions to achieve happiness.

Furthermore, we must recall that for Thomas, the happiness that all men desire is the attainment and enjoyment of God, "who alone by His infinite goodness can perfectly satisfy man's will."[94] In this sense, the natural moral law conducts man to the attainment and enjoyment of God. "Moreover," he writes, "those things are natural to every man, whereby he tends to his natural end: while those which are of a contrary nature, are naturally unbecoming to him. Now, we have proved above[95] that man is by nature directed to God as his end. Consequently those things whereby man is brought to the knowledge and love of God, are naturally right: and whatever things have a contrary result, are naturally bad for man."[96] Thus it would seem that there are really two fundamental principles for discerning man's good: natural inclinations and the usefulness of

---

91. Ibid., I-II, 90, 2.

92. Matthew Berke, commenting on the encyclical letter *Veritatis Splendor*, notes that "the commandments are not regarded here as arbitrary, life-denying impositions that are alien to man's real impulses (*VS* 41), being accepted only in order to receive a payoff from God in the next life. Ethical requirements bind the conscience because they are *true*—true, that is, with respect to 'what man is and what he must do' (*VS* 10) in order to flourish and enjoy the fullness of life in this world as well as the next, as an individual and as a member of the social body" ("A Jewish Appreciation of Catholic Social Teaching," 239).

93. *S. Th.*, I, 82, 1.

94. See ibid., I-II, 3, 1. "Happiness is called man's supreme good, because it is the attainment or enjoyment of the supreme good" (ibid., ad 2).

95. *CG*, bk. III, ch. 17, n. 25.

96. Ibid., bk. III, ch. 129, n. 8.

things for bringing man to his final end. This would explain what Thomas means when he says that natural inclinations must be ordered according to right reason.⁹⁷ If particular things to which man is inclined can be directed to his integral good (if they lead to his perfection and ultimately to God), then they are truly good for man and worthy of choosing. Such options that cannot be so ordered are evil and to be avoided. Here it is clear how closely the natural moral law depends on its anthropological foundation: one can understand what is to be done only by understanding man's good, and man's good can be determined only by knowing who man is and what he is for.

The "perfect, ultimate good" of happiness serves as an end but does not in and of itself reveal the means to that end. It is precisely the task of the moral law to indicate the way to attain to this happiness. Moreover, the natural moral law does not address only man's final good, but also those particular goods that pertain to his nature. We have seen that "everything desires its own perfection," and since the good is perfective of nature, everything needed for the perfection of nature will be apprehended as a good.⁹⁸

Are natural inclinations then the source of natural law? Natural inclinations indeed serve as criteria for discovering human goods in a *general* way: life, sexual intimacy, knowledge, friendship, and so forth. But these different goods must be ordered and appropriated according to reason to ensure that they contribute to man's integral good.⁹⁹ The fact that man is

---

97. "As, in man, reason rules and commands the other powers, so all the natural inclinations belonging to the other powers must needs be directed according to reason" (*S. Th.*, I-II, 94, 4, ad 3). It is the role of the virtues to perfect natural inclinations and to order them according to reason.

98. Since goodness is convertible with being, differing only in the aspect of desirability (see ibid., I, 5, 1), to desire goodness is to desire the fullness of being. To desire this end is also to desire the particular means ordered to this end, and for this very reason the means become useful goods and are good inasmuch as they are useful for achieving this end, that is, inasmuch as they are perfective of the person.

99. In this sense it seems clear that an understanding of man's nature is essential for evaluating whether particular perceived goods do in fact contribute to the person's overall good. If we are ignorant of man's nature, we have no point of reference for reason to distinguish true goods from apparent but false ones. Since good means the perfection of being, the particular good of a being will depend on what sort of being we are dealing with. Otherwise, inclinations are our only guide, and human experience confirms that such inclinations do not infallibly lead to man's true good. In this regard, I agree with MacIntyre's critique of the Grisez/Finnis rejection of human nature as guide for discerning true human goods. "Grisez, Finnis, and other

naturally inclined to eat does not mean that eating anything, at any time, in any place is necessarily good, or that refraining from eating at a given time is a negation of that good. By his reason, man understands that eating is not an absolute good but is ordered toward his health and physical well-being; his health and physical well-being, in turn, contribute to his overall human flourishing.[100] If a certain instance of eating should fail to contribute to these personal goods, or worse still, should cause a person harm, it would cease to be a good for him. In like manner, sexual relations are generally good for man because they contribute to the love and union between spouses and allow for the fruit of new life. Deprived of these two goods toward which it is ordered, however, sexual activity, too, ceases to be a good for the person.

Certain basic goods, therefore, such as health and physical well-being, are good in themselves, not as a *means* but as a *constitutive part* of man's overall good.[101] Related goods (such as food) and corresponding activities (such as eating) are good not in themselves but as means to attaining the human goods to which they are directed (in this case, health). Both "eating" and "health" are said to contribute to man's integral good or perfection, but they do so in essentially different ways. Health does so since it forms a part of man's overall good; eating does so inasmuch as it leads to

---

exponents of their position emphasize that their view—that our knowledge of human goods is not and cannot be derived from our knowledge of human nature, but rather is knowledge of what is self-evident to intelligent persons—does not mean that the goods of which they speak are not fulfilling of human nature. But they do repudiate all arguments of the form: Human nature's essential and ordered inclinations are such-and-such; the achievement of so-and-so would be the achievement of that to which human nature is inclined and ordered; therefore so-and-so is a good for human nature; and therefore we ought to respect and to achieve so-and-so" (MacIntyre, "Theories of Natural Law in the Culture of Advanced Modernity," 106–7).

100. "Hence there is an obligation on the human person to respect the movement towards a continued and ever deepening existence which is essential to his nature: the conservation of his life, of his physical integrity, of his liberty insofar as it is the condition for genuinely human activity, the effort to attain a certain level of cultural development and, in general, the conditions of life in default of which human existence degenerates—all of these will constitute inevitable and universal obligations, even though on certain points, such as the last-mentioned obligation, the manner in which they are applicable can vary considerably" (de Finance, *An Ethical Inquiry*, § 185, p. 320).

101. Here the Finnis-Grisez category of basic human goods (values) is helpful. John Finnis lists them as the goods of life (including health and vitality), knowledge, play, aesthetic experience, sociability (friendship), practical reasonableness, and religion (see *Natural Law and Natural Rights*, 85–90).

health, which is a constitutive part of man's overall perfection.[102] Thus Finnis observes:

> The universality of a few basic values in a vast diversity of realizations emphasizes *both* the connection between a basic human urge/drive/inclination/tendency and the corresponding basic form of human good, and at the same time the great difference between following an urge and intelligently pursuing a particular realization of a form of human good that is never completely realized and exhausted by any one action, or lifetime, or institution, or culture (nor by any finite number of them).[103]

---

102. "Recall, first of all, the distinction between the brute fact of an urge (or drive or inclination or tendency) and the forms of good which one who has such urges can think it worth while to pursue and realize, on the ground not that he has the urges but that he can see the good of such pursuit and realization. Secondly, and *a fortiori*, recall the distinction between the material conditions for, or affecting, the pursuit of a value and the value itself. A sound brain and intelligence are necessary conditions for the understanding, pursuit, and realization of truth, but neither brainpower nor intelligence should appear in a list of basic values: knowledge is the relevant value. . . . Thirdly, in listing the basic values in which human beings may participate, recall the distinctions between general value and particular goal, and between ends and the means for attaining, realizing, or participating in those ends" (ibid., 82).

103. Ibid., 84. Though I have been citing Finnis's work regarding basic human goods and find it most helpful, I must register disagreement with certain central components of his theory, especially with the assertion that no objective hierarchy exists among human goods. For instance, he writes that "each one [of these values], when we focus on it, can reasonably be regarded as the most important. Hence there is no objective hierarchy amongst them" (ibid., 92). It seems to me that Finnis confuses hierarchy and incommensurability. Incommensurability merely signifies that different goods cannot be reduced to a common measure and interchanged according to some ratio. But the existence of an objective hierarchy in no wise suggests incommensurability. Hierarchy does not mean that goods possess greater or lesser value along a common scale, which can produce some ratio such as 2:1 or 4:3. It means, rather, that goods exist on different tiers that separate them and render them incommensurable.

Similarly, Finnis also writes: "Each [of the basic values] is fundamental. None is more fundamental than any of the others, for each can reasonably be focused upon, and each, when focused upon, claims a priority of value. Hence there is no objective priority of value amongst them" (ibid., 93). I see at least two problems with this statement. First, Finnis seems to draw a metaphysical conclusion ("hence there is no objective priority amongst them") from a psychological premise ("each can reasonably be focused upon, and each, when focused upon, claims a priority of value"). Second, as regards the premise, certain basic goods, when focused upon, do *not* seem to claim a priority of value. When I eat, I recognize the importance and indeed the necessity of eating, but I also am aware that it is not the most important activity of my life. It is one thing to say that a basic value is in itself a "sufficient reason for acting" in a given instance and quite another to infer from this an equality among all basic values. Some values rightly are accorded a subsidiary status in life, and we judge a person irresponsible or superficial if he absolutizes or exaggerates the importance of one of these. Furthermore, from a Christian perspective, to have fully developed the first six basic values while neglecting the seventh (religion, holiness) is to have utterly failed. "What does it profit a man . . . ?" (Matt. 16:26; Mark 8:36; Luke 9:25).

If these reflections were to end here, the analysis of the content of natural law would be severely lacking. The preceding discussion has focused on man's perfection, the fullness of being, in which is found his happiness where nothing is lacking to him. From this cosmological, objectivist perspective, man is seen as a creature alongside other creatures, albeit the most exalted. Thus his good consists in the perfection of his nature on its different levels: that which it shares with all beings, that which is proper to animal life, and that which is proper to man as man (the use of reason).[104] Moreover, his good—his perfection—is seen as essentially immanent and self-relational, whereby other created realities are valued as goods insofar as they act as perfecting elements of his nature—in other words, as means to his perfection. This analysis would be sufficient if men existed as isolated individuals in a world of things, but this is not the case. The human person is in continual contact with other human persons who, like himself, are consciously pursuing their own perfection (happiness, the fullness of being, the attainment of God). These other persons are not objects alongside other objects, nor are they simply means to be used in one's quest for perfection.[105] They—like me—are persons, not *something*, but *someone*, spiritual subjects of action. The addition of other persons to the equation of human action and human happiness is so crucial that in a sense it throws the preceding analysis out of kilter.

This helps to explain a curious anomaly in Thomas's exposition of the natural law. If one were to construct *ex novo* a series of natural law pre-

---

104. It should be noted that though certain human goods and the actions realized to attain them can be said to be common to man and irrational beings, man's personhood permeates even these goods and these actions, and thus they are distinctly "human." The action of a man dining is entirely different from the action of a horse feeding. Man does not live as an animal on one level and as a human on another, even though determined actions and determined goods resemble those of irrational animals. Thus de Finance observes: "Because of the unity in man of spiritual subject and organism, even his animal activities have a teleology which rises above the purely biological and animal level, and already share in some degree in the teleology which is his as a spiritual subject" (*An Ethical Inquiry*, § 185, p. 321). See also Miranda, *Respuesta de amor*, 91.

105. In Thomas's teleological framework, beings that are lower than man have their place as means to his perfection, and God has "His place" as man's final end and *summum bonum*. Other persons, however, do not fit neatly into this structure and risk being relegated to the realm of mere means to man's perfection, since they cannot be his final end. "Now a twofold order has to be considered in things: the one, whereby one created thing is directed to another, as the parts to the whole, accident to substance, and all things whatsoever to their end; the other, whereby all created things are ordered to God" (*S. Th.*, I, 21, 1, ad 3).

cepts from the analysis just undertaken, one would undoubtedly come up with precepts regarding the ordered use of natural goods to ensure that they always contribute to man's integral fulfillment, and thus to his happiness. They would deal principally with the cardinal virtues of temperance, fortitude, and prudence, and enjoin moderation and good sense in the use of all things.[106] Yet when Thomas himself cites particular moral precepts belonging to the law of nature, these are not the examples he uses. He cites as examples of the most evident moral precepts the commandments "Honor thy father and thy mother," "Thou shalt not kill," and "Thou shalt not steal," all of which, he states, "belong to the law of nature absolutely."[107] Other precepts that are less evident, but belong nonetheless to the law of nature, include respect for the elderly. Finally, Thomas teaches that to reach the knowledge of some precepts human reason needs divine instruction such as the second commandment, which forbids the making of graven images or taking God's name in vain.

In other words, *all* Thomas's examples of particular moral precepts of the natural moral law refer not to ordering man's use of *things* but rather to ordering his relations with other *persons,* only touching upon things as they relate to persons (for example, in forbidding stealing). Thus they do not deal with the ordering of practical reason per se (prudence),[108] or with the ordering of the passions (temperance and fortitude),[109] but instead with the cardinal virtue of justice.[110] Of course, it cannot be inferred from this that the natural moral law governs only man's relationship with other persons.[111] Though natural law embraces the whole of

---

106. Thomas teaches that justice deals with external operations while all the other moral virtues deal with ordering man's internal passions. "The reason for this is that justice is about operations, which deal with external things. . . . But the other moral virtues deal with interior passions" (Ibid., I-II, 64, 2).

107. Ibid., I-II, 100, 1.

108. Thomas devotes only two articles of the *Summa* to "the precepts of prudence," and notes that none of the precepts of the natural law (Decalogue) deals with prudence per se, but rather all with justice, since prudence is about means, whereas the first precepts of the Law are concerned with ends. All of the precepts are related in a general way to prudence, however, in that they all command virtuous acts, and prudence directs practical reason to these acts. See ibid., II-II, 56, 1.

109. See ibid., I-II, 61, 2.

110. "Justice properly so called regards the duty of one man to another: but all the other virtues regard the duty of the lower powers to reason" (ibid., I-II, 100, 2, ad 2).

111. Though according to Thomas human law deals with justice only—whose proper function consists in directing the human community—divine law enjoins the practice of the

natural morality—what should and should not be done—at its core, it deals with justice—that is, with relations with other people.[112] Hence the *Catechism* (following St. Thomas)[113] notes that the principal precepts of the natural law are expressed in the Decalogue,[114] and these are precepts of justice.[115] Furthermore, Thomas notes that the very notion of precept implies duty, and duty in turn "is of one towards another."[116] The virtue that orders relations of one to another is justice. If this is so, then the basic precept of justice ("Give to each his due") underlying all relations between persons must also be one of the fundamental precepts of the natural moral law. This also makes sense when one considers the New Testament teaching that love—which is the perfection of justice—sums up the entire Old Law and the prophets (see Matt. 22:39–40; Rom. 13:8–10; Gal. 5:14; Jas. 2:8).

The *Catechism* furthermore states that the natural moral law, whose principal precepts are contained in the Decalogue, "hinges upon the desire for God and submission to him . . . as well as upon *the sense that the other is one's equal*."[117] In other words, the natural moral law revolves

---

other virtues, since anything commanded by reason is enjoined by the divine law for the very reason that God's image is found in reason. Thus "the Divine law proposes precepts about all those matters whereby human reason is well ordered" (ibid., I-II, 100, 2).

112. "Natural law, like the virtue of justice, is primarily oriented to others, while always including the agent who is also a member of society" (Pinckaers, *The Sources of Christian Ethics*, 453).

113. Thomas asserts that "the precepts of the decalogue are the first principles of the Law: and the natural reason assents to them at once, as to principles that are most evident" (*S. Th.*, II-II, 122, 1).

114. See *CCC*, 1955. The *Catechism* goes on to cite St. Irenaeus: "From the beginning, God had implanted in the heart of man the precepts of the natural law. Then he was content to remind him of them. This was the Decalogue" (St. Irenaeus, *Adv. Haereses* 4, 15, 1; J.-P. Migne, ed., *Patrologia Graeca* [Paris, 1857], 7/1, 1012; hereafter *PG*). Pope John Paul affirms the same when he says that God gave man the light of understanding and the natural law "at creation" as well as "in the history of Israel, particularly in the 'ten words,' the commandments of Sinai" (*VS*, 12). John Paul goes still further, stating that the commandments contain the entire natural law: "These are the goods safeguarded by the commandments, which, according to Saint Thomas, contain the whole natural law" (ibid., 79, citing *S. Th.*, I-II, 100, 1).

115. Thomas states that "the precepts of the decalogue must needs pertain to justice. Wherefore the first three precepts are about acts of religion, which is the chief part of justice; the fourth precept is about acts of piety, which is the second part of justice; and the six remaining are about justice commonly so called, which is observed among equals" (*S. Th.*, II-II, 122, 1).

116. "Now it is altogether evident that the notion of duty, which is essential to a precept, appears in justice, which is of one towards another" (ibid.).

117. *CCC*, 1955; emphasis added.

around our relationship with others: with God and with other persons.[118] Man immediately grasps not only that he is a person, responsible for achieving a transcendent purpose, but also that other human beings are also persons, equal in dignity to himself. According to the Council, man's conscience discovers in his heart a law inscribed by God that calls him "*to love* and to do what is good and to avoid evil."[119] The addition of the words "to love" to the traditional Thomistic formula is significant. It would seem to put love on a par with the first principle of practical reason as a fundamental principle immediately discovered by conscience. Since "love is the fulfilling of the law," one could say that the particular precepts of the Law issue from the one central precept of love.

Again, justice (and love) do not exhaust the whole of the moral life.[120] Their centrality, however, cannot be overemphasized.[121] The importance of justice and love in the moral law does not contradict man's natural desire for happiness, which is fruit of the fullness of being. Indeed, the fullness of being for man is not separate from but includes his relationality with other persons. The nature of the "other" as person is so unique that the other person can never be integrated into a moral scheme of *means* to the end of happiness or human fulfillment. The discovery of another personal good equal to mine and distinct from mine—though somehow related to it—introduces into morality a component that makes the human

---

118. "The natural law, when the senses do not dominate reason, moves us spontaneously to receive all men as our brothers and to come to the aid of those in need; it inspires in us a unanimous will, such that each is happy to give to others what he himself would like to receive. This is what the Lord taught: 'Whatever you wish that men would do to you, do so to them.' Such is the humanity realized in those in whom nature is governed by reason. This manner of life, this way of seeing and hearing, makes them aware of the rational unity of human nature, a unity in which there exists no trace of the laceration of that nature which comes about as the result of selfishness" (St. Maximus the Confessor, "The Three Laws: Question 64 to Thalasius," *PG*, 724–28).

119. *GS*, 16; emphasis added.

120. Wherefore Thomas notes that "since justice is directed to others, it is not about the entire matter of moral virtue, but only about external actions and things, under a certain special aspect of the object, in so far as one man is related to another through them" (*S. Th.*, II-II, 58, 8).

121. "When the Catholic moral tradition and, in its wake, the *Catechism* speak of the nature of man, of the natural law and of behavior in conformity with nature, what is meant is not some form of biologism but behavior that accords with what the Creator has implanted at the core of our being. If we continue this line of inquiry, we discover love as the heart of all morality" (Ratzinger, *Gospel, Catechesis, Catechism*, 16–17).

good thoroughly different from the good of other created beings. Furthermore, the personal good of the other is no mere datum added to the moral equation. The person is open to and made for relation—and not only for relation, but for self-giving and for love. The person realizes himself as a person only when he becomes a gift for others.

KNOWLEDGE OF NATURAL LAW

The promulgation of a law is part of its essence. Since it is directed to reason, if law be unknown it cannot bind, nor can it serve as a guide to human activity.[122] This also holds true for the natural law, since it does not function automatically, as in the case of animal instinct, but by appealing to reason. The natural law, therefore, is also promulgated "by the very fact that God instilled it into man's mind so as to be known by him naturally."[123]

Though the natural law is universal in scope and is in essence identical for all persons and intelligible to all, not all apprehend it equally.[124] Cultural environment, upbringing, intellectual acumen, the disposition and time for serious reflection, openness to moral truth, and previous moral choices may help or hinder a person's comprehension of natural law precepts.[125] Moreover, some of the precepts of the natural law are more read-

---

122. Thomas observes that "a law is imposed on others by way of a rule and measure. Now a rule or measure is imposed by being applied to those who are to be ruled and measured by it. Wherefore, in order that a law obtain the binding force which is proper to a law, it must needs be applied to the men who have to be ruled by it. Such application is made by its being notified to them by promulgation. Wherefore promulgation is necessary for the law to obtain its force" (*S. Th.*, I-II, 90, 4).

123. Ibid., I-II, 90, 4, ad 1.

124. When St. Thomas questions himself as to whether or not all men know the precepts of natural law, he answers with an important distinction. All men feel the inclination to act according to reason, and in this sense, the first precept is always present in them. Yet the application of this first precept can present problems, whether because of objective reasons—such as circumstances that change and do not allow for the same application of a norm—or because of passions, bad habits, and even man's bad natural attitudes. These latter factors can corrupt the process of knowledge of what is right. See ibid., I-II, 94, 4. "The precepts of natural law are not perceived by everyone clearly and immediately. In the present situation sinful man needs grace and revelation so moral and religious truths may be known 'by everyone with facility, with firm certainty and with no admixture of error'" (Pius XII, *Humani Generis:* DS 3876; see also *Dei Filius* 2: DS 3005).

125. What Pius XII wrote in reference to knowing God by the unaided light of human reason can also be applied to the knowledge of the precepts of the natural law. "Though human

ily evident than others. Therefore Thomas, in the context of principles of speculative reason, says that "certain axioms or propositions are universally self-evident to all;[126] and such are those propositions whose terms are known to all, as, 'Every whole is greater than its part,' and, 'Things equal to one and the same are equal to one another.' But some propositions are self-evident only to the wise, who understand the meaning of the terms of such propositions."[127] One could add the further distinction that though everyone naturally knows that a whole is greater than its part, not all would be able to reach a theoretical formulation of this axiom. It is one thing to naturally grasp a truth and even to use it in one's reasoning process and quite another thing to *know* that one is using it. In a similar way, everyone knows that good is to be pursued and evil avoided, and everyone spontaneously acts according to this principle, though not all would be capable of articulating the axiom.

Mention must be made here of the workings of moral conscience, which grasps the first principles of natural law (synderesis) and applies them to concrete situations.[128] According to Thomas, conscience is an act of practical reason in the form of judgment regarding what we have done

---

reason is, strictly speaking, truly capable by its own natural power and light of attaining to a true and certain knowledge of the one personal God, who watches over and controls the world by his providence, and of the natural law written in our hearts by the Creator; yet there are many obstacles which prevent reason from the effective and fruitful use of this inborn faculty. For the truths that concern the relations between God and man wholly transcend the visible order of things, and, if they are translated into human action and influence it, they call for self-surrender and abnegation. The human mind, in its turn, is hampered in the attaining of such truths, not only by the impact of the senses and the imagination, but also by disordered appetites which are the consequences of original sin. So it happens that men in such matters easily persuade themselves that what they would not like to be true is false or at least doubtful" (*Humani Generis*, 561: DS 3875).

126. "The basic principles and norms of the natural law, as *natural*, are addressed to all human beings, and they are held to be accessible to all who are capable of forming the concepts which comprise them" (Boyle, "Natural Law and the Ethics of Traditions," 4).

127. *S. Th.*, I-II, 94, 2.

128. Ibid., I, 79, 13. "Synderesis" refers to a habit of practical reason by which first principles are naturally grasped. "Therefore we must have, bestowed on us by nature, not only speculative principles, but also practical principles. Now the first speculative principles bestowed on us by nature do not belong to a special power, but to a special habit, which is called 'the understanding of principles,' as the Philosopher explains (*Ethic.* vi, 6). Wherefore the first practical principles, bestowed on us by nature, do not belong to a special power, but to a special natural habit, which we call 'synderesis.' Whence 'synderesis' is said to incite to good, and to murmur at evil, inasmuch as through first principles we proceed to discover, and judge of what we have discovered" (*S. Th.*, I, 79, 12). See also *CCC*, 1780.

or propose to do.¹²⁹ It is in conscience, then—"man's most secret core and his sanctuary" where "he is alone with God"—where man discovers the natural law, and the voice of conscience urges him "to love and to do what is good and to avoid evil."¹³⁰ Therefore, "whereas the natural law discloses the objective and universal demands of the moral good, conscience refers to the application of the law to a particular case; this application of the law thus becomes an inner dictate for the individual, a summons to do what is good in this particular situation."¹³¹ In this way, conscience formulates moral obligation in the light of the natural law by acknowledging the universality of the law and its obligation and establishing the law's application in concrete circumstances. Thus "the judgment of conscience states 'in an ultimate way' whether a certain particular kind of behavior is in conformity with the law; it formulates the proximate norm of the morality of a voluntary act, 'applying the objective law to a particular case.'"

Taking a step backward from the judgment of conscience in particular circumstances, in practice, how does man come to grasp the precepts of the natural law? According to Catholic teaching, amply backed up by human experience, man's knowledge of natural law precepts is not innate.¹³² Instead, as in the case of all natural human knowledge, it develops through man's reasoning about what he has experienced through the senses. Knowledge of natural law implies a discovery of a preexisting order, an order of goods. Thus Wojtyła remarks that coming to knowledge of the natural moral law is not a subjective interference of reason in ob-

---

129. St. Thomas describes conscience as an application of knowledge to an individual case, an application that is made in three ways: (1) by witnessing to the fact that the person has or has not done something; (2) by binding or inciting to an action in judging that it should or should not be done; (3) by judging whether an action was well done or badly done and thus accusing, excusing, praising, etc. (See *S. Th.*, I, 79, 13). Similarly, the *Catechism* explains that conscience "is a judgement of reason whereby the human person recognizes the moral quality of a concrete act that he is going to perform, is in the process of performing, or has already completed" (*CCC*, 1778).

130. *GS*, 16.

131. *VS*, 59.

132. "By forbidding man to 'eat of the tree of the knowledge of good and evil,' God makes it clear that man does not originally possess such 'knowledge' as something properly his own, but only participates in it by the light of natural reason and of Divine Revelation, which manifest to him the requirements and the promptings of eternal wisdom. Law must therefore be considered an expression of divine wisdom: by submitting to the law, freedom submits to the truth of creation" (ibid., 41). See also *S. Th.*, I, 79, 3; I, 84, 6.

jective reality; rather, it entails an "attitude of reason discerning, grasping, defining, and affirming, in relation to an order that is objective and prior to human reason itself."[133] At the same time, the first principle of practical reason—that good is to be done and evil avoided—*is* innate, in the sense that it is written into the structure of human freedom and is discovered as the fundamental rule by which man must govern his actions. In other words, just as speculative reason "works" according to certain principles that it necessarily employs, so, too, human freedom is essentially ordered to pursue the good and avoid evil.[134] Likewise, just as the speculative reason proceeds from naturally known, indemonstrable principles to particular conclusions, so it is with practical reason, which proceeds from the general to the specific, from the common to the proper.[135] The various moral precepts of the natural law all derive from the first principle of practical reason, just as the various principles of speculative reason derive from the principle of noncontradiction.[136]

133. Wojtyła, "The Human Person and Natural Law," 184.

134. "Aristotle argued in book Gamma of the *Metaphysics* that anyone who denies that basic law of logic, the law of noncontradiction, and who is prepared to defend his or her position by entering into argumentative debate, will in fact be unable to avoid relying upon the very law which he or she purports to reject" (MacIntyre, *Whose Justice? Which Rationality?* 4).

135. "Now it is to be observed that the same procedure takes place in the practical and in the speculative reason: for each proceeds from principles to conclusions, as stated above (*De libero arbitrio,* i, 6). Accordingly we conclude that just as, in the speculative reason, from naturally known indemonstrable principles, we draw the conclusions of the various sciences, the knowledge of which is not imparted to us by nature, but acquired by the efforts of reason, so too it is from the precepts of the natural law, as from general and indemonstrable principles, that the human reason needs to proceed to the more particular determination of certain matters" (*S. Th.,* I-II, 91, 3).

136. There is a fundamental difference, however, between the dynamics of speculative and practical reason. Speculative reason apprehends first principles and extracts from them necessary conclusions, which hold true always and everywhere for the very reason that they are necessary. The practical reason, on the contrary, deals not with necessary but with contingent things, and consequently its conclusions allow for a greater margin of error in judgment. Drawing conclusions from speculative principles resembles pure deduction, whereas the conclusions of practical reason take the form of an *application* of a general principle to concrete circumstances. Accordingly, we can say with Aquinas that general principles of practical reason are the same for all and readily comprehensible, but the more detailed or specific the application, the greater the margin for error. Wherefore Thomas states that "as regards the general principles whether of speculative or of practical reason, truth or rectitude is the same for all, and is equally known by all.... But as to the proper conclusions of the practical reason, neither is the truth or rectitude the same for all, nor, where it is the same, is it equally known by all.... And this principle will be found to fail the more, according as we descend further into detail" (Ibid., I-II, 94, 4).

Let us take examples of moral precepts offered by Aquinas to see how this understanding comes about in practice. The particular precepts of the natural law cited by Aquinas are principles of natural justice that govern man's relationship with other persons. These are summed up in the commandments of the second tablet of the Decalogue. How, in fact, do the commandments come to be naturally apprehended—as categorical obligations or as the imperative corollary to the acknowledgment of some good to be respected and defended? Though the natural law can be conceived as a series of categorical imperatives, experience does not support this. No one discovers "Thou shalt not kill" emblazoned somewhere on his conscience as a precept innately received. By definition, the content of natural law is rationally accessible, and thus one must be able to reason back to it. "Reasoning back to it," in this case, means tying it into the first principle of practical reason, which enjoins the pursuit of good and the avoidance of evil. If the commandment not to kill forms part of natural law, it can be only because reason discerns that killing a fellow human being is evil and thus "to be avoided."

Though the revealed commandment forbids "killing" in the abstract ("Thou shalt not kill"), without specifying the object of this action, Jewish and Christian tradition has always taken the prohibition to refer exclusively to other human beings, and this interpretation is corroborated by natural ethics. Uprooting poison ivy and squashing cockroaches, which clearly constitute instances of deliberate killing, do not carry the same moral charge of evil as killing another human person. The evil of killing depends directly on who or what is being killed. The deliberate destruction of innocent human life is recognizably evil, whereas the destruction of plant or animal life does not possess the same moral character. Therefore, one must conclude that human life possesses a worth or goodness not possessed by plant or animal life. It would furthermore seem logical to say that if killing another human being is evil, then such an action constitutes an improper or incorrect way to treat another person.

Now, if there is an improper or incorrect way to treat a person, there must perforce be a proper and correct way to treat him. The morality of interpersonal relations, then, will consist in treating other persons in a proper or correct manner. And here the argument returns to the issue of justice, which deals with the question of what is "due" to others. In the case of the precepts of the second tablet of the Decalogue, which treat of man's obligations toward all persons without distinction, the issue is what is due to man simply as man, by the mere fact of his humanity.

The same simple analysis can be carried out with the other moral precepts of the natural law. The second tablet of the Decalogue outlines the sort of behavior that represents an improper way to treat other human persons, and the avoidance of this behavior can be said to be naturally due to others. Behind these prohibitions stand goods to be respected and promoted in others (property, life, marital union, etc.). Certain types of conduct toward others that would violate these goods (stealing, killing, adultery, etc.) is forbidden. In the case of the fifth commandment, for example, it is good that the other *is,* that the other *lives,* and thus to kill the other would be wrong. At least this is how classical Christian ethics has viewed the matter, and it is difficult to think how it could be otherwise, unless the natural law is to be discarded altogether.[137] These relationships between personal good and the natural moral law square with the personalistic principle, which holds up the person as an object of love rather than use.

The workings of the natural moral law in terms of man's perception of his fellows as naturally deserving of a certain sort of treatment lead to questions regarding the inner coherence of the virtue of justice. As the central aspect of the natural law, justice must be shown to indeed be natural. If this can be done, rights as an essential component of justice must surely be natural, too.

---

137. Pinckaers has written that "for St. Thomas the feeling of obligation did not come first. It was rooted in the natural inclinations towards truth and goodness and was based on the attraction and behest of the true good" (*The Sources of Christian Ethics,* 421).

14. NATURAL JUSTICE

THE CARDINAL VIRTUE OF JUSTICE holds the primary place in the matrix of natural law precepts.[1] Human reason is capable of discerning that certain things are naturally due to other human beings by a quality of their humanity termed dignity. To understand how natural rights square with natural law theory, and especially with the classical understanding of natural justice, the concept of justice and particularly the central notion of "due" *(debitum)* must be in harmony with the idea of subjective rights as a moral power to demand one's due.

Several steps are involved in showing this harmony. Thinkers throughout history have offered different and even opposing ideas of justice, and therefore concord between natural justice and natural rights supposes a precise idea as to which concept of justice is in play. Moreover, "justice" is traditionally subdivided into several types, and these taxonomic distinctions also affect justice's relation to rights. The notion of "due," which forms a natural nexus between justice and rights, must also be examined more closely to determine how something can be naturally due to someone else. Finally, the rapport between justice and the other moral virtues reveals much about the relationship between the person, justice, love, and rights and thereby further illuminates some of the conclusions reached in earlier chapters.

---

1. In order for the precepts of justice to form part of the natural law, a natural justice, apprehensible by human reason independent of positive law, must exist. Thus St. Thomas writes: "The wisdom of the divine intellect is the source on which the essence of all justice is primarily dependent. This wisdom constitutes beings in their due relation both to one another and their cause; and it is in this relation that the essence of created justice consists. To say that justice depends purely and simply on the (divine) will is to say that the will is not guided by divine wisdom—and this is blasphemy" (*De Veritate*, 23, 6).

ORDERING HUMAN RELATIONS ACCORDING TO RIGHT REASON

Alasdair MacIntyre has been particularly effective in making the case that there is not one traditional understanding of justice but several diverse and even irreconcilable traditions.[2] In his discussion of justice, C. Henry Peschke groups historical understandings of justice according to three basic theories, which he terms the positive law theory, the social good theory, and the natural right theory.[3] The positive law theory defines justice as conformity to the law, and in so doing equates justice with legality. The social good theory defines justice as "doing what is useful for the social good." In other words, what is just is defined by its consequences for the good of society. The natural right theory, finally, holds that natural right is the ultimate basis of justice.[4] According to this latter theory, writes Peschke, man has rights "not primarily because he has received them by society, but because his nature as a human being confers rights upon him."[5] Otto A. Bird lists twenty-three authors espousing the positive law theory, including Hobbes, Holmes, Kelsen, and Spinoza. For the social good theory, he names nineteen authors, such as Bentham, Hume, Mill, Radbruch, and Sidgwick. For the natural law theory, he enumerates a further forty-two authors, including Aquinas, Aristotle, Augustine, E. Brunner, Grotius, Leibnitz, Locke, Maritain, Messner, Pufendorf, Suárez, Del Vecchio, Vitoria, and Wolff.[6]

Despite deep differences in the way ethical schools understand justice, certain characteristics are generally agreed upon. Bird distinguishes three common notes. In the first place, there is general accord that justice is a social norm, or a rule for guiding persons in their actions toward one an-

---

2. See especially MacIntyre, *Whose Justice? Which Rationality?*

3. See C. Henry Peschke, *A Presentation of Special Moral Theology in the Light of Vatican II* (Dublin: C. Goodliffe Neale, 1978), 213. Here Peschke adopts the findings of Otto A. Bird in his work *The Idea of Justice,* Concepts in Western Thought Series (New York: Frederick A. Praeger, 1967).

4. These three theories basically coincide with those cited by MacIntyre: "Some conceptions [of justice] appeal to inalienable human rights, others to some notion of social contract, and others again to a standard of utility" (*Whose Justice? Which Rationality?* 1). Social contract is a form of positive law, natural rights a derivative of natural right, and social good a form of universalized utility.

5. Peschke, *A Presentation of Special Moral Theology,* 213.

6. Bird, *The Idea of Justice,* cited in Peschke, *A Presentation of Special Moral Theology,* 213n2.

other. Second, justice is understood to be approbative, or virtuous, in the sense that judging an action to be just manifests approval of that action. Third, justice implies obligation, in that judging a certain course of action to be just means that a person in a similar situation ought to do the same thing.[7]

In spite of this real variety, there is clearly a "received teaching" on justice, a core understanding that has been held from the time of the ancient Greek philosophers up to the present with surprisingly little modification on the part of Christian thinkers. From the foregoing synopsis of theories of justice, one readily sees that what Peschke calls the "natural right theory" corresponds to the teaching of perennial philosophy and is most agreeable to a Christian ethics.

According to the classical and Christian understanding, justice constitutes one of the four "cardinal" virtues, together with prudence, temperance, and fortitude,[8] around which all other moral virtues are grouped.[9] Justice is the virtue that directs man in his dealings with other persons.[10] In its most fundamental meaning, justice has been defined since antiquity as the habitual disposition to render to each his own (his due).[11] As a virtue, justice refers to a good *habit,* and therefore the classical definition speaks of "a constant and perpetual will" to render each man his due. The virtue, or habit, of justice, can thus be distinguished from an "act" of justice, which Thomas defines as "nothing else than to render to each one his own."[12]

---

7. See Bird, *The Idea of Justice,* 10ff.

8. These four virtues are praised in the book of Wisdom as the fruit of her labor: "And if anyone loves righteousness, [wisdom's] labors are virtues; for she teaches temperance and prudence, justice and courage; nothing in life is more profitable for mortals than these" (Wis. 8:7).

9. See *CCC,* 1805; *S. Th.,* I-II, 61, 1–5.

10. See *S. Th.,* II-II, 58, 2.

11. Cicero refers to justice as "assigning each his own" *(suum cuique tribuens)* and later reiterates that justice is displayed "in giving each his due" *(in suo cuique tribuendo)* (*De finibus bonorum et malorum,* trans. H. Rackham, vol. 40 of Loeb Classical Library [Cambridge: Harvard University Press, 1994], bk. V, xxiii, pp. 469–70). For his part, Augustine writes: "Iustitia porro ea virtus est, quae sua cuique distribuit" (*De Civitate Dei,* XIX, 21, 2; cfr. *De Libero Arbitrio,* Lib. I, 27 B). Justinian offers the well-known definition: "Iustitia est constans et perpetua voluntas ius suum unicuique tribunes" (*Iustiniani Digesta,* I, tit. 1, leg. 10 [KR I, 29b]; cf. Instit., I, tit. 1, leg. 1 [KR I, 1a]), which Thomas adopts as a point of departure for his own discussion of justice (cited in *S. Th.,* II-II, 58, 1, 1; see also *S. Th.,* II-II, 58, 11; *De Veritate,* q. 1, art. 5, ad 13).

12. "Et ideo proprius actus iustitiae nihil est aliud quam reddere unicuique quod suum est" (*S. Th.,* II-II, 58, 11).

The aim of justice is the establishment and maintenance of a certain equality between persons.[13] Justice therefore rests upon two pillars: equity and impartiality. Justice implies equity, since "the just" refers to "that which is equal or fair."[14] Equity, in turn, demands a certain impartiality that excludes arbitrariness or bias. Thus the virtue of justice is often represented by the figure of a blindfolded woman holding scales in her hands. The scales represent equity, and the blindfold suggests impartiality. Impartiality, or the quality of treating all persons alike and without subjective preferences, derives from the acknowledgment of the fundamental equality of all persons, or at least all within a given group.[15] According to the Christian conception, personhood is a binary function: either a given entity is or is not a person. By the same token, every person is equally a person, and there are no grades or levels of personhood.

By themselves, however, equity and impartiality offer an insufficient standard for justice. Though justice precludes arbitrariness and promotes equality, it goes still further. Neither kindness nor cruelty is in itself more arbitrary than the other, yet one suspects that impartial cruelty toward all would somehow fail to constitute just conduct. Clearly, then, another standard is needed, one that will ensure that one's behavior toward others is not only equitable and impartial but in accord with what the person deserves and therefore truly just.

This standard is *oneself.* True justice extends the principles of equity and impartiality to the moral agent himself and thereby applies to others principles that he naturally applies in his own regard. Justice recognizes

---

13. "For it belongs to justice to establish equality in our relations with others . . . and it pertains to the same cause to establish and to preserve that which it has established" (ibid., II-II, 79, 1).

14. Aristotle, *Nichomachean Ethics,* V, 1:1129a35.

15. Actually, the notion of the equality of persons is of relatively recent origins, and it is fruit of the influence of Christianity. In the past, and still today in some cultures, the equality proper to justice applied not to all persons as persons but to those within a certain select group (freemen, citizens, etc.). Thus Aristotle says that political justice "means justice as between free and (actually or proportionately) equal persons, living a common life for the purpose of satisfying their needs" (ibid., V, 5:1134a26–28). Between people not free and equal, he adds, such justice can exist only in a metaphorical sense. Internally to this group, or among those of equal standing, justice was seen as demanding equality. Some, furthermore, because of other factors (rank, breeding, prominence in the community, etc.), were considered deserving of more than others, but taking into account these elements a fundamental equity was pursued as proper to justice, according to the equality of proportion. Further along, in our discussion of the types of justice, we will examine how this equality was applied.

that the other is another "I," a neighbor who shares in my nature. Therefore, one's legitimate expectations for self become the standard for conduct toward others. "'Do to (or for) others what you would have them do to (or for) you.' Put yourself in your neighbor's shoes. Do not condemn others for what you are willing to do yourself. Do not (without special reason) prevent others getting for themselves what you are trying to get for yourself."[16] Though Christian revelation asserts this principle categorically (Lev. 19:18; Matt. 7:12, 19:19, 22:39; Mark 12:31; Luke 6:31, 10:27; Rom. 13:9; Gal. 5:14; Jas. 2:8), natural justice and consequently the natural moral law likewise rest upon it. Thus the "Golden Rule" turns up in numerous different moral traditions and is not exclusive to Judeo-Christian revelation.[17]

TYPES OF JUSTICE

Aristotle divided justice first into the categories of general and particular, whereby general justice refers broadly to lawfulness and particular justice to fairness or equity (rendering to others their due).[18] He further subdivided particular justice into commutative and distributive justice.[19] Thomas Aquinas adopted the same basic structure, first addressing the notion of general or "legal" justice and then speaking of particular justice, split into commutative (corrective) and distributive justice.[20]

Commutative justice is the virtue that regulates interaction between particular persons, aiming at the establishment and conservation of a just order among them. It is so called because its primary form is "commuta-

16. Finnis, *Natural Law and Natural Rights*, 108.

17. C. S. Lewis cites an ancient Chinese maxim that matches the Golden Rule nearly verbatim: "Never do to others what you would not like them to do to you" (*Analects of Confusius*, trans. A. Waley, xv. 23; cf. xii. 2; cited in Lewis, *The Abolition of Man*, 98).

18. The adjective "unjust," according to Aristotle, can be used to describe the one who breaks the law and the unfair man, who takes more than his due. Therefore, "the just" means both "that which is lawful and that which is equal or fair" (*Nichomachean Ethics*, V, 1:1129a32–35). When we refer to justice in the sense of lawfulness, we refer to the general virtue, and when we speak of justice as fairness or equality (rendering to each is own), we refer to particular justice.

19. See ibid., V, 2:1130b30–35.

20. See *S. Th.*, II-II, 61, 1. Aristotle refers to "corrective" justice, in that its purpose is to equalize what has been made unequal and thus regain the equilibrium proper to justice. See Aristotle, *Nichomachean Ethics*, V, 4:1131b25, 1132a7–8.

tion," or exchange. This exchange extends beyond commerce or the interchange of chattel, however, to include things, persons, or works.[21] In other words, all matter of externals that touch on the interrelation between particular persons is the proper matter of commutative justice. Aristotle calls the equality proper to this form of justice "arithmetic," in that it demands a quantitatively equivalent return for goods or services rendered, as in the cases of commerce, restitution of damage, payment of debt, and so forth.[22] The concept of "particular persons" is not limited to physical individuals; it also includes corporate personalities, associations, and even the state, when the latter acts not as the representative of the public weal but as a private "person" (when, say, the state contracts out work).[23]

Distributive justice refers to the virtue that orders relations between the community as such and its members, aiming at the preservation of a just order in these relationships.[24] It derives its name from its role, whereby it "distributes common goods proportionately" among the members of the community.[25] Unlike the strict arithmetic equality proper to commutative justice, in the Aristotelian-Thomistic scheme distributive justice apportions goods to its members according to a "geometric proportion," in accord with the worth and needs of each.[26] Thomas, referring to the concept of "worth," speaks of more prominent members of the community—where the criterion for prominence will depend on the type of government (aristocracy, oligarchy, democracy)—receiving a greater share than less prominent members.[27] The operative principle here is "to

---

21. "of things, as when one man takes from or restores to another that which is his; of persons, as when a man does an injury to the very person of another, for instance by striking or insulting him, or even by showing respect for him; and of works, as when a man justly exacts a work of another, or does a work for him" (*S. Th.*, II-II, 61, 3).

22. See Aristotle, *Nichomachean Ethics*, V, 4:1132a1–2.

23. See de Finance, *An Ethical Inquiry,* § 199, pp. 350–51.

24. As regards the agent subject to the moral requirements of distributive justice, Finnis notes that this virtue extends beyond the state to anyone who has charge of common goods. "On Aquinas' view, anyone in charge of an item of 'common stock' will have duties of distributive justice; hence any property-holder can have such duties, since the goods of this earth are to be exploited and used for the good of all. In the newer view (now thought of as traditional), the duties of distributive justice belong only to the State or the personified 'whole' community" (*Natural Law and Natural Rights,* 186).

25. See *S. Th.*, II-II, 61, 1.

26. See Aristotle, *Nichomachean Ethics*, V, 3:1131b13; see also *S. Th.*, I, 21, 1; II-II, 61, 2.

27. See *S. Th.*, II-II, 61, 2. According to this understanding, justice's blindfold is removed

each in accordance with the degree to which he promotes the good of the community."²⁸

The third type of justice, called legal or general justice, refers to justice in a broad sense as a virtue that orders a person's acts to the good of all rather than merely to oneself. Since temperance and fortitude and their related virtues order the concupiscible and irascible passions in conformity with right reason, properly speaking they are immanent virtues and directly profit only the individual who possesses them. Since justice is the virtue that orders man's relations with his fellows, in a general way it is seen as perfecting the other moral virtues in that it directs them beyond the immediate good of the moral agent to the common good. The adjective "legal" refers to the fact that this virtue aims at the common good, which is proper to the law.²⁹ The Scholastics, beginning with Cardinal Cajetan, modified this classical understanding of general justice to mean a virtue regulating the duties of the individual person to the community as such, as a sort of reciprocal function to that of distributive justice.³⁰

In the scope of the present study, all three types of justice are of interest. Particular justice, in its two forms of commutative and distributive justice, operates on the principle of rendering to each his due. Distributive justice embraces the obligations of the community or whoever has charge of common goods to render to each of its members what is due to them, by a proportion adjusted to need or worth. Thus formulated, dis-

---

and she considers the relative worth and neediness of the parties involved, albeit respecting principles of equity and judging not by subjective preference or inclination but by objective criteria.

28. De Finance, *An Ethical Inquiry*, § 199, p. 351.

29. See *S. Th.*, II-II, 58, 5. Thomas explains that justice exists as a general virtue, in that all acts of virtue can pertain to justice since the particular good of any virtue contributes to the common good. And because it is proper of the law to direct to the common good, general justice also bears the name of legal justice, inasmuch as it directs the acts of all the virtues to the common good. Aristotle has said much the same, in noting that the various pronouncements of the law aim at the common interest of all (or that of a ruling class), and thus "the just" can be applied in a general way to whatever contributes to the happiness of the political community (See Aristotle, *Nichomachean Ethics*, V, 1:1129b14–18).

30. See Finnis's persuasive criticism of distortions of Aquinas's original bipartite division of justice into distributive and commutative, brought about by Cardinal Cajetan and his followers. The new tripartite classification runs "legal" (of a person toward the state), "distributive" (of the state toward the person), "commutative" (of a person toward another person). As Finnis points out, for Aquinas, legal justice is the fundamental form of *all* justice. (See *Natural Law and Natural Rights*, 184–88).

tributive justice calls attention to the fact that the community as such administers goods for the sake of its members, and an abstract common good seen as somehow separate from and above the good of the persons comprising the community is foreign to this understanding.[31] The community (or state) does not surrender its goods to individuals as an act of condescension or gratuitous benevolence, it does so because this is *due* to them: such goods truly belong to all. If this is the case, then the members of the community have rights vis-à-vis the community, and can therefore morally lay claim to what is *theirs*.

Commutative justice likewise operates on the principle *unicuique suum tribuere*, only in this case it deals not with a relationship between the community and individual members of that community but with the relations of particular persons among themselves. Commutative justice can be *natural* in two ways. First, it is natural in that human inclinations to fairness and equality are natural. Overcharging customers or favoritism in business are naturally perceived as unfair and inequitable behavior. The equity and impartiality demanded by justice are intuitive principles that do not originate in the law; they precede the law and provide a standard by which just laws may be enacted. Second, justice is natural in that all men as persons naturally deserve something from one another. The universal custom of distinguishing between human beings and other creatures and reserving particular behavior for the former is not a mere convention. It reflects an understanding that persons are distinct from nonpersons, and for this very reason in justice one's behavior toward them must vary accordingly.

General or legal justice highlights this aspect of the importance of actions whose object is other persons and therefore the moral superiority of justice to other, merely self-referential virtues. For this reason legal justice elevates the other moral virtues, conferring on them greater nobility by directing them beyond perfection of the moral agent to the good of others. In a sense, general justice grounds particular justice by indicating the excellence of dealing with other persons.[32] Just dealings depend on an ac-

---

31. Finnis observes that "talk about benefitting 'the community' is no more than a shorthand (not without dangers) for benefitting the members of that community" (ibid., 168).
32. Justice, therefore, before dealing with particular precepts or goods to be rendered, begins with the acknowledgment of the excellence of the other. "Justice means recognizing that every person is worthy of respect for his or her own sake" (Spaemann, *Basic Moral Concepts*,

knowledgment of this excellence, since justice may entail personal disadvantage from a purely self-referential perspective.

UNPACKING A DEFINITION OF JUSTICE

The classical definition of justice—a firm and enduring disposition to render to each his due—can be broken into component parts. To define justice as an enduring disposition merely assigns justice to the genus of habit.[33] More important is the second part of the definition—"to render to each his due"—which contains four key elements, at least implicitly. First, implicit to the virtue is the moral agent, the one who possesses the virtue and is called to render something to another. Second, the recipient of the action is the one to whom something is due or rendered. Third, the "thing" rendered forms the content of what is "his" or "due." Finally, the definition reveals a moral relation between the thing rendered and the recipient, by which the thing is "his" or "due" to him.

The latter two elements of the definition are more germane to the present investigation, and for the moment an analysis of the moral agent and the recipient of the action can be left aside. First, what is the duty proper to justice? How can it be said that something is "due" to someone? What does it mean that something "belongs" to someone, or that it is "his" by right? Second, what is the specific content of this debt of justice? What does one person owe another by natural justice?

Unicuique suum: The Meaning of One's "Own" or "Due"

In his exposition of the virtue of justice, Thomas notes that justice "above all regards the aspect of something due."[34] This concept, which forms the nucleus of the definition of justice, contains both the notion of moral obligation and the specific matter that forms the content of the obligation. To express this concept, Thomas speaks variously of what is "his"

---

46). Or, as Caffarra writes, "justice . . . is the recognition of the unconditional value of other human persons simply by virtue of their humanity" (*Living in Christ*, 214).

33. Thomas, drawing from Aristotle's *Metaphysics,* defines habit as "a disposition whereby that which is disposed is disposed well or ill" (*S. Th.,* I-II, 49, 1). A little further along Thomas distinguishes habit from disposition *tout court,* by adding the quality of durability. Thus Thomas notes "that the word 'habit' implies a certain lastingness: while the word 'disposition' does not" (ibid., I-II, 49, 2, ad 3).

34. "Iustitia maxime respicit rationem debiti" (ibid., II-II, 56, 2).

(*suum*) or "due" (*debitum*) or "right" (*ius*).³⁵ He uses these terms as if they were synonyms, interchangeably and without distinction. None-theless, each contributes a different nuance of meaning that helps round out the definition of justice, and each concept merits a separate consideration.

Aquinas teaches that debt or duty arises as the result of a benefit received from another.³⁶ Since commutative—or corrective—justice aims at establishing and conserving a certain equality, duties of justice come into being only when this equality is somehow disrupted. Along with commercial situations where "things" are exchanged, debt may also result from the exchange of less tangible goods, such as service or life itself.³⁷ Thus Thomas employs the examples of a master being indebted to his servant and a child to his father. This latter example illustrates another dimension of the Thomistic conception of debt: the benefit received need not have been requested; the very fact of one benefiting from another gives rise to the debt.³⁸ Therefore, debt results not merely from contract or consent but from the exchange of real benefit.

---

35. For *suum*, see *CG*, bk. I, ch. 93; bk. II, ch. 28; *S. Th.*, II-II, 58, 1; II-II, 58, 11; *Super epistolam ad Romanos*, ch. 14, lectio 2; *De Virtutibus*, I, 12, ad 26. Regarding *debitum*, Aquinas writes: "Iustitia enim . . . ad alterum est, cui debitum reddit" (*CG*, bk. II, ch. 28); or that "iustitia est ad reddendum debitum alteri" (*S. Th.*, II-II, 56, 2). See also *S. Th.*, II-II, 58, 1, ad 6.For *ius*, see, for example, *S. Th.*, II-II, 58, 1; *De Veritate*, q. 1, art. 5, ad 13; *CG*, bk. II, ch. 28.

36. As noted earlier, in a strict sense duty differs from mere obligation because of its relational or "other-directed" character. Duties (what is *due*) are always duties to someone. This becomes still clearer when we consider that the Latin *debitum* can be translated as either "duty" or "debt." Whereas in modern English usage "duty" can refer to a nonrelational obligation, "debt" always refers to an obligation to a second party, and in the absence of such a party, the debt disappears.

Actually, Thomas does not use the word "benefit" but the more generic term "thing," and the word "benefit" is employed here simply because all the examples Thomas uses involve real benefits (See *CG*, bk. II, ch. 28). Nonetheless, one could also say that a debt is incurred when one receives bad things as well as good, since justice in the Aristotelian-Thomistic sense refers to the establishment and conservation of equilibrium. The Old Testament *lex talionis* (which enjoined "life for life, eye for eye, tooth for tooth, hand for hand, foot for foot, burn for burn, wound for wound, stripe for stripe" [Exo 21:23–25]) illustrates well such a strict understanding of justice. An injury gives rise to a debt of justice to render an equivalent injury to the offending party.

37. One way that something becomes due to another, or his own, in a moral sense, comes through the performance of a service for another. Since justice seeks to maintain an equilibrium, the consignment of some good or the rendering of a service creates a debt for an equal value to be returned to the one who yielded it. Thus, reasons Thomas, "a man by working has a right to call his own that which, as an act of justice, is rendered to him by the person who pays him" (*CG*, bk. II, ch. 28).

38. "No one owes something to another except from the fact that in some way he depends

Thomas's analysis of debt as a consequence of beneficence immediately gives rise to a moral difficulty. If a person has a debt or duty only toward those from whom he has profited (or suffered) in some way, man's duties of justice extend not to all persons but only to a relatively tiny portion of humanity.[39] If this is so, then natural justice—based as it is on the notion of debt—would be applicable only in the case of someone having received a real benefit (or injury) from another. Such a hypothesis would seem to contradict human experience, whereby men naturally know that they must treat other human persons differently from the way they treat other beings. This required difference in treatment can be restated as a debt to them that precedes any real benefit (or injury) received from them.

Thomas circumvents this problem by observing that debt may also result when man receives something from a third party, "on whose account he owes something to the other"; consequently, "every man is a debtor to his neighbor for God's sake, from Whom we have received all good things."[40] In other words, man's natural debt of justice toward his neighbor results from the benefits received from God, not from the relationship between man and his fellow.

This answer creates at least two problems of its own, first in terms of the naturalness and cognitive accessibility of such justice, and second in terms of the locus of the debt of natural justice. Though man may come to a natural knowledge of God's beneficence and hence of his own debt of piety and gratitude in God's regard, it seems unreasonable to suppose that man could come to a natural knowledge of such beneficence giving rise to a vicarious debt to other human beings. If X receives a benefit

---

on him or receives something either from him or from a third, on whose account he owes something to the other: for thus a son is a debtor to his father, because he receives being from him; a master to his servant, because he receives from him the service he requires" (ibid., II, 28).

39. It is true that the negative duty of not injuring our neighbor may be present even where no positive duty of beneficence exists. In this sense, the negative precepts of the Law that prohibit killing, stealing, adultery, and the like would lose none of their negative force, since the infringement of these precepts would bring about an imbalance in the equality that justice seeks to conserve. These negative laws would continue to govern man's conduct toward all fellow human beings, regardless of whether or not a previous relation existed. Nonetheless, no positive duty of beneficence would exist unless the moral agent himself had been the cause his neighbor's need.

40. *CG*, bk. II, ch. 28.

from Y, he does not for that reason incur a debt toward Z, unless Y were to formally transfer his entitlement to Z. Such an arrangement could be known only if it were revealed.

Second, if man's natural duty of justice toward neighbor issues solely from his debt toward God, then indeed he owes God and not his fellow man, much the same as he may owe God the exercise of responsible stewardship of creatures and the environment, without having any true debt toward snail darters or the ozone layer (but only a debt to God in their regard). But man naturally experiences that his debt to his fellows differs not only in degree but in kind from his duty toward other creatures. Hence if a debt of natural justice exists among all human persons, it must proceed from another source.

One helpful clue may come from Finnis's observation that distributive justice does not lay an obligation solely on the state or an official representative of the common good; the same obligation applies to any individual insofar as he has charge of common stock. The proper domain of commutative justice is the regulation of relations between particular persons, but distributive justice as well obliges individuals as administrators of the common good.[41] According to the Thomistic understanding of property, what is possessed in surplus does not belong properly speaking to the one who holds it but rather to the community. Therefore, a person who enjoys a surplus of goods has an obligation toward one who is in need, without there being any causality between the former's abundance and the latter's want.[42] The simple fact of his ability to rectify an objective inequality creates a certain obligation to do so. Direct duty is much harder to assign when dealing with distributive justice than when dealing with commutative justice. Further insights can be drawn from the other two terms used by Thomas.

---

41. "The act of distributing the goods of the community, belongs to none but those who exercise authority over those goods; and yet distributive justice is also in the subjects to whom those goods are distributed in so far as they are contented by a just distribution. Moreover distribution of common goods is sometimes made not to the state but to the members of a family, and such distribution can be made by authority of a private individual (Quamvis etiam distributio quandoque fiat bonorum communium non quidem civitati, sed uni familiae, quorum distributio fieri potest auctoritate alicuius privatae personae)" (*S. Th.*, II-II, 61, 1, ad 3).

42. Thomas writes that "whatever certain people have in superabundance is due, by natural law, to the purpose of succoring the poor," and "each one is entrusted with the stewardship of his own things, so that out of them he may come to the aid of those who are in need" (ibid., II-II, 66, 7).

Suum is used to mean "his," or what belongs to the person. In justice, therefore, man is called to render to each what is "his own." Justice, in fact, rests essentially on the notion of possession, or belonging, and discerns between *mine* and *yours*.⁴³ This belonging clearly does not refer to what one possesses *physically* but rather *morally* (or legally): first because one cannot render to another that which he already has in his possession (though one can respect it), and second because a moral obligation can arise only from a moral relation.⁴⁴

Thomas relates *suum* to that which is proper or becoming to a person. Morality has to do with dealing fairly with reality or, in other words, treating each reality in a way suitable or becoming to it. Thus Thomas observes that "in external operations, the order of reason is established ... according to the becomingness [*convenientiam*] of the thing itself; from which becomingness we derive the notion of something due which is the formal aspect of justice: for, seemingly, it pertains to justice that a man give another his due."⁴⁵

How is this "becomingness" to be understood? According to Aquinas, "that which is ordered to a man is what is said to be his own."⁴⁶ Rommen has noted that a man's own is that "which is directed to him, which must be regarded as due or owed to him, from the standpoint of his essential idea."⁴⁷ One's own, in fact, is an extension of the self.⁴⁸ Since according to Thomas's teleological framework, man is not perfect but must move to-

---

43. "Iustitia ... quae secernit suum a non suo" (ibid., I-II, 66, 4, ad 1). Such a separation of property is greatly assisted by the social order. De Finance notes that it is "only in virtue of a social organization, at least embryonic, that the firm outlines of 'mine' and 'thine' will begin to appear" (*An Ethical Inquiry,* § 196, p. 348).

44. Thus, for example, stealing refers to taking something that does not belong to you. Though the object may have changed hands (and consequently physical possession), it still *belongs* to the one from whom it was stolen. The moral obligation of restitution rests on the idea of a moral attachment existing between the person and some specific goods. Physical possession is a circumstantial condition, a mere relation of contiguity, which cannot of itself give rise to moral obligation.

45. *S. Th.,* I-II, 60, 3.   46. Ibid., I, 21, 1, ad 3.

47. Rommen, *The Natural Law,* 182.

48. Wherefore Rommen observes that "one's own is an extension of the ego. Definite things are not of their very nature and forthwith ordered by natural law to this person. On the other hand, it is self-evident that the person has a right to the products created by his labor (with, of course, the proper reservations) and to have these pass into his ownership. The institution of private property is of natural law. In the long run, man cannot exist, cannot make good his right to marriage or to a family or to security of life, and cannot maintain his sphere of individual right to a life of his own, unless he is entitled to ownership through the acquisition of

ward perfection—as what is potential moves to what is actual—a man's "own" refers not only to what he actually possesses but to that which is necessary for him to become fully himself.[49] The quality of "becomingness," therefore, takes on a meaning of perfectiveness. What becomes a man is that which leads him to the fullness of his being. Thus Thomas remarks that "that which is required for a thing's perfection is necessarily due to it: thus it is due to a man to have hands or strength, since without these he cannot be perfect."[50] The just man, therefore, the one who possesses a firm and constant will to render to each his own, at bottom wills that each should be fully himself and is prepared to act to ensure that this is the case.

From this brief explanation, the close tie that binds *suum* to the *debitum* becomes evident since, as Thomas remarks: "To each one is due what is his own."[51] Not everyone acknowledges this close relation. Peschke, for example, has written: "Attention is to be called to the distinction between a person's *own* and *due* by right. Justice for one leaves to every man what is rightfully his own, and for another gives a man what he does not yet own but what is rightfully his due."[52]

Based on earlier considerations, Peschke's separation of *due* and *own* seems somewhat forced. While a certain distinction in emphasis can be drawn, the two concepts are not applied to different situations (holding in possession or deserving to receive) as Peschke affirms. Though the ma-

---

goods. The right to private property follows from the physical, ontological make-up of the individual person, from the body-spirit nature of man" (ibid., 207).

49. "But this prompts the question of what exactly 'his' means. . . . *Having* is often opposed to *being;* but, in fact, it is rather its complement. It involves a certain unity between what is possessed and the one who possesses, but it is a unity in which the distinction between the two is preserved, a unity which implies subordination, finality, completion. What is possessed is related to the one who possesses as the part is related to the whole, the limb to the living being, the instrument to the agent who makes use of it (with whom it forms one dynamic totality) etc. In this sense, one can say that every existing being 'possesses' the principles of being that are intrinsic to it, as well as the accidental qualities which are proper to it: these 'belong' to it, because they are linked with its being in a more profound manner than are the effects which are merely worked upon it from without. In the same way, everything without which a thing could not exist, and could not be what it is, can be said to be 'due' to it" (de Finance, *An Ethical Inquiry,* § 196, pp. 346–47).

50. *CG,* bk. II, ch. 28.

51. *S. Th.,* I, 21, 1, ad 3. Elsewhere he says that "each man's own is that which is due to him according to equality of proportion" (ibid., II-II, 58, 11).

52. Peschke, *A Presentation of Special Moral Theology,* 215.

terial consequences of justice will vary according to whether a person already has what is due to him or has not yet obtained it, these are but two instantiations of a single moral phenomenon, not two different phenomena. As a principle of justice, to be one's "own" signifies not "to have in one's possession at a given time" but rather "to be proper to" or "due to." Likewise, "due" refers not to "yet to be delivered" but rather "belonging to in justice." One could have in his possession what is not due to him, in which case it is not properly his own. Thomas emphasizes this point in still stronger terms. "That which is not due to another is not his properly speaking," since the formal aspect of justice "considers that thing as belonging to this particular man."[53]

The question of "belonging" or "possession" as the kernel of justice also reveals something about what sort of being can be the object of justice or, in other words, the subject of rights. Our phenomenological-linguistic analysis in chapter 1 ascertained that a subjective right is something one has. The object of justice (and subject of rights) can be only such a being as is capable of possessing. In what way can something be said to "belong" to a nonpersonal being?

The word "possession" can be used to denote different realities. A thing is said to possess its parts, such that a mammal "possesses" fur or hair, an analog clock "possesses" hands, or a man "possesses" health or athletic skills.[54] The parts of a thing therefore "belong" to the thing either essentially or accidentally. Next we have the case of de facto physical possession, as when a man is said to "possess" what is in his pocket, or a squirrel "possesses" the store of nuts stockpiled in its nest (in fact, we say "its nest" to signify just this sort of possession, the difference here being that possession is inferred from habitual use). Finally, we have the case of de jure moral possession, for instance when a man "possesses" stock in a company or a piece of real estate that perhaps he has never so much as visited. Unlike de facto possession, de jure possession implies a moral or legal tie that attaches a piece of property to its owner and exacts the respect of other moral agents. It is clear that the mere fact of someone's holding something in physical possession does not in and of itself entail

---

53. *S. Th.*, II-II, 62, 1, ad 1.

54. Thomas explains this sort of possession or "having" as being between two realities, the "haver" and what is had, where there is no medium between them. Such is the sort of possession of components, such as quantity or quality. See ibid., I-II, 49, 1.

this moral or legal tie. When Thomas deals with restitution as a requirement of commutative justice, he speaks of a situation "occasioned by one person having what belongs to another."[55] Here a situation exists where *de facto* possession (having) is at odds with de jure possession (what belongs to another). As this example illustrates, justice deals with de jure possession, not de facto.

Whereas nonpersonal beings are capable of possession in the first two senses described above, it would seem they are not capable of possessing in the moral or *de jure* sense.[56] The moral attachment of property to an owner requires a *moral subject,* and here the previous discussion on the subjectivity proper to the person proves especially helpful. The statement "I own" or "I am due," just as the statement "I act," implies a self-conscious subject of ownership or action. There can be no moral belonging without a moral *self.*[57] This is why justice, properly speaking, refers only to persons. When applied to animals and inanimate things, one speaks of "having" or "belonging" only in an analogical sense, as de Finance makes clear:

Strictly speaking they [such usages] are applicable only where persons are concerned, since it is they alone who are capable of disposing of themselves and their goods in virtue of their free will. Someone genuinely *possesses* only what he is capable of making use of so as to attain goals which he himself has chosen. . . . What someone can call "his" is an extension and complement of the "self" to whom it belongs, and it is only a person who has a "self," since only he is capable of *reflection.* . . . In other words, it is necessary that what is possessed be related to its possessor as one who possesses himself and is capable of disposing of himself, as one who is "for himself," who is a *"self."* If a person can possess things, the reason for this is that he first of all possesses himself, in virtue of his presence to

---

55. Ibid., II-II, 62, 1.

56. For this same reason irrational animals and other nonpersonal beings cannot be the object of the love of benevolence. One cannot wish their good for their own sakes, since they possess no proper good, except in an analogical sense. Thomas asserts that charity "cannot have an irrational creature for its object: first because friendship is towards one to whom we wish good things, while, properly speaking, we cannot wish good things to an irrational creature, because it is not competent, properly speaking, to possess good, this being proper to the rational creature which, through its free-will, is the master of its disposal of the good it possesses" (ibid., II-II, 25, 3).

57. "'Mine,' however, presupposes an 'I,' a person, i.e., a subject whose aims and ends things serve and whose advantage is a goal of the actions of others, solely by reason of being a person" (Rommen, *The Natural Law,* 182).

himself and his power of liberty. The root and condition of possibility of all possession, in the true sense, is this prior possession of oneself, which distinguishes a human being from all other beings on the face of the earth.[58]

In determining what is appropriate or fair in dealing with personal and nonpersonal realities, one final consideration is in order. If nonpersonal realities cannot be the subject of rights or the object of justice, what is appropriate or fair in treating such realities? As a point of departure, Thomas's query as to whether it is unlawful to kill any living thing can prove illuminating. He concludes that it is not unlawful to kill irrational animals, since there "is no sin in using a thing for the purpose for which it is. Now the order of things is such that the imperfect are for the perfect," and thus "it is lawful to kill dumb animals, in so far as they are naturally directed to man's use."[59] According to a Christian, teleological view of creation, all things exist for a purpose: a being can exist for itself (for its own sake) or for the sake of another. The good of a being does not consist solely in being but in being according to the divine purpose and according to its proper finality. A unique quality of persons is existence "for their own sake" or as "an end in themselves," whereas nonpersonal beings, since they do not possess subjectivity, do not have a "sake" or a "self" in the proper sense. Their entire existence is ordered to another, and thus they may be disposed of for the good of the other, since their purpose consists in this.

Thomas also uses the term *ius* in his definitions of justice, often in conjunction with *suum*, as in the case where he defines justice as "habitus secundum quem aliquis constanti et perpetua voluntate ius suum unicuique tribuit."[60] Here *ius suum* can be translated as "his right" or "what is his by right." Since *ius*, for Thomas, refers to the object of justice, which is the establishment and preservation of a certain equality in the relationships between man and his fellows, *ius suum* would seem to refer to that which is due to the individual in order to attain this equality.

For Aquinas, *ius*, or right, forms the object of justice, and is equivalent to "the just" *(iustum)*.[61] Justice, in fact, is the virtue that aims at establishing equality among men, a condition of balance or equilibrium. This

---

58. De Finance, *An Ethical Inquiry*, § 196, p. 347.
59. *S. Th.*, II-II, 64, 2.
60. Ibid., II-II, 58, 1.
61. "Et propter hoc specialiter iustitiae prae aliis virtutibus determinatur secundum se

state of equilibrium equates to the just order, or a situation of objective right *(ius)*. Already in the thirteenth century, Aquinas made note of an evolution in meaning of the word *ius*, which initially was used to denote the just thing itself, then designated the art whereby it is known what is just, later meant the place where justice is administered, and finally became a rule of law.[62]

In his definition of justice, however, Aquinas speaks of "right" not as an objective situation or rule but on the individual level, whereby "right" approaches the more modern notion of subjective right. Aquinas states that "the 'right' or the 'just' is a work that is adjusted to another person according to some kind of equality."[63] It is in this sense that Aquinas places *ius* in his definition of justice, in saying that justice is the habit by which one renders to each his *ius* with a constant and perpetual will.[64] Since Aquinas employs *ius* as an equivalent substitute for the words *suum* and *debitum*, he accords to *ius* the meaning of that which is due to another or that which is his. From this understanding to the contemporary idea of subjective rights requires only a relatively small step. Moreover, though many insist that Thomas employs *ius* solely in an objective sense, others have effectively demonstrated that there are numerous instances where Thomas uses the term in a thoroughly subjective sense.[65] This, too, helps to understand how natural rights fit into the classical structure of natural justice.

---

obiectum, quod vocatur iustum. Et hoc quidem est ius. Unde manifestum est quod ius est obiectum iustitiae" (ibid., II-II, 57, 1).

62. See ibid., II-II, 57, 1, ad 1.

63. "ius, sive iustum, est aliquod opus adaequatum alteri secundum aliquem aequalitatis modum" (ibid., II-II, 57, 2).

64. "iustitia est habitus secundum quem aliquis constanti et perpetua voluntate ius suum unicuique tribuit" (ibid., II-II, 58, 1).

65. H. Hering compiled a very helpful assortment of texts in which Thomas employs *ius* in the manner of subjective right. The references Hering adduces are, from the *Summa Theologiae*, I-II, 58, 2 *(ius contradicendi)*; II-II, 62, 1, ad 2 *(ius dominii)*; II-II, 66, 5, ad 2 *(ius possidendi)*; II-II, 69, 1 *(ius praelationis)*; II-II, 87, 3 *(ius accipiendi)*; II, 46, 3, obj. 3 *(ius in homine)*; II, 57, 6, ad 3 *(ius mansionis caelestis)*; II, 67, 2 *(Ius accedendi ad mensam Domini)*; II, 67, 6 *(ius baptizandi)*; Suppl., 57, 1, ad 7 *(ius successionis)*; Suppl., 64, 1, ad 3 *(Si aliquis redditur impotens ad debitum solvendum . . . mulier non habet ius plus petendi)*; Suppl., 64, 4, ad 1 *(ius petendi)*; Q.D. de virtutibus in communi, q.1, a.4 *(ius et facultatem repugnandi)*; Quodlib. II, 8 *(ius exigendi)*. See H. Hering, "De Iure Subjective Sumpto apud S. Thomam," *Angelicum* 16 (1939).

What Is Due in Justice to Every Person

Though not elaborating on the specific content of the debt proper to justice except in a scattered way, Thomas does give key indications that make it possible to discern this content. The kernel of his teaching, as seen earlier, is that whatever is required for the perfection of a thing is due to it. Aquinas asserts that when God wills a particular thing, He also wills whatever is required for that thing.[66] This is because God wills the perfection—i.e., the fullness of being according to its nature—for all He creates, since He cannot will defects. Hence "that which is requisite for a perfection of a thing is due to it."[67] This principle follows directly on chapter 13's considerations of the natural law, with the difference that those reflections focused on man's good and his subsequent obligation to seek the good, whereas here a thing's perfection is considered from the perspective of what is due to it.

This principle leads to the conclusion that a particular thing will be due to a person in the degree to which that thing is necessary for his perfection. The different levels of goods proper to man according to the natural law, beginning with those fundamental goods necessary for his existence such as food and shelter, provide a helpful guide to understanding what is due to the human being. The more basic goods that ensure the preservation of life are fundamental, not inasmuch as they are most perfective of him but as necessary conditions without which any further perfection is impossible. Man's perfection includes especially those goods that are characteristic of him as a human person called to communion with God and neighbor. As a social animal, man's perfection is bound up with the good of others and their mutual relations, and thus "one man naturally owes another whatever is necessary for the preservation of human society."[68] This, in turn, forms the basis for the natural duty to speak

---

66. *CG*, bk. I, ch. 83.

67. "Quod autem ad perfectionem alicuius requiritur, est debitum unicuique" (ibid., bk. I, ch. 93). See also ibid., bk. II, ch. 28.

68. Thomas writes that "homo est animal sociale, naturaliter unus homo debet alteri id sine quo societas humana conservari non posset" (*S. Th.*, II-II, 109, 3, ad 1). Once again we note that Thomas speaks of a duty with no prior benefit received. Here, however, the matter of the duty cannot be reduced to a negative precept; rather, Thomas speaks of a man owing those things necessary for the conservation of society.

the truth, since deceit would bring about a breakdown in the trust necessary for human society.[69]

According to Thomas, "it is due to every natural being that it have the things which its nature calls for both in essentials and in accidentals."[70] Here once again, "due" acquires the sense of what is proper or becoming to a given being in order for it to fully be what divine wisdom ordained it to be. When God provides for creatures, giving them what corresponds to their nature, He is acting "justly" toward them, not because He owes them anything, strictly speaking, but because His gifts correspond to the requirements of their being according to His own wisdom in creating them.[71] Therefore, there is a gratuitousness found in creation that is not found in God's sustenance of what He has created.

As regards the statement that "whatever is required for the perfection of a thing is due to it," some important distinctions are in order. If debt is understood in a moral sense, this is true only in the case of persons, since nothing is morally due to nonpersonal beings. Man is free to dispose of such creatures not with regard to their good but to his own, in that they are ordered to the good of man and not to their own good. If a man chops down a tree for firewood in order to keep warm, this frustrates the natural perfection of the tree per se but contributes to the perfection of the tree in that it exists not for itself but for man.[72] In a broader sense, when Thomas says that whatever is required for the perfection of a thing is *due* to it, this "due" can be understood to mean suitable or proper to it, but not necessarily due in a moral sense.

Furthermore, in the Thomistic context, the notion of debt admits of degrees. Properly speaking, justice "requires a debt of necessity: since what is rendered to someone out of justice, is due to him by a necessity of right *(ex necessitate iuris).*"[73] But not all debt is of this sort. This can be seen from Thomas's discussion of some of the potential parts (annexed

---

69. "Non autem possent homines ad invicem convivere nisi sibi invicem crederent, tanquam sibi invicem veritatem manifestantibus. Et ideo virtus veritatis aliquo modo attendit rationem debiti" (ibid.).

70. *De Veritate,* 23, 6, ad 3.

71. "Thus also God exercises justice, when He gives to each thing what is due to it by its nature and condition. This debt however is derived from the former; since what is due to each thing is due to it as ordered to it according to the divine wisdom" (*S. Th.,* I, 21, 1, ad 3).

72. See ibid., II-II, 64, 2.

73. *CG,* bk. II, ch. 28.

virtues) of justice. An example is the case of the virtue of liberality: although it "does not consider the legal due that justice considers, it considers a certain moral due. This due is based on a certain fittingness and not on an obligation: so that it answers to the idea of due in the lowest degree."[74] Thomas's distinction offers a mine for further reflection. According to this logic, legal justice demands a debt of necessity, and civil legislation should be limited to this strict understanding of a duty of justice. This makes sense. In order for legal justice to be enforceable by law, it must correspond to strict obligation. But Thomas also speaks of "a certain moral due" that is based on "a fittingness and not on an obligation." A person who could assist another in need or could initiate activity in others (individuals, the community, the state, according to prudential judgment) may have a certain moral duty to do so, although he would not have a strict legal duty. Such distinctions of degree parallel the hierarchy of rights outlined in chapter 11.

THE PREEMINENCE OF JUSTICE AMONG THE MORAL VIRTUES

Justice not only occupies center stage in natural law theory, it also enjoys a certain preeminence among the moral virtues. A habit is a quality by which man is disposed well or ill according to a faculty, an operation, or a passion. The virtues are positive habits, that is, habits that perfect the powers of the soul, whereas vices dispose them negatively. Wherefore the *Catechism* defines virtue as "an habitual and firm disposition to do the good."[75] Virtue enables the person to readily perform good acts and to give the best of himself. The intellectual virtues perfect the intelligence. The moral virtues dispose man toward good action, and among the moral virtues four play a pivotal role and are thus called "cardinal" virtues, as we have seen. Prudence perfects the practical reason, temperance disposes and orders the concupiscible passions, fortitude orders the irascible passions, and justice perfects the will and its operations.[76]

---

74. *S. Th.*, II-II, 117, 5, ad 1.
75. *CCC*, 1803.
76. "Prudence is the virtue that disposes practical reason to discern our true good in every circumstance and to choose the right means of achieving it" (*CCC*, 1806). Prudence is defined by Aquinas, following Aristotle (*Nichomachean Ethics*, VI, 5:1140b, 6–8), as "right reason in action" *(recta ratio agibilium)* (*S. Th*, II-II, 47, 2). "Temperance is the moral virtue that moderates

According to Thomas, prudence, a quasi-moral virtue, "is more excellent than the moral virtues, and moves them"[77] and "is the principal of all the virtues simply,"[78] because prudence helps guide the other moral virtues to their true mean[79] and commands right action.[80] Among the true moral virtues, on the other hand, justice holds pride of place.[81] Justice perfects the will and deals with operations, so that the just person is necessarily good, since he acts well.

Virtue "is that which makes its possessor good, and renders his work good," with good here signifying "in accord with reason."[82] The virtue that makes the person good in the truest sense is justice, since justice orders the will and the will determines the moral quality of human acts as well as the moral status of the person himself. Justice is so essential to man's moral goodness, in fact, that Aquinas, appropriating Tully, says that "good men are so called chiefly from their justice," and that "the luster of virtue appears above all in justice."[83] The intellectual virtues rectify reason, and prudence rectifies practical reason, or reason regarding action. Justice establishes the order of right reason in human affairs. The

---

the attraction of pleasures and provides balance in the use of created goods. It ensures the will's mastery over instincts and keeps desires within the limits of what is honorable. The temperate person directs the sensitive appetites toward what is good, and maintains a healthy discretion" (*CCC*, 1809). "Fortitude is the moral virtue that ensures firmness in difficulties and constancy in the pursuit of the good. It strengthens the resolve to resist temptations and to overcome obstacles in the moral life. The virtue of fortitude enables one to conquer fear, even fear of death, and to face trials and persecutions. It disposes one even to renounce and sacrifice his life in defense of a just cause" (*CCC*, 1808). Thomas speaks of fortitude as firmness of mind, or a firmness in resisting those things that can withdraw the will from following reason, such as in grave danger. See *S. Th.*, II-II, 123, 2–3.

77. *S. Th.*, II-II, 47, 6, ad 3. Properly speaking, prudence is not a moral but an intellectual virtue, since it perfects the practical reason, although it is a quasi-moral virtue in that it presupposes the rectitude of the will and disposes not only thought but thought's application to action (see ibid., II-II, 47, 1, ad 3). According to Thomas's structure, "the subject of the moral virtues is the appetitive part of the soul," or the will (ibid., I-II, 60, 1).

78. Ibid., I-II, 61, 2, ad 1.

79. Ibid., II-II, 47, 7. Therefore "it is called *auriga virtutum* [the charioteer of the virtues]; it guides the other virtues by setting rule and measure. It is prudence that immediately guides the judgement of conscience" (*CCC*, 1806).

80. *S. Th.*, II-II, 47, 8.

81. Thomas asks whether justice is chief among the moral virtues and answers in the affirmative. See ibid., II-II, 58, 12. In this case he considers prudence not as a moral virtue but in its proper sense as an intellectual virtue.

82. Ibid., II-II, 123, 1. See also Aristotle, *Nichomachean Ethics*, II, 6:1106a22–24.

83. See *S. Th.*, II-II, 58, 3.

other cardinal moral virtues—temperance and fortitude—play an ancillary role to justice by removing the obstacles to the establishment of this uprightness in human relations.[84] The human will can be drawn by some object of pleasure to something other than what right reason requires, and this obstacle is removed by the virtue of temperance. The will can likewise be disinclined to follow what reason dictates because of some difficulty that presents itself, and this obstacle is overcome by the virtue of fortitude.[85]

But the true importance of justice, and the characteristic that separates it from all other virtues, is not so much the fact that it perfects the will and its operations as the fact that it deals with man's relations with other persons.[86] "Justice is the virtue that disposes the person to realize interpersonal relations in such a way that the absolute value of other persons is recognized, actualized and promoted."[87] In a certain sense, the other three cardinal virtues and the other virtues attached to them can be seen as subordinate to justice and ordered to justice. One can be supremely moderate in all earthly pleasures, courageous in the face of all dangers, and even prudent as regards choosing effective means to reach one's objectives yet still be unjust, and therefore lacking in virtue.[88] From this

---

84. "While our sense appetite aims at obtaining what will be of advantage to ourselves, our rational appetite enables us to impose restraints on ourselves for the advantage and well-being of others; it is in this self-imposed restraint that the rationality of this appetite is manifested in the highest degree" (de Finance, *An Ethical Inquiry*, § 196, p. 348). These two virtues also clearly play a subsidiary role with regard to the virtue of prudence. Thus Aristotle describes temperance as ancillary to the virtue of prudence (and even derives an etymological definition of temperance *[sophrosyne]* as "preserving prudence"), since "a man corrupted by a love of pleasure or fear of pain, entirely fails to see any first principle, and cannot see that he ought to choose and do everything as a means to this end and for its sake" (Aristotle, *Nichomachean Ethics*, VI, 5:1140b18–20).

85. See *S. Th.*, II-II, 123, 1.

86. Thus Aristotle wrote that "justice is perfect virtue because it is the practice of perfect virtue; and perfect in a special degree, because its possessor can practice his virtue towards others and not merely by himself; for there are many who can practice virtue in their own private affairs but cannot do so in their relations with another" (*Nichomachean Ethics*, V, 1:1129b31–35). Furthermore, "justice alone of the virtues is 'the good of others,' because it does what is for the advantage of another, either a ruler or an associate" (ibid., V, 1:1130a2–5).

87. Caffarra, *Living in Christ*, 168.

88. In the strict sense, as "perfect virtues," all the moral virtues require the others, in that they require a good will in accord with right reason. Virtue by definition makes its possessor good, and his work as well, but one virtue does not make a man entirely good, but only as regards the particular power it perfects. In justice alone, however, is good will proper to the virtue as such. For this reason, the other moral virtues have secondary meanings whereby they

perspective, only justice is truly "virtuous."[89] The other cardinal virtues can be sought and used selfishly, as a mere means of self-perfection, while one remains indifferent to or even disdainful of others, thus trampling charity, the *forma virtutum*. The other moral virtues perfect the person, make him more thoroughly master of himself, but a right will demands above all a proper regard for others.[90] Only justice directs the virtues beyond their proper end to the good of others, the common good.[91]

On the other hand, justice truly demands the possession of the other virtues, at least in some degree.[92] One cannot be just if one is intemperate, since one will prefer one's own pleasure to the good of the other. Likewise, if one lacks courage, he will abandon the other when giving him his rightful due becomes difficult or dangerous. Neither can a man be truly just if he is imprudent, since he will not correctly discern what he must do in order to act justly toward others. For a person to be thoroughly just, he must be temperate, courageous, and prudent.

Justice is thus the interpersonal virtue and perfects that which is most proper to the person, which is relation. For this reason Thomas says that

---

perfect a given power but do not guarantee righteousness. Virtue is adherence to goodness, but this may refer to the Good as such or to partial goods that are the object of powers of the soul. Temperance, for example, disposes one to dominate the natural inclination to pleasure according to reason, but properly speaking it does not imply a completely upright will in other regards. Likewise prudence, "practical wisdom," perfects practical reason to know the good, as when one has a good moral conscience, but one may know the good and still not carry it out.

89. "La justice est la vertu qui rend à chacun son dû. Comment la definir par rapport aux trois autres vertus cardinales? Elle seule est 'vertuese.' Un voleur peut être prudent, tempérant, courageux, il n'est pas juste" (Jean Guitton and Jean-Jacques Antier, *Le livre de la sagesse et des vertus retrouvées* [Saint-Amand-Montrond, Cher: Librairie Académique Perrin, 1998], 149).

90. For this reason Aristotle writes that "justice alone of the virtues is 'the good of others,' because it does what is for the advantage of another, either a ruler or an associate. As then the worst man is he who practices vice towards his friends as well as in regard to himself, so the best is not he who practices virtue in regard to himself but he who practices it towards others; for that is a difficult task" (*Nichomachean Ethics*, V, 1:1130a3–8).

91. Thus Thomas says: "Every virtue strictly speaking directs its act to that virtue's proper end: that it should happen to be directed to a further end either always or sometimes, does not belong to that virtue considered strictly, for it needs some higher virtue to direct it to that end. Consequently there must be one supreme virtue essentially distinct from every other virtue, which directs all the virtues to the common good; and this virtue is legal justice" (*S. Th.*, II-II, 58, 6, ad 4).

92. Aristotle goes on to say that justice, in this sense, "is not a part of Virtue, but the whole of Virtue" (*Nichomachean Ethics*, V, 1:1130a9). This view of justice as comprehensive virtue is not justice in the proper sense, but the very fact that justice lends itself to a broad definition that encompasses all virtue suggests that justice stands at the heart of virtue.

"the other virtues perfect man in those matters only which befit him in relation to himself," and consequently rectitude in the works of the other virtues "depends on its relation to the agent only." On the other hand, "it is proper to justice, as compared with the other virtues, to direct man in his relations with others," and rectitude in a work of justice, "besides its relation to the agent, is set up by its relation to others."[93] It is precisely for this reason that justice stands out as chief among the moral virtues.[94]

Justice, and the love that constitutes its perfection, is more essential to man's nature and more constitutive of his true good than any other virtue. Man was made for interpersonal relation, for love, more than he was made to be a great piano player, an acclaimed writer, or a world-class figure skater—though these qualities, too, may contribute to his integral perfection. By his very nature, the human person is called to love and finds his true personal fulfillment only in love. His moral good depends far more on his relationship with persons than his relationship with things, and even than his success in perfecting himself. If a person fails to develop his natural gifts for art or for mathematics, that is sad. If he never learns to love, he has failed in the essential enterprise for which he was created.

A danger exists among a certain strain of moral eudaimonism according to which the focus and core of morality seems to be the attainment of a perfect self: "integral human fulfillment." John Finnis, for instance, has written that "the fundamental task of practical reasonableness is self-constitution or self-possession; inner integrity of character and outer authenticity of action are aspects of the basic good of practical reasonableness, as are freedom from the automatism of habit and from subjection to unintegrated impulses and compulsions."[95] How such a conception can

---

93. *S. Th.*, II-II, 57, 1.

94. Thomas reasons that justice stands foremost among all moral virtues both because of its subject, since it is perfective of the highest part of man, the rational appetite or will, and because of its object, because it deals with other persons. Thus whereas the other virtues are commendable in respect of the sole good of the virtuous person himself, "justice is praiseworthy in respect of the virtuous person being well disposed towards another, so that justice is somewhat the good of another person, as stated in *Ethic.* v, 1. Hence the Philosopher says (*Rhet.* i, 9): 'The greatest virtues must needs be those which are most profitable to other persons, because virtue is a faculty of doing good to others. For this reason the greatest honors are accorded the brave and the just, since bravery is useful to others in warfare, and justice is useful to others both in warfare and in time of peace'" (*S. Th.*, II-II, 58, 12).

95. Finnis, *Natural Law and Natural Rights*, 168.

be squared with the Christian vision, which sees love as the summit and sum of all virtue, is unclear. In this regard Hittinger has responded that "a eudaimonism that remains on the immanent level of goods flirts precipitously with an understanding of any good as a mere *bonum mihi*. Why this or that should be a good for someone else, and why I am morally obligated to promote that good for the other person, requires answers that are not easily extracted from the Grisez-Finnis system."[96]

The virtue of justice, the permanent disposition to give to each his due, is without doubt perfective of the moral subject who possesses it. By acting justly the moral agent becomes a better person and elevates himself. Nonetheless, a peculiarity of justice as distinguished from the other cardinal virtues is its inherent transcendence. Justice can never remain a merely immanent human value, chosen solely for the sake of the acting subject's self-improvement or perfection. To treat others justly implies the acknowledgment of their personal good, independent of any advantage to oneself. In justice that personal good is affirmed *for its own sake* and not for its utility to the agent, not even the agent's moral utility (i.e., that it makes *me* a better person to act in such a way). In essence, when one acts justly one pursues a good of a wholly different order than the self-perfecting goods that are below man.[97]

Morality concerns itself primarily with free human actions, as constitutive of human moral character. The effect of deliberate choices on the moral agent usually tops the list of the ethicist's concerns. This mode of conceiving ethics or moral theology requires a reworking when passing

---

96. Hittinger, *A Critique of the New Natural Law Theory*, 150. MacIntyre adds a similar criticism, stating that the Grisez/Finnis theory "defines integral human fulfillment in terms of respect for and the achievement of a set of basic goods. It does not understand human individuals as essentially parts of larger wholes—of the family and of political community, for example—wholes apart from membership in which the human individual is incomplete" ("Theories of Natural Law in the Culture of Advanced Modernity," 105).

97. According to Thomas's scheme, particular goods are integrated into one's ultimate good, which is beatitude, perfection of being, the possession of God. Within this teleological scheme, what is good for the moral subject is that which moves him toward his final good. From another perspective, there are basic, incommensurate human goods or values that are constitutive of man's integral flourishing or perfection, and in this sense they could also be called "means" to the end of his perfection. Justice, which regulates relations with other persons, cannot be stretched to fit into this scheme. Doing good to others and avoiding what would harm them (rendering them their "due") cannot be rightly pursued as a means to the perfection of the subject. To be truly just to the person, one must treat him as an end, for his own sake.

from the sphere of self-referential goods to the sphere of justice, where human actions are no longer primarily self-relational but other-relational. Things are below the person and are ordered to his perfection; other persons are equal in dignity to the acting subject and therefore cannot be incorporated into a self-referential framework of perfective goods, but only into a common good, a good possessed by a communal subject of persons.[98] When one treats another person correctly, in a just way, one does so in the first place because the other person deserves such treatment absolutely. It is indeed consonant with right reason to treat him in this way, but in this case one seeks consonance with right reason not because it leads to self-perfection or happiness or integral human flourishing, but primarily for the sake of the other.[99]

---

98. "To act justly towards another is to acknowledge in practice that he is on the same level of existence as you yourself, that you enjoy no privilege in regard to what is his. Between you and him there is, accordingly, a relationship of the type that exists between one being and another insofar as each is actual, as opposed to a relationship of the type which necessarily involves a movement from what is potential to what is actual; you are not treating his as a mere means to the attainment of your ends, nor are you making use of him to obtain what you lack" (de Finance, *An Ethical Inquiry*, § 144, p. 239).

99. "If one harms another person, is the *reason* for the disvalue simply that one has harmed or obstructed one's own potential to be just, or to realize one's potential to enjoy friends? Is there not also an offense to the other person which must fundamentally enter into a description of the disvalue, and hence into a description of the value as such? Insofar as justice involves other persons, one would not be inclined to define it exclusively in terms of an individual's way of adjusting to other goods" (Hittinger, *A Critique of the New Natural Law Theory*, 117–18).

15. NATURAL RIGHTS IN CLASSICAL THEORY

Establishing the central position of natural justice within the global framework of the natural law is vital for locating natural rights within classical ethical theory. It is the essential tie of rights to natural justice that will guarantee the place of natural rights within natural law theory and thus verify the compatibility of rights with traditional ethics.

NATURAL RIGHTS AND NATURAL JUSTICE

Among those of the classical tradition who accept the concept of natural rights, there is nearly universal agreement that rights form part of the virtue of justice.[1] Intuitively, since the virtue of justice orders all interpersonal relations, and rights are ethical principles dealing with the same matter, rights must be principles of justice. Moreover, the very term "natural rights" suggests that such a phenomenon must somehow be distinguished as a part of the natural moral law.[2] Thus Maritain noted that

---

1. The International Theological Commission states: "The rights of the human person depend on justice. Man has a right to all the means necessary to develop himself and attain to fulfillment, subject indeed to the common good" ("Propositions on the Dignity and Rights of the Human Person," 265).

2. Hence we read in the *Catechism:* "The natural law, present in the heart of each man and established by reason, is universal in its precepts and its authority extends to all men. It expresses the dignity of the person and determines the basis for his fundamental rights and duties" (*CCC,* 1956). Pinckaers similarly states: "Natural law is the foundation of human rights, as it roots them in our personal nature. Thus these rights are, in their source, universal and inalienable.... They call forth each one's respect and benevolence in keeping with the virtue of justice, which is a firm determination to give everyone their due" (*The Sources of Christian Ethics,* 452–53).

"natural law and the light of moral conscience do not prescribe merely things to be done and not to be done; they also recognize rights, in particular, rights linked to the very nature of man."[3] For this reason, a "true philosophy of the rights of the human person is therefore based upon the idea of natural law. The same natural law which lays down our most fundamental duties, and by virtue of which every law is binding, is the very law which assigns to us our fundamental rights."

How do rights fit into the structure of natural law and natural justice? As an order of justice, natural law can be seen as an expression of natural right, since the law makes explicit and imperative the sort of conduct necessary for the preservation of the just order. In this sense, natural law would contain those precepts that natural right implicitly demands. From another perspective, and more properly, the natural moral law is broader than natural right and embraces it, because the natural moral law governs all of man's actions according to right reason, and not merely those relating to other persons.[4]

Objective right implies or contains subjective rights, in that if any particular right—a single element of "what is due" to someone—is lacking, a situation of objective right or of objective justice no longer exists. Natural justice forms the core of the natural moral law, and the matter or object of natural justice is natural right. Natural right, in turn, can be "broken down" into natural rights, specific instantiations of "what is due" in justice to all human beings. Put in another way, the "just order" requires the satisfaction of specific precepts of justice, and these precepts, from the perspective of the recipient, are formulated as rights. Natural rights, then, are a central component of the natural moral law. As de Finance has written:

Even though the first question [Are there natural rights?] has been the subject of much controversy, there can be no real problem about the answer, once the existence of a natural moral law is granted. The same line of thought which led us to the conclusion that there is such a law, also leads us to the conclusion that there are such rights. Prior to all positive laws, certain relations between human beings are objectively in conformity with the judgments of right reason; other relations

---

3. Maritain, *The Rights of Man*, 37.
4. "Natural moral law . . . embraces the whole natural moral order. From this natural moral law must be distinguished natural right, which only covers that segment of natural moral law which is concerned with the realm of justice and the juridical order between men" (Peschke, *A Presentation of General Moral Theology*, 106).

clash with these judgments. In consequence, there arises the obligation to foster relations of the first kind and shun those of the second. But what does this mean except that, prior to all positive laws, there is a just and unjust order which imposes itself categorically on human liberty? Now, a just and unjust order is precisely what is meant by the term "objective rights." Consequently, such rights exist prior to all positive laws. But a right which exists prior to all positive laws is, by definition, a *natural right*. Hence there are natural rights.[5]

Right *(ius)*, as the name indicates, is the object of justice *(iustitia)* and describes a situation wherein everyone receives his due, and everyone is disposed to give others their due. The word *iustitia* denotes a virtue, a habit of the will, that aims at the establishment of *ius*. Justice, therefore, refers to a moral virtue (a firm disposition to render others their due), whereas the right describes the "just order," a situation where de facto all members of the society are just, and thus all receive what is due to them. Virtue lies in the disposition of the will, but objective right—the object of justice—lies not in the will but in a state or situation.

Justice deals with what is due and therefore with desert. In his discussion of justice, Aristotle refers to the principle of "assignment by desert," noting the general consensus that "justice in distribution must be based on desert of some sort."[6] The concept of desert is central to the idea of rights, since a right is simply the moral capacity to claim what one deserves. Since justice rests on the conviction that a person can morally deserve something from someone else, then rights clearly stand at the center of justice. As Hittinger observes: "Until or unless someone can rightfully claim 'this is owed to me [him, or them],' there is literally no issue of justice."[7] Indeed, justice depends on the possibility of determining what is due to another person, that is, what the other person has a right to and what the moral agent's duties are with regard to that other person. To arrive at a situation of justice where everyone receives his due presupposes knowledge of what is in fact due to each.

Whereas natural rights theory, thus understood, represents no deviation from traditional natural law theory as far as *content* is concerned, it does entail a change in *vocabulary* and a shift in *emphasis*. "What is due" can be considered from the perspective of the one who owes or the one

---

5. De Finance, *An Ethical Inquiry*, § 212, p. 376.
6. Aristotle, *Nichomachean Ethics*, V, 3:1131a24–26.
7. Hittinger, introduction to *The Natural Law*, xxix.

who is owed. The same moral phenomenon can be described in terms of rights or duties, though certain cases will lend themselves more to one than to another. Thus there can be a shift in emphasis or perspective without a change in meaning. Instead of describing a moral event or situation from the perspective of the moral agent, rights language describes the event from the perspective of the recipient of the action.[8] It thus complements and enriches more traditional ethical language.

Justice involves both "negative" and "positive" rights, where negative rights are understood as requiring noninterference with another's activities, and positive rights are understood as requiring some positive intervention in favor of the rights-bearer.[9] To not interfere or to provide some benefit are simply two manifestations of what can be "due" to another. Thus Carlo Caffarra states that the order of justice "essentially involves refraining from the violation of another's rights to the goods necessary for his development *(alteri non laedere)* and giving everyone his due *(unicuique suum tribuere).*" For his part, Benedict Ashley writes that justice "concerns a *right,* that is, what is due some person, and this implies a certain *equality* between what the agent does and what is due to the recipient."[10] Or, as Finnis observes, human rights "embody the requirements of justice."[11]

RIGHTS ONLY TO TRUE GOODS

Since justice is rooted in the objective order; "what is due" to each is determined not by what each would like, but rather by what is truly good and necessary for each, in the sense of truly conducive to his perfection

---

8. "In short, the modern vocabulary and grammar of rights is a many-faceted instrument for reporting and asserting the requirements or other implications of a relationship of justice *from the point of view of the person(s) who benefit(s) from* that relationship. It provides a way of talking about 'what is just' from a special angle: the viewpoint of the 'other(s)' to whom something . . . is owed or due, and who would be wronged if denied that something" (Finnis, *Natural Law and Natural Rights,* 205; emphasis in original).

9. This understanding of natural rights is at odds with the Liberal concept, which limited natural rights to negative rights of noninterference. One notes that the Liberal theory of Hobbes and those after him maintains only a tenuous relation between rights and justice in the classical sense, since the essence of justice is an active "rendering" *(tribuere)* and not merely the passive respect of noninvolvement.

10. Caffarra, *Living in Christ,* 221; Ashley, *Living the Truth in Love,* 272–73.

11. Finnis, *Natural Law and Natural Rights,* 23.

or integral flourishing. This conclusion flows logically from Thomas's discussion of the nature of the "debt" proper to justice. One is due what is his own, and "one's own" stems from a relationship of becomingness, not from personal preference. Becomingness derives from one's nature, not from one's subjective interests or desires. To separate rights from human goods is to remove the only objective criterion by which one can distinguish true rights claims from mere declarations of desire or preference. The intelligibility of natural rights, therefore, depends on their relationship with goods.[12] The very idea that some rights are "natural" means that they are apprehensible by human reason as universally predicated to all members of the human race. If this is so, then they must be rooted in human nature, not in individual or collective preferences, convention, or interests.

A distorted understanding of freedom as thoroughly autonomous and disconnected from objective human good has led some to propose rights even to wrong actions. The right to certain morally evil actions is generally defended on the grounds that such rights fall under the aegis of broader rights, such as autonomy, privacy, and self-determination, which encompass them.[13] Robert George devotes a chapter of his work *Making Men Moral* to the question of whether persons can have a right to do wrong, or more precisely, can have a *moral* right to commit *moral* wrong. He argues from two historical cases: the the Lincoln-Douglas debates on the question of slaveholding and New York governor Mario Cuomo's 1984 defense of "the putative moral right to do moral wrong in the case of abortion."[14]

Stephen Douglas asserted that the moral rightness or wrongness of

---

12. "Perfectionist theories of political morality typically ground rights in goods. If an activity or way of life really is a 'positive moral good,' it is certainly wrong to deprive people of it on the basis of a belief that it is wicked or corrupt. And it makes conceptual sense to say that people have a right to something when depriving them of it would be wrong. Moreover, if a right is grounded in the value of that to which it is a right, the right will not appear to be arbitrary. Its intelligibility will be rooted in the intelligibility of the human good it helps to protect or advance" (George, *Making Men Moral*, 145).

13. According to Jeremy Waldron, for instance, the particular right to do something morally wrong is a specific instance of a more general right that necessarily includes a wide range of actions. As Waldron puts it: "What is defended or contested when a general right is in dispute is the claim that choice within a certain range is not to be interfered with" ("A Right to Do Wrong," *Ethics* 92 [1981]: 34, cited in George, *Making Men Moral*, 123).

14. George, *Making Men Moral*, 112.

slavery was not the central issue in the debate but rather the right to self-governance arising from popular sovereignty, by which the terms of social relations are decided upon. To this Lincoln responded: "When Judge Douglas says that whoever, or whatever community, wants slaves, they have a right to have them, he is perfectly logical if there is nothing wrong in the institution; but if you admit that it is wrong, he cannot logically say that anybody has a right to do a wrong."[15] For Lincoln, Douglas has fallen into a logical fallacy, although, as George points out, "Lincoln did not suppose that there is anything illogical in claiming that someone could have a *legal* right to do something that is morally wrong."[16]

George then goes on to cite the case of New York governor Mario Cuomo's keynote address delivered at the University of Notre Dame in 1984. Cuomo declared his belief that abortion is in most cases gravely immoral, but that even so, in a pluralistic society, women are entitled to decide for themselves whether or not to abort. Though Cuomo did not present a detailed explanation of the rationale behind his position, George offers the interpretation that for Cuomo, "the right to abortion is a specific instance of a more general right of persons to govern their lives according to their own consciences and, in particular, to decide what happens in and to their bodies."[17] In other words, a more sweeping right to autonomy could sometimes contain the right to something that is in itself morally wrong.

To rebut Cuomo's argument, George offers a useful taxonomic distinction between what he terms "strong" rights and "weak" rights.[18]

---

15. R. P. Basler, ed., *The Collected Works of Abraham Lincoln* (New Brunswick, N.J.: Rutgers University Press, 1953), 3:256–57, quoted in George, *Making Men Moral*, 111.

16. George, *Making Men Moral*, 111. Moreover, against the strict Lincolnian position, George argues that "there is a sense in which one can, without logical inconsistency, speak of an individual's moral right not to be forbidden to perform, or interfered with in performing, acts that one has a moral duty not to perform" (*Making Men Moral*, 115).

17. Ibid., 113.

18. Some refer to these as "passive" rights and "active" rights. Andrew Tardiff, for instance, writes: "There are active rights (the right to do something) and there are passive rights (the right not to be prevented from doing something)" ("The Traditionalists' Untraditional Ideas about Religious Freedom," *New Oxford Review* [April 2000]: 23). Grotius offers a different angle to the question when speaking of "direct" or "supposed" rights: "The common right relating to acts is conceded either directly or by supposition. It is conceded directly in respect to acts indispensable for the obtaining of the things without which life cannot be comfortably lived" (*De Iure Belli ac Pacis*, bk. II, ch. II, XVIII, 203). Here direct rights could be said to basically correspond to "strong" rights, and "supposed" rights would include activities contained

"Strong" rights are those that refer specifically to a human good or action, whereas "weak" rights are those that fall under the mantle of more encompassing rights or exist as "shadows" of others' duty of noninterference.[19] For instance, catchphrases like "I have a right to think whatever I want" draw immediate consensus but are actually false. If this declaration meant no more than "No one can morally interfere with my thinking what I want," it would be a true statement. In point of fact, however, "I have a right to think whatever I want" means, at a minimum, "It is morally right for me to think whatever I want," which is simply not true.[20] Some thoughts are good, others permissible, others stupid, others sinful. No one has a moral right to think a sinful thought, just as no one has a moral right to perform an immoral act.

The confusion here stems from the tendency to think of the categories of "right" and "subject to legal proscription" as cumulatively exhaustive of all possibilities, whereas in fact a large range of activities exists to which no right is attached yet which should not be outlawed.[21] Not all immoral activities ought to be prohibited by law, but one cannot infer from this that since such activities are not illegal, they are therefore somehow protected by natural rights.[22] Rights to action ("liberties") are not

---

under the umbrella of broader rights, without attempting to posit strong rights to such activities.

19. See George, *Making Men Moral*, 115.

20. De Finance declares that by the very fact of my having a right, "my exercise of it is in accordance with right reason and is, in consequence, morally good, provided I have complied with the other conditions which are requisite for such activity" (*An Ethical Inquiry*, § 194, p. 344).

21. The subtle passage from a right not to be unduly harassed, even when this means that one cannot be prevented from performing an immoral action, to an ostensible *right* to perform the immoral action itself, has crept into decisions of the Supreme Court in the United States, as documented by Mary Ann Glendon. Glendon writes that "in declaring privacy an individual right, the Court had taken a momentous step. *Eisenstadt v. Baird* not only put the right squarely on an individual basis, but it marked a shift from privacy as 'freedom from surveillance or disclosure of intimate affairs,' to privacy as 'the freedom to engage in certain activities' and 'to make certain sorts of choices without government interference'" (Glendon, *Rights Talk*, 57, citing Michael J. Sandel, "Moral Argument and Liberal Toleration: Abortion and Homosexuality," *California Law Review* 77/521 [1989]: 527–28).

22. Thus when Thomas asks whether human law should repress all vices, he responds that they forbid "only the more grievous vices, from which it is possible for the majority to abstain; and chiefly those that are to the hurt of others, without the prohibition of which human society could not be maintained: thus human law prohibits murder, theft and such like" (*S. Th.*, I-II, 96, 2). George offers the important observation that the "question of whether an act is right

automatically deduced from the fact that others have no right to interfere. In these cases the duty not to interfere proceeds from some other cause than a presumed right to perform a given action.[23]

A right not to be prevented from doing something is just that: a right to noninterference (or privacy) and not a right to a given activity. Here the right itself proceeds not from the relationship between the right-bearer and a given activity but from another, broader right that somehow encompasses the possibility of that activity.[24] Therefore, it is inexact and confusing to speak of a right to the activity as such, when in reality no such "active" or "strong" right exists. A true right can be justified only by its relation to a perfective good. Rights cannot be derived from other, broader rights, nor can they be extrapolated by saying that if one has a right to a particular good, he thereby has a right to any means necessary to procure it.

Thomas Hobbes asserted that man has a natural right to everything.[25] In a certain sense he was correct, and in another sense he was clearly mistaken. According to the Liberal understanding of rights (where another's nonright to interfere constitutes my right to act or possess), man does indeed possess a natural right to everything. It is unjust to arbitrarily interfere with another's action, and the burden of justification falls on the one who seeks to interfere rather than the one being interfered with. It may often happen that a person does something that is morally wrong (and that, consequently, he has no moral right to do), without it being right for the government (or anyone else) to interfere.

---

or wrong and the question of whether it is right or wrong for the government (or, for that matter, some private party) to interfere with someone's performing that act are *always* distinct questions" (*Making Men Moral*, 118).

23. George offers the example of lying to distinguish between legal tolerance and moral right, affirming that "someone can recognize compelling reasons for tolerating non-defamatory lying without supposing that people have any sort of strong moral right to spread non-defamatory lies" (*Making Men Moral*, 126).

24. Such general rights such as the right of association or free speech or the press include the possibility that people will use these rights in an immoral way, and though certain more egregious abuses of these rights should not be permitted, other abuses must be tolerated when closer supervision would constitute undue interference in the internal affairs of individuals and associations. Though no "strong" right to such abuses exists, one could argue that here a "weak" right (understood as the right not to be interfered with in such activities) is operative.

25. Thomas Hobbes, *The Elements of Law Natural and Politic: Part I, Human Nature, Part II, De Corpore Politico, with Three Lives*, ed. J. C. A. Gaskin (New York: Oxford University Press, 1999), part I, ch. XIV, 10, 80.

This line of reasoning highlights the difference between freedom (or liberty) and rights. The statement "I am *free* to do such and such" is equivalent to the proposition "I have a *right* to do such and such" only when freedom is taken to mean the absence of coercion and when rights are understood as the absence of another's right to interfere. In reality, however, to say "I am free to do such and such" is an assertion about the limits of others' rights ("No one has a right to stop me") rather than about one's own rights. "I am free to do such and such" does not mean "I have a right to do such and such," only "No one else has a right to keep me from doing such and such."

Just because a third party does not, cannot, or must not intervene to prohibit a certain type of action does not lead to the logical conclusion that one has a right to perform such an action.[26] Rights do not proceed from others' duty not to interfere. An emblematic example is anti-sodomy laws. To say that no one has a (moral or legal) right to prevent consenting adults from engaging in homosexual acts in the privacy of their home is not the same as saying that someone has a right to such activities. There is no exact correspondence between rights and duties here, since one's duty of nonintrusion originates in a source other than the other's putative right to perform an immoral act.

Arguments attributing strong rights to a range of activities possible in the exercise of liberty or under the blanket of more general rights likewise fail in that such arguments beg the question of why people should respect others' liberty or privacy in the first place.[27] In reality, arguments of this sort make the implicit assumption that liberty and privacy are themselves basic human goods worthy of respect. Although proponents of these the-

---

26. "Opportunities for immoral choice inhere in the human condition. They are, in a certain sense, ineradicable. They could be eliminated only by destroying the human capacity for free choice that is a condition for practical deliberation, judgment, and choice with respect to morally permissible possibilities.... We need not embrace the idea of a moral right to do moral wrong on any strong sense to ensure that people will have available to them valuable opportunities to test their moral mettle and (further) develop their moral character" (George, *Making Men Moral*, 128).

27. "Any theory that posits rights to liberty and privacy but fails to link these putative rights to basic human goods, invites, but cannot answer, the question, 'Why should I respect the rights of others?'. This question can be easily answered, however, by a theory that prizes liberty and privacy *because*, and only in so far as, they enable people to realize reasonably for themselves and their communities *intrinsic* goods whose realization would be prevented or seriously hampered by the lack of liberty or privacy" (ibid., 192; emphasis in original).

ories often reject the idea that goods underlie rights, in reality they implicitly assert that liberty and privacy constitute the basic goods that should be protected under the law.[28] Regardless of the particular arguments advanced, some notion of the good always lies at the base of any theory of rights.[29]

THE COMPLEMENTARITY OF RIGHTS AND DUTIES

Rights as a moral category involve various complementary relationships. The relationship of the rights-bearer to the thing or activity that is the object of the right—a relationship of "becomingness" or "due"—is critical for distinguishing true rights from spurious claims. Yet a moral relationship also exists between the rights-bearer and another person or persons, which qualifies the rights-bearer to make a moral claim on the other party. The "satisfier" of the right bears a moral duty toward the rights-bearer. What exactly is the relationship between rights and duties?

In analyzing this relationship, three fundamental issues merit investigation. The first involves the correlativity of these two moral categories. What constitutes the relationship between them? Does one necessarily imply the other, or can they exist independently of one another? In the second place, does an order or priority exist between them? Does one proceed from the other, or do they both arise from some other principle? Third, and finally, how does one go about attributing duties to particular rights? Especially in the case of more general, two-term rights where no

---

28. "How is this process of specification and demarcation [of rights] to be accomplished? . . . one needs some conception of human good, of individual flourishing in a form (or range of forms) of communal life that fosters rather than hinders such flourishing" (Finnis, *Natural Law and Natural Rights*, 219–20).

29. Waldron, for example, suggests that it is the *importance* of an action to one's self-constitution that determines the right. The more important an action for the identity of the person, the stronger the right to perform the action. If this criterion is divorced from any sense of the objective good of the person, what elements remain for determining the *importance* of a given decision? Only the subjective weight we choose to give it. It is important because it seems important to me, or it is important because I say it is important, according to the identity I have chosen for myself. Thus Charles Manson could conceive of his identity as essentially a mass murderer. To forbid him to commit murder would become a violation of his right of self-determination. We would be forbidding what is, for him, the most important, self-constituting act. The crux of the matter is that importance, if it is to assume an objective character and transcend the assertion that something matters to me, necessarily falls back on the notion of the good. See Waldron, "A Right to Do Wrong," 34, cited in George, *Making Men Moral*, 123.

rights-satisfier is explicitly mentioned, the task of assigning this duty poses particular problems.

The Correlativity of Rights and Duties

As regards the first point, Maritain states: "The notion of right and the notion of moral obligation are correlative. They are both founded on the freedom proper to spiritual agents."[30] Grisez affirms that rights "do not constitute a basic category but are correlative to duties, which are the social aspects of one's moral or legal responsibilities."[31] Indeed, Grisez binds rights and duties closely together, such that they do not exist as separate entities but rather as two dimensions of a single reality. Right and duty, he asserts, "are the same reality, 'right' signifying its bearing upon the person or group affected by the action which the duty specifies (see *S. Th.* 2-2, q. 57, a. 1; cf. 1-2, q. 100, a. 2)."[32] From this, Grisez correctly draws the conclusion that "there are as many meanings of 'rights' as of 'duties,' and all distinctions made concerning duties must also be made concerning rights."

Rights and duties coincide in the idea of moral debt. The same proposition of moral debt can be stated in the active or passive voice without altering its sense. To say that "A owes B" (duty) is the same as to say that "B is owed by A" (right); the syntactical inversion of subject and predicate does not affect the content of the proposition. Moreover, the addition of the "thing" owed (the content or object of the right) does nothing to alter this correlativity. Any true debt implies a debtor, a creditor, and a content of the debt. Furthermore, the statement that "B is owed (X) by A" necessarily entails B's moral capability to claim or demand X from A. In other words, as Grisez observes, to speak of rights or duties is to speak of the selfsame moral reality from two different perspectives: that of the debtor and that of the creditor.

This correlativity forms a part of all rights, even when the assignment of duty is unclear. For example, even in the case of so-called two-term

---

30. Maritain, *The Rights of Man*, 37. From earlier discussion, it is clear that this statement is not altogether precise. Whereas "duties" are correlative to rights in that duties—strictly speaking—always involve at least two persons, "moral obligations" may exist on an individual basis, outside of the scope of justice. In these cases, no rights correspond to moral obligation.

31. Grisez, *Christian Moral Principles*, p. 924.

32. Ibid., 10.E, p. 264.

positive rights where the right is expressed in terms of a given good (such as the right to an education) without reference to the rights-satisfier, a corresponding duty is always implied. Otherwise it would be improper to speak of a right; one could only speak of a need or a desire.

Since duties and rights are correlative, neither can exist without the other. This is true as long as one avoids crossing over between different *types* of rights. Here Grisez's distinction between "natural duties" and "positive duties" proves useful. Of the former, Grisez writes: "Duties existing prior to any choice whatsoever can be said to pertain to human nature itself; thus a duty of this sort can be called a 'natural duty.'"[33] Duties, however, which arise not out of human nature but out of one's own commitments or the decisions of someone in authority, can be called "positive duties." Though a natural moral right cannot exist without a corresponding natural moral duty, a *natural moral* right may exist without a correlative *legal* right and hence without a corresponding *legal* duty. In similar fashion, a *positive moral* duty or a *legal* duty may exist without a corresponding *natural moral* right. Person A may have a duty to treat person B in a certain way, not because B deserves (or has a natural right to) such treatment but for some other reason, such as a divine command or a civil law that requires such treatment. Here a real duty (legal or positive) exists with no real (natural) right.

There is yet another way in which rights are said to correspond to duties. Not only does a reciprocal relationship exist between the one owed and the one who owes (creditor and debtor); one can also speak of duties that correspond to the rights of the rights-bearer himself. Caffarra, for instance, states that rights "always presuppose duties: the duty, first of all, of the person possessing the right in question to achieve a certain end and ultimately to attain the end for which he exists as a human person."[34] In other words, according to this reasoning the right to something supposes a prior duty of the right-bearer himself to attain a certain end.

Pope John XXIII expresses a similar idea in *Pacem in Terris,* where he affirms that natural rights are "inextricably bound up with as many duties, all applying to one and the same person." He goes on to exemplify this principle, stating that "the right to live involves the duty to preserve one's life; the right to a decent standard of living, the duty to live in a be-

---

33. Ibid.
34. Caffarra, *Living in Christ,* 221.

coming fashion; the right to be free to seek out the truth, the duty to devote oneself to an ever deeper and wider search for it." Furthermore, the Pontiff adds later, "man's awareness of his rights must inevitably lead him to the recognition of his duties. The possession of rights involves the duty of implementing those rights, for they are the expression of a man's personal dignity. And the possession of rights also involves their recognition and respect by other people."[35]

How is this text to be understood? One can surely accept that in a *general way*, man's rights are bound up with his own duties. Man clearly has a moral duty as well as a natural inclination to pursue his own perfection, and the goods due to man (what is "his") are due precisely because they are "becoming" to him and are conducive to his perfection. If man is obliged to pursue his perfection, then he is also obliged to pursue those particular goods that are *necessary* to his perfection, though he is not obliged to pursue every good that *could* contribute to his perfection. Whereas man's broad duty to perfect himself can be realized in a variety of ways by pursuing a number of different human goods, his rights necessarily embrace *all* of those ways and goods. Therefore, a one-to-one correspondence between personal rights and duties does not exist. When John XXIII speaks of the possession of rights involving "the duty of implementing those rights," this can be understood only in a general way.

This becomes clear when we take examples of specific natural rights from the same encyclical. For instance, the Pontiff speaks of the right of meeting and association and then the right to emigrate and immigrate.[36] Obviously, one cannot deduce from these rights that man has a moral duty to form associations or to emigrate from his country. Similarly, the right to marry can in no wise be construed to entail a corresponding *duty* to marry.

No strict obligation exists on the part of the rights-bearer to exercise all of his rights, and care must therefore be taken not to conflate rights and duties. The concept of rights speaks of moral possibility, a possibility that must be respected by others. On the other hand, natural rights that are properly qualified as "inviolable" impose the same characteristic of inviolability on the rights-bearer himself. Thus a person cannot morally

35. *PT,* 8, 9, 44.
36. Ibid., *23–24*, 25.

justify taking his own life on the grounds that he chooses not to "exercise" his right to life. Precisely as an inviolable right, the right to life cannot be waived.[37] It would be more correct, however, to say that since man has an obligation to seek his own perfection, and existence is the essential *conditio sine qua non* of perfection, he has a moral obligation to preserve his own life: self-destruction is not a moral option. The more essential a given good is to a person's perfection, the more closely personal rights and obligations coincide.

The Origin of Rights and Duties

A second question regards whether an order of priority exists between rights and duties, either of the selfsame subject or between persons. Does either one—rights or duties—come first? Does one proceed from the other, or do they both originate in another principle?

Clearly, if a person has an obligation to do something (for example, to seek the truth), then a fortiori he has the right to do so. No one may legitimately hinder another from fulfilling his obligations. In the language of justice, one's obligation in this case corresponds to what is "becoming" to a person, or what is "his." It is in this sense that it is due to him. Yet one's moral obligations are not the only source of what is proper or becoming to him, and therefore they are not the ultimate foundation of human rights. If they were, those persons who have no duties (such as the unborn) would also enjoy no rights. All persons, regardless of their duties, possess certain rights by the very fact that they *are* persons. What is due to them as persons cannot depend on prior obligations on their part. This is especially evident on the part of the divinity, where His rights can in no way be seen as deriving from any prior duties. Thus Maritain notes that the "notion of right is even more profound than that of moral obligation, for God has sovereign right over creatures and He has no moral

---

37. The language of rights, however, is not well suited to moral questions involving one person, since rights are an aspect of justice, and justice orders relations among persons. Strictly speaking, no one "owes" anything to himself, and thus, as Aristotle and Thomas observe, no one can be unjust toward himself (see Aristotle, *Nichomachean Ethics*, V, 11:1138a4–28; *S. Th.*, II-II, 58, 2). Suicide, for example, is not an act of injustice toward oneself; it is an injustice toward God and toward the members of the human community and a usurpation of a power over one's life that does not belong to oneself. In a broader sense, however, one can speak of justice toward oneself, just as one speaks of loving oneself. In this sense, we can speak of one's duty to respect one's own inviolable rights.

obligation towards them (although He owes it to Himself to give them that which is required by their nature)."[38]

Therefore, assertions like Caffarra's of a priority of duties over rights are unacceptable, since rights sometimes exist before any moral obligation can be attributed to the rights-bearing person, and indeed independent of any such obligation. Though moral obligations always give rise to rights (one who is lawfully commanded to do something by that very fact acquires the right to do so), not all rights are the product of moral obligations. If one's own obligations are not the ultimate source of one's rights, much less are one's rights the source of one's obligations. As we have seen, the right to do or possess something does not necessarily carry with it an obligation to exercise that right.

The other possibility is that one's rights generate duties in *others*. Because a perfect correlation exists between these rights and duties, since they represent two ways of expressing the same moral proposition, perhaps one has priority over the other, and one takes its origin from the other. Some, indeed, place rights as anterior to duties. Ashley, for example, states: "Because rights and duties are mutually correlative, my right places on others an obligation to respect it, and my moral obligation in justice (not *all* moral obligations) arise from someone else's rights."[39] In this view, rights preexist duties and give rise to them.

Though initially plausible, this hypothesis does not stand up to close examination. A right cannot come into existence on its own and only afterward give rise to the creation of a duty. Rights describe how persons are to treat others and be treated by others in relation to determined goods. Again, to say "A owes X to B" and to say "B is owed X by A" is to say the same thing. One cannot precede the other, because each is already present in the other. This holds true for both legal rights and natural rights. In the case of legal rights, the same law that mandates a certain sort of treatment simultaneously confers rights and duties. In the case of natural rights, the same human nature determines what is "due" or "becoming" to the person and thus gives rise to both rights and duties. In this regard, Canavan has written that both "the rights and the obligations depend upon the teleology inherent in man's nature and supernatural

---

38. Maritain, *The Rights of Man*, 37.
39. Ashley, *Living the Truth in Love*, 275.

destiny; the obligations are derived not from the rights but from the goods that are the goals of human nature."[40]

In a broader and less proper sense—and perhaps Ashley meant rights in this sense—rights can give rise to duties, but only when rights are understood analogically as a simple relation between rights-bearer and some particular good. This occurs, for example, when general two-term rights (for example a person's right to an education) become proper three-term rights, when a duty-bearer is identified as responsible for satisfying the right. The first element of a right (which is not yet a right in the true sense)—the relationship of "becomingness" or "due" between a subject and a perfective good—gives rise to a moral relationship of right and duty when another person is brought onto the scene. Before this other party enters the picture, however, a right exists only in an analogical sense, in the same way that the virtue of justice can be invoked only in an analogical sense: It is "right" for X to do or to have such and such; it is "just" for X to do or to have such and such. Since rights and duties (in the strict sense) are moral principles of justice, they truly exist only when at least two persons are involved.

Similarly, one may discover the personal good of another human being as worthy of a certain treatment generally and thus come to grasp one's *personal* duty to treat him in that way. This would seem to be the meaning of de Finance's assertion of the primacy of right over duty. "If we consider a relation," he writes, "between a particular duty towards a definite person and the corresponding right that he has, it is the latter which is primary so that the duty is determined by it. Because Peter owns this car, Paul, Andrew, etc., have the duty of not using it without his permission."[41] A general right that "others" respect one's ownership of what is "his" gives rise to a specific duty for concrete individuals who come in contact with this reality. Even here, however, there is only a cognitive process of discovery but not a genuine generation of a duty from a right.

---

40. Canavan, "The Image of Man in Catholic Thought," 20.

41. De Finance, *An Ethical Inquiry*, § 203, p. 358. He adds: "Rather than seek to establish whether, on the plane of relations between human beings, duties are anterior to rights or rights to duties, it is much better to acknowledge that both arise simultaneously from our human condition as sharers in the Value. But if one wishes to be very exact, one could also maintain here that right is prior to duty, inasmuch as 'being' expresses what is more fundamental than 'participated being'" (ibid., § 203, p. 359).

The Assignment of Duty for Positive Rights

The third issue to be explored in the relationship between duties and rights deals with the attribution of duty for positive rights. In the case of negative rights, the assignment of duty poses no problem, since everyone bears an identical duty of respect and noninterference toward the right-bearer. For negative rights, since no one may morally interfere in their exercise, the same universal duty is predicated of all human beings. Moreover, at least implicitly such negative rights are seen especially as limiting government interference in citizens' activities, since government may be more inclined than individuals to try to regulate such activities.

Positive rights, on the other hand, do not allow for such an easy attribution of duties. Often two-term, natural rights to things such as food, healthcare, education, employment, and participation in society are enumerated without naming a corresponding rights-satisfier. In these cases, on whom does the corresponding duty devolve?

The facile answer is government, since the public authority has charge of the common good, and such an assumption is nowadays so widespread that attempts to defend positive rights are often taken as a call for an increase in state programs to meet these rights. The tendency to omit other social mediating institutions from the rights calculus often results in an enthusiastic and sometimes indiscriminate endorsement of social assistance programs on the part of those with greater sensitivity to the plight of the weakest and less fortunate, while often leading those who would minimize government intervention—convinced of the inefficacy of political bureaucracies and wary of government control—to reject the idea of these positive, two-term rights altogether.[42]

The distinction between moral and civil rights helps surmount this apparent impasse. Though they are closely intertwined, moral rights and civil rights exist on separate planes. Thus the assertion of a moral right does not necessarily imply a correlative *civil* duty, but simply a moral duty. Moreover, as opposed to classical Liberal theory, the moral rights we are speaking of do not exist exclusively between the public authority and citizenry; as principles of justice they span the entire gamut of interpersonal relations.[43] It cannot be assumed, therefore, that the duties cor-

---

42. See previous discussion on two- and three-term rights in chapter 2.
43. Classical Liberalism conceived rights nearly exclusively as limiting government vis-à-vis

responding to positive rights necessarily fall on the shoulders of government. According to Catholic social teaching, public authority is indeed constituted for the custody and promotion of the common good. In this regard, government must certainly ensure that basic rights are satisfied, but this responsibility may or may not mean that government should assume this task directly.

If commutative justice fully exhausted this cardinal virtue, the assignment of duty would be a simpler affair. Commutative justice demands an arithmetic equality: what is taken (or at least its equivalent) must be given back, and thus equality is restored. In the case of distributive justice, however, we are obliged to deal with a "geometric proportion," a determining of others' true needs and possibilities and one's own possibilities to assist. When a person possesses in excess of his own need, such possessions cease to belong to him strictly speaking, and he finds himself in the uncomfortable situation of administrating the common stock of society.

Where gross material inequality exists, to take a concrete example, what duties do those who possess an abundance have toward those who experience want? Must they "sell all (or nearly all) and give the money to the poor" (Luke 18:22) and thus reestablish equality? Is some inequality in fact morally permissible, or does justice exact a strict balance? May they invest the money where such investment will create jobs and benefit the state of the economy as a whole? And, passing from the purely material realm to the cultural and spiritual, do the same concepts of distributive justice apply? Is the one who received an abundance of human talents obliged in justice toward those who received little? The resolution of these and similar questions clearly requires recourse to the virtue of prudence. It also requires a fresh look at the Church's proposal of an ethics of solidarity.

---

citizens, and many today continue to view human rights through this prism. "Natural rights theory," Gerard V. Bradley writes, "is primarily about the relationship of coercive public authority and individuals. Natural law theory is about rectitude in all human choosing, both the choices made by public authority and also those of private persons in everyday affairs" ("Moral Truth, the Common Good, and Judicial Review," in *Catholicism, Liberalism, and Communitarianism: The Catholic Intellectual Tradition and the Moral Foundations of Democracy*, ed. Kenneth L. Grasso, Gerard V. Bradley, and Robert P. Hunt [Lanham, Md.: Rowman & Littlefield, 1995], 121). As has been made clear, this view does not coincide with a personalistic conception of natural rights. While it may be true that natural rights theory is *in practice* invoked primarily as protection of the individual vis-à-vis the state, the scope of natural rights extends well beyond individual-state relations to embrace the totality of interpersonal morality, i.e., the entire realm of the virtue of justice.

PART FIVE

TOWARD AN ETHICS OF SOLIDARITY

The personalist approach to explaining the foundation of human rights opens the door to a new brand of ethics, one centered on actively promoting the good of one's fellow men instead of just refraining from doing them any harm. The Church has come to designate this proactive vision of human rights as the virtue of "solidarity." It has its roots in the Gospel, where Christ sums up the Law in the two commandments of loving God and loving neighbor. But the Gospel narration doesn't stop there. Jesus offers an intriguing reply to the follow-up question "And who is my neighbor?" (Luke 10:29). Familiarity with this Gospel passage has, perhaps, tarnished both the inadvertent incisiveness of the question and the far-reaching implications of the answer. A detailed examination of how the Church has interpreted the passage shows the deep theological consonance between personalism and Christian charity. But it also highlights personalism's broader ethical appeal: by rooting human rights in human dignity properly understood, personalism enables the call of Christian charity to resound far beyond the reach of Christianity to all men and women of goodwill.

16. WHO IS MY NEIGHBOR?

THE PERSONALIST APPROACH affirms that every human person, regardless of intelligence, talents, social class, skin color, religious affiliation, or other distinguishing characteristics, has a right to be loved. Basic natural rights, beginning with the right to be loved for one's own sake, are predicated universally of all human beings. The radical difference between persons and nonpersons leaves no room for distinctions among persons on this level, since "personhood" does not admit of degrees : either one is, or is not, a person. No one is "more" a person than anyone else. For this reason, all human beings are essentially equal in dignity and command equal regard qua persons. The idea of denying members of the human race the respect due to all is completely foreign to the personalist approach.

Yet is this same universality present in Christ's commandment to love one's neighbor as oneself? Does not the very expression "love of neighbor" make a distinction between neighbor and outsider, implicitly excluding the latter? Does not Christ himself at one point refer to the Old Testament imperative: "Love thy neighbor and hate thy enemy?" (Matt. 5:43), which clearly distinguishes between "neighbors" and "others"? If Christ had wished to include all human beings, why didn't he simply say so, instead of opting for the word "neighbor"?

This question has been asked and answered by many saints and doctors of the Church. Two of the most complete and penetrating answers come from St. Augustine and St. Thomas. In their commentaries on the preceding passage, both, in fact, reach the identical conclusion: that Christ's use of the word "neighbor" is meant to include all persons. Their reasoning sheds an intense theological light on personalism's explanation of the universality of human rights.

In his consideration of the second great commandment, St. Augustine offers three reasons why no person can be excluded from the category of "neighbor." First, such exclusion would contradict Christ's conduct.[1] Though he was sent "only to the lost sheep of the house of Israel" (Matt. 15:24), Christ himself exercised a universal love. Second, drawing from the parable of the Good Samaritan, Augustine associates "neighbor" with "one in need," summarizing the moral of the parable by saying that "he is our neighbor whom it is our duty to help in his need, or whom it would be our duty to help if he were in need." Finally, Augustine contends, how could anyone be omitted from the reach of love, when the most extreme cases—our enemies—are explicitly included?[2] The commandment to love even one's enemies, arguably the least worthy of love, clearly implies a commandment to love all people.

Aquinas reaches the identical conclusion, reasoning from a different angle. The word "neighbor," he points out, comes from the root meaning "near."[3] Thus when Christ says "love your neighbor" he means love whomever is "near to you." This nearness does not mean just physical proximity but also all those who, like oneself, were made in God's image and destined for eternal glory. "The reason for loving," Thomas asserts, "is indicated in the word 'neighbor,' because the reason why we ought to love others out of charity is because they are nigh to us, both as to the natural image of God, and as to the capacity for glory. Nor does it matter whether we say 'neighbor,' or 'brother' according to 1 John 4:21, or 'friend,' according to Lev. 19:18, because all these words express the same affinity."[4] Charity, then, involves acknowledging another as neighbor, as like and near to oneself. Since all human beings are "near," because all share the same nature and the same personal dignity, all fall within the scope of the charity each is bound to give his neighbor.

---

1. "[T]hat He who commanded us to love our neighbor made no exception, as far as men are concerned, is shown both by our Lord Himself in the Gospel, and by the Apostle Paul" (St. Augustine, *De Doctrina Christiana*, bk. I, ch. 4, pp. 530–31).

2. "And, again, who does not see that no exception is made of any one as a person to whom the offices of mercy may be denied when our Lord extends the rule even to our enemies? . . . it is clear that every man is to be considered our neighbor, because we are to work no ill to any man" (ibid.).

3. This holds true both for the English word "neighbor," which comes from the Old English *nēah*, meaning "near," and for the Latin *proximus*, meaning literally "the nearest," and derivatively, "neighbor" or "fellow man."

4. *S. Th.*, II-II, 44, 7.

Christ's own illuminating reply to the lawyer who asked, "And who is my neighbor?" provides a final consideration. Instead of responding with a simple definition of neighbor, Jesus recounts a parable of a man who falls in with robbers and is left half dead by the roadside. After a priest and a Levite pass by without stopping, a Samaritan happens by and takes pity on the man, dressing his wounds and taking him to an inn where he can be cared for. As an illustration of "neighbor," Jesus chooses the most unlikely of candidates, a man whom tradition has handed down under the title "the Good Samaritan." He was in no way a brother, in the sense of a fellow Jew, or a fellow countryman, but rather a reprobate and a pariah.[5] In selecting a Samaritan to exemplify "neighbor" in the second great commandment, Jesus underscores the universality of the precept of charity, as he does earlier when enjoining his followers to love even their enemies.[6]

At the same time, Jesus draws attention away from the identity of the man who had been beaten and robbed. In the parable, the neighbor is not the man in need, but the man who helps.[7] Thus in choosing whether to help someone in need, Christians are not called to distinguish among persons as if only some were neighbors; rather, they are to *be* neighbors to all. Thus "neighbor" describes not only the one in need, but also the one who helps.

RIGHTS TALK AND CHRISTIAN SOLIDARITY

The summons to be a neighbor to all finds a conceptual expression in the Christian virtue of solidarity, a concept that clarifies why rights talk is both valuable in itself and compatible with Catholic Christianity. Solidarity has a particular relation to "positive" (as opposed to "negative")

---

5. Samaritans were descended from Jews who had intermarried with pagan Assyrians and subsequently developed their own form of Judaism and built their own Temple. They were bitter enemies of the Jews in Palestine at the time of Christ.

6. Jesus proposes the Father's universal goodness toward men as the example to be followed: "I say to you, 'Love your enemies and pray for those who persecute you, so that you may be children of your Father in heaven; for he makes his sun rise on the evil and on the good, and sends rain on the righteous and on the unrighteous'" (Matt. 5:44–45). See also Luke 6:27–35.

7. See the commentary on Luke's Gospel by Robert J. Karris in *The New Jerome Biblical Commentary*, ed. Raymond E. Brown, Joseph A. Fitzmyer, and Roland E. Murphy (London: Geoffrey Chapman, 1989), 702.

rights, a dimension of the rights question that can point the way to real progress in protecting human rights against threats both new and old.

Assigning responsibility for meeting rights claims poses a dilemma. Rights correspond to duties, but often, especially in the case of "two-term" rights (rights to "things" such as food or healthcare), it is impossible to attribute a one-to-one correspondence between right-bearer and duty-bearer. A frequent objection against the very idea of positive rights is the practical difficulty, in many cases the *impossibility*, of correlating rights to moral agents responsible for meeting them. A neighbor's right to food and housing, for instance, combined with a lack of the wherewithal to procure them for himself, surely relates to a corresponding duty—but whose? Formulating long lists of rights—critics suggest—merely encourages illusory expectations, which place ever greater burdens on society and foster personal irresponsibility. Especially among those with a more conservative political bent, such rights-mongering smacks of a thinly veiled argument for a welfare state. In the end, it would seem, the satisfaction of rights with no corresponding providers always end up falling on the shoulders of government.

If the satisfaction of basic human rights cannot be turned over wholesale to the state, a solution must be sought elsewhere. When a one-to-one correspondence of rights to duties cannot be established, three possible courses of action could be followed. First, one could abandon the concept of positive, two-term rights altogether as unworkable and fatally problematic, concentrating instead on negative rights (the right to do certain things without hindrance from others) or simply on concepts such as duties and virtue, omitting reference to rights altogether. Second, one could ignore the assignment of duties by concentrating solely on rights, with the attendant risk of stripping rights of their moral and legal clout or of inviting the state to absorb all such obligations. Finally, one could insist on the objective moral force of positive rights and appeal to the conscience of individuals and the human community as a whole to work out concrete solutions. Though this latter course is the most challenging, it alone squares with the ethical demands both of human dignity understood in light of personalism and of the Gospel command to love one's neighbor as oneself.

The very difficulty experienced in assigning personal responsibility for satisfying rights claims points—paradoxically—to one of the strong advantages of rights language in ethical discourse. Exclusive concern with duties, which by their nature are strictly and minimalistically defined, may subtly lead to a situation where subjectively everyone is acting justly, while objectively gross injustices endure. Everyone is fulfilling his "duty," and at the same time others are suffering great want, which is "nobody's fault." Imagine a school cafeteria scene where one child has left his lunch bag at home. The other children merrily eat their own meals in the subjective certainty that they are not accountable for their lunchless peer's unfortunate state. Yet unless someone does something, unless the "community" takes up its responsibility, the child will continue the school day with an empty belly. A greater emphasis on moral rights can help remedy this situation. Here the starting point is not the individual rectitude of the moral agent, defined as "doing nothing wrong" or "fulfilling one's strict duty," but the concrete situation of others for whom all are in some way responsible. That starting point allows for the development of a type of ethical behavior that can overcome the supposed impracticality of "rights-mongering."

SINS OF OMISSION

Personalistic love, in treating other persons as an end, wills the good for them. In order to be true, such benevolence cannot remain at the level of a vague feeling of goodwill but must express itself in action. Benevolence must blossom into beneficence, good intentions into good actions. In light of this principle, love not only requires actions to be benevolent ("Whenever you deal with a person, do so in such and such a way"), it also, at times, commands action itself.[8] Stated in another way, love often dictates positive action, and in those cases the *failure* to act may sometimes constitute a mistreatment of persons—and even an injustice.

Culpable inaction, according to the traditional moral lexicon, goes by the name of the sin of omission. Sometimes individual persons are morally obliged to do something, and when they do not, their inaction constitutes wrongdoing. Thus negative moral absolutes ("Thou shalt not . . .") are not the sum total of morality. The Ten Commandments and

---

8. Here we must hasten to recall that we are dealing on the level of moral duty, which cannot necessarily be translated into civil legislation. The following arguments appeal not to lawmakers but to moral conscience.

other negative precepts not only forbid specific acts, but by so doing they also hold up basic human goods as worthy of protection. Love, from the personalist perspective, focuses on the good of the person; it does not merely avoid all that could harm him. In point of fact, the obligation to shun evil is not more absolute in itself than the obligation to do good. It is, of course, possible to pinpoint certain actions as evil in themselves and hence always to be avoided, whereas actions that are good in themselves are to be done only depending on the circumstance of each person. No one is required to do all possible good, only the good enjoined on each. Yet the positive command to do good, to actively love God and neighbor, is as absolute as any moral precept.

The crux of the sin of omission, and the key characteristic which distinguishes *culpable* inaction from simple inaction without a moral charge, lies in the moral obligation to perform certain good acts. Thus Thomas states that "omission signifies the non-fulfilment of a good, not indeed of any good, but of a good that is due."[9] The human person is not responsible for doing the greatest possible good in every moment, which would demand an impossible running calculus of options and consequences, but the good required of each.[10] Nonetheless, it is not always easy to distinguish between a good action that is due and a good action that is merely elective. What seems clear is that despite its natural indefiniteness, the moral category of omission merits more attention than it generally receives.

In the Gospel Jesus lays exceptionally heavy emphasis on the sin of omission, a characteristic of his message often overlooked by preachers and students of the Bible alike. Though he doesn't use the word "omission," Jesus places the sin of culpable inaction at the center of some of his more forceful parables and moral teachings. Three such instances illustrate the point especially well.

The first is, once again, the parable of the Good Samaritan (Luke 10:29–37), where Jesus in a sense defines "neighbor" (i.e., the one who ef-

---

9. *S. Th.*, II-II, 79, 3.

10. "Criminal negligence is the omission of something which ought to have been done. If we were responsible every moment for everything that we were not doing at that moment, and if we had to examine every single alternative course of action and choose the best one every single time we acted at all, the demands on us would be impossible" (Spaemann, *Basic Moral Concepts*, 55).

fectively loves and fulfills the commandment) as one who comes to the assistance of another in need. In this parable, Jesus does not contrast doing evil on the one hand and avoiding it on the other—between, say, the robbers who assaulted the Samaritan and the passers-by who refrained from violence. The "neighbor" here is not identified with one who minds his own business and does no wrong to others. Rather, Jesus contrasts those who positively act on behalf of others and those who neglect to act. In representing love for neighbor, then, Jesus presents the fundamental difference as between action and inaction, doing or failing to do.

The parable of the rich man and Lazarus (Luke 16:19–31) bears a striking resemblance to that of the Good Samaritan. Here the story takes place at the house of a wealthy man. The narration is straightforward. There was a rich man who "dressed in purple and fine linen" and "feasted sumptuously every day." Meanwhile, at his gate lay a poor fellow named Lazarus, "covered with sores," who "longed to satisfy his hunger with what fell from the rich man's table." His misery extends to the point that "even the dogs would come and lick his sores." Both Lazarus and the rich man die, yet while Lazarus is carried off to the bosom of Abraham, the rich man finds himself tormented in Hades.

Why the drastic difference in their fates? The scant data offered in the Gospel account only reveal the rich man's financial state and a bit about his lifestyle. The reader cannot assume that his wealth was ill gotten, that he oppressed his workers, or that he was unfaithful as a husband and family man—just that he was rich and dressed and ate well. Of Lazarus the parable shows only that he was poor, took up residence at the gate of the rich man, and suffered from sores and hunger. Again, there are no grounds to assume that he was a religious man, or that he was particularly kind to his fellow beggars or patient in his suffering, or that he possessed other virtues in any exceptional degree. The only explanation offered, in fact, comes from Abraham's words to the rich man: "Child, remember that during your lifetime you received your good things, and Lazarus in like manner evil things; but now he is comforted here, and you are in agony." It would seem that the reason for Lazarus's salvation and the rich man's condemnation stems purely from the fact that the rich man led a pleasant earthly existence and Lazarus a miserable one.

There is, however, another piece of information in the Gospel passage that must be taken into account, and that is the juxtaposition of the two men. Lazarus is not just a poor man scraping out a difficult existence in a mountain hamlet and the rich man a successful businessman in a big city far away. The two men's lives touch; the rich man saw the poor beggar lying at his gate and day after day *chose* not to come to his assistance. In this regard, the dogs' licking of Lazarus's wounds stands in contrast with the rich man's inaction: even the irrational beasts seem to possess more compassion than this man. From the parable's perspective, the rich man's wealth conferred on him a responsibility that he failed to assume, and his negligence in the face of his neighbor's need brought about his condemnation.[11]

A third parable of Jesus highlighting the importance of positive action deals once again with judgment, this time with the last judgment (Matt. 25:31–46). Here the Son of Man is presented in glory, seated on a throne and surrounded by angels. Before him are gathered "all the nations," and he divides them into two groups, assigning one a place at his right hand, the other at his left. He first invites those at his right hand to take possession of the kingdom prepared for them "from the foundation of the world." He associates their blessed destiny with their conduct while on earth: "for I was hungry and you gave me food, I was thirsty and you gave me something to drink, I was a stranger and you welcomed me, I was naked and you gave me clothing, I was sick and you took care of me, I was in prison and you visited me." He conducts a similar procedure with those at his left, only this time he banishes them from his presence "into the eternal fire prepared for the devil and his angels." Once again, their fate is shown to be the direct result of their earthly activities: "for I was hungry and you gave me no food, I was thirsty and you gave me nothing to drink, I was a stranger and you did not welcome me, naked and you did not give me clothing, sick and in prison and you did not visit me."

The striking feature of this judgment scene is precisely the kind of behavior being evaluated. Here the damned are not taken to task for their fornications, murders, extortions, and drunkenness, nor are the blessed

---

11. Cardinal Ratzinger writes: "Power and possession are not evil as such, nor are they to be rejected as a matter of principle. However, they are not an end in themselves but a means that not only imposes on man an increased responsibility but also involves an increased risk for him.... [The rich man] will stand before God as a poor man, and he will be rich only to the extent that his possessions have become a means of service and love" (*Gospel, Catechesis, Catechism*, 45).

praised for avoiding such misdeeds. The blessed are received into the kingdom because of their love for Christ, made manifest in their works of charity for their neighbors. Moreover, the faithful appear to be unaware that they were loving Christ at all—they were conscious only of having come to their neighbors' aid. Hence their surprise when Jesus tells them of their service to him: "Lord, when was it that we saw you hungry and gave you food, or thirsty and gave you something to drink? And when was it that we saw you a stranger and welcomed you, or naked and gave you clothing?" The condemned, in turn, are charged only with having failed to love in this way, that is, for having omitted the positive actions inherent to love. The centrality of man's obligation to care for his fellow man comes across with exceptional clarity in this scene-indeed, it forms the sole basis for judgment as presented in this passage.

LOVE AND RESPONSIBILITY

The quality of love that moves a person to act when another is in need and to watch over his good goes by the name of responsibility. Responsibility is the acknowledgment and acceptance that another person has been entrusted to us or put under our care, resulting in a sense of accountability for him. True love is of its very nature responsible. "Love divorced from a feeling of responsibility for the person," writes Wojtyła, "is a negation of itself, is always and necessarily egoism. *The greater the feeling of responsibility for the person the more true love there is.*"[12] A benevolent love involves an identification with the other person, such that the good of the other becomes so identified with one's own good that what happens to the other is experienced as happening to oneself. This is why love is the opposite of indifference. The greater the love, the more what happens to the other *matters* to me, as if it happened to myself.[13]

If a sense of responsibility for others serves as a sure indicator of the

---

12. Wojtyła, *Love and Responsibility*, 131.
13. Thus Thomas affirms that "in the love of friendship, the lover is in the beloved, inasmuch as he reckons what is good or evil to his friend, as being so to himself; and his friend's will as his own, so that it seems as though he felt the good or suffered the evil in the person of his friend.... Consequently in so far as he reckons what affects his friend as affecting himself, the lover seems to be in the beloved, as though he were become one with him: but in so far as, on the other hand, he wills and acts for his friend's sake as for his own sake, looking on his friend as identified with himself, thus the beloved is in the lover" (*S. Th.*, I-II, 28, 2).

presence of love, then a love-based morality will necessarily be suffused with responsibility. Rather than strict duty or a code of legal rules, therefore, the essence of Christian ethics is "the positive sense of responsibility for those goods which were protected by the law and are now positively entrusted to men. This responsibility is above all positive responsibility for one another."[14] Love, which is the only fitting response to the person, cannot be reduced to "do no evil" in his regard or to its corollary, "violate none of his rights." Love is expressed in positive "responsibility" for the other person, as his steward or "keeper" (see Gen. 5:10).

Though in many circumstances "responsibility" is synonymous with "duty," there exists an essential difference with important ethical consequences. Duty readily lends itself to codification since it focuses on tasks, on concrete actions to be performed. "Such and such must be done. Such and such must not be done."[15] Responsibility, on the other hand, deals with goods that are entrusted to a person for him to watch over or projects for him to carry forward to completion.

In general terms, duty deals with means, whereas responsibility deals with ends. Take the simple example of a soccer game. Here one's *duty* is summed up in the rules of play. One has to be in a certain place at a certain time, avoid fouling the other players, keep oneself within certain boundaries, obey the indications of the referee, and so forth. One's *responsibility*, on the other hand, is to score goals and thus win the

---

14. Robert Spaemann, "Christian Ethics of Responsibility," in *Moral Truth and Moral Tradition: Essays in Honor of Peter Geach and Elizabeth Anscombe,* ed. Luke Gormally (Blackrock, Ireland: Four Courts Press, 1994), 138.

15. Duty, which answers the question "What must I do?" is essential to the moral life, but it is not the whole of the moral life. In the exchange between Jesus and the rich young man in the Gospel, the man asks just this question—What must I do to inherit eternal life?—and Jesus replies that he must keep the commandments. The young man, however, is not satisfied with this reply. One could say, rather, that he was dissatisfied with the minimalist way he had framed his own question. Pope John Paul reflects that "even though he is able to make this reply, even though he has followed the moral ideal seriously and generously from childhood, the rich young man knows that he is still far from the goal: before the person of Jesus he realizes that he is still lacking something" (*VS,* 16). A responsible love transcends duty and frees man from legalism. Thus John Paul adds: "It is his awareness of this insufficiency that Jesus addresses in his final answer. Conscious of *the young man's yearning for something greater, which would transcend a legalistic interpretation of the commandments,* the Good Teacher invites him to enter upon the path of perfection: 'If you wish to be perfect, go, sell your possessions and give the money to the poor, and you will have treasure in heaven; then come, follow me' (*Mt* 19:21)" (ibid.; emphasis in original).

game. A duty-based mentality will focus on the rules of play, whereas a responsibility-based mentality will focus on the object of the game. Here it becomes clear that the two virtues of dutifulness and responsibility complement one another and are both necessary. Excessive attention to duty may lead to neglect of the outcome (a clean game with no goals scored), while excessive attention to the outcome may lead to infringement of the rules (many goals but many infractions as well). Still, responsibility is broader in scope than duty and in a sense embraces it. If a player is truly responsible, he will enthusiastically endeavor to win *according to the rules of the game,* since to win otherwise destroys the sense of play.

In the moral sphere, the extremes mentioned above have their counterparts in *legalism* (excessive concentration on the moral code and strict obligation) and *consequentialism* (excessive concentration on the final results of one's actions). Yet here, too, true responsibility both embraces and surpasses duty. As a characteristic of authentic love, responsibility will never be satisfied with the fulfillment of precepts but looks always to the greatest good of the other.[16]

This reflection is confirmed by the subjective experience of responsibility. Jesus' Great Commandment bids each person to "love your neighbor as yourself." The human person naturally loves himself as an end and never treats himself as a mere means. In other words, love of self is always a *responsible* love, because, despite being dependent on other people, one experiences that he has been entrusted to himself and has the ultimate responsibility for himself.[17] For this reason a healthy self-love always focuses on the good of self rather than on a reductive fulfillment of obligations to self.

When a person falls sick, he pursues the means at his disposal to get well. He may take an aspirin, consult a medical encyclopedia, or see a physician. He does this not out of an abstract moral duty or out of a sense of justice toward himself but out of love for himself and hence out

---

16. John Paul notes that "those who are impelled by love . . . feel an interior urge—a genuine 'necessity' and no longer a form of coercion—not to stop at the minimum demands of the Law, but to live them in their 'fullness'" (ibid., 18).

17. Such entrusting is part and parcel of man's freedom and self-determination. John Paul notes that "man himself has been entrusted to his own care and responsibility. God left man 'in the power of his own counsel' (*Sir* 15:14), that he might seek his Creator and freely attain perfection. Attaining such perfection means personally building up that perfection in himself" (ibid., 39).

of concern for the good of health, which contributes to his overall personal well-being. Therefore, he gauges his efforts not by a calculus of what he is morally required to do for himself but by their effectiveness in obtaining the desired outcome. If after taking an aspirin he realizes that it has not produced the anticipated results, he will not cease his search for a successful remedy in the smug satisfaction of having "fulfilled his duty." Again, this is because his interest is directed not toward fulfilling his duty but toward restoring his health.

This experience of natural self-love can be transferred to the sphere of interpersonal relationships. When a person loves another as another "self," then the other's good becomes identified with his own good, and he pursues that good as if it were his own. Just as in the case of self-love, a minimalist ethics of duty does not come into play here. If a mother has a sick child she will do all in her power to help him get well, just as the sick person would for himself. The mother's concern focuses on the good of her child rather than on her duty to the child or her own moral rectitude. The essential difference between strict duty and the responsibility born of love expresses itself in this shift in concern.

RESPONSIBILITY AND SOLIDARITY IN A GLOBALIZED WORLD

The scope of a particular person's responsibility will depend on his understanding of who has been entrusted to him. Obviously one's parents, children, siblings, and close friends will fall into this category. An ethics of "equal regard"—as if people did not have a greater responsibility to those nearest to them—is foreign to traditional Christian ethics.[18] Rather, in defining responsibility as an active concern for those entrusted to one's care, there will be an order to responsibility, since some are en-

---

18. St. Augustine, for instance, sustains this natural order of responsibility. "God teaches him two chief commandments, the love of God and the love of neighbor. . . . Right order here means, first, that he harm no one, and second, that he help whomever he can. His fundamental duty is to look out for his own home, for both by natural and human law he has easier and readier access to their requirements" (St. Augustine, *The City of God*, bk. XIX, ch. 14 [Garden City, N.Y.: Image Books, 1960], 460). In this regard, it should be noted that though "equal regard" or strict "impartiality" do not provide a sufficient basis for ethics, they are necessary principles for civil legislation, which by its very nature must treat all citizens as "equal under the law." Once again, complications arise when the legal and moral spheres are confused.

trusted more particularly than others.¹⁹ Thus Thomas speaks of the order of charity among human persons, which begins with love for oneself and is followed by love for parents, children, those of one's household, and so forth.²⁰ Some of Thomas's particular conclusions are flawed, but on the whole his reasoning is sound and confirms the common experience of mankind.²¹ On the other hand, as Thomas rightly clarifies, preferential love does not imply exclusive love, as if loving one meant not loving another.²² Here again appears the distinction between benevolence and beneficence: *wishing* good to all (benevolence) is a moral obligation; actively *doing* good to all (beneficence) is an impossibility—everyone must choose to whom they will do good. Love is not, however, unequal as regards *what good* is wished to each, as if loving more meant wishing a greater good to some and a lesser good to others. The same integral good must be wished to all, especially the supreme good of eternal life. In this sense one's love for all persons is the same; it varies not in *content* but rather in *intensity* and in its practical manifestations.

But what about those outside the immediate circle of blood relations and friendship? What does it mean to be responsible for them? Here again the concept of "neighbor" as one who is "nigh" proves especially suggestive. The nearness proper to neighbors could be taken to mean anything from physical proximity, to social ties, to common circumstance, to Aquinas's idea of participation in a common nature. In the parable of the Good Samaritan, Christ portrays as a neighbor a person who by happenstance (or providence) finds himself in a situation where he (1) is *physically close* to a fellow human being in need ("came near him"); (2) has *immediate knowledge* of the other's need ("saw him"); and (3) has the *power to respond* to the need in some way ("bandaged his wounds," "poured oil and wine on them," "put him on his own animal,"

---

19. Thus Thomas teaches with regard to almsgiving that "each one must first of all look after himself and then after those over whom he has charge, and afterwards with what remains relieve the needs of others" (*S. Th.*, II-II, 32, 5).

20. See ibid., II-II, 26, 4–13.

21. Thomas erroneously asserts, for instance, that one should love father more than mother (see ibid., II-II, 26, 10).

22. See ibid., II-II, 26, 6, ad 1. This principle was likewise confirmed in the case of the Church's "preferential option for the poor," which focuses on those in greatest need but excludes no one. See Congregation for the Doctrine of the Faith, *Instruction on Christian Freedom and Liberation*, 68.

"brought him to an inn").[23] Of these three characteristics, the first carries the least weight and can be assimilated into the other two, since the Good Samaritan's physical proximity is important only in that it allows for his cognizance of his neighbor's plight and his own ability to intervene.

This third aspect, the ability or power to respond to another's need, includes in turn three other factors. First, one may have talents or skills specially suited to aid another, as in the case of a doctor or a mechanic. Second, one who possesses an abundance of worldly goods may be empowered to offer assistance where others could not. Finally, the degree of the other's need for *me* must be considered, either because no one else is around or no one else is prepared to help.[24]

Without the power to intervene afforded by some combination of these three factors, no one would have a concrete moral obligation to help his neighbor. Even in such a case, however, the *responsibility* for the good of one's neighbor would remain. Although some people can be "nearer" than others (e.g., family members are closer neighbors than anonymous orphans on the other side of the globe) and thus require a more exacting love, this does not mean that anyone is excluded from a particular person's responsibility; in other words, no human person is not "neighbor" to every other human person.

On a global scale, this general responsibility for one's fellow man is designated in Catholic social teaching as "solidarity." In this sense, solidarity refers to the extension of "responsible love" to the entire human race. In the words of the *Catechism,* solidarity is "dictated and imposed both by our common origin and by the equality in rational nature of all men," can be "articulated in terms of 'friendship' or 'social charity,'" and

---

23. The sage moral principle "ad impossibilia nemo tenetur" comes into play in the third aspect here. Though we may be aware of great human need, we are not always in a position to alleviate this need.

24. "If someone has been injured on a ship, people ask if there is a doctor on board. If there is, the doctor is under the obligation to help. There are similar implications regarding other human characteristics. Some people are more far-sighted than others. They owe it to others under certain circumstance to give good advice. Some people have a more highly developed sense of values. One might well reproach those people for doing certain things one would never dream of holding against others. Some people have to accept responsibilities on behalf of others who would not see themselves as being responsible in the same way. This is because the former have simply seen something the others have failed to see" (Spaemann, *Basic Moral Concepts,* 77).

is a "direct demand of human and Christian brotherhood."[25] Through solidarity we see the other "not just as some kind of instrument . . . but as our 'neighbor,' a 'helper' (cf. Gen. 2:18–20), to be sharer on a par with ourselves in the banquet of life to which all are equally invited by God."[26]

Though this principle of Catholic social doctrine has been elaborated in detail only recently, it has long formed part of Christian teaching. It can be found outside the Christian tradition as well. In Cicero's (106–43 B.C.) ethical treatise *De finibus bonorum et malorum,* the Roman orator offers a heartfelt encomium to the solidarity of mankind *(caritas generis humani),* and in so doing, he also presents a classic description of this "modern" virtue. He speaks of a natural affection and affinity that begins with those around us and spreads until it encompasses the whole of mankind:

But in the whole moral sphere of which we are speaking there is nothing more glorious nor of wider range than the solidarity of mankind, that species of alliance and partnership of interests and that actual affection which exists between man and man, which, coming into existence immediately upon our birth, owing to the fact that children are loved by their parents and the family as a whole is bound together by the ties of marriage and parenthood, gradually spreads its influence beyond the home, first by blood relationships, then by connections through marriage, later by friendships, afterwards by the bonds of neighborhood, then to fellow-citizens and political allies and friends, and lastly by embracing the whole of the human race.[27]

In the conception of the Church, however, solidarity is not limited to a generalized affection for humanity or an affinity of interests. Like the charity of which it is an expression, it must be translated into action. Thus solidarity is not "a feeling of vague compassion or shallow distress at the misfortunes of so many people," it is a determination to "commit

---

25. *CCC,* 1939; see also John Paul II, *SRS,* 38–40; *CA,* 10.
26. John Paul II, *SRS,* 38.
27. "In omni autem honesto de quo loquimur nihil est tam illustre nec quod latius pateat quam coniunctio inter homines hominum et quasi quaedam societas et communicatio utilitatum et ipsa caritas generis humani, quae nata a primo satu, quod a procreatoribus nati diliguntur et tota domus coniungio et stirpe coniungitur, serpit sensim foras, cognationibus primum, tum affinitatibus, deinde amicitiis, post vicinitatibus, tum civibus et iis qui publice socii atque amici sunt, deinde totius complexu gentis humanae" (Cicero, *De finibus bonorum et malorum,* bk. V, xxiii, pp. 468–69.

oneself to the common good; that is to say, to the good of all and of each individual because *we are really responsible for all.*"[28]

This last phrase merits special consideration; it ties back to the issue of positive rights. The Pope's assertion that all are "responsible for all" makes some uneasy. Doesn't such an affirmation reflect sloppy ethical reasoning? Moreover, how can anything be accomplished without assigning responsibility to specific individuals or groups? John Finnis, for example, writes:

> For it is becoming common, at least in academic discussion, to propose, in effect, that "everyone of us is responsible for everyone else in every way." Here the feeling that it is difficult or impossible to find norms for definitely apportioning one's effort in differing degrees amongst different potential beneficiaries seems to link up with the assumption that justice is primarily a property of states of affairs and only derivatively a property of particular decisions of ascertained persons.[29]

Contrary to Finnis's analysis, however, a sense of responsibility for mankind deals not with a "state of affairs" but rather with the virtue and moral sensibility of human persons and communities. Pope John Paul's affirmation of universal responsibility does not eliminate differences in degrees of responsibility, it challenges an insular morality that limits personal responsibility to one's closest neighbors. Furthermore, the Pope's use of "we" as the subject of responsibility surpasses the libertarian/socialistic mentality that conceives of a bilevel separation of individuals and the state, with no mediating institutions in between. John Paul does not say that "each individual" is responsible for every other, he says that "we"—that is, the human community, or society—are responsible for all the members of this community. The solidarity conceived of by the Church does not merely entail the care of individuals for all other individuals, it begins with a conception of community that is itself the acting *subject* of solidarity, not only its beneficiary.

Here the distinction between duty and responsibility is especially germane. That all are responsible for all does not mean that each has the duty to intervene on behalf of every other person. The interest of responsibility is not principally with the *task* but with the *person*, not with the *means* but with the *end*. Everyone must be actively concerned for every other member of the human race without exception, which means that

---

28. *SRS*, 38; emphasis added.
29. Finnis, *Natural Law and Natural Rights*, 176.

no one ought to be indifferent to the plight of anyone else. At the same time, practical contributions to remedying neighbors' needs will vary from case to case.

"We are really responsible for all." From this perspective, speaking of two-term, positive rights takes on a concrete meaning. To say that all persons have the right to food, for instance, translates into a responsibility of the human community to see to it that people are fed. No one escapes this ineluctable responsibility. Since each is a "neighbor" to each other, each deserves each other's effective concern and solicitude. When a person cultivates the virtue of solidarity—conceived as a sense of concern and accountability for the entire human family—he grows in his resemblance to God, who is compassionate and hears the cry of the oppressed and afflicted. God's very nature as "merciful love" compels Him to meet the manifold needs of His creatures. Hence Joseph Ratzinger explains Christ's injunction to "be perfect as your heavenly Father is perfect" (Matt. 5:48) as follows: "Be infected by the dynamism of a love that cannot abide in the glory of heaven while the cry of the suffering rises up from the earth."[30] This is solidarity in its purest form.

BACK TO FOUNDATIONS

An increasingly globalized society makes the virtue of solidarity more pressing. One of the primary consequences of globalization is a "shrinking" of the world, such that every person is brought nearer to every other person, both in terms of knowledge of others' situation and needs and in terms of ability to come to their assistance. Hence the Holy Father's continual appeals that the globalization of the economy and culture be accompanied by a globalization of solidarity.

But the solidarity that is needed in a globalized world must be rooted in firmer turf than an uncertain feeling of general goodwill and affection for humanity. In order for society to see solidarity as a demand of justice, not an "extra," the objective foundations of solidarity must be explained and understood. Only if human rights are real, rooted in a solid theological anthropology and metaphysics, can solidarity flourish, which is why an investigation of the ultimate foundations of human rights, of how it

---

30. Ratzinger, *Gospel, Catechesis, Catechism*, 44.

can be said that certain things are due to all human persons—as undertaken above—is so critical.

Grounding human rights consists not in working out a justification for each specific right but rather in showing that the human person deserves a certain sort of treatment from other persons, and that this treatment includes the affirmation of determined goods with respect to the person and excludes behavior that damages any of these goods.

An attempt to ground human rights is essentially an attempt to ground natural justice itself. Discussing in depth how and why something can be due to another person leads to a discussion about the essence of rights—but also, necessarily, to a discussion about the essence of justice. Natural rights, as one aspect of natural justice, do not rest on a foundation distinct from that of justice; they rest on the selfsame foundation. Both natural justice and natural rights depend for their very intelligibility on the reality of personhood, specifically on the notion of a dignity that is at once a quality of persons and an ethical requirement vis-à-vis other persons. In other words, if there is something about the person that makes him worthy of a certain sort of treatment—a quality referred to as human dignity—then this quality forms the bedrock of both natural justice and natural rights.

It is the specific character of Thomistic personalism as the clearest and most cogent defender of human dignity that makes it the best candidate for grounding human rights. Drawing on the strength of Thomas's anthropological metaphysics as well as the more recent contributions of phenomenology and existentialism, Thomistic personalism manifests the excellence of personhood, both on a philosophical and theological level, and clearly distinguishes persons from nonpersons. This distinction brings to light the decisive ethical consequences of personhood and results eventually in the personalist principle, whereby the human person is seen as a creature toward whom the only proper attitude and behavior is love. Love, seen as the affirmation of the person as an end and never just a means, comes to be seen as the central requirement of natural justice, i.e., what is essentially due to every person simply because of his humanity.

These reflections bring to the fore the relationship between love and justice, which is paradoxical in that love may be considered as both undergirding justice and completing it. Love is implied in justice as its first and primary requirement and simultaneously transcends and surpasses it. Once love is accepted as naturally due to the human person, it is relatively easy to show how love of the person as such demands the affirmation of those particular human goods that together contribute to and comprise the person's integral good. If love is not owed to the person, however, the bottom falls out of any attempt to make sense of natural human rights and duties. If the person as such is not to be affirmed, there is little sense in asserting that particular goods are in any way owed to him. Particular goods are precious only insofar as they are perfective of a being who is valuable as an end in himself.

No other human rights theory makes a more convincing case for grounding not only natural human rights but even natural justice itself than the personalist approach. The inherent dignity of the human person as the root of natural rights makes intuitive sense, in that when we suppose the contrary (i.e., that man does not possess this dignity), natural rights lose all solidity and become mere conventions. In other words, natural rights lose their natural character. Moreover, the explanation offered by Thomistic personalism meshes with Catholic social teaching in a way that other natural rights theories do not, thus satisfying both philosophically and theologically.

Recognizing the inherent worth of all human persons, and hence the importance of each human person, is essential for building a culture of solidarity. Solidarity, the virtue that disposes one actively to work for the common good, rests on an appreciation of human dignity and an understanding of man's nature as a being called to communion. Acknowledging the objective importance and worth of all persons, and their fundamental right to love, forges bonds that guarantee the transformation of culture and true progress toward a civilization of justice and love.

SELECT BIBLIOGRAPHY

Ashcraft, Richard. "Locke's Political Philosophy." In *The Cambridge Companion to Locke,* edited by Vere C. Chappell, 226–51. Cambridge: Cambridge University Press, 1994.
Ashley, Benedict M. *Living the Truth in Love: A Biblical Introduction to Moral Theology.* Staten Island, N.Y.: Alba House, 1996.
Aristotle, *Aristotle: Selected Works.* 3rd ed. Translated and edited by Hippocrates G. Apostle and Lloyd P. Gerson. Grinnell, Iowa: Peripatetic Press, 1991.
———. *Nichomachean Ethics.* Translated by Harris Rackham. London: William Heineman, 1982.
Augustine, St. *The City of God.* Edited by Vernon J. Bourke. Translated from the Latin *De Civitate Dei* by Gerard G. Walsh, Demetrius B. Zema, Grace Monahan, and Daniel J. Honan. Garden City, N.Y.: Image Books, 1960.
———. *De Doctrina Christiana.* Edited by Philip Schaff and Henry Wace. Translated by J. F. Shaw. Peabody, Mass.: Hendrickson, 1995.
Balthasar, Hans Urs von. *Explorations in Theology: Spiritus Creator.* Translated by Brian McNeil. San Francisco: Ignatius Press, 1993.
———. "On the Concept of Person." Translated by Peter Verhalen. *Communio: International Catholic Review* 13 (Spring 1986): 18–26.
Balthasar, Hans Urs von, Joseph Ratzinger, and Heinz Schürmann. *Principles of Christian Morality.* Translated from the German *Prinzipien Christlicher Moral* (1975) by Graham Harrison. San Francisco: Ignatius Press, 1986.
Beneton, Philippe. "The Languages of the Rights of Man." *First Things* 37 (November 1993): 9–12.
Benn, Stanley I. "Rights." In *The Encyclopedia of Philosophy,* vol. 7, edited by Paul Edwards. New York: Macmillan, 1967.
Bentham, Jeremy. "Anarchical Fallacies." In *Society, Law, and Morality,* edited by Frederick A. Olafson, 343–79. Englewood Cliffs, N.J.: Prentice Hall, 1961.
Berke, Matthew. "A Jewish Appreciation of Catholic Social Teaching." In *Catholicism, Liberalism, and Communitarianism: The Catholic Intellectual Tradition and the Moral Foundations of Democracy,* edited by Kenneth L. Grasso, Gerard V. Bradley, and Robert P. Hunt, 235–54. Lanham, Md.: Rowman & Littlefield, 1995.
Berns, Walter. "The Need for Public Authority." In *Freedom and Virtue: The Conservative/Libertarian Debate,* edited by George W. Carey, 55–67. Wilmington, Del.: Intercollegiate Studies Institute, 1998.
———. "Taking Virtue Seriously." *Public Interest* (Summer 1997): 122–26.
Bettati, Mario. *Le nouvel ordre économique international.* Paris: Presses Universitaires de France, 1983.

Bird, Otto A. *The Idea of Justice.* New York: Frederick A. Praeger, 1967.
Black, Virginia. "What Dignity Means." In *Common Truths: New Perspectives on Natural Law,* edited by Edward B. McLean, 119–50. Wilmington, Del.: ISI Books, 2000.
Blazquez, Niceto. *Los derechos del hombre.* Madrid: BAC, 1980.
Boyle, Joseph. "Natural Law and the Ethics of Traditions." In *Natural Law Theory: Contemporary Essays,* edited by Robert P. George, 3–30. Oxford: Clarendon Press, 1995.
Braaten, Carl E. "A Response to Russell Hittinger." In *A Preserving Grace: Protestants, Catholics, and Natural Law,* edited by Michael Cromartie, 31–40. Grand Rapids, Mich.: Ethics and Public Policy Center/William B. Eerdmans, 1997.
Bradley, Gerard V. "Moral Truth, the Common Good, and Judicial Review." In *Catholicism, Liberalism, and Communitarianism: The Catholic Intellectual Tradition and the Moral Foundations of Democracy,* edited by Kenneth L. Grasso, Gerard V. Bradley, and Robert P. Hunt, 115–32. Lanham, Md.: Rowman & Littlefield, 1995.
Brown, Chris. "John Rawls, 'The Law of Peoples,' and International Political Theory." *Ethics and International Affairs,* Carnegie Council on Ethics and International Affairs, 14 (2000): 125–32.
Brunner, Emil. *Justice and the Social Order.* Translated by M. Hottinger. New York: Scribner's, 1945.
Buber, Martin. *I and Thou.* Translated from the German *Ich und Du* (2nd ed., 1923) by Ronald Gregor Smith. Edinburgh: T & T Clark, 1987.
Buttiglione, Rocco. *Karol Wojtyła: The Thought of the Man Who Became Pope John Paul II.* Translated from the Italian *Il pensiero di Karol Wojtyła* (1982) by Paolo Guietti and Francesca Murphy. Grand Rapids, Mich./William B. Eerdmans, 1997.
Caffarra, Carlo. *Living in Christ: Fundamental Principles of Catholic Moral Teaching.* Translated from the Italian *Viventi in Cristo* (1981) by Christopher Ruff. San Francisco: Ignatius Press, 1989.
Canavan, Francis S. "The Image of Man in Catholic Thought." In *Catholicism, Liberalism, and Communitarianism: The Catholic Intellectual Tradition and the Moral Foundations of Democracy,* edited by Kenneth L. Grasso, Gerard V. Bradley, and Robert P. Hunt, 15–28. Lanham, Md.: Rowman & Littlefield, 1995.
———. "The Pluralist Game." *Law and Contemporary Problems* 44 (Spring 1981): 23–40.
Carey, George W., ed. *Freedom and Virtue: The Conservative/Libertarian Debate.* Wilmington, Del.: Intercollegiate Studies Institute, 1998.
Cassin, René. "From the Ten Commandments to the Rights of Man." In *Of Law and Man: Essays in Honor of Haim H. Cohn,* edited by Shlomo Shoham, 13–25. New York: Sabra Books, 1971.
Castillo Corrales, E. *Los derechos humanos en la perspectiva de la Iglesia católica.* Mexico City: Imdosoc, 1990.
Cathrein, Victor. "Right." In *The Catholic Encyclopedia,* vol. 13. 1914.
CELAM (reflection team for pastoral theology). *Los derechos humanos: Sus fundamentos en la enseñanza de la Iglesia.* Bogota: CELAM, 1982.
Chapman, John W. "Natural Rights and Justice in Liberalism." In *Political Theory and the Rights of Man,* edited by David D. Raphael, 27–42. Bloomington: Indiana University Press, 1967.
Chappell, Vere, ed. *The Cambridge Companion to Locke.* Cambridge: Cambridge University Press, 1994.
Chomsky, Noam, and Edward Herman. *The Political Economy of Human Rights.* 2 vols. Montreal: Black Rose Books, 1979.

Cicero, Marcus Tullius. *De finibus bonorum et malorum* (44 B.C.). Translated from the Latin by H. Rackham. Loeb Classical Library, vol. 40. Cambridge: Harvard University Press, 1994.
Clifford Richard J., and Ronald E. Murphy. "Genesis." In *The New Jerome Biblical Commentary*, edited by Raymond E. Brown, Joseph A. Fitzmyer, and Roland E. Murphy, 8–43. London: Geoffrey Chapman, 1989.
Composta, Dario. "Prassi e coscienza dei diritti umani nella storia." *Seminarium* 23 (1983): 332–43.
Congregation for the Doctrine of the Faith. *Instruction on Christian Freedom and Liberation (Libertatis Conscientia)*, March 22, 1986. *AAS* 79 (1987):554–99.
———. *Instruction on the Ecclesial Vocation of the Theologian (Donum Veritatis)*, May 24, 1990. *AAS* 82 (1990); 1550–70.
Cranston, Maurice. *What Are Human Rights?* New York: Taplinger, 1973.
Craycraft, Kenneth R. Jr. "Religion as Moral Duty and Civic Right: *Dignitatis humanæ* on Religious Liberty." In *Catholicism, Liberalism, and Communitarianism: The Catholic Intellectual Tradition and the Moral Foundations of Democracy*, edited by Kenneth L. Grasso, Gerard V. Bradley, and Robert P. Hunt, 59–80. Lanham, Md.: Rowman & Littlefield, 1995.
Cromartie, Michael, ed. *A Preserving Grace: Protestants, Catholics, and Natural Law*. Grand Rapids, Mich.: Ethics and Public Policy Center/William B. Eerdmans, 1997.
Cronin, Kieran. *Rights and Christian Ethics*. Cambridge: Cambridge University Press, 1992.
Damico, Alfonso J., ed. *Liberals on Liberalism*. Totowa, N.J.: Rowman & Littlefield, 1986.
Denzinger, H., and A. Schönmetzer, eds. *Enchiridion Symbolorum*. 33rd ed. Freiburg, 1965.
Donagan, Alan. *The Theory of Morality*. Chicago: University of Chicago Press, 1977.
Donnelly, John. "Rethinking Human Rights." *Current History* (November 1996): 387–91.
Dorr, D. *Option for the Poor: A Hundred Years of Vatican Social Teaching*. Dublin: Maryknoll, 1983.
Dubay, Thomas. *The Evidential Power of Beauty: Science and Theology Meet*. San Francisco: Ignatius Press, 1999.
Dulles, Avery. "Human Rights: Papal Teaching, and the United Nations." *America*, December 5, 1998: 14–19.
———. "The United Nations and Papal Teaching." Laurence A. McGinley Lecture, Fordham University, November 18, 1998.
Duston, Robert Allen. "The Rights and Obligations of the Lay Christian Faithful: The Second Vatican Council through the Revised Code of Canon Law." Ph.D. diss., University of St. Thomas Aquinas, Rome, 1986.
Dworkin, Ronald. "Liberalism." In *Public and Private Morality*, edited by Stuart Hampshire, 113–43. Cambridge: Cambridge University Press, 1978.
———. *A Matter of Principle*. Cambridge, Mass.: Harvard University Press, 1985.
———. *Taking Rights Seriously*. Cambridge, Mass.: Harvard University Press, 1977.
Edgar, William. "The Reformed Tradition and Natural Law: A Response." In *A Preserving Grace: Protestants, Catholics, and Natural Law*, edited by Michael Cromartie, 118–30. Grand Rapids, Mich.: Ethics and Public Policy Center/William B. Eerdmans, 1997.
Ellul, Jacques. *Le fondement théologique du droit*. Neuchâtel/Paris: Delachaux and Niestlé, 1946.
Elsbernd, Mary. "Rights Statements: A Hermeneutical Key to Continuing Development in Magisterial Teaching." Extract from doctoral dissertation, in *Ephemerides Theologiae Lovanienses*, t. 62, *308–32*. Leuven, 1986.
Etzioni, Amitai. *Rights and the Common Good: The Communitarian Perspective*. New York: St. Martin's Press, 1995.
Feinberg, Joel. "Duties, Rights, and Claims." *American Philosophical Quarterly* 3/2 (1966).

———. *Freedom and Fulfillment: Philosophical Essays.* Princeton: Princeton University Press, 1992.

———. "Rights, Justice, and Punishment." In *Moral Philosophy: Classic Texts and Contemporary Problems,* edited by Joel Feinberg and Henry West, 310–18. Encino and Belmont, Calif.: Dickenson, 1977.

———. *Rights, Justice, and the Bounds of Liberty: Essays in Social Philosophy.* Princeton: Princeton University Press, 1980.

Filibeck, Giorgio, ed. *Human Rights in the Teaching of the Church: From John XXIII to John Paul II.* Vatican City: Libreria Editrice Vaticana, 1994.

Finance, Joseph de. *An Ethical Inquiry.* Translated from the French *Éthique générale* (1967) by Michael O'Brien. Rome: Editrice Pontificia Università Gregoriana, 1991.

Finnis, John. "Abortion, Natural Law, and Public Reason." In *Natural Law and Public Reason,* edited by Robert P. George and Christopher Wolfe, 75–105. Washington, D.C.: Georgetown University Press, 2000.

———. *Fundamentals of Ethics.* Oxford: Oxford University Press, 1983.

———. *Moral Absolutes: Tradition, Revision, and Truth.* Washington, D.C.: Catholic University of America Press, 1991.

———. *Natural Law and Natural Rights.* Oxford: Clarendon Press, 1980.

Fortin, Ernest L. *Classical Christianity and the Political Order: Reflections on the Theologico-Politico Problem.* Vol. 2 of *Ernest L. Fortin: Collected Essays,* edited by J. Brian Benestad. Lanham, Md.: Rowman & Littlefield, 1996.

———. *Human Rights, Virtue, and the Common Good: Untimely Meditations on Religion and Politics.* Vol. 3 of *Ernest L. Fortin: Collected Essays,* edited by J. Brian Benestad. Lanham, Md.: Rowman & Littlefield, 1996.

Fox Bourne, Henry R. *The Life of John Locke.* 2 vols. London, 1876.

Freedman, David Noel, ed. *The Anchor Bible Dictionary.* New York: Doubleday, 1997.

Frey, Raymond G. *Rights, Killing, and Suffering.* Oxford: Basil Blackwell, 1983.

Galston, William. "Liberalism and Public Morality." In *Liberals on Liberalism,* edited by Alfonso J. Damico, 129–47. Totowa, N.J.: Rowman & Littlefield, 1986.

George, Robert P., ed. *The Autonomy of Law: Essays on Legal Positivism.* New York: Oxford University Press, 1996.

———. "A Clash of Orthodoxies." *First Things* 95 (August–September 1999): 33–40.

———. *Making Men Moral: Civil Liberties and Public Morality.* New York: Oxford University Press, 1996.

———. "Natural Law and International Order." In *Catholicism, Liberalism, and Communitarianism: The Catholic Intellectual Tradition and the Moral Foundations of Democracy,* edited by Kenneth L. Grasso, Gerard V. Bradley, and Robert P. Hunt, 133–50. Lanham, Md.: Rowman & Littlefield, 1995.

———, ed. *Natural Law and Moral Inquiry: Ethics, Metaphysics, and Politics in the Work of Germain Grisez.* Washington, D.C.: Georgetown University Press, 1998.

———, ed. *Natural Law Theory: Contemporary Essays.* Oxford: Clarendon Press, 1995.

———. "Recent Criticism of Natural Law Theory." *University of Chicago Law Review* 55 (1998): 1371–429.

———. "A Response to Joan Lockwood O'Donovan." In *A Preserving Grace: Protestants, Catholics, and Natural Law,* edited by Michael Cromartie, 157–61. Grand Rapids, Mich.: Ethics and Public Policy Center/William B. Eerdmans, 1997.

George, Robert P., and Christopher Wolfe, eds. *Natural Law and Public Reason.* Washington, D.C.: Georgetown University Press, 2000.

Gilleman, Gérard. *The Primacy of Charity in Moral Theology.* Translated by William F. Ryan and André Vachon. Westminster, Md.: Newman Press, 1959.
Gilson, Étienne. *L'esprit de la philosophie médiévale.* Paris: Librairie Philosophique J. Vrin, 1932.
Glendon, Mary Ann. "Catholic Thought and Dilemmas of Human Rights." Address, Higher Learning and Catholic Traditions Conference, University of Notre Dame, October 14, 1999.

———. "Knowing the Universal Declaration of Human Rights." *Notre Dame Law Review* 73/5 (1998): 1153–81.

———. "Rights Babel: The Universal Rights Idea at the Dawn of the Third Millennium." *Gregorianum* 79/4 (1998): 611–24.

———. *Rights Talk: The Impoverishment of Political Discourse.* New York: Free Press, 1991.

———. "Women's Identity, Women's Rights, and the Civilization of Life." In *Evangelium Vitæ and the Law,* 63–75. Rome: Libreria Editrice Vaticana, 1997.

Gormally, Luke, ed. *Moral Truth and Moral Tradition: Essays in Honour of Peter Geach and Elizabeth Anscombe.* Blackrock, Ireland: Four Courts Press, 1994.
Gormley, W. Paul. *Human Rights and Environment: The Need for International Cooperation.* Leyden, the Netherlands: A. W. Sijthoff, 1976.
Grasso, Kenneth L. "Beyond Liberalism: Human Dignity, the Free Society, and the Second Vatican Council." In *Catholicism, Liberalism, and Communitarianism: The Catholic Intellectual Tradition and the Moral Foundations of Democracy,* edited by Kenneth L. Grasso, Gerard V. Bradley, and Robert P. Hunt, 29–58. Lanham, Md.: Rowman & Littlefield, 1995.

———. "Catholic Social Thought and the Quest for an American Public Philosophy." In *Catholicism, Liberalism, and Communitarianism: The Catholic Intellectual Tradition and the Moral Foundations of Democracy,* edited by Kenneth L. Grasso, Gerard V. Bradley, and Robert P. Hunt, 1–14. Lanham, Md.: Rowman & Littlefield, 1995.

Grasso, Kenneth L., Gerard V. Bradley, and Robert P. Hunt, eds. *Catholicism, Liberalism, and Communitarianism: The Catholic Intellectual Tradition and the Moral Foundations of Democracy.* Lanham, Md.: Rowman & Littlefield, 1995.
Griffith, John. "This Bill Should Have No Rights." *Spectator,* February 15, 1997, 18.
Grisez, Germain. *Christian Moral Principles.* Vol. 1 of *The Way of the Lord Jesus.* Chicago: Franciscan Herald Press, 1983.

———. *Living a Christian Life.* Vol. 2 of *The Way of the Lord Jesus.* Quincy, Ill.: Franciscan Press, 1993.

Grisez, Germain, and Joseph Boyle, Jr., eds. *Life and Death with Liberty and Justice: A Contribution to the Euthanasia Debate.* Notre Dame, Ind.: University of Notre Dame Press, 1979.
Grotius, Hugo. *De Iure Belli ac Pacis Libri Tres* (1625). Translated by Francis W. Kelsey. Vol. 2 of *Classics of International Law.* Oxford: Clarendon Press, 1925.
Guilhaudis, Jean-François. *Le droit des peuples à disposer d'eux-mêmes.* Grenoble: Presses Universitaires de Grenoble, 1976.
Guillon, M., ed. *Collection générale des brefs et instructions de notre Très-Saint Père Pie VI relatifs à la révolution française.* Vol. 1. Paris, 1798.
Guitton, Jean, and Jean-Jacques Antier. *Le livre de la sagesse et des vertus retrouvées.* Saint-Amand-Montrond, Cher: Librairie Académique Perrin, 1998.
Haines, Charles G. *The Revival of Natural Law Concepts.* Cambridge: Harvard University Press, 1930.
Hamel, Edouard. "Fondement théologique des droits de l'homme." *Seminarium* 23 (1983): 309–18.

———. "Iustitia et Iura Hominum in Sancta Scriptura." *Periodica de re morali, canonica, liturgica* 69 (1980): 201–17.

Hampshire, Stuart, ed. *Public and Private Morality.* Cambridge: Cambridge University Press, 1978.

Hart, H. L. A. "Bentham on Legal Rights." In *Oxford Essays in Jurisprudence* (2nd ser.), edited by A. W. B. Simpson, 171–201. Oxford: Clarendon Press, 1973.

Hering, H. "De Iure Subjective Sumpto apud S. Thomam." *Angelicum* 16 (1939): 295–97.

Hervada, Javier, and José M. Zumaquero, eds. *Textos internacionales de derechos humanos I: 1776–1976.* Pamplona: EUNSA, 1992.

Hittinger, Russell. *A Critique of the New Natural Law Theory.* Notre Dame, Ind.: University of Notre Dame Press, 1987.

———. Introduction to *The Natural Law: A Study in Legal and Social History and Philosophy,* by Heinrich A. Rommen, xi–xxxii. Indianapolis: Liberty Fund, 1998.

———. "Natural Law and Catholic Moral Theology." In *A Preserving Grace: Protestants, Catholics, and Natural Law,* edited by Michael Cromartie, 1–31. Grand Rapids, Mich.: Ethics and Public Policy Center/William B. Eerdmans, 1997.

Hobbes, Thomas. *The Elements of Law Natural and Politic: Part I, Human Nature, Part II, De Corpore Politico, with Three Lives.* Edited by J. C. A. Gaskin. New York: Oxford University Press, 1999.

———. *Leviathan* (1651). Edited by Richard Tuck. Cambridge: Cambridge University Press, 1991.

Hollenbach, David. *Claims in Conflict: Retrieving and Renewing the Catholic Human Rights Tradition.* New York: Paulist, 1979.

Hunt, Robert P. "The Quest for the Historical Murray." In *Catholicism, Liberalism, and Communitarianism: The Catholic Intellectual Tradition and the Moral Foundations of Democracy,* edited by Kenneth L. Grasso, Gerard V. Bradley, and Robert P. Hunt, 197–218. Lanham, Md.: Rowman & Littlefield, 1995.

Ingram, T. Robert. *What's Wrong with Human Rights.* Houston: St. Thomas, 1978.

International Commission of Jurists. *Development, Human Rights, and the Rule of Law.* Oxford: Pergamon, 1981.

International Theological Commission. "Propositions on the Dignity and Rights of the Human Person (1983)." In *International Theological Commission: Texts and Documents, 1969–1985,* edited by Michael Sharkey, 251–66. San Francisco: Ignatius Press, 1989.

Ishay, Micheline R. *The Human Rights Reader: Major Political Essays, Speeches, and Documents from the Bible to the Present.* London: Routledge, 1997.

Jackson, Robert H. "Closing Address in the Nuremberg Trial." *Proceedings in the Trial of the Major War Criminals before the International Military Tribunal* 19 (1948): 397.

Jenkins, Iredell. "From Natural to Legal to Human Rights." In *Human Rights,* edited by Erwin H. Pollack. Buffalo: Jay Stewart, 1971.

John Paul II. "Address to Participants in the World Congress on the Pastoral Promotion of Human Rights" (July 4, 1998). *L'Osservatore Romano,* English edition, July 29, 1998, 3, 8.

———. "Address to the Congregation for the Doctrine of the Faith" (October 24, 1997). *L'Osservatore Romano,* English edition, October 29, 1997, 2.

———. "Address to the General Assembly of the United Nations Organization" (October 5, 1995). http://www.vatican.va/holy_father/john_paul_ii/speeches/1995/october/documents/hf_jp-ii_spe_05101995_address-to-uno_en.html.

———. "Address to the International Theological Commission" (December 5, 1983). In *Human Rights in the Teaching of the Church: From John XXIII to John Paul II,* edited by George Filibeck, 40. Vatican City: Libreria Editrice Vaticana, 1994.

———. Encyclical letter *Centesimus Annus.* Rome: Libreria Editrice Vaticana, 1991.

———. Apostolic exhortation *Christifideles Laici.* Rome: Libreria Editrice Vaticana, 1988.

———. *Crossing the Threshold of Hope.* Edited by Vittorio Messorio. Translated from the Italian *Varcare la soglia della speranza* by Jenny McPhee and Martha McPhee. New York: Alfred A. Knopf, 1994.

———. Encyclical letter *Dives in Misericordia.* Rome: Libreria Editrice Vaticana, 1980.

———. Encyclical letter *Evangelium Vitae.* Rome: Libreria Editrice Vaticana, 1995.

———. Encyclical letter *Fides et Ratio.* Rome: Libreria Editrice Vaticana, 1998.

———. General Audience of Wednesday, November 24, 1999. *L'Osservatore Romano,* English edition, December 1, 1999, 11.

———. *Gift and Mystery.* Nairobi: Paulines Publications Africa, 1996.

———. *Holy Thursday Letter to Priests.* Rome: Libreria Editrice Vaticana, 1996.

———. *Holy Thursday Letter to Priests.* Rome: Libreria Editrice Vaticana, 1997.

———. Encyclical letter *Laborem Exercens.* Rome: Libreria Editrice Vaticana, 1981.

———. *Letter to Families* (1994). http://www.vatican.va/holy_father/john_paul_ii/letters/documents/hf_jp-ii_let_02021994_families_en.html.

———. Apostolic exhortation *Reconciliatio et Paenitentia.* Rome: Libreria Editrice Vaticana, 1984.

———. Encyclical letter *Redemptor Hominis.* Rome: Libreria Editrice Vaticana, 1979.

———. Encyclical letter *Sollicitudo Rei Socialis.* Rome: Libreria Editrice Vaticana, 1987.

———. Encyclical letter *Ut Unum Sint* (1995). http://www.vatican.va/edocs/ENG0221/_P7.HTM.

———. Encyclical letter *Veritatis Splendor* (August 6, 1993). http://www.vatican.va/edocs/ENG0222/_INDEX.HTM.

Johnson, Paul. *Pope John Paul II and the Catholic Restoration.* New York: St. Martin's Press, 1981.

Johnston, George Sim. "JPII's Personalism Speaks to a Post-Christian World." *National Catholic Register* 73/40 (October 5–11, 1997): 7.

Kant, Immanuel. *Grounding for the Metaphysics of Morals.* Translated by James W. Ellington. Indianapolis: Hackett, 1981.

Karris, Robert J. "The Gospel According to Luke." In *The New Jerome Biblical Commentary,* edited by Raymond E. Brown, Joseph A. Fitzmyer, and Roland E. Murphy, 675–721. London: Geoffrey Chapman, 1989.

Keys, Mary M. "Personal Dignity and the Common Good: A Twentieth-Century Thomistic Dialogue." In *Catholicism, Liberalism, and Communitarianism: The Catholic Intellectual Tradition and the Moral Foundations of Democracy,* edited by Kenneth L. Grasso, Gerard V. Bradley, and Robert P. Hunt, 173–96. Lanham, Md.: Rowman & Littlefield, 1995.

Kilner, John F. "Hurdles for Natural Law Ethics: Lessons from Grotius." *American Journal of Jurisprudence* 28 (1983): 149–68.

Kirk, Russell. *Redeeming the Time.* Wilmington, Del.: ISI Books, 1996.

———. *Rights and Duties: Reflections on Our Conservative Constitution.* Dallas: Spence, 1997.

Lacroix, Jean. *Le personalisme comme anti-idéologie.* Paris, 1972.

Lasanta, Pedro Jesús. *Los derechos humanos en Juan Pablo II.* Madrid: Ediciones Palabra, 1995.

Lasch, Christopher. *The Culture of Narcissism: American Life in an Age of Diminishing Expectations.* New York: Norton, 1978.

Lebech, Anne Mette Maria. "Clarification of the Notion of Dignity." In *The Dignity of the Dying Person: Proceedings of the Fifth Assembly of the Pontifical Academy for Life,* edited by Juan Vial Correa and Elio Sgreccia, 441–55. Vatican City: Libreria Editrice Vaticana, 2000.

Lewis, C. S. *The Abolition of Man: How Education Develops Man's Sense of Morality.* New York: Macmillan, 1947.

———. *The Four Loves.* London: Harper Collins, 1960.

———. *The Problem of Pain*. London: Fount Paperbacks, 1940.
Locke, John. *Two Treatises of Government* (1690). 2nd ed. Edited by Peter Laslett. Cambridge: Cambridge University Press, 1967.
Lubac, Henri de. *The Splendour of the Church*. London: Sheed & Ward, 1956.
Maciel, Marcial. *Salterio de mis días*. Rome: Ediciones CES, 1991.
MacIntyre, Alasdair C. *After Virtue: A Study of Moral Theory*. 2nd ed. London: Gerald Duckworth, 1985.
———. *Are There Any Natural Rights?* Brunswick, Maine: Bowdain College, 1983.
———. "Community, Law, and the Idiom and Rhetoric of Rights." *Listening* 26 (1991): 96–110.
———. *Dependent Rational Animals*. Chicago: Open Court, 1999.
———. "Justice: New Theory and Some Old Questions." *Boston University Law Review* 52 (1972): 330–34.
———. "Theories of Natural Law in the Culture of Advanced Modernity." In *Common Truths: New Perspectives on Natural Law*, edited by Edward B. McLean, 91–115. Wilmington, Del.: ISI Books, 2000.
———. *Three Rival Versions of Moral Enquiry: Encyclopaedia, Genealogy, and Tradition: Being Gifford Lectures Delivered in the University of Edinburgh in 1988*. Notre Dame, Ind.: University of Notre Dame Press, 1990.
———. *Whose Justice? Which Rationality?* Notre Dame, Ind.: Notre Dame University Press, 1988.
MacPherson, C. B. "Natural Rights and Justice in Hobbes and Locke." In *Political Theory and the Rights of Man*, edited by David D. Raphael, 1–15. Bloomington: Indiana University Press, 1967.
Mahoney, John. *The Making of Moral Theology: A Study of the Roman Catholic Tradition*. Martin D'Arcy Memorial Lectures, 1981–1982. Oxford: Clarendon Press, 1989.
Maritain, Jacques. *Man and the State* (1951). Washington, D.C.: Catholic University of America Press, 1998.
———. *The Person and the Common Good*. Translated from the French *La personne et le bien commun* (1947) by John J. Fitzgerald. Notre Dame, Ind.: University of Notre Dame Press, 1985.
———. *The Rights of Man and Natural Law*. Glasgow: Robert Maclehose, 1945.
Massini Correas, Carlos I. "Filosofía y «antifilosofía» de los derechos humanos." In *Razón y libertad: homenaje a Antonio Millán-Puelles*, edited by Rafael Alvira, 378–400. Madrid: Rialp, 1990.
Maximus the Confessor, St. "The Three Laws: Question 64 to Thalasius." In *Patrologia Graeca*, edited by J.-P. Migne, 724–28. Paris, 1857.
May, William. *An Introduction to Moral Theology*. Huntington, Ind.: Our Sunday Visitor, 1994.
McDermott, John M., ed. *The Thought of John Paul II: A Collection of Essays and Studies*. Rome: Editrice Pontificia Università Gregoriana, 1993.
McInerny, Ralph. "Natural Law and Human Rights." *American Journal of Jurisprudence* 36 (1991): 1–14.
McLean, Edward B., ed. *Common Truths: New Perspectives on Natural Law*. Wilmington, Del.: ISI Books, 2000.
McNellis, Paul. "'Rights' vs. Common Good." *Human Life Review* 23/1 (Winter 1997): 79–90.
Meilaender, Gilbert. "Still Waiting for Benedict." *First Things* 96 (October 1999): 48–55.
Melina, Livio. *La morale: Tra crisi e rinnovamento*. Rome: Pontificia Università Lateranense, 1993.

Menken, Yaakov. "Valuing Life." *Jewish World Review,* October 8, 1999, *http://www.jewishworldreview.com/1099/menken1.asp.*
Meyers, D. G. *The Inflated Self.* New York: Seabury, 1981.
Midgley, E. B. F. "Natural Law and Fundamental Rights." *American Journal of Jurisprudence* 21 (1976): 144–55.
Miller, J. Michael, ed. *The Encyclicals of John Paul II.* Huntington, Ind.: Our Sunday Visitor, 1996.
Miranda González de Echavarri, Gonzalo. *Respuesta de amor: Manual de teología moral fundamental.* Vol 1. Mexico City: Nueva Evangelización, 1998.
Montemayor, Giulio de. *Storia del diritto naturale.* Milan: Remo Sandron, 1911.
Montgomery, John Warwick. *Human Rights and Human Dignity.* Edmonton: Canadian Institute for Law, Theology, and Public Policy, 1995.
Mounier, Emmanuel. *Personalism.* Translated from the French *Le personnalisme* (1950) by Philip Mairet. Notre Dame, Ind.: University of Notre Dame Press, 1952.
———. *A Personalist Manifesto.* Translated by the monks of St. John's Abbey. New York: Longmans, Green, 1938.
Murray, John Courtney. *We Hold These Truths: Catholic Reflections on the American Proposition* (1960). Garden City, N.Y.: Image Books, 1964.
Negro, Dalmacio. *La tradición liberal del estado.* Madrid: Unión Editorial, 1995.
Neuhaus, Richard John. *The Catholic Moment: The Paradox of the Church in the Postmodern World.* New York: Harper & Row, 1987.
Nisbet, Robert. "Uneasy Cousins." In *Freedom and Virtue,* edited by George W. Carey, 38–54. Wilmington, Del.: Intercollegiate Studies Institute, 1998.
O'Brien, David J., and Thomas A. Shannon, eds. *Catholic Social Thought: The Documentary Heritage.* Maryknoll, N.Y.: Orbis Books, 1995.
O'Donovan, Joan Lockwood. "The Concept of Rights in Christian Moral Discourse." In *A Preserving Grace: Protestants, Catholics, and Natural Law,* edited by Michael Cromartie, 143–56. Grand Rapids, Mich.: Ethics and Public Policy Center/William B. Eerdmans, 1997.
Olafson, Frederick A., ed. *Society, Law, and Morality.* Englewood Cliffs, N.J.: Prentice Hall, 1961.
Olimon Nolasco, Manuel. *Los derechos humanos.* Mexico City: IMDOSOC, 1987.
O'Neill, Onora. "Justice and the Virtues." *American Journal of Jurisprudence* 34 (1989): 1–18.
Outka, Gene. *Agape: An Ethical Analysis.* New Haven: Yale University Press, 1972.
Paine, Thomas. *Rights of Man* (1791). London: Wordsworth, 1996.
Peeters, Marguerite A. "Playing Games with Human Rights." *Catholic World Report* (November 1996): 44–47.
Pereña Vicente, Luciano. *Los derechos humanos.* Cuadernos BAC 19. Madrid: Biblioteca de Autores Cristianos, 1979.
———. *Derechos y deberes entre indios y españoles en el nuevo mundo según Francisco de Vitoria.* Salamanca: Cátedra V Centenario, 1992.
———. "Proceso a la conquista de América: Veredicto de la escuela de Salamanca, nuevas claves de interpretación histórica." Inaugural lecture of the 1987–1988 academic year in the Leo XIII Faculty of Politics and Sociology, Pontifical University of Salamanca, Madrid, 1987.
Perry, Michael J. *The Idea of Human Rights: Four Inquiries.* New York: Oxford University Press, 1998.
Peschke, C. Henry. *A Presentation of General Moral Theology in the Light of Vatican II.* Vol. 1 of *Christian Ethics.* Dublin: C. Goodliffe Neale, 1977.

———. *A Presentation of Special Moral Theology in the Light of Vatican II.* Vol. 2 of *Christian Ethics.* Dublin: C. Goodliffe Neale, 1978.

Pieper, Josef. *The Four Cardinal Virtues.* Notre Dame, Ind.: University of Notre Dame Press, 1966.

———. *Josef Pieper: An Anthology.* Translated from the German *Josef Pieper: Lesebuch* by Lothar Krauth. San Francisco: Ignatius Press, 1989.

———. *Leisure: The Basis of Culture* (1952). Translated from the German *Musse und Kult* by Alexander Dru. Indianapolis: Liberty Fund, 1999.

Pinckaers, Servais. *The Sources of Christian Ethics.* Translated from the French *Les sources de la morale chrétienne* (1985) by Mary Thomas Noble. Edinburgh: T & T Clark, 1995.

Pollack, Erwin H., ed. *Human Rights.* Buffalo: Jay Stewart, 1971.

Półtawski, Andrzej. "The Epistemological Locus of Moral Values." In *Moral Truth and Moral Tradition: Essays in Honour of Peter Geach and Elizabeth Anscombe,* edited by Luke Gormally, 53–67. Blackrock, Ireland: Four Courts Press, 1994.

Pontifical Biblical Commission. *The Interpretation of the Bible in the Church.* Rome: Libreria Editrice Vaticana, 1994.

Pontifical Council Cor Unum. *Refugees: A Challenge to Solidarity.* Rome, 1992.

Pontifical Council Iustitia et Pax. *Human Rights: Historical and Theological Reflections.* Rome, 1990.

Porter, Jean. *Moral Action and Christian Ethics.* Cambridge: Cambridge University Press, 1995.

———. *The Recovery of Virtue: The Relevance of Aquinas for Christian Ethics.* Louisville: John Knox Press, 1990.

Possenti, Vittorio. "Diritti umani e natura umana." *Rivista di filosofia neo-scolastica* 2 (1995): 249–59.

Raphael, David D., ed. *Political Theory and the Rights of Man.* Bloomington: Indiana University Press, 1967.

Ratzinger, Joseph. *Gospel, Catechesis, Catechism: Sidelights on the Catechism of the Catholic Church.* Translated from the German *Evangelium-Katechese-Katechismus* (1995). San Francisco: Ignatius Press, 1997.

———. *Journey towards Easter.* Retreat given in the Vatican in the presence of Pope John Paul II. Translated from the Italian *Il cammino Pasquale* (1985) by Mary Groves. Slough, England: St. Paul Publications, 1987.

———. *Many Religions—One Covenant: Israel, the Church, and the World.* Translated from the German *Die Vielfalt der Religionen und der Eine Bund* (1998) by Graham Harrison. San Francisco: Ignatius Press, 1999.

Rawls, John. *Collected Papers.* Cambridge: Harvard University Press, 1999.

———. *The Law of Peoples.* Cambridge: Harvard University Press, 1999.

———. *Political Liberalism.* Cambridge: Harvard University Press, 1999.

———. *A Theory of Justice* (1971). Rev. ed. Oxford: Oxford University Press, 1999.

Raz, Joseph. *The Morality of Freedom.* Oxford: Clarendon Press, 1986.

Regan, Thomas. *The Case for Animal Rights.* Berkeley: University of California Press, 1983.

Richards, David A. J. *The Moral Criticism of Law.* Encino, Calif.: Dickenson, 1977.

Rieff, Philip. *The Triumph of the Therapeutic.* New York: Harper & Row, 1966.

Rigobello, Armando. "Personalismo." In *Dizionario teologico interdisciplinare,* 2:726–30. Torino: Marietti Editori, 1977.

———. "Personalismo." In *Studio ed insegnamento della filosofia,* 2:177–90. Rome: AVE-UCIIM Editori, 1966.

Robertson, Arthur H. "The European Convention on Human Rights." In *The International Protection of Human Rights,* edited by Evan Luard. London: Thames & Hudson, 1967.

Robertson, David. *A Dictionary of Human Rights*. London: Europa, 1997.
Rommen, Heinrich A. *The Natural Law: A Study in Legal and Social History and Philosophy*. Translated from the German *Die ewige Wiederkehr des Naturrechts* (1936) by Thomas R. Hanley. Indianapolis: Liberty Fund, 1998.
Rorty, Richard. "Human Rights, Rationality, and Sentimentality." In *On Human Rights*, edited by Stephen Shute and Susan Hurley, 111–34. New York: Basic Books, 1993.
Schaff, Philip, ed. *A Select Library of the Christian Church*. Peabody, Mass.: Hendrickson, 1995.
Schall, James V. "Human Rights: The 'So-Called' Judaeo-Christian Tradition." *Communio: International Catholic Review* 8/1 (Spring 1981): *51–61*.
———. "Second Thoughts on Human Rights." *Faith and Reason* (Winter 1975–1976): 44–59.
Schlesinger, Arthur, Jr. "Human Rights and the American Tradition." *Foreign Affairs* 3 (1979): 502–3.
Schmitz, Kenneth L. *At the Center of the Human Drama: The Philosophical Anthropology of Karol Wojtyła/Pope John Paul II*. Washington, D.C.: Catholic University of America Press, 1993.
Schönborn, Christoph. *God's Human Face: The Christ Icon*. Originally published as *L'icone du Christ: Fondements théologiques élaborés entre le Ier et le I^e Concile de Nicée (325–787 A.D.)* (1976). Translated from the German *Die Christus-Ikone: Eine theologische Hinfuhrung* (1984) by Lothar Krauth. San Francisco: Ignatius Press, 1994.
Shapiro, Ian. *The Evolution of Rights in Liberal Theory*. Cambridge: Cambridge University Press, 1986.
Sheed, Francis J. *To Know Christ Jesus* (1962). San Francisco: Ignatius Press, 1992.
Shoham, Shlomo, ed. *Of Law and Man: Essays in Honor of Haim H. Cohn*. New York: Sabra Books, 1971.
Shrader-Frechette, Kristin. "MacIntyre on Human Rights." *Modern Schoolman* 79 (November 2001): 1–21.
Shute, Stephen, and Susan Hurley, eds. *On Human Rights: The Oxford Amnesty Lectures, 1993*. New York: Basic Books, 1993.
Singer, Peter. *Practical Ethics*. New York: Cambridge University Press, 1993.
———. *Rethinking Life and Death: The Collapse of Our Traditional Ethics*. Oxford: Oxford University Press, 1994.
Smith, Janet. "Rights, the Person, and Conscience in the Catechism." *Catholic Dossier* 3/1 (January–February 1997): 29–37.
Spaemann, Robert. *Basic Moral Concepts*. Translated from the German *Moralische Grundbegriffe* (1982) by T. J. Armstrong. London: Routledge, 1991.
———. "Christian Ethics of Responsibility." In *Moral Truth and Moral Tradition: Essays in Honour of Peter Geach and Elizabeth Anscombe*, edited by Luke Gormally, 133–48. Blackrock, Ireland: Four Courts Press, 1994.
———. *Personen: Versuche über den Unterschied zwischen "etwas" und "jemand."* Stuttgart: Klett-Cotta, 1996.
Spencer, Herbert. *The Man versus the State: With Six Essays on Government, Society, and Freedom* (1843–1891). Indianapolis: Liberty Classics, 1981.
Strauss, Leo. *Natural Right and History*. Chicago: University of Chicago Press, 1953.
———. *What Is Political Philosophy? and Other Studies*. Chicago: University of Chicago Press, 1959.
Stunz, William J. "When Rights Are Wrong." *First Things* 62 (April 1996): 14–18.
Thomas à Kempis. *The Imitation of Christ*. Translated by the Daughters of St. Paul. Boston: St. Paul Editions, 1983.

Thomas Aquinas. *Commentary on the Nichomachean Ethics.* Translated by C. I. Litzinger. Chicago: Regnery, 1964.

———. *Commentary on St. John.* Vol. 1. Translated by James A. Weisheipl and F. R. Larcher. Albany, N.Y.: Magi Books, 1980.

———. *Commentary on St. Paul's Epistle to the Galatians.* Translated by F. R. Larcher. Albany, N.Y.: Magi Books, 1966.

———. *The Disputed Questions on Truth.* 3 vols. Translated by Robert William Mulligan, James V. McGlynn, and Robert W. Schmidt. Chicago: Henry Regnery, 1952–1954.

———. *The Literal Exposition of Job: A Scriptural Commentary concerning Providence.* Translated by Anthony Damico. Atlanta: Scholars Press, 1989.

———. *On Charity.* Translated by L. H. Kendzierski. Milwaukee: Marquette University Press, 1960.

———. *On the Power of God.* Translated by English Dominican Fathers. London: Burns, Oates, and Washbourne, 1932–1934.

———. *Questions on the Soul.* Translated by James H. Robb. Milwaukee: Marquette University Press, 1984.

———. *Summa Contra Gentiles.* Translated by English Dominicans. London: Burns, Oates, and Washbourne, 1934.

———. *Summa Theologiæ.* Translated by English Dominicans. London: Burns, Oates, and Washbourne, 1912–1936; repr., New York: Benziger, 1947–1948; repr., New York: Christian Classics, 1981.

Truyol y Serra, A. *Los derechos humanos: Declaraciones y convenios internacionales.* Madrid: Tecnos, 1994.

Tuck, Richard. *Natural Rights Theories: Their Origin and Development.* Cambridge: Cambridge University Press, 1979.

Vial Correa, Juan, and Elio Sgreccia, eds. *The Dignity of the Dying Person: Proceedings of the Fifth Assembly of the Pontifical Academy for Life.* From an assembly held in the Vatican City, February 24–27, 1999. Vatican City: Libreria Editrice Vaticana, 2000.

Villagrasa, Jesús. "La antropología de la Carta a las familias del Papa Juan Pablo II." *Christus* 4/1 (1994): 101–9.

Villa-Vicencio, Charles. *A Theology of Reconstruction: Nation-Building and Human Rights.* Cambridge: Cambridge University Press, 1992.

Villey, Michel. "Abrégé du droit naturel classique." *Archives de philosophie du droit* 6 (1961): 25–72.

———. *Le droit et les droits de l'homme.* Paris: Presses Universitaires de France, 1983.

Vitz, Paul C. *Psychology as Religion: The Cult of Self-Worship.* 2nd ed. Grand Rapids, Mich.: William B. Eerdmans, 1994.

Waldron, Jeremy. "A Right to Do Wrong." *Ethics* 92 (1981): 21–39.

Watkins, Michelle, and Ralph McInerny. "Jacques Maritain and the Rapprochement of Liberalism and Communitarianism." In *Catholicism, Liberalism, and Communitarianism: The Catholic Intellectual Tradition and the Moral Foundations of Democracy,* edited by Kenneth L. Grasso, Gerard V. Bradley, and Robert P. Hunt, 151–72. Lanham, Md.: Rowman & Littlefield, 1995.

Weigel, George S. *The Final Revolution: The Resistance Church and the Collapse of Communism.* New York: Oxford University Press, 1992.

———. *Soul of the World: Notes on the Future of Public Catholicism.* Grand Rapids, Mich.: Ethics and Public Policy Center and William. B. Eerdmans, 1996.

———. *Witness to Hope: The Biography of Pope John Paul II.* New York: HarperCollins, 1999.

Weinreb, Lloyd L. "Natural Law and Rights." In *Natural Law Theory: Contemporary Essays*, edited by Robert P. George, 278–303. Oxford: Oxford University Press, 1995.
Westberg, Daniel. "The Reformed Tradition and Natural Law." In *A Preserving Grace: Protestants, Catholics, and Natural Law*, edited by Michael Cromartie, 103–17. Grand Rapids, Mich.: Ethics and Public Policy Center/William B. Eerdmans, 1997.
Whitehead, John W. *The Second American Revolution*. Elgin, Ill.: David C. Cook, 1982.
Williams, Thomas D. "Capital Punishment and the Just Society." *Catholic Dossier* 4/5 (September–October 1998): 28–36.
———. "Values, Virtues, and John Paul II." *First Things* 72 (April 1997): 29–32.
Wojtyła, Karol. *The Acting Person*. Translated from the Polish *Osoba i czyn* (1969) by Andrzej Potocki. Dordrecht, the Netherlands: D. Reidel, 1979.
———. "The Family as a Community of Persons." Translated from the Polish "Rodzina jako 'communio personarum'" (*Ateneum Kaplanskie* 66 [1974]: 347–61) by Theresa Sandok. In *Person and Community: Selected Essays*, vol. 4 of *Catholic Thought from Lublin*, edited by Andrew N. Woznicki, 315–27. New York: Peter Lang, 1993.
———. "The Human Person and Natural Law." Translated from the Polish "Osoba ludzka a prawo naturalne" (*Roczniki Filozoficzne* 18/2 (1970): 53–59) by Theresa Sandok. In *Person and Community: Selected Essays*, vol. 4 of *Catholic Thought from Lublin*, edited by Andrew N. Woznicki, 181–85. New York: Peter Lang, 1993.
———. *Love and Responsibility*. Translated from the Polish *Miłość I Odpowiedzialność* by H. T. Willetts. New York: Farrar, Straus, & Giroux, 1995.
———. *Ocena możliwości zbudowania etyki chrześijańskiej przy założeniach systemu Maksu Schelera* (An Evaluation of the Possibility of Constructing a Christian Ethics on the Basis of the System of Max Scheler). Lublin: Towarzystwo Naukowe KUL, 1959.
———. "On the Dignity of the Human Person." A talk broadcast in Polish over Vatican Radio, October 19, 1964. Translated from the Polish "O godnosci osoby ludzkiej" (*Notificationes a Curia Principis Metropolitae Cracoviensis* [1964]: 287–89) by Theresa Sandok. In *Person and Community: Selected Essays*, vol. 4 of *Catholic Thought from Lublin*, edited by Andrew N. Woznicki, 177–80. New York: Peter Lang, 1993.
———. "The Personal Structure of Self-Determination." A paper presented at an international conference on St. Thomas Aquinas, Rome-Naples, April 17–24, 1974. Translated from the Polish "Osobowa struktura samostanowienia" (*Roczniki Filozoficzne* 29.2 [1964]: 5–12) by Theresa Sandok. In *Person and Community: Selected Essays*, vol. 4 of *Catholic Thought from Lublin*, edited by Andrew N. Woznicki, 187–95. New York: Peter Lang, 1993.
———. *Person and Community: Selected Essays*. Vol. 4 of *Catholic Thought from Lublin*, edited by Andrew N. Woznicki. Translated by Theresa Sandok. New York: Peter Lang, 1993.
———. "The Separation of Experience from the Act in Ethics: In the Philosophy of Immanuel Kant and Max Scheler." Translated from the Polish "Problem oderwania przezycia od aktu w etyce na tle pogladow Kanta i Schelera" (*Roczniki Filozoficzne* 5/3 [1955–1957]: 113–40) by Theresa Sandok. In *Person and Community: Selected Essays*, vol. 4 of *Catholic Thought from Lublin*, edited by Andrew N. Woznicki, 23–44. New York: Peter Lang, 1993.
———. "Subjectivity and the Irreducible in the Human Being." A paper sent to an international conference in Paris, June 13–14, 1975. Translated from the Polish "Podmiotowosci i 'to, co nieredukowalne' w czlowieku" (*Ethos* 1/2–3 [1988]: 21–28) by Theresa Sandok. In *Person and Community: Selected Essays*, vol. 4 of *Catholic Thought from Lublin*, edited by Andrew N. Woznicki, 209–17. New York: Peter Lang, 1993.
———. "Thomistic Personalism." A paper presented at the Fourth Annual Philosophy Week, Catholic University of Lublin, February 17, 1961. Translated from the Polish "Personalizm

tomistyczny" (*Znak* 13 [1961)]: 664–75) by Theresa Sandok. In *Person and Community: Selected Essays,* vol. 4 of *Catholic Thought from Lublin,* edited by Andrew N. Woznicki, 165–75. New York: Peter Lang, 1993.

Woznicki, Andrew N., ed. *Person and Community: Selected Essays: Selected Essays.* Vol. 4 of *Catholic Thought from Lublin.* New York: Peter Lang, 1993.

Zalba, Marcellinus. *Theologiae Moralis Compendium I.* Madrid: BAC, 1958.

INDEX

abortion, xv, 4, 77, 89–90, 96, 99, 130, 132, 287–89
actus humanus, 135
Adeo Nota, 33
amor benevolentiae, 166–67, 169–71, 173–74, 181
amor complacentiae, 166–67, 169–70
amor concupiscentiae, 166–67, 169–71, 181
animals and rights, xv, 4, 11, 22, 126–27, 129, 131, 133–34, 136, 142, 144, 149, 158, 205, 207, 210, 219, 241, 246, 254, 271–72
Antigone, 225
Arcanum, 35
Aristotle, 56, 86, 112, 116, 126, 139, 151, 153, 167, 173–74, 176–77, 187, 219, 230, 253, 257, 259–62, 264, 276–79, 285, 296
Aristotelianism, 63, 86, 115, 126, 152–53, 172–74, 239, 261, 265
Ashley, Benedict M., 27, 205, 286, 297–98
assisted suicide, xv, 77
Augustine, Saint, 10, 162–63, 193, 207, 223, 225, 257–58, 302–3, 313

basic human goods, 43, 103, 171–72, 176, 196–97, 244–45, 274, 280–81, 291–92, 307. *See also* values, basic
Bill of Rights, 21, 58
Becker, Oskar, 115
Benedict XIV, Pope, 33
Beneficentia, 193–94
Benestad, J. Brian, xiv
Benn, Stanley I., 12, 16

Bentham, Jeremy, 16, 54, 257
Berke, Matthew, 17, 103, 242
Berns, Walter, 58
Bettati, Mario, 30
Bird, Otto A., 257–58
Black, Virginia, 150, 153
Blondel, Maurice, 112
Bloom, Allan, 79
Boethius, A. M. Severinus, 121, 122, 135, 153
Bonaventure, Saint, 121, 155
bonum mihi, 119, 172, 281
Boyle, Joseph, Jr., 156, 233, 251
Bowne, B. P., 112–13
Braaten, Carl E., 227
Bradley, Gerard V., 300
Buber, Martin, 108, 144–45
Buttiglione, Rocco, 114, 115

Caffarra, Carlo, 74–75, 136, 138, 141, 175, 194, 197, 202, 264, 278, 285–86, 294, 297
Calvin, John, 226–27
Cajetan, Thomas de Vio, 262
Camus, Albert, 112
Canavan, Francis S., 46, 80, 297–98
Cassin, René, 29
Catechism of the Catholic Church, xiv, 20, 23–24, 31, 74–75, 96, 148, 177, 183, 200, 204, 209, 211–12, 222–23, 225–26, 231, 235–36, 238, 248, 249, 251–52, 258, 276–77, 283, 315–16
Cathrein, Victor, 8, 13

Centesimus Annus, 17, 28, 30, 42–43, 103, 153–54, 158, 231, 316
charity, 28, 75, 95, 102, 104, 157, 165, 173, 175, 195, 202, 212, 271, 279, 301, 303–4, 310, 314, 316
Christie, Agatha, 89
Christifideles Laici, 137, 148, 160, 214
Christology, 117, 121
Cicero, Marcus Tullius, 225, 258, 316
Clifford, Richard J., 210
Code of Canon Law, xiv, 31, 209
Commissum Divinitus, 34
common good, 18, 23, 24, 35, 40, 42, 50, 70, 72, 74–75, 82, 85–87, 94–95, 101–2, 120, 174–81, 222, 237, 261–63, 267, 279, 282–83, 299–300, 317, 320
communio, 140, 141, 211
Compagnoni, Francesco, 9
Composta, Dario, 16
Comte, Auguste, 91, 110
concupiscence, 165–70, 173, 177
Conrad-Martius, Hedwig, 115
conscience, vii, 15, 18–21, 38, 40, 44, 88, 90, 99–100, 120, 137, 145, 148, 154, 220, 223, 228–29, 242, 249, 251–52, 254, 277, 279, 284, 288, 305–6; freedom of, 42, 90, 99, 198
Craycraft, Kenneth R., Jr., xiv, 50,
culture, viii, x, xvi, 38, 45, 56, 62–63, 78–79, 133, 219, 226, 228, 236, 245, 259, 318, 320
Cuomo, Mario, 287–88

Darwin, Charles, 111
De Finance, Joseph, 7, 17, 23–24, 73, 93, 110, 159, 170, 182, 185, 227, 244, 246, 261–62, 268–69, 271–72, 278, 282, 284–85, 288, 298
De Molina, Luis, 68
De Rougemont, Denis, 114
De Vitoria, Francisco, 52, 64, 79, 225, 257
debitum, 73, 75, 256, 265, 269, 273–74
Decalogue, 60, 75, 106, 183, 199–201, 203, 247–48, 254–55

Declaration of Independence, 18, 58
Declaration of the Rights of Man and of the Citizen, 33, 58
Dei Filius, 204–5, 250
Dignitatis Humanae, xiii, 18, 24, 31, 39, 41–42, 45, 92, 148, 177
dignity, human, xiv, xvi, 5, 20, 27–28, 37–45, 66, 75, 85, 92, 95, 102, 106–7, 108–9, 111, 112, 116–22, 124, 128–29, 132, 137, 145–48, 152–60, 163–64, 174, 182, 192–93, 198–200, 202–4, 206, 212–16, 230, 233, 256, 282–83, 195, 301–3, 305, 319–20; according to Aquinas, 154–55, 157–60; according to Bonaventure, 155; according to Hobbes, 149; according to Kant, 153–56; and conscience, 90, 137, 154; as bridge between anthropology and ethics, 106, 145–47, 150; as excellence, 150–51, 158, 208; as image of God, 206–9, 212; Christological dimension, 212–16; death with dignity, 149; in *Dives in Misericordia*, 156–57; in *Gaudium et Spes*, 154, 206, 216; in *Veritatis Splendor*, 233; levels of, 207–9; moral, 156–57; of adopted sonship, 208–9; of sinners, 157–60; of work, 176; ontological, 156–57
Diuturnum Illud, 37
Dives in Misericordia, 156–57, 187
Donum Vitae, 132
Douglas, Stephen, 287–88
Dubay, Thomas, 179
Dulles, Avery, x, 41
duty, 13, 15, 18, 23, 26, 37–38, 42, 46, 50, 55, 82–83, 88, 90–96, 104, 266, 274, 289–91, 296, 303, 311; as component of justice, 247, 248, 264, 265, 266, 267, 276; as correlative to rights, 8, 11, 13, 18, 25, 292, 293, 294, 295, 297, 298; assignment of, 25, 299, 300, 305, 306; distinguished from obligation, 7; distinguished from responsibility, 311–13, 317; legal, 16, 19, 276, 294; moral, 15, 18, 19, 24, 39, 60,

87, 89, 276, 288, 292, 293, 294, 295, 306; natural, 15, 59, 60, 61, 267, 274, 294; to love, 182, 185

E Supremi, 36
Edgar, William, 217
Elsbernd, Mary, 32–37
Enlightenment, 10, 65–66, 71–72, 78, 83–84, 91, 150, 217
equality: arithmetic, 261, 300; human, 23, 29, 40, 66, 69, 73, 77, 100–101, 132, 149, 153, 175, 198, 209, 259–60, 272–73, 315
eudaimonism, 180–81
euthanasia, xv, 77, 149
Evangelium Vitae, 43, 157, 210

Feinberg, Joel, 104
Fides et Ratio, 140, 155, 221, 228
finis ultimus, 85, 195
Finnis, John, 3, 24, 26, 64, 100–102, 132, 172, 178, 200–202, 239, 243–45, 260–63, 267, 280–81, 286, 292, 317
First Vatican Council, 204
Fletcher, Joseph, 27
Fortin, Ernest L., 46, 52, 82–100, 153–54, 156, 195, 224–25
fortitude, 247, 258, 262, 276–78,
French Revolution, 29–30, 33, 66
Freud, Sigmund, 111, 113, 220
friendship, 140, 165–70, 172–74, 178, 187, 243–44, 271, 310, 314–16; with God, 196

Galilei, Galileo, 56
Gaudium et Spes, xiii, 31, 39–41, 45, 80, 137, 140, 142–43, 148, 151, 154, 180, 196, 202, 206, 208, 212–14, 216, 236–37, 249, 252
George, Robert P., 25, 69, 72, 76–77, 80, 217, 287–91
Gerson, Jean, 68
Gilson, Étienne, 110, 112, 118, 135–36
Glendon, Mary Ann, xiv, xv, 18–19, 31, 46, 74, 102–3, 289
Goethe, Johann Wolfgang von, 76

Gormley, W. Paul, 30
Grasso, Kenneth L., 49, 50, 72, 154, 206
Graves de Communi, 37
Gravissimo Officii Munere, 36
Gregory XVI, Pope, 34, 228
Grisez, Germain, 9–12, 26, 156, 170–72, 243–44, 281, 293–94
Grotius, Hugo, 9–12, 68, 126, 139–40, 224–25, 257, 288
Guardini, Romano, 108
Guilhaudis, Jean-François, 30

Hamel, Edouard, 32, 204, 208
Hartmann, Nikolai, 115
Heidegger, Martin, 115
Hegel, Georg W. F., 110–12, 116
Hering, H., 273
heteronomy, 233
Hirsch, Shamson Raphael, 210
Hittinger, Russell, 170–72, 227–28, 230, 233, 235, 281–82, 285
Hobbes, Thomas, 58, 64, 66, 68, 72, 78, 82–85, 106, 111, 149–50, 257, 286, 290
Howison, G. H., 113
Humani Generis, 204–5, 250–51
Humanum Genus, 37
Hume, David, 146, 150, 237, 257
Husserl, Edmund, 114–16
hypostasis, 121–22, 154–55

Il fermo proposito, 36
imago Dei, 206–8, 212
Immensa Pastorum, 33
Immortale Dei, 37
immunities, 16, 26
Ingarden, Roman, 115
Inscrutabili, 37
Irenaeus, Saint, 164, 248
ius, 23, 34, 36, 68, 185, 230, 258, 265, 272–73, 285

Jesus Christ, xiv, 38–41, 80, 93, 102–3, 106–7, 117, 143, 171, 182–83, 185, 189–91,

Jesus Christ (*continued*), 195–96, 200, 203–6, 209, 211–16, 301–4, 307–10, 312, 318
John Paul II, Pope, xiv, 17, 20, 24, 26, 28, 30, 41–46, 60, 92, 102–3, 115–18, 137, 140, 143, 148, 153–58, 160, 163–64, 175–76, 180, 183, 186, 188, 193, 200, 206, 211–12, 214, 228, 231, 234–35, 237, 248, 311–12, 316–17
John XXIII, Pope, 18, 23, 28, 37–38, 45–46, 147, 157, 214, 294–95
Johnston, George Sim, 102
justice, 7, 8, 10–13, 16–17, 23–25, 32, 47, 50, 60–63, 66–67, 69, 73–76, 78, 81, 83–84, 90, 92, 94–95, 98, 100, 119, 146, 156, 176, 178, 204–5, 215–16, 218, 227, 230–32, 247–49, 254–87, 296–300, 306, 312, 317–20; according to Rawls, 131; and love, 75, 104, 157, 173, 184–89, 193–97, 248–49, 280, 319; applied only to persons, 271–72; commutative, 73, 260–63, 265, 267, 271, 300; distributive, 73, 260–62, 267, 300; legal, 260, 262–63, 276, 279; political, 230; preeminence of, 276–82; social, 18, 42, 227; theories of, 63, 106, 257–58; toward God, 188–89
Justinian, 258

Kant, Immanuel, 66, 85, 88, 110, 114–15, 119, 153–55, 160–61
Karris, Robert J., 304
Kaye, David, 15
Keys, Mary M., 178, 179, 181
Kierkegaard, Søren, 108, 112
Kirk, Russell, 16–17, 22, 50
Kłósak, Kazimierz, 116
Knudson, A. C., 113
Kuhn, Thomas, 56

Laborem Exercens, 43, 117, 176
Lacrimabili Statu, 37
Lacroix, Jean, 112

Lasch, Christopher, 91
law, 6, 10, 12–13, 67, 69, 73, 95, 262, 311–12; and happiness, 242; anti-sodomy, 191; biological, 229; civil, 15–19, 22–23, 26, 61, 77–78, 224, 263, 276, 289, 292, 294, 297; criminal, 79; definition of, 10, 222–23, 252; divine, x, 9, 58, 61, 64, 66–67, 69, 73–74, 80, 157, 223–24, 230, 233, 247–48; divorce, 17; ecclesiastical, xiv, 31, 209, 224; eternal, 222–23, 233–34, 236–37; evangelical, 224, 226; historical, 110; human, 15–16, 22, 66, 224–25, 230, 234, 247, 313; moral, 15–17, 25, 44–45, 60, 96, 99, 147, 153, 182, 205, 218, 222–24, 226, 228, 233–34, 236, 238, 240, 242–43, 247–49, 252, 255, 260, 283–84; natural, 9, 38–39, 42, 44, 46–47, 59–61, 65–67, 69, 73–74, 80, 83–84, 86, 92, 100, 147, 152, 154, 156, 170, 182–84, 201, 203–5, 216–56, 260, 267–68, 274, 276, 283–85, 300, 313; natural law according to John Calvin, 227; natural law according to Martin Luther, 227; natural law in *Veritatis Splendor*, 234; of nature (physical), 222–23, 228–29, 233; of non-contradiction, 253; of the gift, 142; Old Testament (Torah), 103, 183, 185, 190, 200, 223–25, 248–49, 301; positive, 16, 61, 66, 80, 147, 223–25, 230, 232–33, 256–57, 284–85; private, 70; public, 70; rule of, 17–19, 23, 273; temporal, 222–23; unjust, 231–32; unwritten, 225, 237
Lebech, Anne M. M., 153, 156
Leo XIII, Pope, 35–37, 39, 222–23, 226, 231
Lewis, C. S., 152–53, 165, 219, 232, 238–39, 260
Liberalism, 2, 65–67, 71–72, 78–79, 83–86, 91, 98, 111, 120, 299; the Church and, 32–37
Libertas Praestantissimum, 35, 37, 39, 222–23, 226, 231, 235
liberty, 24, 26, 33, 35, 77, 93, 151, 222, 235,

244, 272, 285, 291–92; as a right, 3, 18, 21, 29, 58, 291; religious, 18, 39, 42, 45, 92, 148, 192
Liguori, Saint Alphonsus, 28
Lincoln, Abraham, 287–88
Locke, John, x, 58, 66, 68, 77–78, 83–84, 86–87, 111, 257
L'Osservatore Romano, 41, 46, 117, 140
Lumen Gentium, 209
Luther, Martin, 227

Maciel, Marcial, 189
MacIntyre, Alasdair C., xiv, 8, 52–65, 139, 152, 172, 214, 230, 241, 243–44, 253, 257, 281
Magisterium, xiii, xvi, 30, 45, 100, 132, 147, 160, 228
Marcel, Gabriel, 112, 114
Maritain, Jacques, viii–x, 72, 108, 110, 114, 126–27, 134, 141–42, 158, 176, 207, 224–27, 235, 237, 240, 257, 283–84, 293, 296–97
Marx, Karl, 111,
marxism, 29, 113, 116
Mater et Magistra, 23, 37, 45, 46, 177
Maximus the Confessor, Saint, 249
Meilaender, Gilbert, 172
Menken, Yaakov, 206, 210
Meshech Chochma, 210
Messori, Vittorio, 20
Meyers, D. G., 91
Milosz, Czeslaw, viii
minimalism: ethical, 15, 186, 306, 311, 313
Miranda González de Echavarri, Gonzalo, 229, 233, 234, 246
Mirari Vos, 34
Mit brennender Sorge, 36, 39
Montgomery, John W., 29–30, 103
moral obligation, 66, 78, 93–94, 99–100, 158, 197, 219, 252, 264, 268, 293, 296–97, 307, 314–15
moral precepts, 28, 98, 235, 238–40, 247, 253–55, 307

moral theology, 9–10, 71, 84, 98–99, 102–3, 115–17, 281
moral virtue(s), 15, 87–88, 247, 249, 256, 258, 262–63, 276–80, 285
Mounier, Emmanuel, 113–14, 143
Murphy, Ronald E., 210–11
Murray, John Courtney, 15–16
Muslim, 8

neighbor, xi, 19, 75, 95, 101, 145, 175, 195–97, 200–201, 260, 266–67, 302–5, 307–9, 314–16, 318; love of, 28, 97, 165, 182–83, 186, 189–91, 195–97, 199–202, 214, 237, 274, 301–3, 305, 307–8, 312–13
Neo-Thomism, 82
Newton, Sir Isaac, 56, 110
Nietzsche, Friedrich, 79, 91, 111–13, 116, 220
nominalism, 52, 95, 102, 114, 225
Non abbiamo bisogno, 36
Nos es muy conocida, 36
Nostra Aetate, 40
noumenon, 110, 115

Ockam, William, 230
O'Donovan, Joan Lockwood, 52, 65–74, 76–81, 83, 91
omission: as moral category, 15, 27, 306–10
Optatam Totius, 102

Pacem in Terris, 18, 23, 28, 37–39, 45–46, 147, 157, 177, 214, 231, 294, 295
Paine, Thomas, 58
Pascal, Blaise, 108
Pascendi Dominici Gregis, 36
Paul VI, Pope, 92, 132
Perry, Michael, 148
Personalism: as anti-ideology, 112, 120, 140, 143; as intellectual movement, 108; characteristics, 117–20, 128, 140, 143, 152, 179, 202; Christian, 190, 204; history, 110–17; in broad sense, 109, 123; in France, 112–14; in Germany, 114–15; in Poland, 115–17; in the United States, 114;

Personalism (*continued*), in strict sense, 109, 123; manifold expressions, 108; of Emmanuel Mounier, 113–14, 143; of Karol Wojtyła, 115–17, 120, 124, 138–39, 146; of Martin Buber, 144; origin of term, 112; relation to theism, 108; Thomistic, x, xvi, 104–5, 110, 115, 120, 123, 125–27, 146, 156, 179, 202–4, 206, 217, 319–20

Peschke, C. Henry, 205, 234, 257–58, 269, 284

Phenomenology, 4, 109, 114–16, 118, 135, 319

phronesis, 63

Pieper, Josef, 76, 177–78

Pinckaers, Servais, 28, 95, 102, 186, 248, 255, 283

Pius VI, Pope, 33

Pius IX, Pope, 34–35

Pius X, Pope, 35–37

Pius XI, Pope, 36–37, 39

Pius XII, Pope, 18, 39, 179, 204–05, 250

Plato, 86, 112, 219

Platonism, 86, 114

Poirot, Hercule, 89

Populorum Progressio, 92

Porter, Jean, 197

Possenti, Vittorio, 6, 78

possession: as moral ownership (*de iure*), 268–72; of faculties (contrasted with exercise), 130–32; of free will, 136; of rights, 5, 55–56, 62, 104, 131, 295; of self, 69, 76, 134, 138, 141–42, 272, 280

prudence, 90, 98, 100, 205, 239, 247, 258, 276, 277, 278, 279, 300; precepts of, 247

Quadragesimo Anno, 36
Quanta Cura, 34
Qui Pluribus, 34
Quo Graviora, 34
Quod Aliquantum, 33

rational animal, 126, 236
Ratzinger, Joseph, 184, 212, 249, 309, 318

Rawls, John, 131
Redemptor Hominis, 25, 41, 180, 214, 215
Regan, Thomas, 22
relatio subsistens, 212
religion: virtue of, 188–89
religious freedom. *See* liberty, religious
Renouvier, Charles B., 108, 112
Rerum Novarum, 35, 37
Respicientes, 34
Rieff, Philip, 91
rights: absolute, 14, 26–28, 55, 73–74, 90, 98–99, 195, 197, 199, 206–7; as immunities, 16, 26; civil, 14, 18, 21–23, 29, 36, 69, 70, 77, 198, 299; cultural, 29, 198; hierarchy of, 27–28, 45, 197–99, 276; human, vii–xv, 1–5, 13–14, 16, 18–22, 29–33, 37–39, 41–46, 49–51, 53–55, 57, 59, 63, 66–67, 71–72, 74–75, 78–79, 81–82, 84, 86, 90–92, 94–95, 97–98, 101–6, 114, 116, 118, 124–25, 128, 143, 145–49, 156, 160, 163–64, 176, 182, 192–93, 197–98, 200–2, 204, 206, 216–17, 227, 257, 283, 286, 296, 300–302, 305, 318–20; inalienable, 5, 14, 28, 101, 193, 198, 257, 283; legal, 10–22, 103, 149, 288, 291, 294, 297, 305; moral, 5–20, 24–25, 27, 32, 38, 44–45, 54, 61–62, 87–88, 95, 103, 130, 197, 200, 285–95, 297–99, 305–6; natural, 14, 19–22, 24–25, 27–28, 32–35, 37–40, 44, 46–47, 52–54, 58–59, 61, 64, 68–70, 77–79, 82–84, 92–93, 100, 106, 159, 195–96, 199, 203–4, 217, 223–24, 226, 231–32, 256–58, 273, 283–87, 289–90, 294–95, 297, 299–300, 302, 319–20; negative, 14, 18, 26–28, 58, 286, 299, 305; political, 23, 29, 66–67; positive, 14, 18–19, 21, 26–27, 69, 231, 286, 294, 299–300, 305, 317–18; relative, 27–28, 99, 197; solidarity, 29; subjective, 23–24, 66–68, 70, 72–74, 87, 218, 256, 270, 273, 284; three-term, 24–25, 298–99; to education, 3, 6–8, 25–26, 29, 35, 37–38, 40,

196, 294, 298–99; to life, xv, 3, 20, 26, 28, 38, 43, 45, 76–77, 80–81, 94, 99, 130, 192, 198, 296; to work, 29, 43; two-term, 24–25, 292–93, 298–99, 305, 318
Rigobello, Armando, 109
Rommen, Heinrich A., 179, 180, 224, 268, 271
Rorty, Richard, xvi
Rosenzweig, Franz, 108
Rousseau, Jean-Jacques, 58, 66

Sandel, Michael J., 289
Sartre, Jean-Paul, 112
Schall, James, xiii, 3
Scheler, Max, 115, 116
Scholasticism, 114, 118
Second Vatican Council, x, xiii, 18, 31, 39, 41, 46, 80, 82, 92, 102, 117, 140, 147, 154, 206, 209, 213
self-consciousness, 122–24
self-determination, 30, 70, 128, 135–39, 141, 151, 233, 287, 312
self-ownership. *See* possession, of self
Shrader-Frechette, Kristin, 53
Sidgwick, Henry, 57, 257
Sijthoff, A. W., 30
Simcha, Meir, 210
Simon, Yves, 110
Singer, Peter, 130–31, 133–34
socialism: Marxist 29; National, 36, 111
Socrates, 88
solidarity, 175, 300–301, 304, 313, 315–18, 320
Sollicitudo Rei Socialis, 30, 316–17
Sophocles, 225
sophrosyne, 278
sovereignty, 30, 45, 66, 70, 288
Spaemann, Robert, 20, 101, 110, 118, 126, 137, 145, 161, 186, 190, 193–94, 202, 220, 263, 307, 311, 315
Stefanini, Luigi, 112
Stein, Edith, 115
Stoics, 140, 219, 225
Strauss, Leo, 91, 231–32

Suárez, Francisco, 52, 68, 225, 257
subjectivity, 24, 69, 118–19, 123–24, 126–28, 133–35, 141, 144, 179, 216, 271–72
summum bonum, 85, 195, 246
suppositum, 122, 134, 155
suum, 10, 75, 193, 258, 263–65, 268–69, 272–73, 286
Syllabus, 34
synderesis, 251

Tao, 152, 232, 238
Tardiff, Andrew, 288
teleology, 58, 64, 85, 91, 138, 151, 172, 195, 239, 241, 246, 268, 272, 281, 297
temperance, 247, 258, 262, 276, 278–79
Ten Commandments. *See* Decalogue
theological dissent, 90, 99, 227–28
Thomas à Kempis, 189
Thomas Aquinas, Saint, 7, 15, 17, 23, 27, 105–6, 110, 112, 116–18, 120–29, 135–36, 139–40, 142, 146, 153–55, 157, 159, 163, 165–73, 186, 188–90, 197, 205, 207–11, 213–15, 222–25, 230, 235, 237–43, 246–58, 260–62, 264–77, 279–81, 287, 290, 296, 302–3, 307, 310, 314, 319
Thomism, xi, 115, 118
Tuck, Richard, 68

Une fois encore, 36
UNESCO, viii–ix, 29
United Nations, viii, 31, 41, 43–44, 114, 227
Universal Declaration of Human Rights, vii, 16, 21, 29, 31, 42–43, 114, 227
Ut Unum Sint, 117
utilitarian, 54, 101, 149, 156, 166–67, 169, 175, 194

Value(s): basic, 139, 245, 281; contrasted with dignity, 118–19, 149, 155; ethics of, 115; infra-moral, 93; instrumental, 168; moral, 17, 102, 138, 152; of human person, 42, 109, 112–13, 118–19, 160, 176, 184, 187, 192–93, 207, 215, 278

Vatican II. *See* Second Vatican Council
Veritatis Splendor, 60, 92, 96, 154, 156, 193, 201, 226, 228, 231, 233–35, 237, 242, 248, 252, 311
Vasak, Karel, 29
Vehementer Nos, 36
Villey, Michel, 52

Vinogradoff, Paul, 12
virtue(s): cardinal, 94, 119, 247, 256, 258, 276, 278–79, 281, 300; intellectual, 276–77; moral, 15, 87–88, 247, 249, 256, 258, 262–63, 276–80, 285; quasi-moral, 277

Who Is My Neighbor? Personalism and the Foundations of Human Rights was designed and composed in Adobe Garamond by Kachergis Book Design, Pittsboro, North Carolina; and printed on sixty-pound Natures Natural and bound by Thomson-Shore, Inc. of Dexter, Michigan.

www.ingramcontent.com/pod-product-compliance
Lightning Source LLC
Chambersburg PA
CBHW031405290426
44110CB00011B/261